Archie Bunker for President

ARCHIE BUNKER FOR PRESIDENT

How One Television Show Remade American Politics

OSCAR WINBERG

THE UNIVERSITY OF NORTH CAROLINA PRESS ★ CHAPEL HILL

This book was published with the assistance of the Luther H. Hodges Jr. and
Luther H. Hodges Sr. Fund of the University of North Carolina Press.

© 2025 The University of North Carolina Press
All rights reserved
Manufactured in the United States of America

Designed by Lindsay Starr
Set in Calluna, Bebas Neue, and Cooper Black by codeMantra
Cover art courtesy Wikimedia Commons.

Library of Congress Cataloging-in-Publication Data
Names: Winberg, Oscar, author.
Title: Archie Bunker for president : how one television show
remade American politics / Oscar Winberg.
Description: Chapel Hill : The University of North Carolina Press,
[2025] | Includes bibliographical references and index.
Identifiers: LCCN 2025015430 | ISBN 9781469690896
(cloth ; alk. paper) | ISBN 9781469690902 (pbk. ; alk. paper) |
ISBN 9781469686462 (epub) | ISBN 9781469690919 (pdf)
Subjects: LCSH: All in the family (Television program)—Influence. | Television and politics—United States—History. | Political culture—United States—History—20th century. | Political culture—United States—History—21st century. |
BISAC: HISTORY / United States / 20th Century | SOCIAL SCIENCE / Media Studies
Classification: LCC PN1992.77.A483 W56 2025 | DDC 791.45/72—dc23/eng/20250526
LC record available at https://lccn.loc.gov/2025015430

For product safety concerns under the European Union's General Product
Safety Regulation (EU GPSR), please contact gpsr@mare-nostrum.co.uk or
write to the University of North Carolina Press and Mare Nostrum Group
B.V., Mauritskade 21D, 1091 GC Amsterdam, The Netherlands.

For my kids—Vincent, Liv, Vivan, and Will

Television is democracy at its ugliest.

—PADDY CHAYEFSKY

CONTENTS

LIST OF ILLUSTRATIONS → VIII

INTRODUCTION: This Monster Must Be Stopped → 1

ACT I. AUDIENCES AND ACTIVISTS

CHAPTER 1. Ready for Prime Time → 13

CHAPTER 2. More Good Than Harm → 31

CHAPTER 3. Advocacy on the Air → 46

ACT II. CANDIDATES AND CAMPAIGNS

CHAPTER 4. Richard Nixon Meets Archie Bunker → 67

CHAPTER 5. Archie Bunker on the Campaign Trail → 89

ACT III. FRIENDS AND FOES

CHAPTER 6. Mrs. Bunker Goes to Washington → 109

CHAPTER 7. Stopping Immorality on TV → 126

CHAPTER 8. Battle Royale → 142

CONCLUSION: Archie Bunker in the White House → 159

ACKNOWLEDGMENTS → 167

NOTES → 171

BIBLIOGRAPHY → 229

INDEX → 251

ILLUSTRATIONS

Cast of *All in the Family* → 6

All in the Family ratings → 16

All in the Family Emmy Awards → 17

Edith Bunker on *All in the Family* → 56

Norman Lear on the set of *All in the Family* → 61

Archie Bunker on *All in the Family* → 69

Richard Nixon with Taft Schreiber and Tina Cole → 78

Richard Nixon with Charles Colson and Ken Clawson → 81

Carroll O'Connor advertisement for John Lindsay → 94

Jimmy Carter with *All in the Family* cast → 104

Jean Stapleton at the National Women's Conference → 122

Norman Lear → 146

Archie Bunker
for President

INTRODUCTION

THIS MONSTER MUST BE STOPPED

In the middle of the contentious presidential election between former secretary of state Hillary Rodham Clinton and businessman Donald J. Trump in the fall of 2016, television producers, writers, and actors gathered at a CBS sound stage in Studio City. The prospect of a Trump presidency fed a sense of unease, even dread, among many television producers in Hollywood.[1] The hosts of the evening's event, Max Mutchnick and David Kohen, the producer duo behind *Will & Grace* (NBC, 1998–2006), had decided that "this monster must be stopped."[2] To do so, they relied on what they knew best: television entertainment.[3] So they invited their friends to the sound stage for a surprise. "When the curtain went up," television director James Burrows remembered in his memoir, "the audience went crazy."[4] On the stage were Will Truman (played by Eric McCormack) and Grace Adler (Debra Messing), the eponymous main characters of *Will & Grace*, sitting in their living room complaining about recent events—the first time the actors had returned to their popular roles since the show's finale ten years earlier.

Onstage, more characters joined and the conversation turned to politics as Grace, who favored Clinton, and Karen Walker (Megan Mullally), a Trump voter, attempted to convince Jack McFarland (Sean Hayes) to vote for their preferred candidates in the upcoming presidential election. Neither Karen's fearmongering nor Grace's pathos appealed to Jack. Instead, Will settled the debate by informing Jack that the pop star Katy Perry liked Hillary Clinton. "I'm with her," Jack announced, and the appeal "#votehoney" appeared on the screen. The ten-minute video, released online hours before Clinton and

Trump's first debate, became "a runaway YouTube hit" with millions of views.[5] It was deliberately political. "The core of our skit was to just get involved, make your voice heard and vote," Messing, a strong supporter of Clinton, reasoned.[6]

Following the election of Trump, NBC—which had not been involved in the making of the online video—promised the show would return to television the next season. With Trump in the White House, the new *Will & Grace* (NBC, 2017-20) was more political than ever. In fact, the president was "osmotically omnipresent" in the show.[7] *Will & Grace* was not the only sitcom eager to mix the worlds of politics and entertainment. Waking up the morning after the 2016 election, Kenya Barris, the producer of *Black-ish* (ABC, 2014-22), recalled thinking, "I have to write about this election."[8] "To the extent the people are talking about issues," producer Garrett Donovan of *Superior Donuts* (CBS, 2017-18) acknowledged, "we'll have our characters [do the same]."[9] Bruce Helford, one of the producers behind the return of *Roseanne* (ABC, 1988-97, 2018), spoke openly about a wish to "bring a kind of dialogue back" in a moment of division.[10] Producer Nahnatchka Khan of *Fresh off the Boat* (ABC, 2015-20) seemed to agree, saying that the election results "just sort of confirmed to us that this is a dialogue that needs to happen."[11] Behind the return of *Murphy Brown* (CBS, 1988-98, 2018-19) to prime time was, according to producer Diane English, a desire "to give a voice to the resistance."[12] Nor were the producers and writers alone in their appreciation of television entertainment as a political forum.

Advocacy groups were happy to support television producers and writers developing stories that furthered their agenda. For example, when the undocumented character Mateo Liwanag (played by Nico Santos) faced deportation on the sitcom *Superstore* (NBC, 2015-21), the producers and writers worked with the advocacy organization Define American to make sure the script resonated.[13] Advocates also recognized the political value of representation. Gay rights organizations welcomed the return of *Will & Grace* as "an aggressive counterweight to Trump-era intolerance."[14] Advocacy groups led a campaign to save *One Day at a Time* (Netflix, 2017-19; Pop TV, 2020) when Netflix considered dropping the show after two seasons. The National Hispanic Media Coalition called the sitcom about a Cuban American family navigating life in Trump-era Los Angeles "a guiding light."[15]

Even politicians turned to sitcoms to broaden their appeal and promote their values. Hillary Clinton made a surprise appearance on the first episode of the new *Murphy Brown*.[16] On *Black-ish*, Rainbow Johnson (played by Tracee Ellis Ross) befriended former First Lady Michelle Obama.[17] Meanwhile in the White House, Trump praised Roseanne Barr, a supporter of his, for *Roseanne*'s strong ratings.[18] And when Messing and McCormack of *Will & Grace* condemned the president and attendees at a Beverly Hills fundraiser for him, Trump called for NBC to fire Messing.[19]

The dawn of this new political reality, many concluded, was the political rise of Donald Trump. Trump, after all, was a television character. "TV wasn't an adjunct to Trump's career," the *New York Times*' television critic observed, "it was his career."[20] Having turned his career in New York real estate into appearances on television comedies such as *Suddenly Susan* (NBC, 1996–2000) and *The Drew Carey Show* (ABC, 1995–2004) before becoming a kind of symbol of business success on the reality show *The Apprentice* (NBC, 2004–17), Trump established himself as a political figure on television through appearances on Fox News.

Rather than something new, however, Trump represented the culmination of a process long in the making. For decades, ambitious and media-savvy politicians such as Ronald Reagan, Bill Clinton, and Barack Obama had used entertainment television to broaden their appeal and reach new audiences. Nor were elected officials alone in this: Liberal advocacy organizations worked with television producers and writers in their portrayals of such themes as substance abuse, mental health, and recycling, while conservative activists mobilized in organizations such as the National Federation for Decency, the Parental Television Council, and Americans for Responsible Television to remake prime-time entertainment. These various political officials, campaigns, and movements turned to prime time to deliver them success because of a shared belief: that television entertainment could sell not just consumer products but candidates, legislation, and values.

The implications of the belief in the political power of television remain with us today. It is evident whenever a politician turns up on a sitcom: then–vice president Joe Biden meeting with Leslie Knope (Amy Poehler) on *Parks and Recreation* (NBC, 2009–15) or presidential candidate Hillary Clinton visiting Abbi Abrams and Ilana Wexler (played by Abbi Jacobson and Ilana Glazer, respectively) on *Broad City* (Comedy Central, 2014–19). Or whenever a television star turns up in a political campaign: Julia Louis-Dreyfus (of *Seinfeld* and *Veep*) and Tracee Ellis Ross (of *Black-ish*) hosting the Democratic National Convention in 2020 or the cast of *Parks and Recreation* doing a "town hall" reunion to fundraise for the Democratic Party. Or whenever conservative politicians and activists celebrate the support of television stars such as Tim Allen (*Home Improvement*), Roseanne Barr (*Roseanne*), or Scott Baio (*Charles in Charge*) while at the same time decrying prime-time entertainment for promoting "immorality" or "liberal values." And it is evident in how political campaigns follow the logic of television entertainment: grandstanding for the cameras in Congress;

hosting media events accompanied by catchy sound bites; and making primetime announcements to present public policy to the nation.

These developments can be traced back to the attempts by political candidates, strategists, and activists to understand the power of television entertainment many decades earlier. In a moment of change, both in politics and broadcasting, in the 1970s, *All in the Family* (CBS, 1971–79) became the most popular and most discussed show on television. Attempts to understand the new situation comedy and to leverage the popularity of the show for political agendas bring into sharp relief the emergence of a shared conviction that television entertainment can sell politics. This book is about *All in the Family*, but more than that it is about how that shared conviction took hold among political elites (the people who are elected to public office, run their campaigns, or mobilize in activist movements) as well as among entertainers (the producers, writers, and actors who create television shows) and how it came to transform political life in the image of television entertainment. It is about how *All in the Family* can help us understand how we got to where we are today.

In our current moment of media fragmentation, it is difficult to appreciate the reach and popularity of *All in the Family*. In the early 1970s, one-third of all households in the nation tuned in to watch it each week. In the middle of the 1971–72 season, as many as 60 percent of all televisions sets in use were tuned to *All in the Family*.[21] It ran for nine seasons, and for a record-breaking five consecutive seasons it was the most popular show on the air. Four individual episodes made it on to the list of the twenty-five broadcasts with the largest audiences in the history of American television, alongside Super Bowls, the Beatles' 1964 appearance on *The Ed Sullivan Show*, and the 1976 broadcast of *Gone with the Wind*.[22] Without streaming services or home video recorders available, *All in the Family* was appointment television even before the term was coined. If you missed a show, you had to wait for a potential rerun months later. And so Americans declined dinner invitations to stay home on Saturday night with *All in the Family*. Archie Bunker was the most recognized face in the nation. Terms such as "dingbat," "stifle," and "meathead" became a part of the popular vocabulary. Books and records of the show sold out, as did T-shirts, bumper stickers, board games, and buttons. The cast graced the covers of *TV Guide* but also of *Newsweek*, *Time*, and *Ebony*. It became, according to the Smithsonian Institution, a "part of the nation's cultural legacy."[23] In fact, the show's influence was never limited to culture.[24] It was the topic of conversation, and heated debate, not just in living rooms or at work but in the op-ed pages, on late-night talk shows, in classrooms, and in Sunday sermons. It was discussed at the kitchen table of grassroots activists, in the offices of interest groups, on Capitol Hill, and in the Oval Office. *All in the Family* was, it seemed in the 1970s, everywhere.[25]

When *All in the Family*, created by producer Norman Lear, was first broadcast by Columbia Broadcasting System (CBS) in January 1971, it took the traditional domestic situation comedy and then added life in all its unvarnished reality. On 704 Hauser Street in Queens, New York, Archie (played by Carroll O'Connor) and Edith Bunker (Jean Stapleton) lived with their daughter Gloria (Sally Struthers) and son-in-law Mike Stivic (Rob Reiner). Arguments filled the house. Civil rights, feminism, Vietnam, welfare, homosexuality, inflation, drugs, discrimination, cancer, sexual violence, Richard Nixon, and Watergate were all on the table for discussion. The show did not shy away from engaging the issues that defined modern life. In fact, it charged headfirst into these issues which long had been verboten on prime time.[26] "The kinds of topics Archie Bunker and his family argued about . . . were certainly being talked about in homes and families," Norman Lear later recalled. "They just weren't being acknowledged on television."[27]

Archie Bunker was a middle-aged working stiff with an absent-minded yet warmhearted wife, providing room and board for their spirited daughter and son-in-law while the latter went to college. Archie Bunker was a gruff yet lovable husband and father, but he was also a reactionary bigot. Edith Bunker was slow but also the moral conscience of the household. Gloria Stivic was still finding herself, while Mike Stivic was a liberal looking to change the world, starting with his father-in-law.

When Archie spouted off on race, gender, or society, the others challenged him. Condemning changing values on sex, a blustering Archie in the pilot episode explained to Mike: "When your mother-in-law and me was goin' around together—it was two whole years—we never—I never—I mean there was nothin'—I mean absolutely *nothin'*—not till the wedding night." Seemingly lost in her own memories of the night, Edith inadvertently delivered the punch line: "Yeah, and even then . . ."[28] The studio audience erupted in laughter as the camera cut to a close-up of Archie looking the fool, equal parts befuddled and annoyed.

The arguments in the family were heated, loud, and uncompromising. Archie made a habit of calling his son-in-law a meathead ("dead from the neck up"); Mike did not hesitate to call his father-in-law a bigot; Gloria called both her husband and father male chauvinists; and even Edith at times raised her voice. The neighbors, Lionel (played by Mike Evans), Henry (Mel Stewart), George (Sherman Hemsley), and Louise Jefferson (Isabel Sanford) or Irene (Betty Garrett) and Frank Lorenzo (Vincent Gardenia), wholeheartedly joined

Cast of *All in the Family*: Mike Stivic (Rob Reiner), Gloria Stivic (Sally Struthers), Archie Bunker (Carroll O'Connor), and Edith Bunker (Jean Stapleton). CBS/Photofest.

in the various arguments. And Archie, for all his bluster and indignation, was always the fool, even as "Archie's expressions [mirrored] everything going on."[29] For example, when Archie condemned "subversion," "radical, liberal garbage," and "dropouts," Mike pushed back.

> Archie: They got the greatest country in the world. Highest standard of living, the grossest national product. Now what more do they want from us anyhow?
>
> Mike: Peace.
>
> Archie: One thing they ain't got and right away they drop out.
>
> Mike: How about pure air, how about clean water, how about noncontaminated food, how about confidence in their government—

> Archie: Alright, will ya. We ain't perfect, I mean this is the United States of America. It ain't the perfect states of America.[30]

Cue the studio audience laughter.

While conflicts—between generations, between genders, between races—were at the heart of the show, the love within the family was never in doubt. In the sixth episode of the show, Archie went from being furious over Gloria being pregnant to finding joy in becoming a grandfather, only to learn that she miscarried. By her bed, a heartbroken Archie struggled to express himself, only to have his daughter put his emotions into words: "You love me? I love you too, Daddy."[31] Some weeks later, Archie worried all night about losing his job in announced layoffs, about losing his role as provider, and about losing the respect of his family.[32] Archie, such episodes made clear, was not a creature of hate; he was, Norman Lear later remarked, "just afraid of change," and around him everything was changing.[33]

The show wasn't *about* bigotry or politics, but in depicting real life—including the sounds of belches and toilets flushing—it dealt with everything from redlining to wage and price controls, from the oil shock to gay liberation, from crime on the subway to menopause, from birth control to tax evasion. This was something new for television. By the late 1960s, a few shows, such as *The Smothers Brothers Comedy Hour* (CBS, 1967–69), *Julia* (NBC, 1968–71), and *The Mod Squad* (ABC, 1968–73), were starting to engage the unrest and unease of the sixties, but more often than not television still offered audiences escapism with talking horses, flying nuns, and shipwrecks on desert islands.

As business and technological advancements resulted in new demands by advertisers and audiences by the turn of the new decade, however, some executives at the networks started to recognize that television needed to change. To remain relevant, television needed to move past programming produced for the lowest common denominator to "entertain, amuse and isolate."[34] *All in the Family*, with its frank discussions of social and political themes, was the answer. The conversations around the show, first in reviews and then in columns, op-eds, think pieces, sermons, political addresses, and court hearings, signaled a consensus that television was no longer—as the iconic television newsman Edward R. Murrow had warned in the late 1950s—"nothing but wires and lights in a box."[35]

But the merging of politics and entertainment in the 1970s was not inevitable.[36] It was the result of elected officials, political activists, network executives, and entertainers experimenting with new modes of communication.

Television entertainment and politics came together in a contested process made possible by a changing television industry and a shifting political landscape because both believed they needed the other for relevance, profit, and power. If the 1960s ushered in the belief that television mattered, the 1970s ushered in the idea that television entertainment did.[37]

This book is divided into three acts. The first focuses on audiences and activists grappling to understand the influence of *All in the Family* and how to make use of the show to promote political values and agendas. Bigotry and the influence television entertainment had on social values and political attitudes dominated these discussions around *All in the Family*. Civil rights activists, aware of the importance of television to combat prejudice, engaged in both private and public debates about the show. While there was disagreement among activists, as well as in research on the subject, the elite consensus that formed suggested that the show did more good than harm. Today, many remember *All in the Family* as a prime example of selective exposure, arguing that people saw what they wanted to see in the liberal satire, forgetting that the public conversation, including by community and religious leaders, made the intended satire clearer for audiences. Advocacy organizations recognized in the bold handling of controversial material previously banned from prime-time entertainment an opportunity to influence how issues such as reproductive health care and sexual violence were portrayed. *All in the Family* broke ground in terms of both the subjects that were being addressed and the collaboration with advocates behind the scenes. While some celebrated the honest engagement with sensitive themes, others fretted over television entertainment bringing about a permissive or weak society.

The second act turns to politicians as they worried about the power of television entertainment and struggled with finding ways to use it to their own advantage in political campaigns. One of the first politicians to recognize the power of *All in the Family*, Richard Nixon relied on close friends in Hollywood to understand television and use it to his advantage. Convinced of the power of television, he hoped Archie Bunker would benefit his reelection campaign of 1972. But at the same time, Nixon, certain that television news undermined him with critical coverage, nurtured a deep hatred for the networks. Perceptive of the business model of broadcasting, he did not hesitate to target television entertainment in his efforts to control his own image and influence television news. While Nixon wanted Archie Bunker on his team, however, it was his Democratic challengers who won Carroll O'Connor's endorsement and recorded advertisements with the most recognized face in the nation to attract media attention and appeal to different voter segments. Politicians probably underestimated voters in believing that television entertainment could make or break campaigns, but even so this belief changed campaign structures and strategies.

The third act explores how activists and politicians came together to mobilize support in efforts, on the one hand, to use television entertainment and entertainers to win political power and, on the other hand, to leverage political power to control prime time. For the women's movement it meant working with Jean Stapleton to use Edith Bunker to campaign for the ratification of the Equal Rights Amendment. For conservative activists it meant using the most popular show on television as a foil to mobilize against the things they deemed "immoral." With increasing demands on television programming from activists across the political spectrum, Congress pressured the Federal Communications Commission to clean up television entertainment. The result was a censorship policy, adopted by the National Association of Broadcasters and the networks in league with the commission, called the family viewing hour. When producers and writers sued over government infringement of their First Amendment rights, it became a political fight along familiar fault lines. The liberal creative community won in court, but the conservative activists against *All in the Family* found in prime-time entertainment an issue that brought attention, funds, and mobilization.

So while Donald Trump loomed large over the sound stage in Studio City where *Will & Grace* returned both to television and to political life in an attempt to sway the 2016 election, another figure loomed even larger over the entire evening. In the audience sat ninety-four-year-old Norman Lear. The evening was marked by the work and legacy of the legendary producer who introduced the nation to a "lovable bigot" on prime time and revolutionized the relationship between television entertainment and politics. When he created *All in the Family* almost fifty years earlier, he did not plan to transform American political life but instead to remake American television. But with political candidates, strategists, and activists all looking to leverage television entertainment for their own agendas at the same time that producers, writers, and actors were gaining a political voice, he ended up doing both.

Act I

AUDIENCES AND ACTIVISTS

Chapter 1

READY FOR PRIME TIME

"Is this antisemitic?" Robert "Bob" Wood, president of CBS Television, asked with caution. Wood was sitting in a screening room in the Eliel Saarinen–designed CBS building on West Fifty-Second Street in Midtown Manhattan known as Black Rock. At the urging of his programming department, he'd agreed to watch a pilot about a bigot called Archie Bunker. On the show, the character used words such as "hebe," "Yid," and "that tribe" when talking about Jews.[1] These were words not heard in polite company in 1970, let alone on national television. But amid the laughter, Wood's fellow executives calmed him. "There are three fat Jewish men sitting here," programming executive Irwin Segelstein remarked. "Don't worry about [antisemitism]."[2] The show was satire; the bigot was constantly played for a fool. Wood later recalled how he was drawn to the honesty and controversy in the show: "It was time TV dared to do something like this."[3] Wood had, in fact, been looking for something new, and in that dark screening room he recognized that he had found that something.

Television in the 1960s had been mostly predictable and safe. To be sure, there were new shows in the late 1960s, such as the variety comedy of *The Smothers Brothers Comedy Hour*, science fiction such as *Star Trek* (NBC, 1966-69), dramas such as *The Mod Squad*, and even situation comedies like *Julia*, introducing a new edge to prime time.[4] Yet while a different business model had allowed late-1960s movies, theater, music, and literature to experiment with new styles and themes in reaction to the civil rights movement, the war in Vietnam, student unrest, and calls for women's liberation, television still offered audiences established favorites such as Lawrence Welk, Ed Sullivan, and Jackie Gleason.

Success in television depended on attracting an enormous audience; numbers that would result in triumph in the film or music industry were often not enough to keep a prime-time show on the air. When *Love Story*, the Ryan O'Neal and Ali McGraw romantic drama film, made $2,463,916 in its first weekend in wide release in December 1970, the studio took out a full-page advertisement in *Variety* calling it "the biggest first 3 days in the history of the motion picture industry."[5] Successful television shows were expected to attract more than ten times that audience—every week.

In most households, the television set was on for hours on end with the whole family spending time together watching prime-time entertainment. In an age without remote controls and only a handful of options, audiences often spent the whole night with a single channel. Unless, of course, something bad enough to provoke a reaction came on. Thus, "a good program executive always played it safe."[6] The least objectionable programming theory—that because most people made a habit of watching television (rather than specific shows) in the evening, the main purpose was not to attract viewers so much as to avoid repelling them—shaped all decisions at the networks. As a result, the most popular shows of the 1960s were *Bonanza* (NBC, 1959-73), *The Lucy Show* (CBS, 1962-68), *The Beverly Hillbillies* (CBS, 1962-71), and *The Andy Griffith Show* (CBS, 1960-68). Intended as escapist entertainment, these popular shows only rarely addressed real life and real challenges in the United States in the 1960s. With some exceptions, the tumult of Richard Nixon's first term in office, marked by protest and polarization, could—on television—be found on the evening news.

Before ascending to the presidency of CBS Television, Wood made a name for himself running KNXT, the Los Angeles affiliate owned and operated (O&O) by the network. KNXT was one of the five stations the Federal Communications Commission (FCC) allowed CBS to own. From there he advanced to the CBS Television Stations division in charge of all five O&O stations. When Wood was named president in 1969, he had ample experience with the network and, in particular, with how CBS did in the major media markets of New York, Los Angeles, Chicago, Philadelphia, and St. Louis, where the O&O stations were located. These five stations were incredibly valuable. In fact, the O&Os accounted for as much as 70 percent of the network's pretax earnings in 1970.[7]

Wood had witnessed firsthand how CBS could be the number one network nationally and still struggle in these valuable markets. The most popular shows on CBS when Wood assumed the presidency in the late 1960s were old favorites such as *Gunsmoke* (CBS, 1955–75), which had been on air since Dwight Eisenhower's first term in office; *Mayberry R.F.D.* (CBS, 1968–71), a spin-off of the popular *Andy Griffith Show*, which premiered before John F. Kennedy was elected; and *Here's Lucy* (CBS, 1968–74), the newest vehicle for Lucille Ball, television's darling since the days when Harry Truman was still in the White House. While these shows all enjoyed high ratings nationally, they failed to attract audiences in the major media markets where CBS could make real money. Wood wanted to rid the network of these old favorites in a move that became known as the "rural purge" and replace them with something new that, he hoped, could win over new audiences.[8] Sitting in the screening room watching Archie Bunker break every taboo of television, using words such as "spics," "spades," "Polacks," and "pinkos" while discussing race, class, and religion, Wood became convinced it was the vehicle he was looking for to bring CBS into the 1970s.

And it worked. The liberal satire of *All in the Family* resonated with critics and members of the Academy of Television Arts and Sciences, which nominated it for best comedy nine years in a row (it won four times), because it represented the maturation of the medium that had for years been derided as the "boob tube." Audiences followed. *All in the Family* became the highest-rated show on television, and along with other new shows such as *The Mary Tyler Moore Show* (CBS, 1970–77), *M*A*S*H* (CBS, 1972–83), and *The Waltons* (CBS, 1972–81) it brought the network record ratings and critical acclaim by elevating the quality of the medium.

Bob Wood wanted television entertainment to matter. Yet while he was celebrated by broadcasters, critics, and producers alike for turning television respectable with the success of new highbrow fare, television in the seventies changed not because of any individual man but because of changes in the economic, legislative, and technological structures of the industry. In the tumultuous last decade of the network era, no other programming signaled the transformations within broadcasting like the most popular show. *All in the Family* marked television's move away from lowbrow programming intended to appeal nationally by avoiding anything controversial or objectionable. It was intentionally controversial and included objectionable lines, characters, and story lines. Most important, it reflected real life. In the process, it marked the changing relationship between television and political life as activists, advocates, candidates, legislators, and presidents came to recognize the political power of television entertainment. Over the decade, they attempted to use, and at times abuse, the characters and experiences presented on prime time to influence real life outside television. But the first step in the process was convincing society that television entertainment was not mindless pap but actually mattered.

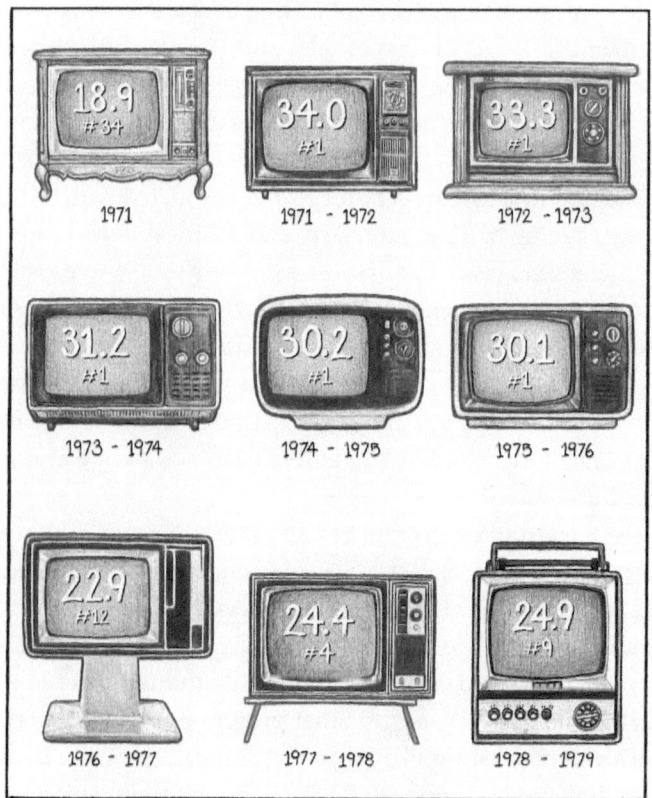

All in the Family ratings. Illustration by Sage Goodwin.

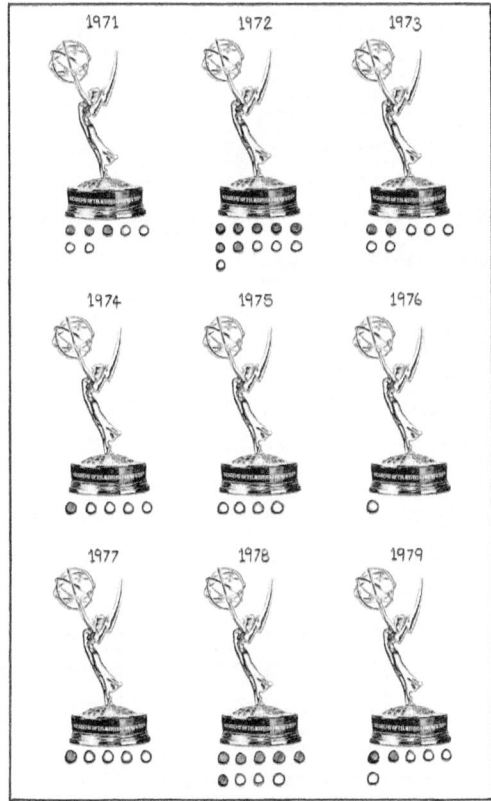

All in the Family Emmy Awards. Illustration by Sage Goodwin.

Even if Wood, along with the programming department, was convinced that *All in the Family* was exactly what he needed to reinvent the network, other executives remained wary of the controversial material. CBS was, in the early 1970s, still founder and chairman William S. Paley's candy store and nothing went on the air without his approval. Paley did not appreciate Archie Bunker. Michael Dann, the longtime head of the programming department, remembered the Jewish chairman saying he would never accept the use of the word "Yid" on his network.[9] According to Dann's successor, Fred Silverman, not only did Paley dislike the show—he despised it.[10] So did John Schneider, the third highest-ranking executive at the company. "I hated it," he later recalled.[11] To understand Wood, his commitment to *All in the Family*, and how he was able to prevail over opposition from his higher-ups requires an appreciation of the state of broadcasting in 1970.

By 1970, television had come of age and the new decade would mark the last days of the network era in which men such as Paley at CBS, David Sarnoff at National Broadcasting Corporation (NBC), and Leonard Goldenson at American Broadcasting Company (ABC) could rule television as their own fiefdom. Since the dawn of the medium some twenty-odd years earlier, broadcasters had established a lucrative and protected television industry with the help of friends in Washington, DC. The seventies, however, were a time of peril in television, with alarming new technology, new legislation, new court decisions, and new regulations shaking the business of broadcasting. In 1970, the powers that be in television felt under assault from all sides.[12]

Television in the United States was developed at the intersection of private and public, following the example set by radio decades earlier. Rather than funding a public broadcasting corporation, the government initially entrusted private enterprises with television. The technology, however, depended on public airwaves, and to guarantee strong signals, the federal government regulated the airwaves through the FCC. Even the strongest signal served only a limited community. The broadcast networks wanted a national audience. Because the FCC, cautious of media domination, limited the networks' ownership of television stations, they depended on affiliation agreements with hundreds of stations across the country for a national reach.

While the stations affiliated with the networks had hitched their wagons, quite literally, to the networks' stars, the relationship was also inherently adversarial. Affiliation was profitable for both parties. The networks provided a feed of programming free of charge and sold most of the advertising minutes in prime time. Still, the advertising dollars allotted to the affiliated stations were enough to make the owners very wealthy. Network executives developed and scheduled prime-time programming, but it was the station manager who decided if and when to air the network feed.[13] Hence, for a show to be successful, the network needed the affiliates to actually air the feed, because the ratings, the be-all and end-all of broadcasting, were national.

The station owners were, more often than not, conservative local businessmen with strong ties to local political power structures and an interest in making money that far exceeded their interest in public service.[14] In public, it was network executives, such as Dr. Frank Stanton of CBS, who were the recognized statesmen of broadcasting arguing in front of Congress that investments in news, public affairs, arts, and sports signaled a commitment to meeting the formal license requirement of serving the public interest. Yet among station owners and managers there was a deep mistrust of these network executives, who were viewed as suspect elites: liberals, Jews, and New Yorkers.[15] Yes, the founders of all three networks, Paley of CBS, Sarnoff of NBC, and Goldenson of ABC, were all Jews living in New York. No, they were neither liberals nor born-and-bred New Yorkers. In fact, most people who made up the higher strata at the networks were gentiles, conservatives, and not from New York. Some, including Bob Wood, were decidedly conservative.[16] Still, a mix of antisemitism, anti-intellectualism, and conservative anger over perceived television news bias fueled a suspicion toward the networks.[17] And so the mistrust lingered.

The same kind of suspicion marked the station managers' and owners' views of the creative community that wrote and produced the shows they were broadcasting. Hollywood was often seen as a nest of immorality and subversive political thought, even a decade after Red Scare blacklists had driven left-leaning writers, directors, and actors either underground or out of the business completely. Broadcasters were particularly worried about permissiveness in the sexual and racial norms presented on popular shows. In the South, for example, many broadcasters in the 1950s and 1960s made a habit of refusing to air the network feed when Black entertainers such as Nat King Cole and Sammy Davis Jr. appeared.[18] Station owners depended on both the networks in New York and the producers in Hollywood to provide them with high-quality and popular entertainment shows. Still, in no small part because the broadcasters were more dependent on political goodwill and thus particularly wary of controversy, they distrusted both.

After all, it was the broadcaster as the licensee, not the networks or the producers, whom the FCC held responsible for the content shown over public airwaves. With licenses only awarded for a period of three years at a time, the stations were never at ease about meeting the commission's standard of serving the "public interest, convenience, and necessity."[19] In the early network era, the commission's commitment to "public interest" was, at best, uneven. Newton Minow, nominated to chair the commission by President John F. Kennedy in 1961, strengthened that commitment. With a notorious speech decrying television as a "vast wasteland" and robust regulatory action, Minow signaled to broadcasters that their licenses could be on the line if they failed to serve the public interest.[20] A television license was, in the words of media activist Everett C. Parker, "perhaps the most valued gift our nation bestows on a citizen."[21] Thus, the broadcasters wanted to avoid any controversy in their community that might result in a challenge when it came time to renew the license. Although the commission tended to renew, rather than award the license to a rival, any challenge was costly and brought uncertainty. A decade-long campaign by the United Church of Christ against WLBT, the ABC affiliate in Jackson, Mississippi, over discriminatory practices set an example for citizen groups for how to successfully take on licensees. In a major victory for the media activist campaigns, a federal appellate court in 1966 found that members of the public had a right to partake in FCC hearings "in order to safeguard the public interest in broadcasting."[22] This, along with the commission's 1965 policy statement on comparative criteria, paved the way for license challenges by media activists. In 1969, the commission stunned the broadcasting industry by revoking the license of WHDH, estimated to be worth around $50 million, in Boston and awarded it instead to a competing applicant. "The door is thus opened for local citizens to challenge media giants in their local community at renewal time with some hope for success before the licensing agency where previously the only response had been a blind reaffirmation of the present license holder," commissioner Nicholas Johnson concluded in a concurring statement.[23] Broadcasters recognized they could no longer count on friends at the regulatory agency for easy renewal every three years.

Nor was it only the license process that gave broadcasters cause to worry at the beginning of the 1970s. New regulatory action by the FCC began to undermine the power of broadcasters and strengthen the position of television producers. Following years of "regulation by raised eyebrow" in the form of public statements by chairmen decrying television as an "electronic Appalachia," the FCC overcame industry opposition to new regulations in 1970.[24] With a policy known as the Westinghouse rule, the FCC crafted two distinct regulations: the Financial Interest and Syndication Rules and the Prime Time Access Rule. Both intended to circumscribe the influence of the networks. The former, known colloquially as the fin-syn rules, sought to constrain network ownership of television programming. Targeting vertical control of television entertainment, the rules limited "oligopoly power" by restricting the networks' interest in the production and syndication of entertainment shows.[25] Prior to the rules, the networks argued that airing shows contributed to their value and thus should give them an ownership stake in the programming they aired. As a result, the networks held financial and syndication interests in almost all shows even if they did not participate in the production process. The new policy, which left the networks out of the lucrative syndication business, represented a shift at the FCC and a direct threat to network control of television.[26] By restricting the power of the networks, the fin-syn rules ushered in an era of independent production companies. Grant Tinker and Mary Tyler Moore's MTM Enterprises, Aaron Spelling and Leonard Goldberg's Spelling-Goldberg Productions, and Norman Lear and Bud Yorkin's Tandem Productions rose to prominence. "Without the [fin-syn] rules," Lear later explained, "we might never have been able to build the company we built."[27]

In combination with the fin-syn rules, the commission attempted to limit network control over television entertainment with the Prime Time Access Rule. The idea was to foster diversity in programming by prohibiting stations in the fifty largest markets from airing the network feed in the first hour of prime time. Without the network feed available, the commission reasoned, local stations would produce local programming. While only stipulating limits on the largest markets, the rule led to networks giving up the hour across all markets due to the limited profits available without the major media markets in play.[28] But while the rule faced vehement opposition from the networks, which faced an estimated loss of around $200 million annually, it benefited local stations.[29] In a sign of withering network influence over the regulatory agency, the policy was adopted over the objection of the conservative FCC chairman, Dean Burch, who called it a "Pollyanna" rule unlikely to achieve the desired goal.[30]

When the networks challenged the rule in court, the commission's policy was upheld in a decision affirming government control over television content.[31] Nor was it the only court case which gave broadcasters cause for concern. In 1969, the Supreme Court confirmed in *Red Lion Broadcasting Co. v. Federal Communications Commission* that broadcasters did not enjoy full First Amendment rights, akin to the press or the film industry, because of the scarcity of public airwaves.[32] In a decision authored by Justice Byron White, a unanimous court held that "it is the right of the viewers and listeners, not the right of the broadcasters, which is paramount," and concluded that it was "the right of the public to receive suitable access to social, political, esthetic, moral, and other ideas and experiences."[33] To safeguard the rights of the public, the courts agreed, the federal government was allowed to limit the free speech rights of the broadcasters. While the case focused on personal attacks and the fairness doctrine, the decision was understood by network executives and broadcasters as "a bleak benchmark in regulation."[34] An editorial in *Broadcasting* warned that "it will be both the excuse and the incentive for future regulation."[35] The sense of concern within the industry was palpable.

Broadcasters had long cultivated relationships in Washington, both at the commission and in Congress. In control of the most powerful medium in history, broadcasters had considerable pull over legislators, as most members of Congress were eager to stay on the good side of the station managers and owners in their own communities. Through interest organizations such as the National Association of Broadcasters, once described as "an organization dedicated to combating change," the industry fought—often successfully—any regulatory or legislative demands.[36] Regulatory capture, when government agencies become subservient to the very industry they are expected to regulate, made the FCC into "the parent to whom the broadcaster runs to protect him."[37] Most commissioners made money in broadcasting either before or after their term as regulators. Many key allies in Washington, most notably President Lyndon B. Johnson, also shared in the success of the broadcasting industry.[38] And the broadcasting lobby was recognized as among the most powerful in Washington, even if its power was beginning to wane in the 1970s. For decades, Congress and the FCC had provided broadcasters with protection against rivals looking to build alternatives in the form of pay-per-view, community television, and cable television.[39] In the new decade, political interest in new technology was growing, including from President Nixon, who understood cable television as a way of hurting the networks, and cable was emerging as a major disruptor threatening network dominance over television.[40] At the networks, the bottom line was believed to be under attack.

Congress was also moving forward with other forms of legislation that damaged the networks' business model. Responding to activist pressure, the legislative branch attempted to hold broadcasters responsible for the adverse effects programming and advertising had on audiences. After a presidential commission on the causes and prevention of violence concluded that "violence on television encourages violent forms of behavior, and fosters moral and social values about violence in daily life which are unacceptable in a civilized society," congressional hearings looked at the impact on society, especially children, of violence on television entertainment.[41] This development signaled government interest in meddling in programming decisions in a way that many broadcasters considered blatantly unconstitutional. Nor did legislators believe broadcasters enjoyed the same freedom as the press when it came to advertising. In an extraordinary move that panicked broadcasters, Congress in 1969 banned all broadcasting advertisements for cigarettes.[42] Tobacco companies were and had long been among the most important advertisers on television, accounting for around $200 million in revenue annually by the end of the sixties.[43] Many broadcasters feared that similar bans on automobile and oil industry ads would follow in the "not-too-distant future" and erode their lucrative business model.[44] Even though broadcasting profits were still good, by the 1970s, network executives believed they were under siege. Insiders called it "without doubt the harshest and most uncertain year in two decades."[45] It was in this moment of crisis that Bob Wood looked to reform the number one network, CBS, by gambling on a new show that would come to be known as *All in the Family*.

In 1966, the talk of the town in London was a new comedy series on the British Broadcasting Corporation called *Till Death Us Do Part* (BBC, 1965–75). Provocative and outrageous, the show focused on a working-class bigot named Alf Garnett (played by Warren Mitchell) and his contentious arguments with his wife (Dandy Nichols), daughter (Una Stubbs), and son-in-law (Anthony Booth).[46] Bud Yorkin, a television director who in 1958 had formed the production company Tandem Productions with his friend Norman Lear, was also in London and he told his business partner back home in California about the funny yet controversial show. Lear recognized in the concept his own relationship with his father. "We never agreed about anything; we fought about everything," Lear later recalled. "I'd tell him he was a bigot; he'd call me a goddam bleedin' heart liberal."[47] Lear wanted to bring the show to the United States; Yorkin thought he was crazy.[48]

Lear went about securing the rights, writing a script, and developing a pilot initially titled *Justice for All* for ABC. Programming executives at the network, in particular Martin Starger, were excited about the project, but Starger's bosses balked at the controversial material. Running far behind their rivals as the perennial loser in the ratings race, ABC was in no place to reinvent television in 1968. Executives worried about losing affiliates and were convinced stations would refuse the controversial material.[49] "We in senior management are going to pretend this pilot never happened," Tom Moore, the president of ABC, was said to have told the programming department after leaving a screening of the show.[50] A second pilot, now named *Those Were the Days*, was also rejected by ABC. Now Lear and Yorkin were free to take it to the other networks. At CBS, programming head Michael Dann loved it. That is how the show found its way to Bob Wood.

Wood also had superiors eager to reject the controversial show. To convince the highest echelon of executives at CBS of his strategy to renew the prime-time lineup, he had to stake his presidency on the gambit. Not only did Paley and Schneider hate the show, but the research department also warned that it tested below average among audiences. Still, Wood was confident that he understood television better than test audiences, who tended to consist of people brought in off the street for a small fee.[51] Television was changing in ways that made Wood, a college graduate from Los Angeles with an executive position in New York, a more valued member of the audience than the average man on the street. Television was, as a business, a device to deliver audiences to advertisers. For decades, the *size* of the audience had determined the rate. The networks, stations, and advertisers all relied on the ratings delivered by the "fourth great force in American broadcasting": the A. C. Nielsen Company.[52] But by the 1970s, almost every single household in the country had a television set and advertisers were increasingly interested in certain demographics. Thus, the *quality* of the audience became more important than the size. Signaling the institutionalization of this development, Nielsen, in the fall of 1970, introduced more detailed demographic categories for advertisers and broadcasters.[53] The baby boomers, born in the postwar baby boom years between 1946 and 1964, were emerging as full-fledged members of the "consumers' republic" and becoming the most sought-after audiences.[54] Now, advertisers were ready to leave behind the large, but old and rural, audiences that still loved Lucille Ball, Red Skelton, and Jackie Gleason.[55] Since advertisers wanted to find young, urbane, and affluent audiences with money to spend, the networks were focusing on that very demographic.[56] "Just because the people who buy refrigerators are between 26 and 35 and live in Scarsdale," Michael Dann objected, "you should not beam your programming only at them."[57] But to Wood this was simple business.[58]

Wood's business arguments won him the support of other executives. To win Paley's okay for his renewal of the prime-time lineup, he appealed to the aging chairman's vanity. According to Wood, the choice was to either watch the industry move forward from a rocking chair or take charge so that "you won't just be watching it[,] you'll be leading it."[59] Paley conceded, and Wood moved forward.[60] But, everybody recognized, the show would define Wood's position at CBS. "It's got my name all over it," Wood concluded.[61] From that moment forward, he followed the production process closely and acknowledged freely that "my ass is on the line with this show."[62]

A requirement for any show to succeed was for the affiliates to air it. Convinced that its affiliates would reject the controversial comedy, ABC had passed on it. Now it fell to Wood to sell the show to CBS's affiliates. Without them airing it, the show would fail, and Wood would be out. Many of the affiliates knew Wood well from his years at KNXT and the CBS Television Stations department. He was, in a way, one of them, and when he told them of the need to attract new viewers, they trusted him.[63] At the annual affiliate meeting in the spring of 1970, Wood declared a new direction for the network, announcing that "we have to hold the audiences we have; we have to broaden our base; we have to attract new viewers of every generation, reflecting the educated and sophisticated in American life, people who live in every part of the country."[64]

Asking them to join him in a leap of faith, Wood concluded that "it is better to try something new than not to try it at all and wonder what would have happened if we had."[65] Most of them agreed.[66]

Ahead of the midseason premiere of *All in the Family* in January 1971, Wood screened the show for affiliates over closed circuit. "I think you will agree," Wood observed in a wire to affiliates, "that nothing quite like this series has ever been done on American television."[67] While presenting the new comedy as a daring experiment, he stressed in strong terms that the foremost purpose was "to entertain."[68] To the press, Wood explained how executives long had talked about "a show like this" but then "would not do anything more about it" and called it "an answer" to critics who call television "bland."[69] Wood's close attention to the show illustrated a lingering caution over how to court controversy without offending affiliates, advertisers, and audiences. *All in the Family* was buried in what Fred Silverman of the programming department called "the *worst* time period," on Tuesdays at nine thirty, following the rural variety show *Hee-Haw* and opposite movies on both ABC and NBC, in an attempt to "sn[eak] it on the air."[70]

The network's hesitation over the controversial content also showed up in its production and advertising. The programming department struggled with how to present the show and selected the name *All in the Family* because it was, according to one executive, "the least offensive of all the things we had."[71] The sales department was having a hard time promoting the show and in turn finding advertisers interested in buying time on it.[72] The law department insisted on a disclaimer at the start of the show.[73] The standards and practices department (the network censors) went back and forth with Norman Lear over the language on the show. Only hours before the first broadcast on January 12, 1971, Wood and Lear argued over which episode to air first. The former preferred a less contentious episode, while the latter believed the outrageous pilot episode introduced audiences to the characters better. Lear refused to compromise and told the network it would either air as written or not air at all.[74] He won. Less than an hour later, an advisory message came on the screen: "The program you are about to see is *All in the Family*. It seeks to throw a humorous spotlight on our frailties, prejudices, and concerns. By making them a source of laughter, we hope to show—in a mature fashion—just how absurd they are." Then a voice announced "From Television City in Hollywood," before Archie and Edith Bunker appeared on-screen, singing in front of the piano: "Boy, the way Glenn Miller played, songs that made the hit parade, guys like us we had it made, those were the days . . ." *All in the Family* was finally on the air.

Expecting a tsunami of complaints, and prepared with additional telephone operators at the network, executives at CBS were surprised at the still waters following the debut of *All in the Family*. No more than around 1,000 calls came in nationwide and, even more surprising, over 60 percent of them were laudatory. In Chicago, the CBS affiliate WBBM-TV reported 135 calls in favor and only twenty against.[75] In Philadelphia, it was ninety for and fifty-two against. In Los Angeles, the calls ran three to one in favor. Cities such as Cleveland, Detroit, and Indianapolis all reported few complaints and, even more surprising, many laudatory calls.[76] The only exception to the generally favorable response was in New York, where a slight majority condemned the show for "vulgarity" and "prejudice."[77] Even there, however, the calls were far fewer than anticipated. "We were all geared for a big onslaught of reaction," Wood recalled later, "and precious little of it came in."[78] Critics had promised it would be *the* topic of conversation, yet most people paid no attention to the show. "It was the biggest anticlimax of my life," remarked John Schneider.[79]

In the *San Francisco Examiner*, a review of *All in the Family* concluded it would be the "talk of the country tomorrow morning."[80] It was not. People did not *talk* about the show because they had not *seen* it. It was that simple. It failed to even break into the top forty in the first week's Nielsen ratings.[81] Audiences were not yet paying attention. Television critics, on the other hand, were delivering reviews, columns, and think pieces on the new show. After all, they had been paid not only to see it but also to write about it. Initial reviews were mixed.[82] *TV Guide* described it as "not just the best-written, best-directed and best-acted show on television, it is the best show on television."[83] The television critic for the Associated Press deemed it "a half hour of vulgarity and offensive dialogue."[84] For every critic who loved it, there seemed to be another one who hated it. Take the reviews in *Variety*, for example. While *Variety* praised the show as "the best tv comedy since the original 'The Honeymooners,'" the *Daily Variety* panned it as a "sick joke."[85] Norman Lear leaned into the controversy. Tandem Productions bought a full-page advertisement in *Variety* to reprint the reviews. "It is a controversial show," the ad acknowledged and asked readers, "Which *Variety* do you read?"[86]

Within a week, *All in the Family* was described as "one of the most talked about television series around the country."[87] Coinciding with a period of rising interest in the power of the medium, marked by the recent publication of books exploring the role of television in modern life, the conversations reflected a highbrow interest in prime time.[88] Media and communications departments were proliferating at universities as television was becoming a serious matter of study for sociologists such as Stuart Hall and theorists such as John Fiske.[89] *All in the Family* emerged as a representative for new entertainment, turning prime time into "quality" television by providing highbrow viewers an imagined distance from mass audiences and thus permission to enjoy a form of entertainment traditionally considered lowbrow.[90]

This shift was evident in how the press covered the show. The paper of record published no less than three reviews of the show in a period of six weeks in the winter of 1971. The initial review in the *New York Times* rejected the show as lacking "taste" and relying on "shock value."[91] The second opinion confirmed the conclusion, blasting it as "vulgar and silly" while suggesting it was making bigotry more acceptable.[92] The final verdict, however, came from none other than Jack Gould. Having owned the television beat at the *New York Times* since the 1940s, Gould came to the aid of the satire in a review that focused on the persuasive power of the medium. Noting the tendency of television to look away from social issues, he remarked that *All in the Family* represented new potential for the medium to combat bigotry with laughter. "Some of Archie's words may chill the spine," Gould concluded, "but to root out bigotry has defied man's best efforts for generations and the weapon of laughter just might succeed."[93] This mattered. Gould was widely understood as the conscience of the broadcasting industry and enjoyed respect both among critics and executives.[94] A review from the grand old man of television criticism essentially declaring that *All in the Family* "should not be written off precipitously" gave credibility to the show. A few weeks later, producer Norman Lear jumped into the conversation with a reply to the reviews in which he admitted that no television comedy could eradicate bigotry, an impossible standard applied in some reviews, but explained that their intent was "to hold a mirror up to our prejudices."[95] The unusual amount of ink the editors at the *New York Times* were willing to spill on a new prime-time show suggests *All in the Family* had become a vehicle for discussions about the role of the medium in modern life.

Most critics agreed that it "marks the first major social departure for this commercial genre."[96] Television critics, assigned a beat covering a medium that seemed to avoid experimentation and rely on imitation whenever possible, were eager to engage with the innovative show and its implications for the medium. "For years we have been snowed under with nonsensical pap which masqueraded as 'situation comedy' on television," the critic for the *Los Angeles Sentinel* acknowledged.[97] In *All in the Family*, they now found the promise of television to provoke public conversation on subjects of societal importance. "Certainly, it stands alone in American television," they concluded.[98] The biggest question, according to the reviews, was not whether the show was funny—even many of the negative reviews conceded that it was—but whether audiences would be "ready for Archie Bunker."[99]

Thus, the message of the show became the focus as the conversations continued in reviews, columns, and letters to the editor. The public disagreement over the show among critics resulted in even more conversation. Two months after the January premiere, a second round of reviews looked at it. Critics, *Newsweek* concluded, "are now jumping on the bandwagon."[100] One critic admitted to "beginning to change my mind once more" after having watched the show for a while and appreciating the "complexities within its characters."[101] In her syndicated column, Cynthia Lowry of the Associated Press addressed the "great debate" about the show and acknowledged that "much that is written about the series, including mail to this column, seems more concerned with its message than its laughs."[102] Following the lackluster initial ratings, *All in the Family* won the Emmy for Outstanding Comedy Series in May 1971. With audiences now finding reruns of the comedy that everybody seemed to be talking about, it became the number one show in the country within a month of the Emmys.[103] With the growing success, it became even more important to reckon with television's influence on society and, in particular, to address whether satirizing bigotry worked.

Leading the first charge against the show was Laura Z. Hobson. The aging author had enjoyed wide success by exploring the issue of antisemitism in *Gentleman's Agreement*, a best-selling novel turned into an Academy Award–winning picture starring Gregory Peck, in the 1940s. She had deliberately avoided speaking or writing on prejudice ever since. Until now. Disturbed by *All in the Family*, she wrote a 5,000-word takedown of the show for the *New York Times*. Rejecting the very concept of a "lovable bigot," she charged that the producers were, in fact, whitewashing the hatred of prejudice by avoiding the most offensive slurs on the show. To her, "exposing" viewers to the bigotry of Archie Bunker was nothing less than "cruel" and served only to normalize prejudices.[104]

It sparked an intense debate in the pages of the *New York Times* and beyond.[105] The following week, John J. O'Connor, a respected television critic and reporter for the paper, dismissed Hobson's argument. Calling the show "one of the funniest," he suggested that "dealing humorously with an unpleasant fact of life, the program is at least a step in the right direction."[106] Further illustrating that television mattered, the paper printed no fewer than twenty letters to the editor in response to the essay in the Sunday edition a couple of weeks later. According to the editors, the published letters constituted only a small sampling of the mail the subject had provoked.[107] Around 80 percent of the letters sided with Hobson. Letters came from both those uneased about the show from the beginning and those claiming to have been "brought . . . to my senses" by Hobson.[108]

Others claimed that satire "exposing bigotry" worked and defended the show.[109] Among them were John Rich, director of *All in the Family*, who dismissed Hobson's criticism and suggested that she contributed nothing of value to the conversation.[110] The following week, producer Norman Lear joined the debate with a lengthy reply to Hobson. Bigotry, he argued, comes in many forms. Archie Bunker was *his* "honest portrayal of the bigot next door." For decades, he suggested, movies, books, and other mediums had portrayed bigots as villains. "We've had these bigots through the years—one-dimensional, stereotypes—ad nauseam."[111] The purpose of *All in the Family* was to show a bigot in whom "we see a little of ourselves." The bigotry, however, was always rebutted by the other characters. "Archie at best will work out some kind of convoluted logic to make a point," Lear argued, "but it's always foolish. Totally foolish."[112]

The attention provided by the confrontation between Hobson and Lear moved the conversation around *All in the Family* from reviews and op-eds to long-form articles looking at the controversy surrounding the show and offering a conclusion on its efforts to combat bigotry. *Newsweek* returned without a verdict, concluding that no show could be asked to "speak explicitly and directly to the issue of American racism."[113] While acknowledging the wide range of opinion on the issue, the *New York Times* handed down a verdict that sided with the producers: "Fifty million Americans are being told, week after week, it does you no good to be a bigot."[114] An elite consensus was emerging: *All in the Family* was all right.

When gambling on *All in the Family*, Bob Wood had wanted to start conversations about television.[115] He sought to make broadcasting relevant. Now, everybody was talking about Archie Bunker. "We can't turn it off," Wood told a journalist and, recognizing the value of the public conversation, added, "not that we want to."[116] In fact, it was no longer only television critics talking about the show. On late-night talk shows, Carroll O'Connor was taking on the "lady in New York," who was making "a big thing in the *New York Times* about Archie being a lovable bigot." Satire, he explained, could work where one-dimensional stereotypes had failed.[117] On Johnny Carson, O'Connor described the character as a fool and a loser.[118] Appearing on David Frost's show, Norman Lear talked about the value of satire.[119] Merv Griffin hosted Lear and the cast in conversation about the show and the intended message.[120] The conversations in the *New York Times* and *Newsweek* might have given more credibility with elites on the East Coast, but talk shows tended to attract a wider audience.

Nor was it only in the media, whether print or broadcasting, that conversations about *All in the Family* took place. It was the source of discussion in schools and universities, in churches, temples, and synagogues, and in government offices, corporate boardrooms, and union halls. And in living rooms across the country. By the end of the second season, a television writer proclaimed *All in the Family* "the phenomenon of the decade in the television world."[121] The conversations around the show, however, would soon elevate it to a *political* phenomenon as civil rights activists, advocacy groups, and political interests all came to recognize that television entertainment mattered and then turned to influence it and use it for their own campaigns.

Nobody had really expected Bob Wood to change television. He did not come to the network presidency with a reputation as a trailblazer nor with a mandate to transform CBS. In fact, the network dominated in the ratings. Or so it seemed. But because of his background working in the major media markets, Wood recognized that the national ratings failed to tell the whole story. *Gunsmoke* might have scored big in the heartland, but to win in New York or Los Angeles Wood needed something new.

Without the structural changes that were shaking the broadcasting industry at the start of the 1970s, however, network executives would never have put *All in the Family* on the air. Wood's gambit was a direct response to challenges wrought by technological advances, economic realities, and new regulatory policies. The "peak television" of the 1970s (think *All in the Family*, *The Mary Tyler Moore Show*, *The Bob Newhart Show*, *M*A*S*H*, and *The Carol Burnett Show* all shown in one night) was not the result of new talent finding their way into the medium but rather of a new business model taking over. When advertisers turned from buying the biggest audience to buying the best audience, highbrow fare that engaged with real life came in vogue.

Television critics, tired of the fantasyland of *Gilligan's Island* (CBS, 1964–67) and the homespun corn of *Mayberry R.F.D.*, welcomed the turn toward highbrow entertainment and the sophisticated satire of *All in the Family*. Keen to see the medium live up to its potential to inform public conversation on issues of relevance in society, critics turned discussion about the show into a conversation about television in modern life. *All in the Family* became everything to everyone, all at once. For Wood, it was a way of finding new audiences by changing the conversation about television. For Norman Lear, it was a way of reckoning with the bigotry of, and his love for, his father. For television critics, it was a daring new experiment into the power of a conservative medium. For audiences, it was simply the best show on television. For civil rights activists, however, it was either a threat or an opportunity.

# Chapter 2

MORE GOOD THAN HARM

Rabbi Arthur J. Lelyveld was disturbed. In the spring of 1972, the father of five noticed with growing concern that his own children were bringing home Polack jokes from middle school. Even worse, the jokes had been told to them by their teachers. The real culprit, however, was Archie Bunker. The most popular show on television, Lelyveld believed, was teaching children bigotry. He was not alone in his worry. "Everybody from cab drivers to doctors of psychology has a theory as to just what Archie Bunker is *really* saying," an editorial in *Television Quarterly* remarked.[1]

Neither a cab driver nor a doctor, Lelyveld was a recognized crusader for civil rights. He even had the scars to prove it. Andrew Goodman, one of the three civil rights activists murdered in 1964 in Mississippi, had been a close family friend, and in response to the news of the activists' disappearance Lelyveld traveled down south to spend "freedom summer" registering voters. On his fourth day in Mississippi, Lelyveld was attacked by segregationists wielding a tire iron, leaving him bloodied and bruised.[2] He had almost lost his life in the fight against bigotry and now, not even a decade later, television seemed to be the next front line. Lelyveld, now president of the 50,000-member advocacy organization American Jewish Congress, offered a scathing rebuke of *All in the Family*. Arguing that "it has created a new freedom to be offensive," he warned that after the Polack jokes would inevitably come slurs about "cheating kikes."[3]

Concerned about the influence of television on his children, Lelyveld argued that less sophisticated viewers—*others*—were being influenced by the show.[4] This idea, which sociologists today call the "third-person effect," informed much of the early criticism of *All in the Family*.[5] "The key, most agreed, was the level of sophistication of the viewing audience," one article on the early reactions to *All in the Family* noted.[6] Lelyveld, like Laura Hobson before him, was not worried about his own ability to recognize intended satire or dismiss Archie Bunker's bigotry. Instead, critics, including Hollywood legends such as Jerry Lewis, warned of "dangerous people eating it up alive."[7] The real problem was that the show reached an audience of up to 100 million people. Such an enormous audience included viewers, in particular children and people with little education, whom critics deemed "not sophisticated enough" to discern the message and thus regarded as "dangerous."[8]

Concerns over mass audiences had informed cultural, political, and even legal understandings of media for decades.[9] By the 1970s, however, elitist distrust of mass audiences was in decline. Television, the foremost *mass* medium, was talked about with new respect.[10] For sure, there were still some who insisted that they never watched the "boob tube" or prided themselves on not owning an "idiot box."[11] But they were fewer and fewer as the television set in the average household was on for almost six hours every day.[12] "Americans," one critic noted, "are a people very much committed to television."[13] Even "serious people ... stopped scorning [television]" in the new decade.[14] The new form of quality television that *All in the Family* represented gave television highbrow credibility.

So despite his position within the civil rights community, Lelyveld failed to engage a coalition of organizations and activists against the show. "There are those," he acknowledged, "who are ready to say that *All in the Family* does a great deal of good."[15] It turned out that these outnumbered him not only among the general audience but also within civil rights organizations. Campaigns to challenge *All in the Family* never turned into mass movements because most people appreciated the show. Lelyveld's failure, paradoxically, illustrates the earlier success of civil rights campaigns, which informed an understanding that *All in the Family* was doing more good than harm. This idea that prime-time entertainment influenced hearts and minds convinced a wide variety of activists and political interests to turn toward *All in the Family* to achieve their own objectives in the coming years.

"How do most blacks feel about Archie Bunker?" a reader asked in a letter to entertainment columnist Hy Gardner.[16] There was a sense of unease in the question. While clear that people, including people of color, were watching the show, it remained anybody's guess what they were thinking. Therein lay the source of the unease. *Broadcasting* magazine made it explicit in a cartoon of a white man watching television with his wife, with the caption "I know that Archie Bunker is really kidding but I wonder if the niggers do."[17] With *All in the Family* the most popular show on the air by the summer of 1971, it was clear that it mattered. It was not only the message the show was sending but also the reception of that message by different audiences that mattered. In particular, network executives, civil rights activists, and intellectuals worried over how people of color, on the one hand, and prejudiced whites, on the other hand, understood the show.

Without reliable empirical evidence available, beyond the Nielsen numbers, which indicated that the show was popular with all demographics, much of the conversation was speculative. Initial reviews in the Black press gave the show high marks.[18] "[Archie's] ranting serves an important purpose," a review in the *Los Angeles Sentinel* remarked. "I hope these upset liberals or uptight viewers won't lose sight of that fact."[19] Laudatory reviews in the Black press reassured white liberals that they could enjoy the show without any guilt by suggesting that the message resonated with minorities.[20]

Soon, however, the conversation changed. Whitney M. Young Jr., executive director of the National Urban League, delivered a stinging rebuke of the show in the *Los Angeles Sentinel* in February 1971. Blasting the show for "spreading the poison [of bigotry] and making it—by repetition—more respectable," he lambasted the writers, producers, and network executives. This was the first time a civil rights leader with a national standing spoke out on the show. His broadside predated Lelyveld's efforts by a year. And Young was not just criticizing the show; he seemed to suggest action against it. "The only message that comes through is that such a program ought to be taken off the air and relegated to wherever they're storing the old Amos 'n' Andy programs," he observed.[21] Two decades earlier, civil rights activists under the leadership of the National Association for the Advancement of Colored People (NAACP) had launched an eventually successful campaign of boycotts against the television adaptation of the popular radio show *Amos 'n' Andy* (CBS, 1951–53).[22] Now the leader of a major civil rights organization, a man who enjoyed respect both in the Black community and on Capitol Hill, seemed to be alluding to similar tactics. Due to his standing within the civil rights movement, any campaign Young suggested warranted serious consideration. Then something unexpected happened. While in Lagos, Nigeria, for a conference, Young drowned on March 11, 1971.

Young was not the only critic of *All in the Family* within the Black community. Such prominent figures as Tony Brown (executive producer of television's *Black Journal*), Charles L. Sanders (editor of *Ebony* magazine), Dr. Alvin F. Poussaint (of Harvard Medical School), and actor and comedian Bill Cosby all voiced disapproval of the show. None of them, however, had the same standing within the civil rights movement as Whitney Young. And those who did were unwilling to lead a campaign against it. The reason was not that they did not care about the show or its influence. Rather, they happened to like *All in the Family*.

"[It's] really very funny," Dr. John Morsell of the NAACP concluded in a sentiment shared by many.[23] Even Kwame Ture, the former Student Nonviolent Coordinating Committee chairman and honorary prime minister of the Black Panther Party who previously went by the name Stokely Carmichael, seemed to approve of the show. Producer Bud Yorkin later recalled receiving a call from the Black Power activist praising it for honestly depicting racism in the United States.[24] Many Black viewers writing to the production company echoed this idea.[25] No letters, however, seemed to come to civil rights organizations. Prominent leaders within the Black civil rights movement, including Roy Wilkins (NAACP) and Bayard Rustin (A. Philip Randolph Institute), noted that they had heard no voices of protest from their communities.[26] Indeed, despite much of the early conversation about the bigotry on the show focusing on the Black community, it was Jewish groups who protested the loudest.

Looking for a kind of consensus, representatives of various civil rights groups met to discuss the show and "compare notes."[27] The American Jewish Committee brought a diverse coalition of groups together in April 1971. On the agenda was one item: *All in the Family*. The meeting suggests the interest in the power of television among civil rights activists yet came about after a chance encounter with actress Sally Struthers. Since the first broadcast, the cast had taken an active role in explaining the purpose of the show—to satirize bigotry—in interviews, on talk shows, and at events. Thus, Struthers represented the production at the meeting hosted by the American Jewish Committee. Among the participants were also representatives for the Anti-Defamation League of B'nai B'rith, the Urban Coalition, the National Conference of Christians and Jews, the City Commission on Human Rights, the A. Philip Randolph Institute, and the Coalition of Italian-American Societies. Views varied considerably ahead of the meeting. Some groups had already condemned the show, while the host had praised it in public.[28] Without a clear consensus going in or coming out, no shared position emerged from the meeting.

Many groups declined to take any official position on the show.[29] A few months after the meeting, the leadership of the American Jewish Committee sent memos to area offices noting the lingering disagreement among civil rights groups on the effect of *All in the Family*. Still, their own position remained positive. "It is my own view," Irving Levine concluded, "that 'All in the Family' is an important breakthrough and serves to deflate bigotry."[30]

The debate between Laura Z. Hobson and Norman Lear in the pages of the *New York Times* in the fall of 1971, however, sparked further interest. In her essay, Hobson had criticized civil rights activists for failing to protest the show. In response, in a letter to the *New York Times*, Benjamin R. Epstein, national director of the Anti-Defamation League of B'nai B'rith, explained that the organization was careful not to appear interested in censorship but still had publicly condemned the show. He referred to comments by Arnold Forster, the organization's general counsel, saying that repetition of bigotry only reinforced such sentiments.[31] In fact, the internal correspondence within the organization illustrates an environment of uncertainty and competing views. Following comments by Forster, leaders within the organization questioned the stand. Oscar Cohen, the national program director, expressed an appreciation for the show.[32] Convinced that *All in the Family* succeeded in combating bigotry, Rabbi Jay Kaufman, of the Washington office, concluded that "we should distribute it, not condemn it."[33] In private, Epstein seemed to side with Kaufman, describing a recent episode as "hilarious," explaining that "we are not doing anything about [it]" and acknowledging that if it "succeeds in making prejudice ridiculous and laughable then it can have tremendously worthwhile results."[34] By the summer of 1971, a representative of the organization in private observed that "there has been substantial differences of opinion among staff and lay leadership" and concluded that it is "almost impossible" to say which view is right.[35]

Yet following Hobson's dress-down of the show, Epstein proclaimed in public that "we do not believe that it is possible to combat bigotry by laughing at a central bigoted figure who evokes the sympathy of the audience."[36] Indeed, Epstein echoed Hobson's criticism that the show was making "derogatory epithets" acceptable again.[37] Soon thereafter, the organization produced fact sheets stating that no research supported the theory of combating prejudice with humor and announced the position of the leadership against the show's stereotypes and slurs.[38] This was before social scientists had completed research on the subject, and in the absence of empirical data civil rights activists were key voices on the issue.

Even though Rabbi Lelyveld, along with Julius Kogan of the Jewish Centers Association and Rabbi Marc H. Tanenbaum of the American Jewish Congress, shared Epstein's public view, no organized opposition to the show materialized. Instead, supporters of the show, such as Robert E. Segal, executive director of the Jewish Community Relations Council in Boston, continued to "stubbornly cling to the view that [it would] do much more good than harm."[39] The lack of a united front, combined with the popularity of the show, allowed an elite consensus to form around the idea that *All in the Family* was successful in combating bigotry. The cast and producers were honored and praised for their efforts in the fight against prejudice and bigotry. The Eddie Cantor B'nai B'rith Lodge in Hollywood honored Carroll O'Connor, with Milton Berle proclaiming that "Archie Bunker has done a lot for us [Jews]."[40] Producers Norman Lear and Bud Yorkin were honored with the Image of a Challenge Award by the NAACP for having "challenged all [of] America to face these conflicts and to search our souls for healing remidies [sic] on how to live together as one nation."[41]

Critics within the civil rights community balked at their colleagues rewarding the show with awards. While not publicly condemning the decision, Epstein sent a tense note to the leadership of the NAACP requesting an explanation for the decision to celebrate Lear and Yorkin with an Image Award. While explaining that the awards were given out by the local branch of the organization and thus outside of his jurisdiction, in his reply John Morsell went out of his way to express his disagreement with Epstein. "I emphatically do not share your apprehensions regarding [the show]," he wrote. "I am very fond of it, would not miss watching it, and suspect that its net effect, if any, is a good one."[42]

The arguments in public conversation, closed meetings, and private correspondence illustrate the lingering disagreement within the civil rights community even as a consensus celebrating *All in the Family* was taking hold in public imagination. Even before these discussions, considerations about the power of television had permeated the production process, at both Tandem Productions and CBS, ever since Bob Wood first screened the pilot.

When *All in the Family* came on the air in January 1971, *TV Guide* had predicted that the "abrasive language and subject matter" would "keep the cards and letters pouring in."[43] Following the publication of Rabbi Lelyveld's denunciation of it the following year, people across the country wrote him to voice their agreement. One woman concluded by volunteering to write to "any particular company or organization" in an effort to help get the show off the air.[44] And yet, no significant letter-writing campaigns ever materialized. This failure was, in a way, evidence of the success of the civil rights movement of previous decades. By the 1970s, overt bigotry and racial discrimination were no longer socially acceptable in the corporate culture of broadcasting. In fact, anxiety over the offensive lines on *All in the Family* was the reason that ABC had passed on the project and high-level executives at CBS were hesitant to air it. Many critics, including Whitney Young and Laura Hobson, thought it was nothing short of irresponsible for the network to broadcast derogatory remarks about ethnic minorities. Some even charged network executives with not caring.[45]

On the contrary, the standards and practices department—the industry euphemism for "censor"—vigilantly monitored any use of ethnic slurs and expressions of prejudice. While appreciating the intent to satirize bigotry, the department still frequently attempted to tone down excessive examples of bigotry or offensive remarks. But even as conflicts between producer and network concerning sexual content are well known, the constant back-and-forth over Archie Bunker's use of derogatory epithets is less known. When the network found out that an episode in the fall of 1971 would focus on Mike's struggle with stress-induced impotence, they became concerned. Bob Wood himself flew out to California to meet with Lear.[46] "You're doing a show, a family show, on television, about he can't get it up?" the network head asked.[47] The censors, however, not only challenged the vulgarity in the episode but also demanded that lines they viewed as unnecessary ethnic remarks be removed from the script.[48] But while the fights over the former have been retold at length, the negotiations over the latter have been forgotten.

Lear was notoriously stubborn when it came to network demands on the script. "I automatically resisted Program Practices' position when they asked for something to be removed from a script," he later recalled.[49] Before the first episode aired, he issued his first ultimatum to the network. It would not be the last.[50] "He wore me out!" William Tankersley, the longtime head of the standards and practices department at CBS, known among colleagues as Mr. Prohibition, later recalled.[51] The executives at the standards and practices department cared about the content that went out over the airwaves, but they also cared about the success of the network. Norman Lear himself conceded that their suggestions at times led to conversations that in the end improved the show.[52] Still, as Perry Lafferty of CBS remembered, "They didn't talk Norman Lear out of doing much."[53] This was especially true after *All in the Family* climbed in the ratings. "Nobody fucks with success," Lear observed later.[54]

The cast, writers, and producers of the show also cared about "the mission."[55] The rule was, according to director John Rich, "that all black people, as well as anyone else whom Archie's bigotry had assaulted, would triumph in the end."[56] This was central to the show. Another central idea was that everybody could contribute to the script during rehearsal. If a line felt uncomfortable or offensive, actors, writers, director, and producer would sit down and discuss. Sometimes lines were cut because Mike Evans, the young Black actor who played Lionel Jefferson, objected.[57] Another rule was that Archie Bunker's ethnic slurs were always rebutted or challenged. "At least when Archie says it," writer Michael Ross observed about offensive remarks, "we hit him hard for it."[58] The writers, producers, and director used a variety of techniques to strengthen the understanding of Archie as the fool, including malapropisms, close camera shots, and the laughter of the studio audience.[59]

Whenever something slipped past the cast and the writers, the editors at the standards and practices department demanded stronger objections from the other characters.[60] Even when Gloria and Mike rebuked Archie over his remarks, editors and producers discussed which terms would work best.[61] For example, the network suggested that the term "blackie" was too shocking for audiences. Instead, they suggested a compromise in the form of "darky" because it was "more clearly recognized as part of a now discarded vocabulary."[62] While neither the network nor the production company would admit to any list of words that were unacceptable for *All in the Family*, both were comfortable nixing certain lines.

When Laura Hobson in the *New York Times* demanded that for Archie Bunker to be real he would have to use the most offensive slurs imaginable, Lear answered that he was uncomfortable with words "that connote real hatred."[63] Certain slurs—the worst ones—were simply unacceptable.[64] Indeed, no single offensive remark was allowed to overshadow the story. In the much-awaited first episode of the 1971 fall season, a frustrated Archie Bunker was faced with the challenge of organizing, and paying for, the funeral of a distant relative. "If it's cheaper, you can slip him in between a couple of coons," he remarked to the undertaker in the script. Taping the show in front of a live studio audience, the line provoked roars of laughter.[65] But when Bob Wood, who had heard of the offensive remark but nothing else about the show, congratulated Lear and Rich on the hilarious line the following day, they realized that it had to go. An offensive line could not upstage the actual story.[66]

Nor did the production company and network care only about individual words; no matter how offensive, they cared about demeaning stereotypes. "As written, we feel that the character of EMANUEL is demeaning to

Hispanic-Americans," a memo noted about a script introducing Archie Bunker's Puerto Rican coworker. Asking for a level of "self-respect and dignity" in the portrayal, the memo demanded that "the dialect should be accurate, avoiding exaggeration and stereotyped words and phrases." Finally, it asked the producers to cast a Puerto Rican actor in the role.[67] The role was eventually played by Rafael Campos, born in the Dominican Republic.[68] Another script featured two Black men (played by Cleavon Little and Demond Wilson) burglarizing the Bunker household.[69] The program practice department warned that they should be played "in such a way as to avoid ridicule of their race" and recommended adding the character of Lionel Jefferson to the episode as an example of "a law-abiding Black."[70]

The concern over the portrayals of ethnic minorities and of offensive slurs signaled the success of previous civil rights campaigns.[71] In the early 1970s, the standards and practices departments at the networks were more than just censors. They were the clearinghouse for all kinds of public relations, community outreach, and voices of protest. Pressure on the networks was growing as media reform organizations and special interest groups mushroomed in the late 1960s and early 1970s.[72] With them came newer groups representing white ethnic communities without a long tradition of campaigning for civil rights. Executives in the standards and practices department, however, were not as aware or concerned about jokes targeting them. Still, the most persistent, and angry, efforts protesting *All in the Family* came not from the Black or the Jewish community. They came from the Polish American community.

"Sticks and stones may break my bones," Archie told his son-in-law in an October 1971 episode, "but you are one dumb Polack."[73] This was neither the first nor the last Polack remark made by Archie Bunker. In fact, because the character of Mike Stivic had Polish American roots, sneers about Polacks were common on the show. Writing to Rabbi Lelyveld, one woman lamented that her kids go around echoing the line from *All in the Family*. "For me," she concluded, "the bloom is off the bigot."[74] While unsuccessful, the efforts of figures within the Polish American community to cancel the show illustrate both the rapid expansion of attention to media campaigns among newer interest groups and the work required to take on television entertainment.

From the premiere of the show, leading figures within the Polish American community protested the barrage of "Polish jokes." Denouncing the slurs and jokes directed at them, Eugene Kusielewicz of the Kosciuszko Foundation claimed they hurt the reputation of Polish Americans across the nation. According to the mail received by the production company, however, only "a few" of the letters on the issue condemned the show as offensive. "Others say, 'thank goodness, it's out in the open,'" Norman Lear claimed.[75] Both Carroll O'Connor and Sally Struthers acknowledged that they received a lot of mail from the Polish American community, including critical correspondence.[76] Still, the letters did not necessarily reflect a mass movement but rather the work of a small number of committed activists. "Ordinary Polish-Americans and Dr. Kusielewicz are Poles apart," one observer concluded.[77] An anthropologist studying Polish American communities in Western Pennsylvania mill towns reached the same conclusion. Polish Americans reacted to Archie Bunker's jabs with a shrug or a laugh.[78] Most Americans, after all, did.

Leonard Jarzab, however, did not laugh. He had already made a name for himself in the community by condemning mass-media portrayals of Polish Americans. In the late 1960s, his Polish-American Guardian Society had joined forces with the group Americans of Italian Descent to pressure Hollywood and Washington, DC. The goal was to convince the entertainment industry to refrain from negative depictions of white ethnics via legislation that would give the Federal Communications Commission (FCC) power to enforce the National Association of Broadcasters' (NAB) Television Code.[79] The Television Code, the industry fig leaf of self-regulation intended to avoid government censorship, was, in practice, not enforced by anybody.[80] Nothing came of the proposal in Congress. But Jarzab established his own position as a leader willing to take on the television industry.

When *All in the Family* came on the air with a barrage of Polish jokes, Jarzab took notice. Appreciating the structures and interests of broadcasting in the United States, he went after the bottom line. The show, he believed, was in violation of the Television Code's stipulation that "racial or nationality types shall not be shown on television in such a manner as to ridicule the race or nationality."[81] To him, it seemed obvious that *All in the Family* was in violation of the rule. Archie Bunker, after all, let loose with terms such as "Polack," "hebe," "chink," or "spade" on a weekly basis. First, Jarzab turned to the FCC. The successful license challenge led by Rev. Everett C. Parker of the United Church of Christ a few years earlier had fostered a growing awareness among media activists of how to use the system to go after discriminative practices. Yet it was arduous work. Successful challenges, such as Reverend Parker's, relied on documentation of patterns over all broadcasts by a licensee, an intricate knowledge of the license procedure, and considerable funds for drawn-out litigation.[82] Jarzab relied on his own conclusion that *All in the Family* was patently offensive.[83] That was not enough. Furthermore, the Television Code was a matter for the NAB, not the FCC. In fact, the commission had neither the right nor the intention to censor specific program material. Especially not the most popular show on television. The offensive language of the show, according to the law and the judgment of the commission, enjoyed "the protection of the Constitutional guarantees of free speech."[84] Jarzab, however, did not give up.

In his crusade against Archie Bunker, Jarzab turned from the FCC to the NAB. But he had no more luck with the industry body than with the government agency. The people at the NAB appreciated both the show and its mission. Nor were they likely to pick a fight with CBS. In disagreement with Jarzab's conclusion that it ridiculed any certain race or nationality, the NAB rather believed that the show mocked Archie Bunker for his prejudice. Holding that the ethnic slurs "were for the specific purpose of combating prejudice and racial bigotry," the Code Authority refused to sanction CBS.[85] Charging a "malicious campaign of defamation and degradation . . . against the people of Polish extraction," Jarzab claimed that no other group was as targeted by the show and demanded a meeting with CBS officials. He also threatened the network with congressional hearings.[86] The Code Authority suggested that the issue should be raised with CBS and directly with Norman Lear.[87] Even though Lear often did take time to answer questions from critics, including members of the Polish American community, there is no record of a meeting with Jarzab ever taking place.[88]

With Polish American community leaders such as Jarzab and Kusielewicz saying that protests against the show were necessary, members of Congress in districts with large Polish American populations paid attention.[89] In particular, representatives from Chicago, including Edward J. Derwinski (R-IL) and Frank Annunzio (D-IL), elevated the criticism on Capitol Hill.[90] Annunzio, in fact, campaigned for years for Congress to act against entertainment that would "defame, stereotype, demean or degrade ethnic, racial, and religious groups."[91] While these endeavors remained unsuccessful, the efforts of leaders within the Polish American community illustrate the emerging fervor to take on the television networks over prime-time entertainment. At the same time, their failure highlights the challenges facing any organized campaign against the juggernauts of television. Even with a coalition of respected civil rights groups behind the campaign, it would have been an uphill battle.

And yet complaints to the FCC ballooned dramatically during the show's heyday, climbing from around 2,500 in 1972 to 33,000 in 1973.[92] Challenges to station licenses also increased rapidly, from two in 1969 to sixty-eight petitions against a total of 108 stations in 1972.[93] This increase was *not* due to *All in the Family* but rather due to a recognition of the power of television. New groups started monitoring and protesting prime-time entertainment. And they modeled their efforts on the successful campaigns of liberal civil rights activists in the 1960s and the lessons of such liberal media activists as FCC commissioner Nicholas Johnson and Rev. Everett C. Parker. Rather, *All in the Family* was a vehicle for conversations about the relationship between activists, interest groups, and political interests, on the one hand, and television entertainment, on the other hand.

In the middle of the debate between Laura Hobson and Norman Lear in the pages of the *New York Times* over Archie Bunker's influence on audiences, one reader suggested a simple solution: "Ask the people."[94] This was easier said than done. While the A. C. Nielsen Company delivered numbers on audiences, including breaking them down into demographic categories, it could not tell you whether, or how, television entertainment influenced audiences' attitudes or social values. Nobody could.[95] And yet everybody wanted to know.

Even before there was any empirical research on the subject, many concluded that *All in the Family* had two different audiences: one laughing *at* Archie Bunker and the other laughing *with* Archie Bunker.[96] "The Silent Majority roots for Archie," *Saturday Review* claimed, "the liberals for all those who oppose him."[97] Following the public debate around the show with keen interest, executives at CBS, either disturbed by the idea of bigots liking the show or eager to capitalize on the public good it was doing, depending on whom you believe, ordered a study on it.[98] It was never published, and many assumed, incorrectly, that this was due to its conclusions.[99] Not so. In fact, it found that minority groups appreciated the show, and viewers who found a hero in Archie Bunker consisted of no more than about 5 percent of the audience.[100] Some suggested that any research furnished by CBS was suspect and claimed the researcher behind it "is looked upon with widespread disrespect" among the academic community.[101] Without publicly available research, however, speculation, not evidence, continued to drive the conversation. "We still have no way of knowing what effect a television performance has on attitudes and values," one article concluded in 1972.[102]

It would take until 1974, when the idea that *All in the Family* was doing more good than harm had already taken hold, before a significant study on audience reaction to Archie Bunker was published in a prestigious academic journal. Relying on the concepts of "selective perception" and "selective exposure," or the idea that people with high prejudice understood and enjoyed the show in different ways from other audience members, social psychologists Neil Vidmar and Milton Rokeach suggested that critics were right to worry about *All in the Family*. "In general," the paper concluded, "the data seem to support those who have argued that the program is not uniformly seen as satire and those who have argued that it exploits or appeals to bigotry."[103] It came too late to change the contemporary conversation around the show. But it, more than anything else, came to inform scholars' understanding of how audiences viewed Archie Bunker.[104] Thus, it cemented the idea of *All in the Family* as a kind of racial Rorschach test for years to come.

It was, however, always a flawed conclusion. Subsequent studies either contradicted the results or failed to replicate them.[105] Even more disturbing, it appears that the researchers anticipated finding a considerable portion of bigoted viewers cheering on their hero. This belief shaped and, possibly, distorted the design, implementation, and results of the study. Looking at a wide range of studies conducted in the 1970s, it appears that an overwhelming majority of viewers understood Archie Bunker as a bigot. While they might have liked the character, audiences did not agree with him.[106] Most people recognized him, quite simply, as a fool.

Some people, of course, never understood the satire.[107] Around the same time Vidmar and Rokeach's study was published in 1974, *All in the Family* director John Rich received a letter protesting that the producers in a recent episode had gone "too far" in trying "to tell us that a black man is smarter than Archie Bunker." He was disturbed by the letter.[108] Carroll O'Connor shared the sentiment whenever somebody approached him in public to applaud him, or rather his character, for telling it like it was.[109] "Of course a lot of bigots enjoy our show," O'Connor said in interviews, "but they must get the message that Archie is an unhappy man."[110] The number one rule on the show had always been that "Bunker loses, the maligned minorities win."[111] It registered with even the most hateful viewers. "It didn't escape the notice of any of those 'Right on, Archie!' people," Lear observed in his memoirs, "that the point of view of the show was that the man was foolish and his attitudes were harmful."[112]

Besides, *All in the Family* did not exist in a vacuum. Even if some viewers struggled to recognize the satire, they could hardly escape conversations about it in the paper or on *Johnny Carson*. Nor was it only in newspapers and on talk shows that the message of *All in the Family* was discussed. In churches, synagogues, and temples across the country, religious and community leaders turned to Archie Bunker to tackle the evils of prejudice and discrimination. Television, they realized, could be a teaching aid. Giving a sermon on "Jesus Christ and Archie Bunkerism," Methodist minister Dr. Kermit L. Long acknowledged that "some of us think there is more Christian gospel being preached from that program than from many churches and temples." Then he added, "If we get the message."[113] The message, however, was much easier to get when community leaders were guiding the audiences. "Archie is always the loser," Long announced, "in God's eternal plan."[114]

"Thank you for giving us the Bunkers to serve as tools for getting to know ourselves," a Presbyterian pastor wrote to Norman Lear.[115] All around the nation, ministers, rabbis, and reverends used Archie Bunker as a vehicle to preach about the wrongs of prejudice.[116] It was discussed in religious newspapers, newsletters, and magazines.[117] These conversations are often forgotten when attempting to gauge the influence of the show or looking to understand how audiences viewed the characters. And yet, they were a central part of how people in various communities experienced *All in the Family*.

All in the Family was not just entertainment; it was—by design—a tool to deal with prejudice in society. In churches, synagogues, and temples, yes, but also at work. Organizations and corporations, including army and navy bases, deployed the show in antidiscrimination work.[118] Western Electric turned it on during seminars on discrimination at work, while Detroit Bank & Trust counted on it to educate management about "patterns of prejudice."[119] Interest came from "schools, churches and non-profit groups concerned with sociological issues" to engage with the material.[120] The messages of the show reached far beyond prime time.

Yet conversation often started in the home. Indeed, one woman writing to Rabbi Lelyveld reminded him of the opportunity to "correct that error learned by television influence through subsequent family discussions."[121] While media activists recognized that television had a larger influence on values in modern society than even the church did, viewing prime-time entertainment did not need to be a passive pastime.[122] The idea of *All in the Family* was to foster conversation around difficult issues. Not just about prejudice but around illnesses, sexuality, and politics. "Conversation in the home," Norman Lear remarked in the *New York Times*, "how bad can that be?"[123]

In September 1978, around the start of the ninth and last season of *All in the Family*, Senators Alan Cranston (D-CA), William Proxmire (D-WI), and James Abourezk (D-SD) celebrated the show on Capitol Hill. Claiming that the show had done more to fight bigotry than almost anything else in the last decade, Proxmire observed, "I think it is very, very hard for us to really appreciate the effect of this kind of satire."[124] His remarks illustrated the elite consensus that had formed around the sentiment that the show did, in fact, combat bigotry. Without a united front of civil rights leaders against the show, and in the absence of any conclusive empirical research on the influence of the show, the various efforts to take on the most popular show on television never amounted to anything serious.

It remains unclear whether *All in the Family* succeeded in diminishing prejudice and bigotry in society. "If anybody thought he was going to erase prejudice with a situation comedy," Lear once remarked, "he'd have to be an asshole."[125] Importantly, even as it was the source of much discussion, bigotry was "merely a facet of the entire [show]."[126] Still, the very conversation about the influence of *All in the Family* illustrated a respect for the power of television and a search for understanding it. And the action it sparked from a variety of community leaders, intellectuals, and activists signaled a recognition that political campaigns needed to reckon with mass media. If *All in the Family* could sell not just Volkswagens, Alka-Seltzers, and 7 Ups but actual values and beliefs, various activists and political interests reasoned, then it was time to engage television entertainment.

"I suppose you would rather be known as a 'social commentator' than a 'preacher,'" a Methodist minister observed in a letter to Norman Lear, "but your social comments make good sermons."[127] Lear wanted, first and foremost, to entertain.[128] But he also wanted to engage and enlighten. "He *loved* to make statements," a former coworker observed.[129] Soon, activists recognized that *All in the Family* was the biggest soapbox in the nation. Even more important, they recognized that Norman Lear was happy to use it.

Chapter 3

ADVOCACY ON THE AIR

Standing in the office of Norman Lear, Virginia Carter felt out of place. The feminist leader was not an avid television viewer. In fact, she had been a vocal critic of television entertainment for years.[1] Television, Carter charged publicly, had hurt the women's movement by selling a "stereotyped image" to audiences.[2] When fellow feminist Frances Lear suggested Carter meet with her television producer husband, she did not recognize the name. Norman Lear might have been the cover story in magazines such as *Time*, appeared as a guest on *Dick Cavett*, and been *the* most talked about producer in television, yet to Carter he did not even register. After all, she did not have any dreams of making a life in entertainment and felt out of place among the glamour of Hollywood.

Then again, Carter had felt out of place most of her life. Raised Protestant in overwhelmingly Catholic small-town north Quebec, she had gone on to study math and physics at McGill University at a time when women were few and far between both in the natural sciences and at universities. She was equally out of place when she arrived for graduate work at the University of Southern California and even more so among the men that found employment in the booming defense industry at the Aerospace Corporation. While the men she worked with seemed to ride an escalator of promotions, Carter grew frustrated with a culture of discrimination stymieing her opportunities.[3] Being gay in an age when homosexuality was still viewed as a mental disorder further strengthened her identity as an outsider.

She found a home in the emerging women's liberation movement, rapidly rising to the presidency of the Los Angeles chapter of the National Organization for Women (NOW).[4] It was there that she met and befriended Frances Lear. And it was out of loyalty to Frances that she agreed to meet Norman. She had no expectations for the one-on-one with the producer. "He's a big muckymuck in Hollywood," Carter recalled thinking, "and I'm a physicist!"[5]

Television, however, was changing. Norman Lear and Tandem Productions were eager to strengthen their position in relation to both the networks and various activist organizations distrustful of television. Carter's activist experience and connections, Lear understood, were an asset at a time when feminist activists and progressive advocates were increasingly challenging television.[6] The networks eschewed controversy, yet the success of Tandem Productions depended on engaging, and occasionally enraging, audiences by courting it. Taking over some of the networks' responsibilities of audience contact at the production company made sense.[7] It strengthened Tandem vis-à-vis the networks while serving liberal causes. It was a way of doing good by doing well.

Within a few years of her first meeting with Lear, Carter was one of the most influential women in television entertainment. Her activist voice, or at least her voice echoed by the characters on *All in the Family*, was heard by tens of millions of people gathered around the television on Saturday nights. The outsider was brought inside. From the inside, she would work not just with producers, writers, and executives but with advocates and activists. The independent production companies, the real engine of 1970s television, would do what the networks had refused to do for decades: open the doors to outsiders. In the process, Carter and Lear remade the relationship between television entertainment and political institutions and campaigns.

In the network era, broadcasting dominated public life.[8] While film and theater enjoyed a higher cultural status, television entertainment enjoyed a vast audience. Where a movie could become a success with only a couple of million tickets sold in a weekend, even the worst shows in prime time drew an audience in the tens of millions every week. All the same, network executives imagined that national audience to be pretty bland. "Let's face it," a studio executive remarked, "the squares have always been the television audience and always will be."[9] As a result, most television entertainment in the late 1950s and the 1960s was made for "the squares."

In theory, broadcasters were bound by the production code of the National Association of Broadcasters.[10] In practice, the networks ruled the industry. CBS, NBC, and ABC all placed the responsibility for program content and viewer relations within their own broadcast standards and practices departments. "Standards and practices" and "program practices" were industry euphemisms for censorship. Over the first decades of television, writers were frustrated time and time again by network editors (the preferred title of the censors) limiting what they could and could not write for a television audience. Any suggestion of sexuality was off-limits in the 1950s and 1960s. Even the word "pregnant" was forbidden when Lucille Ball was expecting on *I Love Lucy* (CBS, 1951–57) in 1953, and almost a decade later the married couple on *The Dick Van Dyke Show* (CBS, 1961–66) could still not share a bed.[11] Real life was often prohibited from the air. The censorship lingered into the 1970s. Network executives, for example, refused to accept the idea of Mary Tyler Moore's character being divorced on *The Mary Tyler Moore Show* in 1970.[12] Minorities were also excluded from the airwaves. Black audiences were not even considered by the networks before the late 1960s and early 1970s.[13] Thus, there were no racial minorities in the 1960s prime-time small towns of Mayberry, North Carolina (*The Andy Griffith Show*), or Hooterville, Missouri (*Petticoat Junction*).[14] Even the word "Jewish" was verboten as Austin "Rocky" Kalish and Irma Kalish discovered in the late 1960s when writing for *The Flying Nun* (ABC, 1967–70).[15] The lack of real life on television comedy in the 1960s was not, however, a reflection of the writers' creative interests. Rather, it was the result of the business interests of the network executives.[16]

The rise of the independent production company, sparked by the fin-syn rules, and various citizens' groups and advocacy organizations changed the power balance in broadcasting. "The simple, crucial fact about American broadcasting," industry scribe Les Brown remarked, "is that it cannot be reformed from within."[17] The networks would never cede the remarkable power they enjoyed. Change would have to come from the outside. Neither insiders nor outsiders, independent production companies such as Tandem Productions opened the doors for outside advocates and activists eager to reform broadcasting.

With *All in the Family*, Norman Lear set out to engage audiences and did so with controversial subject matter. In the very first season, the show dealt with homosexuality, premarital sex, women's liberation, and residential segregation.[18] This was the kind of material that standards and practices departments had shunned for decades. Beyond enraging executives at CBS, it engaged activists and advocates around the country.[19] Assuming some of the responsibility of standards and practices at the production company made sense, strengthening Lear's hand in relation to the network and giving him an opportunity to tackle any form of organizing against the show.

Yet it was *Maude* (CBS, 1972–78), a spin-off of *All in the Family*, that made both Tandem Productions and advocacy organizations sit up and take notice. No single incident came to shape the relationship between advocacy or activist groups and television more than Maude Findlay (Beatrice "Bea" Arthur) finding out that she was pregnant in a first-season two-part episode aired in November 1972. It was both the result of advocacy work and a turning point for future activist campaigns.[20] The episode illustrates the power of collaboration in shaping television entertainment, the value of elite allies, the importance of countering protests, and the need for coalition-building.

Arthur had originally played the role of Maude, Edith's liberal cousin and Archie's nemesis, on a December 1971 episode of *All in the Family*.[21] Before the episode ended, Fred Silverman, head of programming at CBS, called Lear insisting on a show featuring the charismatic Arthur.[22] An immediate success was born. Yet despite strong ratings, executives recognized that *Maude* was controversial. "Maude breaks every rule of television from the start," Bob Wood noted.[23] Engaging feminist issues and featuring a strong woman in the lead was enough to make it a lightning rod for controversy.[24]

The worst storm hit early. In November 1972, only two months into the first season, Maude faced a dilemma as she found herself unexpectedly pregnant at age forty-seven. She did not want another child. Her adult daughter Carol (Adrienne Barbeau) encouraged her mother to consider an abortion: "We finally have the right to decide what to do with our own bodies."[25] Abortion was indeed legal in New York state, where the story was set.[26] But the show was broadcast some two months before *Roe v. Wade*, the landmark Supreme Court decision recognizing a constitutional right to abortion in the nation, and the procedure was still outlawed in most of the country. In the end, Maude and her husband Walter (Bill Macy) recognized that another child was not the right choice for them and together decided on an abortion.

While writer Susan Harris, who would go on to develop *Soap* (ABC, 1977–81) and *The Golden Girls* (NBC, 1985–92), shared credit for the episode with the writing duo Rocky and Irma Kalish, advocacy campaigns also played a part. It was the Population Institute, under the leadership of David O. Poindexter, that fostered acceptance for such a daring subject among the top echelons of network executives and among the creative community.[27] "David got Maude pregnant," Norman Lear later quipped.[28] It was not far from the truth.

A reverend in the Methodist Church, the liberal Poindexter had headed up the broadcasting and film commission of the ecumenical National Council of Churches in the 1960s before moving to the Population Institute.[29] Poindexter often stood out among the creative community with his religious zeal, yet he moved between Hollywood and the Eastern establishment in New York and Washington, DC, with ease. His work at the broadcasting and film commission had given him a keen appreciation of the structures of television. Furthermore, it offered access to an impressive network of contacts in the business. His advisory group at the Population Institute was a venerable who's who of broadcasting. Members included Robert Lewine, president of the Academy of Television Arts and Sciences; Thomas W. Sarnoff, son of David and brother of Robert and charged with running NBC's West Coast division; and Lou Cowan, former president of CBS.[30] These were names that mattered in the executive suites and boardrooms in New York.

Poindexter cultivated a top-down strategy for his advocacy work. In 1971, he organized a luncheon for network executives and political leaders at the Waldorf Astoria in New York, using his personal friendships to engage the President's Commission on Population Growth and the American Future for the event.[31] The commission was headed by John D. Rockefeller III—a name that commanded respect among elites in both New York and Washington, DC.[32] Serving on the so-called Rockefeller Commission was Robert Packwood, a young, liberal Republican from Oregon who had cultivated a reputation as a champion of women's rights in the Senate.[33] Packwood also happened to be Poindexter's friend from college.[34] Through Packwood, Poindexter got Rockefeller to serve as host for the luncheon. With invitations from Rockefeller, it was no problem getting the highest executives from the networks, including Frank Stanton of CBS, to attend.[35] This was the Eastern establishment in action.

Years later, Poindexter recalled the meeting as a success. After hearing from Packwood on the importance of population control, Stanton responded with a gentle rebuff. Assuring the commission that all agreed on the importance of the issue at hand, Stanton suggested that the network executives were the wrong audience and that they should "be out on the Coast talking to the creative people."[36] Poindexter, however, knew that producers in Hollywood were unlikely to court controversy without explicit support from the executives in New York. He also recognized that both Hollywood and New York could avoid making any commitments by blaming the other. Prepared for the executives to deflect, he presented a letter from Harry Ackerman. Ackerman was a veteran of broadcasting whose résumé included stints as vice president at both Young & Rubicam and CBS as well as executive producer of shows such as *Dennis the Menace*

(CBS, 1959–63) and *Bewitched* (ABC, 1964–72). Poindexter read aloud the key sentence in Ackerman's letter: "What a group of well-intentioned writers and producers might offer or suggest could prove to be meaningless without a climate of approval and support having been established at the networks."[37] He called Stanton's bluff or, depending on the perspective, schooled the president of CBS on the structures of broadcasting. In any case, Stanton conceded the point and Poindexter left the meeting with a commitment from all three networks to air "quality programs dealing with aspects of the population issue."[38] With the promise from the East Coast, he turned to the West Coast.

In California, Poindexter teamed up with the Academy of Television Arts and Sciences to host conferences introducing television producers and writers to experts on population issues. The events were intended to provide the creative community with research and to spark conversation on how entertainment could be used for good.[39] Following initial disappointment with the hesitation in Hollywood to address political and social issues, Poindexter was excited by the success of *All in the Family*.[40] "I believe that you are making a number of substantial contributions through this program and am delighted with it," he wrote to Norman Lear.[41] The most popular show on television, Poindexter believed, could bring about a change in the creative community. After all, television was a business that rewarded imitation.

The Population Institute established awards with cash prizes for programs addressing topics of sexuality and birth control, recognizing the importance of building prestige as well as financial incentives to engage the creative community.[42] The awards proved successful, with a total of four separate shows in the fall of 1972, including *Maude*, featuring stories related to population control.[43] Many writers brought their ideas to Lear. "This year half a dozen writers came in with late-life pregnancy ideas," he noted.[44]

It was not, however, a question of the advocacy group bribing writers and producers. Rather, the green light from network executives and advocacy organizations allowed writers to tell stories derived from real life—the kinds of stories standards and practices departments had deemed unacceptable for decades. Many writers now embraced the permission, from both the networks and independent production companies, to touch on social and political issues. The abortion episode of *Maude* was pitched by Rocky and Irma Kalish, the same writers who a few years earlier were told they could not identify a character as Jewish on *The Flying Nun*, who were eager to "challenge" the networks and enjoyed the new freedoms Lear provided.[45] Lear himself embraced the honest engagement with the subject and made the call to have Maude, and not a friend of hers, face the dilemma.[46] Staff writers Bob Schiller and Bob Weiskopf, veterans of *I Love Lucy*, in which even the word "pregnant" had been considered inappropriate two decades earlier, were charged with rewriting the scripts, and later recalled the challenge of finding comedy in abortion but feeling that the work was "worthwhile."[47]

The real challenge, however, came after the broadcast of the episodes. Hundreds of angry phone calls lit up the switchboard at CBS. Viewers wrote to the producers, the local stations, the network, and the Federal Communications Commission (FCC), and the episode was debated in the press and in living rooms across the country.[48] Following the first episode of the two-parter, three stations announced they would not air the second segment but in response found themselves under fire from supporters of the show.[49] In Champaign, Illinois, the decision not to broadcast the second part resulted in 400 phone calls over two days. Both opponents and proponents organized against the show, the production company, the local stations, and the networks. While the National Council of Catholic Bishops demanded "equal time" from the FCC, NOW filed a lawsuit seeking an injunction to force the station to air the show.[50] Both were unsuccessful. Yet the action signaled the need to handle advocacy and activist organizations if you wanted to engage social and political subjects on the air.

And so Virginia Carter's baptism by fire came in the summer of 1973, when the reruns of *Maude* were about to hit the airwaves. Since the first broadcast of the episodes in November 1972, the *Roe v. Wade* landmark Supreme Court decision had come down. In response, antiabortion organizations mobilized across the country.[51] Ahead of the summer reruns, antiabortion movements, especially through the Catholic Church, organized alliances to oppose the show and protest both the network and individual CBS affiliates.[52] The pressure was considerable. Lear recalled in his memoirs that "zealots across the country made thousands of phone calls; seventeen thousand similarly worded letters of protest were received by CBS; hundreds in the South and Midwest picketed their local TV stations; and in New York City protesters la[id] down in front of William Paley's car as the chairman of CBS was driving into his network's garage."[53] This was an all-hands-on-deck kind of event for both Tandem Productions and CBS. And Virginia Carter was running point at Tandem.

Aware of the organizations and movements engaged in the fight for women's rights and birth control, Carter drew on her own connections to build coalitions and coordinate the response. She, along with Norman Lear, met with Poindexter in the summer of 1973 to talk about common interests and collaboration. Poindexter described the meeting as "extremely worthwhile for the concerns of the Population Institute," which would become a key ally, along with NOW and the National Association for the Repeal of Abortion Laws (NARAL).[54] NARAL had already warned members and allies of "a massive, organized campaign ... to intimidate the network, Maude, and its sponsors."[55] By the summer, the coalition of supporters of the show adopted the tactics of media activists: phone calls, letters, and pickets. "[We] hesitated to launch a counter-attack," Lawrence Lader of NARAL wrote, "until it became obvious that the official Catholic Church was determined to show it could bend the media to its will, and at the same time, impress Congress with its power."[56] Prime time had emerged as a proxy arena for a political fight.

Affiliate stations around the country balked at the controversy. Advertisers such as Pepsi-Cola and J. B. Williams Company abandoned the show.[57] And yet Frank Stanton held firm in his commitment to air quality shows on population control.[58] With the word of the president of the network, combined with William Paley's personal interest in the show, the structure of broadcasting allowed the personal interests on the executive floor to override short-term business interests.[59] Advertisements were still the source of revenue, but by the 1970s individual advertisers were no longer able to dictate standards to the networks. Not a single sponsor ended up buying time on the shows. "That's a million dollars down the drain, right there," Virginia Carter remembered years later, "but they did it. I had such respect for [the CBS executives] for going through with that."[60] It was the result of both advocacy organizations and activist mobilization.

The brouhaha over *Maude* highlighted the need for Carter to assume the role of a one-person standards and practices department within Tandem Productions because, more often than not, Lear's eagerness to challenge the audience with real subject matter put him at odds with the networks. He could not always count on them to have his back. To take control, Lear needed Carter to do due diligence on controversial subjects, develop collaborative strategies with advocacy groups, build coalitions with different movements, and foster relationships with activists.

As Virginia Carter settled in at Tandem Productions, she screened all the shows of *All in the Family* and received the scripts in development with the instructions to give notes. To her surprise, the scripts were changed in accordance with her comments. "I was stunned," Carter later recalled, "I thought, 'Who am I?'"[61] She was hired at Tandem not because she was friends with Frances Lear but because of her activist background within the women's movement. She became, in effect, an in-house standards and practices department, and while her official titles varied from special assistant to vice president for creative affairs, she was soon recognized as "second only to Lear" when it came to social and political issues on the shows at Tandem.[62]

Carter recognized her influence. "I can change one sentence in a TV script," she remarked in interviews, "and thousands of viewers will receive the impact."[63] The production process behind *All in the Family* rested on a number of staff writers—in the early days primarily Don Nicholl, Bernie West, and Michael Ross—but many of the ideas came from outside writers such as Rocky and Irma Kalish.[64] Most of the writers were middle-aged Jewish men with résumés that included classics such as *I Love Lucy*, *Your Show of Shows* (NBC, 1950–54), and *The Steve Allen Show* (NBC, 1956–60). They had worked for comedy legends such as Jack Benny, Milton Berle, and Bob Hope. There were, however, no more than a handful of women or people of color in the writers' room for the early seasons of *All in the Family*. So Carter brought new perspectives and lived experiences to the writing and rewriting process.

All in the Family was notorious for its many rewrites.[65] Before and after an idea was assigned to writers for a full screenplay, it was worked over in story conference with the staff writers, the producers, and the director. Everybody, including the actors, was encouraged to give notes, and rewrites followed. "We never stop working on this show," Don Nicholl described the process.[66] It could take months or even years before a script was deemed ready.[67] The notes and rewrites, a sort of collaborative process once described as "creative communism," continued up until the taping of an episode.[68] This created the perfect environment to include the voice of Virginia Carter. She brought with her research on controversial subjects, messages from advocacy organizations, and—importantly—a feminist perspective.[69] And a commitment to make the most of it. After all, Carter remarked, "to waste that valuable air space I'd have to be a crazy lady."[70]

Norman Lear wanted *All in the Family* to tell real stories about real people. The writers' room was furnished with all the major newspapers to keep the writers aware of current events and spark their interest. Even more important, Lear instructed the writers "to come to work prepared to talk about their marriages, kids, family problems, health problems—their lives in the context of what was going on in their communities and the world."[71] Writers, and the cast, brought their own experiences of issues such as infidelity, welfare policy, antiwar protests, and illness to the show.[72] When the show presented Edith as a victim of sexual violence, Lear explained in the press that they were "taking something right out of our national life and dealing with it."[73] Dealing with important matters on a comedy show required a deep understanding of the subject at hand.

Virginia Carter was brought on to "make sure we were on the right track with women."[74] She became responsible for research on all topics addressed on the show. When writers suggested a story line about Mike having a vasectomy, Carter consulted with the Population Institute.[75] "Hundreds of men get vasectomies every day right in the doctor's office," Gloria told her husband in the broadcast episode. "It's as easy as one-two-three, snip-snip-snip."[76] When developing an October 1977 episode in which Edith was assaulted, the production company reached out to the Santa Monica Hospital Rape Treatment Center asking what they would say "if you could talk to 40 million people about rape."[77] Working on an episode featuring LGBTQ+ characters, Carter—herself in a committed same-sex relationship—corresponded with the National Gay Task Force to avoid harmful stereotypes.[78] Similarly, when Sally Struthers was expecting, the writers suggested a story line about Mike's vasectomy having failed but decided against it after consultation with the Population Institute.[79] It was not just about being funny: the message mattered, too.

While the primary consideration was to make shows that people would watch, the conversations in the writers' room and in story conferences made it very clear that their considerations were not limited by business imperatives or laughs. At the first story conference on the show in which Edith was attacked, Carter set the agenda: "What we can do most wrong about rape, I think, is to simply rescue Edith."[80] When writers suggested different story devices that would save Edith—including a broken window, a hanging plant, a broken stove, or a broken chair knocking out her attacker—Lear objected. "These organizations," he said referring to the rape treatment centers they had collaborated with on research, "do have things they would love women to know."[81] Following extensive writing and rewriting, Lear rejected solutions that depended on something beyond Edith's control. "There's a million reasons for doing the show," he maintained, "but one of the original reasons was, a woman can save herself if she does the right thing."[82] The message was more important than the comedy. In the broadcast episode, Edith slammed a scorching hot cake right from the oven into her tormentor's face and kneed him in the groin before escaping to safety amid boisterous applause from the studio audience.[83]

Bringing new perspectives and research into the development of shows was just one part of Carter's work at Tandem. She also invited advocates and activists to bring any objections to her and promised to hear them out personally. Her open-door policy signaled an interest in different perspectives and at the same time placated any organized protests of the show because she met with critics in person.[84] Often it worked, but at times it invited heckling or threats.[85] Importantly, it fostered relationships with advocacy groups and

Edith Bunker (Jean Stapleton) is attacked by Lambert (David Dukes) on *All in the Family*, 1977. CBS/Photofest.

activist organizations. For producers eager to engage social and political issues, it made business sense.[86] Carter herself explained, "If there's one person who is boiling enough to get through my door, there's probably 10 million behind him."[87] Again, doing good while doing well.

Building on her own personal network within the women's movement, Carter bridged the divide between feminism and television entertainment.[88] While most early public conversations on *All in the Family* focused on bigotry and prejudice, feminists—including Frances Lear and Peggy Yorkin—were uncomfortable with the show's portrayal of women.[89] Both producers and writers seemed to take the criticism to heart.[90] "Watch us closely next year," Lear wrote in reply to audience criticism months before Carter was hired, "and see if you haven't been influential in some changes we are planning."[91] Bringing in Carter, with feminist bona fides beyond reproach, was a first step toward change at Tandem.[92]

Carter also started hosting special advance screenings of shows for activists and representatives of advocacy groups. For example, she invited her friends in the women's movement to attend the screening of an episode in which Gloria and Mike fight about "women's lib," calling it a "fantastic feminist show."[93] The idea, she explained, was for her friends to "confirm (or reestablish) my feminist perception."[94] Most likely, she was looking both to assess their perspectives *and* to signal a new spirit of collaboration at the production company. Even if Carter was now working in television entertainment (the enemy camp), her standing within the movement vouched for her work. "I trust your perspective," one of her friends wrote in declining the invitation.[95] Beyond Carter's personal friends, and illustrative of the emphasis she put on coalition-building, the invitation list for the advance screening also included representatives from Planned Parenthood, the Population Institute, and NARAL.[96] These were all allies from the fight over *Maude* earlier in the year. In fact, David Poindexter was on the list even though he was not an authority on feminism, nor was the Population Institute a feminist organization. Instead, established relationships and elite contacts guaranteed him a seat at the table.

Soon, the advance screenings became a vital component of Carter's work, establishing personal relationships with movements, acknowledging their position and interests, and—importantly—assimilating them in an effort to avoid any action against the production company. Carter served as a one-woman standards and practices department. Awed by her power working on the most popular show on television, and a desire to do good, she went further than the departments at the network had ever gone.[97]

Writers and producers on *All in the Family* engaged social and political issues to attract and retain an audience. In an era without home video recorders or streaming services, audiences could view the show only when it was broadcast or wait for reruns in the summer or in syndication after a couple of years. Many in the viewing audience, especially those people working on the issues the show took on, appreciated the power of storytelling and of the Bunker household to raise awareness and educate. In general, they found an ally in Virginia Carter. "What I do," she explained, "is try to make the public contact of our shows last longer than the 30 minutes they're on the air."[98] This was a new measure of success for television entertainment—not only selling advertising minutes or amusing audiences but having an impact on their lives.

Years before the notorious episode in which Edith is assaulted, Rocky and Irma Kalish had written a show in which Gloria survived an offscreen attempted rape.[99] Among letters to Tandem Productions from viewers recounting their own experiences of sexual violence were requests from the Women's Coalition on Rape Prevention in Wisconsin for a copy of the show to help in its work of raising awareness and to "provoke discussion."[100] Carter was happy to oblige and not only sent the group a copy but also promised to reach out to her contacts at NOW with the "hope that your fine example will inspire them to action."[101] She even agreed to remove the advertisements from the taped copies on Tandem Productions' dime, illustrating how the good cause mattered above and beyond the bottom line.[102]

Over a year after the original broadcast of the show, it was still being used for educational and advocacy purposes. Carter made it available to a criminal justice training and education center for use as part of a crisis intervention course for law enforcement.[103] In between sessions with law professors, gynecologists, psychiatrists, pathologists, and a female police sergeant, participants were shown the episode to understand the emotional and mental health of a victim.[104] This was not just business as usual.

When the show returned to the subject of sexual violence a few years later with Edith's assault, Carter was eager to work closely with advocacy groups to reach the right audiences. Together with antirape activists and feminists, she organized screenings around the country.[105] For example, a screening was arranged with the coordinator of the victim services at Boston City Hospital. Among the 120 guests for the evening were staff from the hospital as well as from rape crisis centers and from other hospitals in the metropolitan area and the suburbs. In the press, the hosts praised the show and the positive response among the guests.[106] Centers across the nation worked with the production company to raise awareness around the issue with pamphlets and tapes of the show.[107] Carter made sure that the impact of *All in the Family* would not be limited to half an hour, with advertisements, once a week. She made the most of the freedom brought by the show's success.

Norman Lear was more than willing to violate the old Hollywood adage "If you have a message, call Western Union."[108] He had done the sort of comedy that offended nobody while writing on shows such as *The Colgate Comedy Hour* (NBC, 1950–55), *The Martha Raye Show* (NBC, 1954–56), and *The Tennessee Ernie Ford Show* (NBC, 1956–61). But with *All in the Family*, he intended to send a message. The success of the show, combined with the increased influence his independent production company enjoyed following the adoption of the fin-syn rules, gave him the freedom to send (almost) all the messages he wanted.

Initially, Lear defended himself against charges of peddling liberalism in the guise of entertainment by insisting that it was only comedy.[109] Soon enough, his reasoning evolved as he became more comfortable acknowledging his liberal perspectives and his interest in bringing them to his work.[110] That comfort came with the success of *All in the Family*, evident in ratings and awards.

Speaking at the International Radio and Television Society's ceremony in May 1973, where he was honored with the award for Broadcaster of the Year, Lear confronted the issue head on.

> Some of the print media question whether we have the right to express social opinion in a situation-comedy format. I think we do. And I do not believe we are breaking precedent in doing so. Throughout the years Newton Minow was calling television a wasteland, there were dozens of situation comedies on the tube. I remember the biggest problems those sitcom families faced. The boss is coming to dinner and the roast is ruined. Or daddy's about to take the car out of the garage and only Sis and Junior know that mom dented the fender that very afternoon. I'd like to suggest that there was a great deal of social opinion in that. America was being told that the biggest problem it faced was that the roast was ruined, which could only mean that there was no urban crisis, there were no problems between the races, and Vietnam was a word made up by Walter Cronkite.[111]

All in the Family was forcing a reckoning with the power of television entertainment. It was made possible by the business success of Tandem Productions. In the 1972–73 television season, it had not only the number one show on television in *All in the Family* but also the number two show with *Sanford and Son* (NBC, 1972–77). *Maude* was number four. Within two years, *Good Times* (CBS, 1974–79) and *The Jeffersons* (CBS, 1975–85) joined them among the ten most popular shows. *All in the Family* broke records, selling advertisements at a rate of $120,000 a minute.[112] In other words, Lear was basically printing money for CBS. Or, as CBS broadcast president John A. Schneider put it, Lear was "a 2,000-pound gorilla."[113] And he was willing to throw his weight around.

Television was still a conservative business, and though Lear was remaking prime time, other producers struggled with network restrictions. *All in the Family* could engage issues ranging from menopause to miscarriage and impotence. But CBS refused to grant the same freedom to less successful shows. So when in 1973 the producers of *The New Dick Van Dyke Show* (CBS, 1971–74) wanted to do an episode about a young child walking in on her parents in the middle of an intimate moment, the network refused. According to producer Carl Reiner, the decision came directly from Bob Wood and resulted in Reiner vowing never to work with the network again.[114] Even though the original *Dick Van Dyke Show* in the 1960s had made Reiner and Dick Van Dyke into royalty at CBS, the numbers for the new show were not there for the network to give them the freedom Lear enjoyed.[115]

Television is, fundamentally, a producer's medium.[116] As producer, Lear provided his writers with unusual freedom. When the network complained, he defended them.[117] Screenwriters flocked to Tandem Productions because of the opportunities Lear gave them to engage real life.[118] Recalled writer Bernie West, "It's nice to be with a show where we can be as free as we are."[119] Fellow producers and writers viewed their colleagues at Tandem as trailblazers who provided them with cover. The producers behind *M*A*S*H*, for example, understood *All in the Family* as "a real breakthrough" that allowed them to go further in their own work.[120] It gave successful shows on CBS, such as *M*A*S*H* and *The Mary Tyler Moore Show*, license to push the envelope.[121] James Komack, the producer of *Chico and the Man* (NBC, 1974–78) and *Welcome Back, Kotter* (ABC, 1975–79), remarked that *All in the Family* signaled to others that "if we had something better and more to say, the door was open."[122] In response, situation comedies started dealing with more controversial subject matter such as alcoholism, homosexuality, and equal pay.[123]

Nor were television producers and writers the only ones who noticed the prominence of Tandem Productions. When advocacy groups or activists approached the creative community, fellow producers tended to urge them to involve Lear or Carter.[124] In various advocacy campaigns and collaborative projects, Virginia Carter was often identified as a key ally.[125] Advocacy organizations honored Lear with awards and accolades for his work to further issues ranging from civil rights to population control.[126]

The press recognized Lear as pivotal in the growing influence in broadcasting of advocacy groups. Trade papers such as *Variety* and *Broadcasting* observed that he held a "special status" among both the networks and the "outside pressure-group[s]."[127] By the mid-1970s, *Newsweek* noted that listening to outside groups was "an obligation that comes with the franchise" and highlighted Lear as an example for producers and advocates.[128] In a cover story in *Time*, Lear and his business partner Bud Yorkin were declared to be the "catalysts" for change in television entertainment.[129] While Yorkin focused on motion pictures, *Sanford and Son*, and the business at Tandem Productions, Lear emerged as the first really famous television producer.[130] Soon, *Time* crowned him "King Lear," while Bob Hope joked that "we can all be proud of TV and its owner, Norman Lear."[131]

Network executives, however, were not looking to give away the keys to what they still perceived as their kingdom. Throughout the late 1960s and early 1970s, broadcasters looked askance at the growing influence of the public to

Norman Lear talking with Carroll O'Connor and Jean Stapleton on the set of *All in the Family*. CBS/Photofest.

voice demands on television. Broadcasters had built a business that put profits above service, even though it all depended on the public airwaves.[132] They had long enjoyed considerable freedom through regulatory capture of the FCC.[133] By the 1970s, they felt under assault from all sides: The FCC had imposed new rules on both syndication and prime-time access, congressional action against tobacco advertisements hurt the bottom line, the courts held that broadcasters did not enjoy full First Amendment rights, President Richard Nixon used television as a political punching bag, and grassroots activists were organizing to demand changes. Defiantly, the network bigwigs declared their refusal to bow to outside pressure.

So in the fall of 1973, after the intense fight over *Maude* had engaged all kinds of advocacy groups, the networks were on the defensive. In the network era, entertainment provided broadcasters with profits, and the news division provided them with power.[134] If outside groups successfully exerted pressure on the networks over entertainment programming, the executives feared, they could soon influence the news department.[135] Executives shared a belief in their own judgment and a distrust of the creatives out in Hollywood, the politicians and regulators in Washington, and the audiences around the nation. Giving in to pressure from advocates would, according to John Schneider, mean surrendering power to "a small minority whose only qualification to wield such power is that it is vocal, it is persistent and it has the capacity to cause us trouble."[136]

He seemed not to appreciate the irony. Only a couple of years earlier, Vice President Spiro Agnew had declared that it was time to question the power "in the hands of a small and unelected elite" at the networks.[137]

Hesitant to give Lear more power, network executives put the kibosh on his attempt to include an advisory message with mental health information at the end of an episode of *Maude* dealing with depression. Entertainment television, Wood said in a 1975 open letter to the producer, "should not propagandize. It should not proselytize. It should not advocate political or social positions."[138] While unable to include the message in the first broadcast, such pronouncements did not inhibit Lear and Carter from continuing to push the envelope. Two years later, Robert Wussler, Wood's successor, announced that television should "always remain a half or three-quarters of a step behind society." At Tandem Productions, the remark by the new president of CBS Television was roundly mocked. "Fellars," Lear announced to his writers, "we're going to have a hard time being any funnier than this today."[139] The incident, which found its way into the *Boston Globe*, illustrated the reluctance among executives to cede control to outsiders, yet it also highlighted how independent producers defied the networks.

The rise of outside groups eager to remake television according to their own agenda was not single-handedly the result of Norman Lear's work. By the 1970s, television quite simply had grown up and with it came increased political, social, and intellectual scrutiny. Yet the popularity of *All in the Family*, and Lear's commitment to engage social and political issues, made his shows *the* arena of advocacy and activist television campaigns. For Tandem, the bottom line grew when the writers and producers were engaging and, yes, enraging the audience. *All in the Family* was not the most popular show on television *despite* its willingness to address subjects such as menopause, birth control, sexual assault, and impotence. Rather, *All in the Family* was the most popular show on television *because* it engaged with real life experiences. Both Lear and Carter knew it and let it guide their work with advocacy groups and activists. But they also went beyond just catering to their business interests by trying to use the show to advance a good cause on and off the air.

The shift in the power balance between the networks and independent production companies made it possible for Lear and Yorkin to build their own miniature standards and practices department at Tandem Productions. The one-woman department of Virginia Carter stood in stark contrast to the larger standards and practices departments at the networks. There, broadcasting insiders concerned with protecting the status quo in order to secure the bottom line ruled. The heads of the standards and practices departments at the networks—William Tankersley of CBS, Herminio Traviesas of NBC, and Alfred Schneider of ABC—all came up through the business side of broadcasting before moving into their roles as censors. These were vastly different starts than that of Virginia Carter, an outsider in all walks of her life who came into television to break the very same status quo that the men at the networks wanted to protect. "The doors have not been opened enough," Lear declared in 1976.[140] But with Carter he wanted to break them open for other outsiders who wanted a voice in the stories television told. Nor was it only outsiders who recognized the power of television entertainment. Insiders in Washington, DC, were hoping that Archie Bunker could help them win elections.

Act II

CANDIDATES AND CAMPAIGNS

Chapter 4

RICHARD NIXON MEETS ARCHIE BUNKER

Richard Nixon often said that he never watched any television.[1] Yet for all the talk of his predecessors, particularly John F. Kennedy, being "the first television president," nobody in national politics was as consumed by television as Nixon.[2] Appreciating the vast political power of the medium, Nixon intended to either master or dismantle it. Beloved television figures such as Walter Cronkite, Johnny Carson, and Archie Bunker, Nixon reasoned, could either make or break his presidency. And so his keen understanding of television, often influenced by his trusted friends in Hollywood and in the White House, resulted in a media strategy that was both stick and carrot. Nixon was Dr. Jekyll, fostering relationships with the power brokers of television and eager to use the medium to his advantage, *and* Mr. Hyde, intimidating television executives and intent on hurting the networks. Nixon's first encounter with Archie Bunker, however, was all Mr. Hyde. It was by happenstance that Nixon first came across *All in the Family*. He was hoping to catch a baseball game on television in May 1971 only to find it was rained out. Instead, he found himself watching Archie Bunker and was stunned. "The damnedest thing I've ever seen," he told his aides.[3]

The episode Nixon stumbled upon explored prejudice, with a focus on Archie's views of Gloria and Mike's effeminate friend visiting the household. "His friend Roger," the homophobic Archie announced on the show, "is as queer as a four-dollar bill and he knows it."[4] Gloria protested her father's antediluvian attitude while Mike objected to his views on masculinity: "Just because a guy is sensitive, and he's an intellectual and he wears glasses, you make him out a queer." Soon, the tables were turned on Archie, as his own friend—masculine, strong, and handsome—was revealed to be gay. Nixon did not approve.

Fuming over the show, Nixon discussed it in the Oval Office with his closest aides, White House chief of staff H. R. Haldeman, and Domestic Affairs Advisor John Ehrlichman. "Goddamn it," he exclaimed heatedly, "I do not think that you glorify on public television homosexuality." While Ehrlichman was unfamiliar with the show—it had been on the air for only a couple of months at that time—Haldeman had been watching it. Haldeman described an earlier episode in which both Mike and Archie write a letter to the president, and he suggested the intent was to ridicule Nixon's political base.[5] "Usually, the general trend of it is to downgrade [Archie]," Haldeman explained, "make the square hard hat out to be bad."[6] The show was unacceptable, an exasperated Nixon declared. "I turned the goddamned thing off, I couldn't listen to any more."[7]

Nixon went on ranting about homosexuality and the influence of television. "Goddamn it," he remarked, "what do you think that does to kids?" Progressive values on sex and sexuality broadcast to living rooms across the nation constituted, according to the president, a moral problem. He continued his tirade by arguing that the values presented on television entertainment threatened the very foundations of society. "You see, homosexuality, dope, immorality in general: these are the enemies of strong societies," he declared. "That's why the communists and the left-wingers are pushing the stuff: they're trying to destroy us." Haldeman and Ehrlichman agreed with their boss, the latter lamenting the influence of television on society. Later that same day, Nixon—still vexed by the show—returned to the subject with Haldeman.[8] More than indicative of Nixon's temper and his conspiracist obsessions with suspected left-wingers out to undermine the United States, the conversation illustrated his understanding of the reach and influence of television entertainment. It marked a paradigm shift for both Nixon and the Republican Party—who had relied on the star power

Archie Bunker (Carroll O'Connor) and Steve (Philip Carey) on *All in the Family*, 1971. CBS/Photofest.

of Hollywood and the media advice of television producers and advertisement executives to win elections for decades—to a politics of animosity toward the entertainment industry as well as the news media over perceived "liberal bias."[9]

Richard Nixon is remembered as "a man alone," with many enemies but few friends.[10] Yet for all the talk of Haldeman and Ehrlichman as a kind of Berlin Wall around the president, throughout his career Nixon sought the counsel of friends and associates.[11] An ardent student, constantly taking notes on yellow legal pads, Nixon came to understand the power of television early on by befriending actors, producers, and executives in the industry. Having entered public office in 1946, representing California's Twelfth Congressional District for four years before leveraging his anticommunist reputation into a Senate seat and, two years later, receiving the Republican Party's vice presidential nomination, Nixon's rise—buoyed by right-wing bigwigs in Hollywood providing funds and glitter to his campaigns—coincided with the rise of television.[12]

Long before most people even had television sets, Nixon quizzed a television producer named Edward Rogers about the potential of the new medium and was impressed enough to bring him on as a political consultant. In the fall of 1952, when Nixon turned to television to fight for his political future amid a scandal over a slush fund threatening his place as vice president on the Republican ticket, it was Rogers who advised him on the technical aspects of the televised delivery of the so-called Checkers speech.[13] "He saw that night what television can do and he was in awe," Rogers later remarked.[14] And in the televised debates against Kennedy eight years later, Nixon—still advised by Rogers—learned the power of television not only to lift up but to tear down.[15] In defeat, Nixon became even more convinced that mass media was the key to success in modern political life.[16] The fault was not with the candidate, Nixon and his media advisers later concluded, but with the media image of the candidate.[17]

It was after his loss to Kennedy that Nixon met and befriended Paul W. Keyes of *Tonight Starring Jack Paar* (NBC, 1957–62). During an early 1962 visit on the popular late-night program, Jack Paar introduced the former vice president to Keyes and remarked that the latter was "an Irish Catholic from Boston who voted against JFK in 1960."[18] Television and conservative politics became the foundation for their close friendship. Only months after they met, in the middle of the 1962 California gubernatorial race, Nixon suggested Keyes look over campaign material and provide feedback.[19] Keyes gave comprehensive and detailed notes on television appearances, covering everything from makeup and lighting to Nixon's warmth.[20] In his role as a liaison, Keyes not only arranged for movie and television stars to appear on telethons for Nixon but provided notes on how they might best articulate their support for the candidate.[21] Keyes even wrote questions that were, falsely, presented as coming from audience members of the telethons.[22]

But the 1962 gubernatorial election was another disaster for Nixon. Two years earlier he had been so close to winning the White House and before that spent eight years as vice president; now he could not even win statewide office in his home state. Yet even in defeat, Nixon relied on Keyes to mold his public image. For while Nixon had publicly sworn off politics in his virulent "last press conference" and moved to practice law in New York, he never gave up his political ambitions. In private, Nixon and his most trusted advisers, including Keyes, never stopped planning his political comeback.[23]

To keep him in the limelight and rehabilitate his image, Keyes orchestrated an appearance on the prime-time *Jack Paar Program* (NBC, 1962–65) within six months of Nixon's defeat in California.[24] Nixon recognized the importance of the opportunity and corresponded with Keyes, who was a producer on Paar's new show, on both questions and answers of interest.[25] For example, Keyes suggested Paar might ask about which person in government was doing the best job and offered J. Edgar Hoover, the longtime conservative head of the FBI, as the best answer.[26]

The appearance was a success, with Nixon at ease, playing the piano. "You asked just a moment ago whether I had any future political plans to run for anything," Nixon joked, "and if last November didn't finish it, this will, because believe me the Republicans don't want another piano player in the White House."[27] If Nixon had shown that side of himself on television three years earlier, media theorist Marshall McLuhan believed, he would have won the White House.[28]

Nixon continued to use talk show appearances to rebuild his public persona in the run-up to the election year of 1968. The key, Nixon's aides recognized, was to "poke fun at the questioners and at yourself, and at the general scene."[29] As a guest on *The Tonight Show Starring Johnny Carson* (NBC, 1962–92), for example, Nixon seemed relaxed and made several self-deprecating quips. "I'm an expert on how to run for president," a smiling Nixon remarked before delivering the punch line: "Not how to win but how to run."[30] That was a variation of a Keyes line.[31] Nixon even kiddingly offered to run for vice president if the beloved Carson would run for president, noting that "I'm the expert on how important [television image] is."[32] The show was another success for Nixon.[33]

Convinced of the power of television, and equally convinced the press was out to get him, Nixon and his team wanted to control their campaign in 1968 by producing and directing it from within a studio. Television was "the perfect isolation booth," offering complete control.[34] Keyes wrote, or rewrote, questions attributed to voters—a practice even a young Roger Ailes admitted was a "sort of semiforgery"—for Nixon's tightly choreographed television events.[35] The president's celebrity supporters, including Jackie Gleason of *The Honeymooners* (CBS, 1955–56), endorsed Nixon on telethons with words written by none other than Paul Keyes.[36] The zenith of Nixon's entertainment campaign came on Keyes's own show, *Rowan & Martin's Laugh-In* (NBC, 1968–73). While campaigning in Burbank, California, Keyes convinced his friend—apparently over the objections of his other campaign aides—to visit the zany variety show. The most popular show on television in the fall of 1968, it combined youth culture aesthetics with the conventional style of the eponymous comedy duo of Dan Rowan and Dick Martin. The concept was "absolutely balls-out nothing but comedy"; the result was an endless fusillade of jokes, quick cuts, and nonstop punch lines.[37] It was, in short, both funny and popular.

It was not, however, very presidential. Still, with *Laugh-In* returning for a second season in September, Nixon shocked the audience with a surprise appearance on the show. Amid the rapid-fire comedy, he came on the screen to utter one of the show's signature catchphrases: "Sock it to me?" No longer than a few seconds, the guest spot marked a new recognition of the political importance of entertainment and, importantly, of Keyes's influence on Nixon.[38] Without Paul Keyes, it is safe to say, there would have been no "sock it to me" from Nixon. When recording, the set was cleared except for the producers and Nixon's closest advisers, as the presidential candidate struggled to deliver a four-word line without coming across as aggressive rather than incredulous.[39] His performance on *Laugh-In* depended on his friend delivering an opportunity to gamble on entertainment in a safe setting. "Nobody would have ever been able to get Nixon to come on the show and say 'sock it to me,'" Dick Martin later acknowledged, "other than Paul Keyes."[40]

Left-leaning producers repeatedly attempted to persuade the Democratic Party candidate, Vice President Hubert Humphrey, to also appear and quip, "I'll sock it to you, Dick!"[41] Humphrey refused, deeming it risky and failing to understand the benefit of entertainment television in a mediated political race. "That kind of muddle-headed thinking ... cost Humphrey the election," Martin later observed.[42] Democrats agreed. Humphrey himself would later attribute his narrow defeat to not going on *Laugh-In*.[43] The election of 1968, one of the closest elections in modern history, played out against the backdrop of war in Vietnam, political assassinations, protests in the streets, and unprecedented twists and turns, and it was far more complex than a one-liner on *Laugh-In*.[44] Yet to many media strategists the impression was that Nixon had come across as warm and in on the joke while Humphrey was left outside in the cold. And so Nixon arrived in the Oval Office more convinced than ever that television entertainment could revolutionize political life.

When *All in the Family* returned for a second season in the fall of 1971 as the highest-rated show on prime time, the conversation around the power of television entertainment to change attitudes and promote social values captivated the nation. In Hollywood, everybody seemed to have an opinion not just on the laughs but at whom viewers were laughing. There was no real consensus, but many believed the show failed to change hearts and minds. In Washington, political columnists such as William S. White, Rowland Evans, and Robert Novak speculated about the political power of "the Archie Bunker vote."[45] White concluded in early 1972 that the show was "no doubt intended to be only entertainment" but now was "becoming far more than merely amusing."[46] Nixon, however, had learned not to worry about *All in the Family*.

"Archie's for us!" a happy Nixon announced in the middle of a meeting with H. R. Haldeman and press secretary Ronald Ziegler in early 1972.[47] Then he dived into a story he seemed to have told several times before, asking Ziegler if he had heard the story of *All in the Family*. According to Nixon—apparently informed by Keyes, whom he briefly mentioned—the "Jewish" men behind it "wrote this show for the purpose of making the hard hat look [bad]." They did not, however, expect audiences to find in Archie Bunker a "hero." Nixon claimed that was exactly how viewers understood the character and suggested that the producers were "utterly shocked" by this reaction. "They don't know what the hell to do with it," he laughed and insisted that they were desperate to change the situation. Now, Nixon continued, they were exploring ways of detaching viewers from Archie's politics by either having him "see the light" or by making him into a monster to repel audiences. Either way, he concluded with glee, "they've screwed themselves." Dismissing their failure, Nixon suggested that the producers now subscribed to the notion that "it doesn't have any social message, like they thought it would, all it is is pure entertainment." Laughing, Nixon proclaimed that "it isn't that at all!"[48] Whether or not Nixon, or Keyes out in Hollywood, read the situation correctly, this belief that *All in the Family* failed to reach audiences with liberal satire informed his thinking about the show.

Still, Nixon remained convinced that producers and writers were using entertainment television to push a political agenda. Since his earliest days in national politics, Nixon had believed that entertainment could, and should, promote certain values and, more important, condemn others. Way back in 1947, Nixon had used his position on the House Un-American Activities Committee to challenge the entertainment industry, going so far as to suggest to the head of the Motion Picture Association of America (MPAA) that Hollywood should tell audiences about "the evils of totalitarian communism."[49] His long-held belief that entertainment should reflect societal values informed his early anger over *All in the Family* ridiculing the values of his silent majority.

Satire, Keyes had convinced him, was not only powerful but also dangerous.[50] In private conversations, Nixon worried about "satire and other stuff." With Haldeman, the president debated various actions to be taken against writers and directors responsible for ridiculing him in literature and films. "When someone does good satire," Haldeman conceded, "it can be devastating."[51] Not only did Nixon worry about the devastating effect of comedy, but he was also convinced that comedians and writers were out to hurt him politically. "The way to get the other side," he insisted, "is to laugh at them."[52] And Nixon was determined not to let anybody get him.

Furthermore, Keyes had convinced him that Hollywood was full of liberals and Jews. Nixon's deep suspicion of entertainment was often tinged with overt antisemitism. The secret recording system installed in the White House captured Nixon's inquiries about whether perceived enemies in Hollywood, including television talk show host Dick Cavett and the producers behind the satirical film *Millhouse*, were "all Jews."[53] In conversation with Billy Graham, the prominent Southern Baptist minister and informal adviser to the president, Nixon laid out the reasoning behind his concern about Jewish producers. He complained about all the "filth" in television and movies, calling it all "extremely dangerous."[54] Both men agreed the mass media was controlled by Jews, and both viewed it as a problem. "They're the ones putting out the pornographic stuff and putting out everything," Graham exclaimed. A little later, he suggested that "this stranglehold has got to be broken or this country is going to go down the drain."[55] Nixon told Graham that Keyes had informed him of the Jewish domination of television entertainment. "He says it's true of every show in Hollywood," Nixon remarked. "Eleven out of twelve writers are Jewish."[56] It was not the only time Nixon or his friends engaged in the antisemitic trope of Jewish control of the media.[57] A close friend, businessman Elmer Bobst, warned Nixon of "the malicious action of Jews in complete control of our communications."[58] And Vice President Agnew's infamous attacks on the networks carried antisemitic undertones that provoked "an avalanche of sick mail."[59] Distrust of the three television networks, headed by William Paley, David Sarnoff, and Leonard Goldenson, had long been fueled by antisemitism.[60] Despite Nixon's conspiratorial condemnation of Jews and "filth" on television, including the conversation around homosexuality on *All in the Family* that angered him, his most pressing concern remained the image of his political movement.

When talking to Haldeman and Ziegler in January 1972, he reflected on a recent episode of *All in the Family*. This one revolved around Mike struggling with stress-induced bouts of impotence.[61] It was a controversial topic for a network show in the 1970s. From the beginning, censors at CBS were anxious over the intimate nature of the topic at hand, saying that "the comedy treatment of such a personal subject . . . requires unusual care."[62] Norman Lear argued that the episode did indeed show unusual care.[63] CBS wanted to keep any sexual references to a minimum and reminded him that "the network cannot abdicate its responsibility to decide for itself what is in acceptable taste and what is not."[64] Defiant as always, Lear pushed ahead even after censors requested changes in the script.[65] With producer and network at a standoff, Bob Wood, the president of CBS Television, flew out to California and after hours of discussion, at times heated, agreed to broadcast the episode.[66]

Nixon was not bothered by the sexual comedy. In fact, in the privacy of the Oval Office, Nixon, Haldeman, and Ziegler laughed at how Archie approached his neighbor Henry Jefferson (played by Mel Stewart) to ask for remedies for his son-in-law's intimate problem. Archie, in his ignorance over race and sexuality, thought his Black neighbor might have the solution. The problem for Nixon was how Archie Bunker and Henry Jefferson were portrayed. While the white man was played for a fool, the Black man was, according to Nixon, presented as a "Harvard-educated" man with an "Oxford accent."[67] In fact, Jefferson had neither an Oxford accent nor a Harvard education, but presenting a person of color as superior to a white bigot was a deliberate choice. The comedy hinged on a basic premise: Anybody maligned by Archie Bunker's bigotry would triumph.[68] Yet Nixon wanted Archie, the representative of his silent majority, to win.

To Richard Nixon, everything was political. Since his election to the White House, Nixon had invested time and effort in attracting entertainers, including Art Linkletter and Red Skelton, to join him at the White House for dinners, events, meetings, and even sleepovers. While some stars had become actual friends of Nixon's over the years, this was first and foremost a strategic move. He was determined to play Mr. Nice Guy to win endorsements, contributions, and votes. Memoranda within the White House highlighted the need to curry favor with "a letter, a call, or even possibly a White House invitation" if a celebrity "does something newsworthy which might be of interest to the President."[69] In one memo, Nixon himself suggested inviting talk show hosts Johnny Carson, Merv Griffin, and Mike Douglas for evenings at the White House, "even though I don't like most of these people," as a strategic move to win goodwill among the popular talk show hosts. "This could pay off in great measure to us," he concluded.[70]

Nixon's old friends in Hollywood, the stars he had relied on for decades—Ginger Rogers, George Murphy, and John Wayne—were, well, old. Hollywood was no longer the same industry it had been when Nixon was coming up and the studio system ruled the entertainment world. Old Hollywood was giving way to New Hollywood, where stars no longer looked with the same kind of deference to studio executives before taking a stand on issues such as civil rights, the war in Vietnam, or presidential elections.[71] Nixon's trusted supporters—Bob Hope, Lucille Ball, and Jackie Gleason—while still popular among large segments of the population, were remnants of the studio system and the least objectionable programming era of television.

Nixon's team realized that beyond the cadre of celebrities of yesterday, they needed to win over the stars of today.[72] But the Warren Beattys, Goldie Hawns (the breakout star of *Laugh-In*), and Barbra Streisands tended to support Nixon's challenger Senator George McGovern. They lined up behind McGovern, Nixon's men believed, only for the "publicity potential" of supporting "extreme candidates."[73] Thus, the campaign needed to either convince stars that Nixon was their man or make clear that supporting the president would benefit their careers. To do this, they needed to pay attention not only to the celebrities themselves but to the powers that be in Hollywood.

Many of the old tycoons Nixon had counted on throughout his career were either gone or no longer as powerful as they once were. Samuel Goldwyn was ill, Darryl F. Zanuck was off in Europe with his lover, and Jack Warner had lost control of Warner Bros. To make sure studio executives and other power brokers were committed to the president, Nixon used communications policy to align himself with their interests. In this, Taft Schreiber of the talent agency/media conglomerate MCA emerged as a key ally. Lew Wasserman was king at MCA, but Schreiber, the number one Republican, was prince.[74]

Schreiber, who by the 1970s was in his sixth decade at MCA, was a man with considerable influence in the entertainment industry. He had gained a role in GOP politics by turning Ronald Reagan from a young liberal actor struggling to book roles into the conservative governor of California.[75] Schreiber contributed six-figure sums to political campaigns and could deliver millions more from his personal networks. In 1968, he coordinated fundraising efforts for Nixon in California and became close with the candidate.[76] Since then, he had become Nixon's jack-of-all-trades in Hollywood.[77] He was pivotal in the fundraising campaign and provided connections for whatever the president needed.[78] In exchange, Schreiber was given a voice on communications policy, serving as a liaison between the industry and the administration.[79]

Schreiber convinced Nixon to meet with leaders from the entertainment industry. In April 1971, Nixon hosted two dozen representatives at his home in San Clemente, California. They—men such as Charlton Heston of the Screen Actors Guild, Jack Valenti of the MPAA, and Ted Ashley of Warner Bros.—felt squeezed by declining revenue and foreign competition. Many of the executives and leaders in Hollywood shared an enemy with Nixon: the television networks. Nixon viewed them as liberals, Schreiber and his friends understood them as rivals and looked to Nixon for relief through policy changes regarding Federal Communications Commission (FCC) regulation, cable television, antipiracy measures, copyright protection, and tax reform.[80]

Following a fundraising party Schreiber hosted in August 1972, Nixon delivered what *Broadcasting* called his "most provocative statement yet on television programing" by taking a stand against reruns.[81] In a letter to the head of the Screen Actors Guild, he announced that "the increasing number of reruns on the networks in prime time constitutes an economic threat to the talented men and women of the American film industry."[82] Neither the FCC nor the White House had shown any particular interest in the issue before Nixon became involved. In fact, Brian Lamb with the Office of Telecommunications Policy at the White House had concluded only months earlier that it is not "the government's job to tell the media how to run their business."[83] In private conversation, Nixon made it clear that he viewed the issue as a way of both hurting the networks and winning favor in Hollywood.[84] The politics behind it was obvious to all and openly acknowledged in the trade press.[85]

Winning over the bigwigs was a way of sending a message to stars in Hollywood: "An entertainer who commits to the President will have some friends at the top of their industry."[86] That is why Nixon sent the media darlings of the administration, including Henry Kissinger, John and Martha Mitchell, and First Lady Pat Nixon, as well as old friends such as John Wayne and Zsa Zsa Gabor, to fundraising parties Schreiber hosted.[87] The idea, rather naïve, was to "make it the 'in' thing for Hollywood stars to support the President."[88] Schreiber and Keyes were charged with making connections with young actors and actresses, while influential producers such as Jack Warner and Richard Zanuck signaled potential career benefits associated with supporting the president.[89]

Based on information his friends provided, Nixon knew which stars would bring the most attention and positive reaction to his reelection campaign. He hoped to broaden his political coalition via celebrity endorsements.[90] To win Black voters, he leaned on Sammy Davis Jr.[91] To win disillusioned Democrats, Frank Sinatra.[92] To win middle America, Johnny Carson. To win the white working class, Archie Bunker. Convinced that the silent majority Nixon wanted to claim as his base viewed Archie as their hero, the *All in the Family* character loomed large in his political strategy. Haldeman went as far as calling Archie "the best campaign commercial we could've had."[93] Another aide remarked on the "power Archie has with [liberals]."[94] And so the reelection campaign launched a fervent crusade to win an endorsement from Archie Bunker in the fall of 1972. "Several big names in the movie industry, powerful names who were friends of Nixon's," the press reported, "made a major effort to get [Carroll] O'Connor to come over to the President."[95] Recognizing the importance of television entertainment and the connection viewers had with the popular

Richard Nixon with friend Taft Schreiber and actress Tina Cole (*My Three Sons*). Oliver Atkins/Richard Nixon Presidential Library and Museum.

representative of the white working class, they wanted Bunker/O'Connor to play a considerable role in the campaign. "They wanted to paper the country just before the election with photos of Nixon and Archie Bunker shaking hands," sources claimed.[96]

That was where Nixon's powerful friends in Hollywood came into the picture. Schreiber was one of the allies Nixon depended on to make personal pleas to talent.[97] When popular entertainers such as Johnny Carson and Merv Griffin told the president's men that they were for Nixon but could not endorse him, it was Schreiber who leaned on them to go public.[98] Billy Graham also suggested to Carson that he could help Nixon with more favorable treatment on his show.[99] Carson was popular enough to dismiss the pressure and stayed on the sidelines. Carroll O'Connor was even more popular and, in contrast to Carson, a loyal liberal. To him, Nixon was anathema. There would be no pictures of Nixon shaking hands with the most popular representative of his silent majority.

While Nixon could play nice when needed, he did not hesitate to play hardball. He had long nurtured a deep hatred of the media and was convinced that the feeling was mutual. His closest confidants recognized Nixon's vengeful outbursts as temporary moments of weakness.[100] But some advisers were happy to play the role of the devil on Nixon's shoulder, to encourage his vindictiveness, and to become the personification of his "dark side."[101] The problem, according to one of the president's longtime advisers, was "Colson and his band of merry men taking instructions that were meant to be denied and running with them like crazy."[102] Charles "Chuck" Colson was not exactly popular in the White House. Most of his colleagues regarded him as both brilliant and something of a son of a bitch—an "evil genius," a "hit man," and a "hatchetman."[103] The prevailing opinion in and beyond the West Wing was that Colson would walk over his own grandmother for Nixon.[104] He played to Nixon's worst instincts to win influence in the administration, becoming the president's "special assignment man" who answered only to Nixon.[105] With Colson, Nixon left Dr. Jekyll behind and embraced Mr. Hyde. And as Mr. Hyde, Nixon wanted to hurt the powerful, and in his view liberal, television networks.

The initial idea was to control Nixon's image by controlling the newsmen.[106] On the campaign trail in 1968, Haldeman had frustrated the press by keeping the candidate "wrapped in cellophane" and the reporters at bay.[107] In the White House, Haldeman continued to make life hard for the men and women of the media. The former advertising executive at J. Walter Thompson became Nixon's "media magician" and the "President's S.O.B."[108] The president depended on him to such a degree that even close aides acknowledged that it "was hard to tell where Richard Nixon left off and H. R. Haldeman began."[109] Haldeman controlled the press shop and installed a fellow ad man, Ron Ziegler, as press secretary. Ziegler, it was understood, would serve as "hardly more than a Pinocchio puppet whose nose does not grow when he fibs."[110] In control of communications, public relations, and the press office, Haldeman would sell Nixon's image and media campaigns.[111] According to Dan Rather, White House correspondent for CBS News, Haldeman "made a lifetime study of the techniques of manipulating my business."[112]

When control failed, vindictiveness took over. A White House memo from early in the administration outlined wide-ranging actions: deploying the FCC, the IRS, and the Justice Department and targeting the networks with monitoring, regulatory action, antitrust lawsuits, and audits.[113] The first real salvo in the war on the media came in November 1969 when Vice President Spiro Agnew, known as "Nixon's Nixon" for his tendency to serve as mudslinger, was assigned to fire a vicious broadside against the television networks.[114] In front of a crowd of Midwestern Republicans in Des Moines, Iowa, and broadcast to tens of millions over all three networks, Agnew charged the television networks with liberal bias.¹¹⁵ Portraying the news executives and reporters at the networks as an elitist cabal in Manhattan, he labeled them "a tiny, enclosed fraternity of privileged men elected by no one."¹¹⁶ Agnew issued veiled but ominous threats of government action unless the networks became "more responsive to the views of the nation and more responsible to the people they serve." Network executives, including CBS president Frank Stanton, and anchormen, in particular Walter Cronkite, all recognized the speech as an attempt to intimidate the media and vowed to stand strong.¹¹⁷ If intimidation would not work, Nixon wanted to hurt the networks. "We can't kill the news and make it go away," he recognized in private, "[but] I want the networks to know that we're going to kick them in the goddamn ass."¹¹⁸ That meant going after the bottom line with no distinction between news and business.

In the fall of 1972, Nixon frequently discussed different ways to damage the networks' business. In private conversation, Colson told Frank Stanton that the administration "[will] bring you to your knees in Wall Street and on Madison Avenue."¹¹⁹ To do so, they went after entertainment television through antitrust lawsuits brought by the Department of Justice. The cases were discussed in the White House, and widely recognized, as political retribution over television news.¹²⁰ In private conversation, Haldeman told the president that nobody could call regulation of reruns intimidation of the news department, because it targeted entertainment shows.¹²¹ But the business model of all television, including television news, depended on the revenue generated by prime-time entertainment shows and reruns. By hurting the bottom line, Nixon and his men hoped to intimidate the networks' news departments.

Haldeman also suggested going after the networks' other cash cow: the licenses of the handful of stations that they were allowed to own and operate.¹²² Nixon wanted more: to destroy the very business model that placed the networks at the top of the food chain of mass media by using cable television policy to "break up networks."¹²³ In private, Nixon explained that "it must not appear that you're trying to affect the network's news content." He acknowledged that "that's what you do" but stressed that "you must not appear to be doing that."¹²⁴ To Nixon, all communications policy became a weapon against the seemingly all-powerful television networks. His primary target was CBS. Memoranda within the White House identified the network as "an ideological monopoly with iron control of one of the most powerful weapons of communication in history."¹²⁵ And so the network of Walter Cronkite, Dan Rather, and Daniel Schorr was the foremost enemy.¹²⁶ It was also the network of Archie Bunker and, before *All in the Family* had come on the air, Tom and Dick Smothers.

Richard Nixon with advisers Charles Colson and Ken Clawson.
Oliver Atkins/Richard Nixon Presidential Library and Museum.

From his very first months in office in 1969, Nixon was prepared to use intimidation to combat any political comedy he deemed dangerous or harmful. His first target was the popular, yet outrageous, *Smothers Brothers Comedy Hour*. Before Nixon's election, the radical, antiwar politics of Tom Smothers—which permeated the show—provoked infighting with network executives as well as condemnation from President Lyndon B. Johnson.[127] Annoyed by the show, Johnson called William Paley to complain.[128] The president was also close friends with Stanton and applied pressure on him regarding the antiwar comedy on the show.[129] When Nixon succeeded Johnson, the show's ridicule became his problem. And both Smothers brothers were eager and willing to turn the new president into a joke.

Only months into Nixon's first term, a joke on the show listed all the troubles facing the nation, making the idea of Nixon solving them the punch line. "That's really funny," Dick Smothers remarked. It was not a particularly funny joke, but it was enough to provoke Nixon. Informed by advice from Paul Keyes, the producer of the rival *Rowan & Martin's Laugh-In*, Nixon recognized the power of satire and called for action and the "necessity to monitor television programs."[130] He stressed that such monitoring should not be limited to news and public affairs but also include "the entertainment programs on which there are deliberately negative comments which deserve some reaction on the part of our friends."[131] It is not clear what friends Nixon was referring to, but he went on to suggest "that is the kind of line that should receive some calls and letters strenuously objecting to that kind of attack."[132]

Under Nixon, the White House developed a system of astroturf operations in which groups and organizations outside of the administration, including local party machines, were deployed to flood the media with pro-Nixon mail.[133] His aides were also in the habit of using a number of conservative columnists to get their talking points across.[134] Furthermore, Tom and Dick Smothers were among those scrutinized by outside investigators under orders from the White House and audited by the IRS well before Watergate.[135] The brothers later described themselves as "the prototype for the enemies list."[136] A month after Nixon called for repercussions for the ridicule, and following extensive and escalating fights with network executives, CBS fired the brothers in a move widely understood as an olive branch to the new administration.[137] "If Humphrey had won, we'd still be on," Tom Smothers later claimed.[138] Considering the brothers' struggles with censors and network executives, the end might have been inevitable, but the White House likely hastened its arrival.[139] Even after the Smothers brothers left television and turned to motion pictures, Nixon's friends in Hollywood turned the screw. In 1972, Tom Smothers produced a movie satirizing Nixon and Agnew called *Another Nice Mess*, ruffling feathers in the White House.[140] Taft Schreiber used his considerable power in Hollywood to make sure the film never went into wide distribution.[141]

Dick Cavett, the erudite host of an eponymous talk show on ABC, was another target of the intimidation campaigns developed in the White House. Cavett had a sharp wit and, even worse, had the gall to provide a platform to controversial figures such as actress and antiwar activist Jane Fonda, Black Power activist Kwame Ture (formerly Stokely Carmichael), and consumer protection activist Ralph Nader. These were people Nixon viewed as enemies. Hence, within the White House Cavett came to be understood as something of an adversary.

In particular, the men at the White House worried about Cavett's tendency to give room to antiwar activists to voice their criticism of the administration's foreign policy. In the summer of 1971, Cavett invited John Kerry, a young veteran and leading voice of Vietnam Veterans against the War, to debate proadministration veteran John O'Neill about the war.[142] Following another episode about the war in June 1971, Colson sent a memo to Haldeman accusing Cavett of having the deck "badly stacked" against the administration.[143] The following day, Nixon and Haldeman discussed their problem with Cavett. "Is he just a left-winger? Is that the problem?" Nixon asked. "I guess so," Haldeman answered.[144] A few days later, with Colson in the room, the president turned vindictive and asked about action to be taken against Cavett. "Well, is there any way we can screw him? That's what I mean. There must be ways," Nixon inquired.[145] Colson was immediately on the same page. "We've been trying to," he replied.[146] Nixon was irked by the "son of a bitch" and wanted to see him hurt.[147]

It is not clear which efforts to hurt Cavett Colson was referring to, but action by the White House suggests the tactics were similar to those used against *The Smothers Brothers Comedy Hour*. Calls went out to executives at ABC; Cavett was investigated by the FBI; staff at the show were audited by the IRS; the Republican National Committee requested logs of the show for a complaint with the FCC.[148] The pressure was enough to make Cavett believe he was on Nixon's infamous enemies list.[149]

A few months later, Colson told the president, with glee, that Cavett's contract would not be renewed by ABC. Always eager to win Nixon's favor, he claimed it was a "direct result" of their efforts. Nixon asked whether "we raised hell about him," and Colson told him he had called James Hagerty, vice president of ABC and formerly President Dwight Eisenhower's press secretary, and Leonard Goldenson, founder and president of ABC, to complain "once a week, sometimes twice a week." "Good!" Nixon replied.[150] Colson, however, was celebrating too soon, as an improvement in ratings led ABC to renew *The Dick Cavett Show* (ABC, 1969–75) a couple of weeks later.[151] Cavett survived, but the campaign against him illustrated how important television entertainment seemed to the White House.

At the end of the day, television was a business, and to the men (and they were almost exclusively men) in the executive suites in New York, ratings outweighed irate phone calls from Chuck Colson. Since Colson's influence in the White House derived from Nixon's view of him as a ruthless problem solver, he had every reason to inflate his own capability to influence decisions at the networks. But the fact was that *The Smothers Brothers Comedy Hour* was slipping in the ratings and was axed; *The Dick Cavett Show* was climbing and lived to laugh another day. And at the top of the ratings in the early 1970s sat *All in the Family*.

When *All in the Family* returned for a third season in the fall of 1972, in the middle of the presidential election between Richard Nixon and George McGovern, it included some surprisingly sharp jabs at the president. Complaining about the economy, Archie turned sour on Nixon. When Gloria remarked that "Nixon's wage and price freeze was supposed to fix everything," a bitter Archie shot back, "Oh, it's fixing me good!"[152] Tens of millions of people followed along as

Archie, the embodiment of Nixon's political base, criticized the president. In the middle of another argument over Nixon and the economy, Archie thundered, "Listen, if anybody criticizes Nixon around here, it'll be me. He's hurting me, not you!"[153] While Archie lost faith in Nixon, Mike and Gloria championed McGovern.

Nixon and his supporters did not approve. "The average viewer," one letter charged, "was made to feel that anyone in favor of Mr. Nixon was narrow minded, bigoted, thoughtless, stupid and a fool."[154] Furthermore, conservative viewers felt the producers and writers were pushing a political message in the form of entertainment. "You are taking unfair advantage of your viewers by shoving Geo. McGovern down their throats," one letter claimed.[155] The editor of the *Ridgewood Times*, a local paper in Queens, New York—real-life Archie Bunker land—denounced the show and called for action in a front-page editorial. "Just because a program masquerades as 'comedy' we see [no] reason why its picture of American patriots as boobs and pot shots at politicians, political parties and the government should go unanswered," the editor in chief remarked.[156] He charged the producers with intentionally portraying Archie, and the political movement he represented, as silly. To counter the image created by *All in the Family*, the editorial suggested equal time should be provided for a rebuttal and raised the possibility of a boycott.[157] It went on to ask whether the show was in fact "a form of undercover campaigning against the president and Americanism in general."[158] An angry rant in an outer-borough paper was not likely to matter to the producers in Hollywood or executives in Manhattan, but two important follow-up letters to the editor should have caught their attention.

The first, signed by Ken Clawson, a communications aide in the White House, suggested the presidential seal of approval. "[Nixon] appreciated hearing from you," it stated, "and knowing of your concern regarding the content of 'All in the Family' program."[159] After the election, another letter from the vice president's office gave further support to the idea of holding the network accountable for the show: "Your analysis of the Bunker program has been right on the mark."[160] Agnew was already a champion for conservatives dismayed by liberal values and permissiveness on television, and the correspondence from the administration carried ominous undertones.[161] It would have been understood by network executives only as part of Nixon's war on the media.

The most direct criticism of Nixon on the show and the most blatant intimidation from the White House came only days before the election in November 1972. The presidential contest was the source of a heated debate in the Bunker household, when Mike unexpectedly inherited some money and decided to donate it to George McGovern's presidential campaign. Archie objected. Mike defended himself. Archie objected again. Mike decried the imbalance between the campaign chests of the two parties, explaining that the Republicans were flush with funds while the Democrats were struggling "just to keep their heads over water."[162] Furthermore, he described the implications of such financial dominance in a media-driven political environment: "The party with the money can afford to buy TV and radio time to get their message across to the people, the other party doesn't stand a chance. Before you know it, you've lost the two-party system." Frustrated with his son-in-law's progressive politics, Archie demanded to know where he came across such "commie crapola," only to learn that President Eisenhower, a Republican whom Nixon had served as vice president, had warned about such a development four years earlier. The show also included direct and pointed ridicule of Nixon. Gloria, endorsing McGovern, questioned Nixon's performance in office: "Nixon hasn't kept any of his promises; he promised to end the war; to reduce unemployment; to stop inflation." A flustered Archie shot back, "Don't be picking on the man over minor details like that!"[163] The studio audience erupted in laughter.

The response was immediate. In letters to CBS, Tandem Productions, and local stations, viewers protested the "not-so-subtle way of injecting ballyhoo for Mr. McGovern" into an entertainment show.[164] Within a month, the episode had provoked more than twice as much viewer mail to the producers as any of the other shows in the fall of 1972. According to Tandem Productions' internal tally, some 92 percent of the letters criticized the political nature of the show.[165] Describing the show as "tricky," "nauseating," "repulsive," and "unfair," viewers across the nation objected to the imbalanced portrayal of the two presidential candidates.[166] Far from seeing Archie as a hero, they saw a mockery of conservatives and President Nixon. And they resented the liberal satire. Whereas McGovern was endorsed by both Mike and Gloria as the noble underdog, Nixon was championed by what they understood as the "dimwitted remarks" of an ignoramus.[167]

The problem, according to Nixon's supporters, was not just that the show made fun of their president. To them, it looked like political propaganda. "You might as well have given Mr. McGovern a free half hour of television," one irate viewer wrote before concluding that the candidate himself "couldn't have done as well" as the show in presenting his case to the public.[168] Indeed, angry viewers suggested that *All in the Family* should have included a disclaimer stating—incorrectly—that "this is a paid political advertisement for George McGovern."[169] Anxiety over the power of television was nothing new, but by the early 1970s it was an acute worry for both the political left and right. Scholars and journalists warned of the influence inherent in the medium.[170] With "so much responsibility to the public" and "vast power," detractors charged, CBS abused its authority by broadcasting such political entertainment.[171] "This is a public show for all people all over the United States," one viewer claimed, protesting a show broadcast not by public television but by a private business in the free enterprise system.[172]

Central to the criticism was distress over the prospect that the "biased misuse of prime time" would benefit McGovern at the ballot box.[173] Even though Nixon looked to be on the cusp of a landslide victory, his reelection was not guaranteed. Four years earlier, Nixon had used *Laugh-In*, then the most popular show on television, to strengthen his standing in the 1968 election. Now, on the eve of the 1972 election, the most popular show on television seemed to come down against Nixon. Nobody knew if it would impact the vote, but many feared it could. "You surely gave Mr. McGovern's campaign a boost," one disappointed viewer remarked.[174] That fear drove some of the angry fans to take a page out of Nixon's playbook and threaten the producers and the network. Recalling Agnew's suggestions of government action against the networks, one viewer remarked, "If Mr. Agnew blasts [CBS] and you for this don't be surprised."[175] Others wrote about changing channels, boycotting sponsors, filing lawsuits, and promoting various government sanctions.[176] "Perhaps it should be illegal to use a situation comedy to campaign for a Presidential candidate," one letter writer suggested in a thinly veiled threat.[177]

Most disturbing, however, was the reaction at the White House. The week before the episode aired, *CBS Evening News with Walter Cronkite* had taken an extensive look at the "Watergate caper" that had grown into the "Watergate affair."[178] The White House considered the report "shoddier [and] more irresponsible" than any other news broadcast in the last couple of years.[179] A fuming Chuck Colson berated both Stanton and Paley following the first of two installments of the report, threatening them with government sanctions and, ultimately, succeeding in censoring parts of the second installment of the report scheduled to air the week before the election.[180] And now, *All in the Family* was enraging the White House anew with lines that sounded like an endorsement of McGovern. Two days after the election, Rob Reiner told Johnny Carson on *The Tonight Show* about "violent phone calls" the recent episode had provoked. Then, almost casually, he noted that "even President Nixon asked for a transcript of the script, which is unusual, you know."[181] Within the White House and at the networks in New York, it was a recognized strategy of intimidation.

It remains unclear who in the White House called the production company asking for a transcript and who orchestrated the administration's letters to the

Ridgewood Times. There is, however, strong reason to believe it was Colson's handiwork. He believed in requesting transcripts of news broadcasts to scare the networks, and he was known to use Ken Clawson, the author of the first letter to the editor, as a pawn.[182] The infamous enemies list was also Colson's project, and Norman Lear was on it.[183] Yet it was Nixon himself who fostered the environment in which the media, both news and entertainment, was understood as the enemy. And it was Nixon who created a White House culture that encouraged abuses of power to punish enemies.

When Watergate consumed Nixon's second term, he was unable to move forward with the most vindictive plans to limit the power of the networks.[184] At the same time, the president's abuses of power came to forever overshadow his attempts to befriend and collaborate with allies in Hollywood such as Paul Keyes and Taft Schreiber. The eager student of the mass media was forgotten while the would-be abusive master was remembered. The Nixon administration marked a divide between a Republican Party fostering relationships with media barons, studio tycoons, television producers, advertising executives, and popular actors and actresses and a Republican Party condemning the news media for "liberal bias" and television entertainment as "immoral filth." No more Dr. Jekyll, only Mr. Hyde.

Still, Nixon's White House was not an all-powerful, antimedia leviathan making or breaking shows, reporters, producers, and executives at the networks. For all the talk of Chuck Colson as brilliant and ruthless, he failed in his efforts to bring down CBS. As far as media mastery went, he was best at building his own image as the "bad cop" of the administration.[185] When updating Nixon on his angry calls or threats delivered face-to-face to network executives, Colson always came off as the man in charge.[186] Only on occasion, however, did Nixon's war on the media inform decision-making at the networks. Under heavy pressure in the days before the 1972 election, CBS News did compromise its standards to appease the administration. Broadcasting was, after all, licensed by the government. But first and foremost, broadcasting was a business. The entertainment shows made real money, and when Nixon left the White House in disgrace, Archie Bunker and Walter Cronkite were still the most popular faces on television.[187]

There is nothing in the archival record to suggest that the attempts by the administration to intimidate the actors, writers, producers, and executives behind *All in the Family* worked. The success of the show shielded it, more than other shows, from network interference. Nothing indicates that the standards and practices department changed its approach to the show following the public and private signals sent from the White House.[188] Decades later, Norman Lear did not even recall the attempted intimidation.[189] But the potential chilling effect is difficult to measure. Nixon's men reminded the executives at the networks of the sword of Damocles. "When we get through with your guys, they'll be jumping off the thirty-second floor," Colson once told a representative of the network.[190] "The fact it hasn't happened isn't important," Richard Salant, CBS News president, once observed of the White House's threats of action. "Even if the sword hanging over your head hasn't fallen, you never know when it might."[191]

Nixon, fueled by resentment over perceived liberal bias in news and entertainment television, presented himself as a victim of the powerful mass media even as he tried to play hardball with the executives behind the scenes.[192] Thus, he cemented the idea of conservatives as under attack in a war with the media and an understanding of the entertainment industry as a modern-day bête noire. Though the confrontational style mostly failed to subdue the news media, not to mention the entertainment media, the performative tough-guy stand against television became a core tenet of both the Republican Party and the broader conservative movement.

Chapter 5

ARCHIE BUNKER ON THE CAMPAIGN TRAIL

George McGovern was in trouble. It was late October 1972, with the presidential election right around the corner, and opinion polls suggested Richard Nixon was sure to win a second term in the White House. So in the final weeks of the campaign, McGovern turned to Archie Bunker to deliver the white working-class voters that had won the Democratic Party elections for decades. Around the country, voters came across a familiar face in political advertisements for McGovern. "Hello, I'm Carroll O'Connor," the person most viewers recognized only as Archie Bunker announced on television, "a conservative man speaking against radicalism, against the radicalism of the present administration." Even though the support came from Carroll O'Connor, the liberal actor, it was presented as an endorsement by the popular conservative character. "I, as a conservative man," the bona fide liberal concluded, "am going to vote with confidence for Senator George McGovern."¹

The Archie Bunker advertisement may look like a curiosity of 1970s showbiz politics, but it actually signaled a transformation of the Democratic Party's electoral campaign strategy.² Having dominated national politics since the days of Franklin Delano Roosevelt in the 1930s, the party found itself in the midst of a paradigm shift in the sixties. The New Deal coalition, in essence an economic consortium, crumbled under its own weight, giving way to alliances based on shared identities, emotions, and experiences. This turn to a politics of entertainment depended not only on a move to a party of diverse interests and factions but on a reformed nomination process of primaries and caucuses in small states such as New Hampshire and Iowa. The new nomination process, the result of the so-called McGovern-Fraser Commission on party structure and delegate selection, opened up the party after the chaotic national convention of 1968, in which party bosses nominated Vice President Hubert Humphrey over the candidates who had run in primaries across the nation.³ More transparent and media driven, these new presidential campaigns ingrained the role of professional consultants and entertainers into party politics.

While the media strategies of the Republican Party were marked by Nixon's obsession with mastering television, the Democratic Party lacked an obvious champion of mass media in the 1970s. Stuck in the shadow of a president consumed with mass media, liberals needed new strategies to reach voters increasingly found in front of the television set. Convinced that Nixon's success lay in his media and image craft, as captured in the best-selling *The Selling of the President*, political strategists working for Democratic candidates set out to further blur the line between television news and entertainment. Their new strategies came to cement the importance of television on the campaign trail and the role of Hollywood within the Democratic Party. But that process took time and experimentation. In fact, the first candidates to turn to Archie Bunker were resoundingly beaten at the ballot box. Even in defeat, however, they transformed the Democratic Party.

John Lindsay was perfect for television. Tall, young, and good looking, the patrician Lindsay had an air of glamour, a quality that suggested he was made for either the rolling hills of Hollywood or the neoclassical halls of Washington, DC. It was his looks, historians have suggested, that made it possible for him to run for, and win, public office via television.⁴ After making a name for himself in Congress representing New York's Seventeenth District, the "silk stocking district" that housed the affluent Upper East Side of Manhattan, Lindsay returned to New York as a rising star for the mayoral race of 1965. Defeating both Democratic Party candidate Abraham Beame and Conservative Party challenger William F. Buckley Jr., he became the first Republican mayor since Fiorello La Guardia in the 1940s. This was a time when the GOP in New York was still dominated by liberals, people such as Senator Jacob Javits and Governor Nelson Rockefeller, who believed in civil rights and good government and viewed the situation in Vietnam with unease.[5]

The 1965 run for mayor was a showcase of a modern campaign. Lindsay charmed reporters, politicians, and voters through his use of television, personality, and celebrity.[6] His campaign seemed to be best captured in the slogan "He is fresh and everyone else is tired."[7] By the end of 1971, Lindsay was neither fresh nor Republican.[8] He was still, however, the media darling and believed television could catapult him into the White House. In December 1971, Lindsay announced his run for the Democratic Party nomination to challenge Richard Nixon for the presidency. Having registered as a Democrat only four months earlier, he lacked a strong base of support within the party. His liberal bona fides were beyond dispute, and Democratic voters had helped carry him to Gracie Mansion twice. Still, compared to his fellow presidential hopefuls—party stalwarts such as Senators Hubert Humphrey of Minnesota, Edmund Muskie of Maine, and Henry Jackson of Washington—Lindsay's connections within the party were scant. He also lacked the regional support of Southern segregationist George Wallace or the demographic appeal of New York representative Shirley Chisholm. Without established ties to the different segments of the Democratic Party, Lindsay turned to television to carry his candidacy.[9]

Following the end of the smoke-filled rooms of earlier nominating conventions, the reforms of the McGovern-Fraser Commission meant the candidacy in 1972 would be won in open state primaries and caucuses.[10] The new rules, and the opportunity to remove Richard Nixon from the White House, attracted a dozen candidates. Lindsay stood out among the crowd in one particular aspect of the "New Politics": generating media attention. "Television is where Lindsay is by far the best of the field," a campaign aide explained. "We work to get maximum media attention."[11] The Lindsay campaign believed it could develop an emotional connection between voter and candidate by leveraging the media attention showered on him. Forgoing the hand-shaking and baby-kissing retail politics of freezing small-town New Hampshire, with its first-in-the-nation primary, the campaign focused instead on Florida. The Sunshine State was everything to everyone all at once. To George Wallace it was the South. To Hubert Humphrey it was a state full of migrants from the Midwest. To Henry Jackson it was a state fueled by the defense and aerospace industries.

To Shirley Chisholm it was a minority state. To John Lindsay, however, it was a media state, and he worked to use his television skills to broaden his appeal and establish himself as the front-runner.[12] The momentum, the campaign reasoned, would then carry him through the coming Midwestern primaries. For help, Lindsay turned to Archie Bunker.

The popularity of *All in the Family* made Archie Bunker an icon. He was *the* representative of the white blue-collar cultural conservatism that was embedded in the realignment of American politics that both parties were grappling with in the 1960s and 1970s.[13] Archie Bunker represented the conservative white ethnics behind the political success of Democrats such as Frank Rizzo in Philadelphia, Sam Yorty in Los Angeles, Louise Day Hicks in Boston, and Mario Procaccino in New York.[14] The success of figures such as Spiro Agnew signaled that Republicans were eager to contest the same demographic.[15]

Ahead of the 1972 presidential election, "the Archie Bunker vote" came up again and again in political columns, editorials, and off-the-record discussions.[16] This was by design; Norman Lear wanted to start conversations with *All in the Family*. The character was no mere political gadfly but rather appreciated as a powerful political voice.[17] Indeed, one poll found Archie Bunker the most recognized face in the nation.[18] The reach of the show—over one-third of all households turned on CBS every Saturday night to hear the heated arguments on *All in the Family*—carried serious implications. "The most thoroughly practical of politicians are now in private discussing 'The Archie Bunker Vote,'" conservative columnist William S. White observed. "Some of the most influential and sophisticated couples in Washington . . . are declining attractive Saturday night dinner bids to stay home in the family with 'All in the Family.'"[19] It was not just a question of Archie Bunker as shorthand for socially conservative workers; politicians were trying to understand the connection viewers had with Archie Bunker and experimenting with how to use it to their own advantage.

Lindsay, the quintessential limousine liberal, went all in on Archie Bunker. Showbiz politics had served him well over the years. Having established a strong record on civil rights during his time in Washington, Lindsay had enjoyed the support of Black stars such as Sammy Davis Jr., Ossie Davies, Ruby Dee, and Jackie Robinson in his 1965 mayoral race.[20] In his reelection bid four years later, the liberal mayor again won the endorsements of entertainers such as Harry Belafonte, Dustin Hoffman, and Barbra Streisand.[21] While the campaign welcomed and touted such endorsements, aides also recognized that celebrity praise might enhance the public perception of Lindsay as "too Manhattan."[22] Over the years, he received much criticism portraying him as a show pony rather than a workhorse. Robert Moses, the legendary public official in

New York, dismissed the mayor as a "matinee-idol."[23] Nor was Moses alone in castigating him as nothing more than a celebrity. "I am still not a movie star," former mayor Robert Wagner announced in a direct jab at his successor, "but then, New York is not a movie."[24] Echoing the line, Mario Procaccino, another challenger in the 1969 race, denounced Lindsay as an "actor who went on television and smiled while the city burned."[25] Even political reporters acknowledged that "God knows John Lindsay was a TV celebrity."[26]

Lindsay's record as mayor, however, was mixed at best. He especially struggled in the white, blue-collar neighborhoods of the outer boroughs.[27] To win these voters during his reelection campaign in 1969, he connected his candidacy to middle-class heroes, notably the New York Mets, who against all odds won the World Series only weeks before the November election.[28] On television, viewers could not help but notice the mayor celebrating with the team.[29] Three years later, with his eye on the presidency, Lindsay and his strategists hoped Archie Bunker would play the role the Mets had and give the liberal candidate credibility with new voters. The local appeal of the sports team was swapped out for the national appeal of *All in the Family*.

The actor made famous as Archie Bunker was in fact the polar opposite of the beloved character. Classically trained, Carroll O'Connor was a staunch liberal with a keen interest in politics. For years, O'Connor, who had studied at the University of Montana before continuing his education in Europe, used to write to longtime Senate majority leader Mike Mansfield (D-MT).[30] Stridently opposed to the war in Vietnam and a strong supporter of the civil rights movement, O'Connor's politics were not unlike those of the meathead on *All in the Family*. "Oddly enough," Rob Reiner recalled later, "I think that Carroll O'Connor personally was even more liberal than I was."[31] Norman Lear later remembered the actor as completely dedicated to "the mission" of the show and believed portraying the failures of the character would make clear the poison of bigotry.[32] And so O'Connor did not hesitate to use the character of Archie Bunker as a vehicle to promote his liberal politics in Lindsay's campaign in 1972.[33]

Ahead of the Florida primary in early March, Lindsay announced Carroll O'Connor's endorsement. The actor issued a statement presenting the patrician liberal as a hero of the common people. "When you're in John Lindsay's shoes you see people and their problems at eye level—a worker out of a job, a neighborhood struggling painfully for hope, a family who lost a boy in a war nobody wants and nobody really comprehends."[34] The chairman of the campaign welcomed the endorsement, describing O'Connor as somebody who "enjoys such exceptional respect and affection within his own profession and among the public."[35] Accustomed to embracing celebrities, Lindsay knew the actor

Carroll O'Connor in a television advertisement for John Lindsay's 1972 presidential primary campaign.

might do more than just capture the attention of voters. He also hoped that fellow entertainers would join the bandwagon and open up their checkbooks.[36]

With the filming of the second season of *All in the Family* coming to a close, O'Connor could put in the time for his candidate. He worked with the campaign to record several advertisements in which the actor explicitly channeled Archie Bunker in support of his fellow New Yorker. "He can't actually endorse him in character, but he uses some language that will make it recognizable," explained a Lindsay spokesperson to the press.[37] Without ever mentioning Archie Bunker, O'Connor blurred the lines between actor and character. And that character mattered: a conservative from Queens was giving credibility to the Manhattan liberal.

Television viewers in Florida were greeted by a familiar face as O'Connor appeared onscreen to support Lindsay. "Hello, I'm Carroll O'Connor. If you are a young American, listen to an old-fashioned one," the actor remarked at the beginning of a sixty-second ad. Immediately, he evoked Archie Bunker. Explaining Lindsay's position on the war in Vietnam, describing the conflict as violent, radical, and illegal, the actor then morphed completely into his popular character. Leaning back, O'Connor put a cigar in his mouth and adopted the characteristics and voice of Archie Bunker. "So, if you're a young person," that famous Queens accent declared, "will you listen to me for a change?"[38]

Illustrating the importance of the character for the campaign, both the sixty-second ad and two additional ten-second spots included the actor transforming into the lovable bigot. Emulating Archie Bunker's penchant for malapropisms, O'Connor encouraged the viewers to "you know, stick with me as part of the Lindsay contiguancy." In the notoriously thick outer-borough accent, O'Connor playfully warned the viewers in another ad, "I'm sures gonna be watchin' yas down dere."[39]

Media attention followed, further amplifying the message. "Archie Bunker for Lindsay," announced a headline in the *Boston Globe*.[40] In the *Washington Post*, an article remarked that Carroll O'Connor was known from television's *All in the Family* and went on to conclude that "Archie Bunker" presents John Lindsay as the solution.[41] According to the political reporter Martin Nolan, the advertisements said "a lot about politics, media manipulation and American culture."[42] Left unsaid was what it meant: the growing entanglement of television entertainment and politics.

Despite his efforts, Lindsay placed fifth in the crowded field in Florida and, in the words of one journalist, "limped home."[43] The poor showing was hardly Archie Bunker's fault. Rather, it was, campaign scribe Theodore White concluded, the result of a "blundering political campaign" and the fact that the New York mayor split the liberal vote with at least George McGovern, Hubert Humphrey, and Shirley Chisholm.[44] Even before Lindsay announced his run, columnist William S. White called talk of him as a formidable candidate for president "the sheerest of moonshine."[45] Indeed, the campaign never stood a chance. "John, you're going to be a fucking disaster," a friend had responded when Lindsay announced his run.[46] But even as Lindsay's campaign floundered, his challengers mirrored its media strategy—relying on television and celebrity politics to foster a relationship with the electorate in the primaries and caucuses around the country by presenting a forward-looking and cool image in the mass media.[47] In fact, Lindsay's main rival for the nomination appropriated his strategy and made even better use of Archie Bunker in the quest to defeat Richard Nixon.

George McGovern knew he needed television. Unlike the attractive John Lindsay, nobody would confuse McGovern for a Robert Redford or a Warren Beatty. Tall, with a receding salt-and-pepper hairline and a natural sternness, McGovern had the appearance of the former preacher and college professor he was. He often struggled to excite audiences with his nasal voice and tendency to turn campaign speeches into lectures or sermons. On television, however, McGovern found himself at home. Political reporters noted that McGovern "paradoxically is more himself on television than in person."[48] This was the result of hard work. Even gonzo journalist Hunter S. Thompson recognized that "McGovern had taken his time and learned how to use the medium—instead of letting the medium use him."[49]

Using television to launch his campaign for the presidency some fourteen months before the first primary contest of 1972, the South Dakotan faced an uphill battle.[50] According to the notorious Las Vegas bookmaker Jimmy "The Greek" Snyder, McGovern's odds were 200–1.[51] In the polls, McGovern struggled to attract more than a couple percent of support.[52] But he did have support in Hollywood, which proved critical in lifting him up.

Two years earlier, Shirley MacLaine, impressed by the liberal crusader picking up the mantle of the assassinated Robert F. Kennedy at the 1968 Democratic National Convention, had campaigned for McGovern's senate reelection. Now Hollywood provided the money that gave McGovern a fighting chance in the battle for the presidential nomination. "They carried most of the early financial burden," campaign director Frank Mankiewicz acknowledged.[53] More important, however, the candidate himself came to appreciate the value of celebrities in a mediated campaign. "I began to visualize what they could do," the prairie statesman reflected, "particularly on the fundraising end, but also in lending a certain amount of appeal or charisma and interest in the campaign."[54]

While Nixon courted the Old Hollywood of studio moguls, McGovern depended on New Hollywood.[55] This gap was reflected in their support from TV stars. Among the president's supporters were the stars of television of yesteryear, people such as Red Skelton, Martha Raye, and Desi Arnaz. The popular stars of the day, such as Goldie Hawn, Tom Smothers, and Leonard Nimoy, lined up behind his Democratic challenger.[56] Beyond celebrity politics at events and fundraisers, the campaign welcomed both MacLaine and her brother Warren Beatty into the inner circle.[57] Beatty in particular contributed to campaign strategy and political considerations, operating as "a ghost in the machine."[58]

Recognizing the importance of television in the campaign, the McGovern camp attracted media attention with its cadre of young stars. They also understood film and television celebrities as providing a "personal," or rather an emotional, connection to viewers. Eager to make the most of the star power, the campaign offered television shows "well-known personalities" such as MacLaine, Beatty, or Robert Vaughn as campaign surrogates.[59] On Dick Cavett's or Merv Griffin's talk shows, the Hollywood luminaries could promote their candidate to broad audiences.

Featuring celebrities at McGovern events large and small also attracted news cameras and coverage.[60] At the same time, the campaign drew on the media-monitoring techniques of liberal broadcast activists to gain access to the medium under the equal-time rule.[61] The playbook for left-wing media activists at the time, written by the radical young Federal Communications Commission (FCC) commissioner Nicholas Johnson, urged activists to "use the FCC" by monitoring broadcasts and filing requests for equal time when appropriate.[62] McGovern aides and volunteers recognized that airtime was the name of the game in the television age of political campaigns.[63]

While Edmund Muskie, the stoic senator from Maine and the party's vice presidential nominee in 1968, was the early front-runner, he struggled to live up to the expectations that came with the designation. It was not that he was bad at television; he just never seemed to adjust to the new reality of a mediated primary campaign.[64] Muskie invited strict scrutiny from the press while challengers such as McGovern garnered considerable (and often favorable) media attention with cadres of young activists and Hollywood stars. Even when Muskie won the first primary of the season in New Hampshire, the media deemed his 46–37 percent margin over McGovern a failure.[65] "Muskie was destroyed *in* the press," one political reporter acknowledged, "if not *by* the press."[66] Instead, McGovern became the story. Media coverage, in turn, provided the campaign with momentum.[67] "The press didn't create the McGovern juggernaut," a reporter noted, "but they sure as hell *helped* create it!"[68]

The rise of the modern primary system resulted in a dramatic change to the way mass media covered political campaigns with a turn toward dramatic horse race coverage.[69] McGovern played to the cameras and was rewarded with more coverage.[70] In fact, one of the rules for the campaign was that "anytime you appear on radio or television you automatically have more listeners than at any scheduled appearance at an event at the same hour."[71] Hollywood stars, who per definition depended on broad audience appeal, proved valued allies in the new political environment. Celebrities were able to both attract media attention and reach various segments of the party coalition. "In 1972, as never before," the cover story in *Newsweek* noted in September, "the stars are mounting the stump."[72]

But relying on star power came with risks. Early in the campaign, McGovern's trusted adviser, documentary filmmaker and media strategist Charles Guggenheim, highlighted a major challenge for the candidate. For decades, the Democratic Party had counted on working-class voters in Northern urban centers, and now, Guggenheim warned, these same voters don't "know what to make of George McGovern of South Dakota."[73] White working-class Democrats had supported Muskie, Humphrey, or Wallace in the primaries. Moving beyond liberals, and especially antiwar students, to build a broad McGovern coalition was both necessary and challenging within a fractured party. In the Wisconsin primary, McGovern finally began to reach what campaign director Gary Hart described as "the most important politically, the 'Archie Bunker' vote."[74] The blue-collar whites who supported the war and were tired of civil rights remained an important bloc within the Democratic Party, crucial for success in November.[75]

But the old New Deal coalition that had carried the party since the 1930s— workers, farmers, minorities, intellectuals, and segregationists—was coming undone in the aftershocks of the sixties. The white South, having lost its de facto veto power over the party nominee and party platform in the 1960s, was leaving the party. Now another segment of the party, organized labor, was realizing its power was waning, too, as McGovern bested Humphrey, labor's darling, in the primaries. At the same time, new interests closely aligned with the Democratic Party were gaining a voice, especially the movements for civil rights and women's liberation.[76] By the summer's nominating convention, McGovern's liberal crusade had secured him the nomination. To win the presidency, however, he needed to reunite a broader coalition.

The glitter of Hollywood celebrities surrounding the McGovern campaign, some strategists worried, could alienate the traditional Democratic base of blue-collar workers. Warning of a growing dependence on showbiz politics, one adviser urged the candidate to "ditch the movie stars, celebrities, moneyed crowd, etc."[77] The worry was that McGovern, like Lindsay before him, was becoming too Hollywood, that the stars would make McGovern seem like a representative of the elite.[78] Enter Archie Bunker.

The campaign addressed the concerns by adjusting its media strategy. Media wiz Charles Guggenheim presented the candidate in cinema verité advertisements among voters and blue-collar workers.[79] In a five-minute spot showing the candidate in conversation with representatives of small businesses in Milwaukee, McGovern defended himself against charges of radicalism.[80] "Every leader throughout our history who has advocated change in the way things are at a given time has been called a radical," McGovern remarked.[81] Another way to ease the minds of the blue-collar electorate was to turn to the most prominent symbol of the working class.[82] In the general election, just as Nixon's strategists had feared in the summer, the campaign embraced Archie Bunker—the character, not the actor.[83] The idea was that Archie Bunker would reach the workers that the Democratic Party had relied on for years and that McGovern was struggling to convince.[84]

Both Republicans and Democrats leaned on Carroll O'Connor in the fall of 1972. Despite repeated pleas from prominent Hollywood champions of the president, O'Connor never seriously considered endorsing Nixon. The McGovern campaign implored the actor to support the liberal standard-bearer. In a signal of how much the strategists valued Archie Bunker, McGovern personally talked with O'Connor. "I posed some hard questions," O'Connor later remarked. "I received some straight forward answers."[85] It was only after John Lindsay, O'Connor's friend and favorite in the primaries, gave his support to his fellow liberal that the actor seriously started considering McGovern.[86] In October 1972, Archie Bunker announced his support for George McGovern.

In the minds of many television viewers Carroll O'Connor was Archie Bunker, and so the campaign leaned into the conservative angle—intentionally blending the two personas. Media interest in celebrity and entertainment helped. "Archie Bunker," the press reported, "is casting his vote for McGovern."[87] An Associated Press headline read "Archie Bunker Backs McGovern."[88] Associated Press political reporter Walter Mears, one of the most respected journalists on the campaign beat, even highlighted the support of Archie Bunker before that of the former vice president (and McGovern rival in the primaries) Hubert Humphrey.[89] The coverage made it clear that the strategy of presenting O'Connor as a representative of working-class Queens, rather than another embodiment of Hollywood, was working.

In television advertisements for McGovern, O'Connor went even further than he had in Lindsay's ads to present himself in character. Thus, he presented himself as a conservative man for McGovern, not as the lifelong liberal that he actually was. Outtakes from the recording reveal the importance of having the conservative Archie Bunker back McGovern. "Never mind," O'Connor exclaimed in frustration in the middle of one of the takes when he forgot the most important line. "I got to get the conservative in."[90] Indeed, in one of the sixty-second ads he recorded, O'Connor described himself as conservative no less than three times, while repeatedly describing the Nixon administration as an example of radicalism.[91]

Beyond the television spots, O'Connor also campaigned in person for McGovern, joined by his fellow liberal cast member Rob Reiner for additional impact.[92] "McGovern's not the perfect candidate," Reiner remarked at a campaign event during the primaries, "but he's the closest."[93] Even though Reiner had supported McGovern since the spring, the campaign did not tout the endorsement as coming from *All in the Family*'s meathead. Yet in telethons for the candidate, McGovern himself thanked O'Connor for his support while at the same time intentionally conflating the actor with the character: "The only thing we ask is that all of you who like Archie Bunker vote for George McGovern and Sargent Shriver."[94]

For many television viewers, the political campaigns and the prime-time comedy blurred. It was not just on campaign telethons that Archie Bunker expressed doubts about the president. It was a constant theme on Saturday night's *All in the Family*. Since it returned for a third season in September 1972, the characters had engaged in direct conversations, often turning into heated debates, about the upcoming election.[95] "The whole world will be talking about the election," director John Rich observed in the press. "Why couldn't Archie Bunker?"[96] Of course, Rich denied any interest in promoting a political agenda. Instead, he argued that political debates on the show were "an advocacy of character."[97] For the characters to feel real, the argument went, they would have to fight about politics the same way they fought about everything else.

While Nixon's campaign and supporters disapproved of the political turn on the show, liberals welcomed it.[98] "At last," one viewer wrote when an early episode mocked the president, "a show dared criticize Nixon."[99] In the fall of 1972, Mike loudly promoted McGovern and his policies on the show. Archie Bunker's defense of the president, however, was convoluted and flawed. "I know how tough it's getting with higher prices and higher taxes," Mike explained in a September 1972 episode, praising "a man like McGovern . . . with a program."[100] Archie Bunker's response, a silly criticism of the candidate's tax proposals, was met with laughter from the studio audience. At times, Mike's passionate support of McGovern sounded like a campaign message. "There's a real emergency, can't you see," Mike proclaimed in a heated exchange in a November episode. "The election is only two weeks away and they need the money desperately!" Again, Archie Bunker's convoluted and halfhearted defense of Nixon provoked laughter, while Gloria joined her husband in endorsing the Democrat: "McGovern *should* be president!"[101] With the stars wading into politics both on the show and on the campaign trail, the lines dividing news and entertainment became hazy.

Many viewers connected the political debates on the show with O'Connor's campaign for McGovern. "If that weren't Pro-McGovern propaganda I don't know what is," a dismayed woman wrote, "especially with Mr. Carroll O'Connor making commercials saying he is a 'conservative for McGovern.'"[102] Another woman noted "Carol O'Conner's [sic] ridiculously underhanded and mud-slinging campaign speech during a recent football game" as further evidence that the producers were "using Archie to personify the alleged stupidity of anyone who holds views opposed to those of your writers."[103]

And yet, the angry letters connecting the political comedy of *All in the Family* with O'Connor's politics attest to the reach of his political endorsements. Condemning the ads, critics were convinced of their persuasive potential. One viewer called O'Connor's advertisements for the candidate "the strongest made by any star (I don't include Jane Fonda)."[104] The political comedy on *All in the Family* and the public political endorsements by Carroll O'Connor reinforced each other and, in the minds of many in the audience, were inseparable from each other.

Archie Bunker's strength as a political icon was evident in the thinking of campaign strategists. Convinced of the political influence of the character, rather than the charm of the actor, campaigns looked to translate the blue-collar appeal into votes. But they failed. George McGovern went down to a landslide defeat, as Nixon, winning everywhere but Massachusetts and Washington, DC, coasted to reelection. Yet even as McGovern became a symbol of liberal defeat, the blurring of politics and entertainment would continue to grow. In September 1972, R. W. "Johnny" Apple Jr., the influential political reporter at the *New York Times*, wrote of the concern that McGovern relied too much on television.[105] In the coming years, however, candidates came to rely more, not less, on television.[106] Soon, McGovern's use of television would seem quaint.

The most prominent impact of the transformations wrought by the McGovern campaign was not measured at the ballot box but within the party itself. In particular, the campaign further entangled Hollywood with the Democratic Party. Conservatives, convinced they were left in the cold, built rival institutions to expand the reach of their ideology.[107] But the diverse Democratic coalition did not depend on ideology but rather on a variety of interest groups, and so Hollywood became a key partner to build the party. At the height of the network era of broadcasting, television reached beyond demographic divides, regional boundaries, and socioeconomic barriers. Both Lindsay and McGovern shared an understanding of the influence of television entertainment. Or they were desperate enough to experiment with new forms of appeals. Either way, their campaigns cemented the institutional role of liberal Hollywood within the party. Four years later, however, the success of an unknown Southerner illustrated that showbiz politics no longer depended on the candidate's own interest in Hollywood.

Following Nixon's fall from grace in 1974, slick and packaged politics were out of favor.[108] The opprobrium of Watergate made all politics suspect. In 1976, Jimmy Carter, a former governor of Georgia, offered himself as an outsider for the White House. "I'll never tell a lie," the maverick candidate proclaimed in his efforts to distance himself from politics as usual.[109] And yet Carter recognized that television had replaced older forms of campaigning, and he structured his run around the medium. But his television strategy was first and foremost an "(un)celebrity campaign."[110] Running in all the primaries, with a particular focus on the Iowa caucus, Carter bogarted media coverage by feeding its constant hunger for drama.[111] The fresh-faced Southerner provided the media with an outsider and underdog story. Recognizing the structures of broadcasting and the demands of television news in an age when attracting television coverage was, according to journalist Jules Witcover, the "*sine qua non* of each day's plan" made Carter competitive.[112] Television won Jimmy Carter the nomination and, in November, the White House.[113]

"Jimmy Carter actively avoided Hollywood," recalled one of his campaign strategists. "He just didn't see where it added anything."[114] While Carter's team closely studied how George McGovern had won the nomination in 1972, they did not believe celebrities would launch Carter's long-shot campaign to prominence. Instead, they focused on another sort of celebrity: the political reporters and newscasters who, in the post-Watergate environment, seemed capable of making or breaking a campaign.[115] Appreciating the cynicism among both the electorate and the press, Jimmy Carter deliberately sold himself as unpackaged and unproduced.[116]

Instead, it was the other candidates, including a young Jerry Brown, governor of California, and populist Fred Harris, senator from Oklahoma, who courted Hollywood. Aware of the role stars played in boosting McGovern four years earlier, strategists turned to movie and television stars for endorsements, funds, and glamour. On the marathon campaign trail along small towns in Iowa, New Hampshire, and Wisconsin, Hollywood celebrities were a big deal. Furthermore, post-Watergate campaign finance reforms served to strengthen the fundraising role of Hollywood in liberal politics.[117]

Fred Harris was, according to reporter Jules Witcover, "equal parts brilliant, friendly, shrewd, impulsive, folksy, aggressive, and ambitious."[118] Early on, Harris recognized coverage on television news and talk shows as "the highest priority."[119] Exhibiting his appreciation of the popularity and power of Archie Bunker, he hoped to use television entertainment to attract television news. A campaign aide suggested Carroll O'Connor would "be super in Iowa," concluding that "he'd probably do tremendously well as Archie Bunker."[120] The candidate agreed on turning to television entertainment, noting how "we could get good press and sign additional people up if we could get Carroll O'Connor or Dennis Weaver [of television's *McCloud* (NBC, 1970–77)] or Will Geer [of television's *The Waltons*] for small town meetings in various Iowa towns."[121] There were a lot of liberals in Hollywood, but not many television characters as popular, plainspoken, and down-to-earth as Sam McCloud, Zebulon Walton, and Archie Bunker.

While the radical Harris won many Hollywood endorsements, Carroll O'Connor was perceived as the most important name. The strategists wanted to find a celebrity to serve as a coordinator of entertainment for the campaign, like Warren Beatty had done for McGovern and Shirley MacLaine for the Democratic National Committee in 1972. "The perfect man, in my opinion, would be Carroll O'Connor (Archie Bunker)," wrote one aide, "who is as liberal-radical as they come, and obviously outshines everybody else mentioned here both in 'stardom,' and in really ability for work, initiative, imagination, and persistence."[122] Measured in either star power or political savvy, O'Connor could not compete with Beatty. The real strength of Carroll O'Connor was as Archie Bunker. Yet while the strategists talked about the power of the character, in the end they favored more traditional showbiz politics.[123]

Neither Carroll O'Connor nor Archie Bunker could save the Harris campaign. With Mo Udall, Sargent Shriver, Birch Bayh, and latecomers Jerry Brown and Frank Church all vying for the position as the liberal champion against the moderate Jimmy Carter, Harris failed to break through in the media. Indeed, he attributed his failed campaign to his struggles to attract television attention or the funds and credibility that accompanied such coverage. Still, even in defeat he remained convinced of the medium's power and the potential of showbiz politics.[124] He shared that belief with many within the party. In fact, showbiz was becoming an institutional part of the party.

Carter did not care about Hollywood. Nor did Carter care *for* Hollywood. "He considered them frivolous, immoral people and mostly avoided them," one of his speechwriters concluded.[125] When Warren Beatty hosted a fundraiser for the Democratic nominee at the Beverly Wilshire Hotel, Carter told an audience full of stars, including Carroll O'Connor and Norman Lear, that he had a responsibility to "bypass the big shots, including people like you."[126] Amid the glamour, Tony Randall joked to the candidate that "you've never met people at this level." "That's how I won the nomination," Carter quipped back.[127] Like many in the room, the host of the evening Warren Beatty preferred "more orthodox liberal candidates," and the former governor had indeed won the nomination without the support of Hollywood.[128] But the Democratic Party and Hollywood did care about each other even if Carter was the de facto standard-bearer of the party. For the general election campaign in the fall, the stars lined up behind the candidate. Carroll O'Connor teamed up with Rob

Jimmy Carter with the *All in the Family* family (*clockwise from Carter*): Jean Stapleton, Rob Reiner, Peggy Marshall (Reiner's wife, back to camera), Norman Lear (back to camera), Peggy Yorkin (Bud Yorkin's wife), William Rader (Struthers's husband), Sally Struthers, and William Putch (Stapleton's husband). Jimmy Carter Presidential Library and Museum.

Reiner in "public service" television advertisements for the voter registration drives of the Democratic Party. Playing on the animosity of their characters, the ads pitted them against each other: "If people like you are going to register and vote, I'm going to register and vote just to even the score."[129]

In the White House, Carter came to appreciate the cultural reach and political power of television entertainment. Following a short inaugural address on the "new spirit" in American life, Jimmy Carter became the first president to walk in the inaugural parade from Capitol Hill to the White House. It represented the culmination of the carefully crafted image of Jimmy Carter as the nonpolitician. Later in the evening, television viewers took part in the inaugural celebrations with performances by prime-time stars such as Redd Foxx (*Sanford and Son*), Freddie Prinze (*Chico and the Man*), and *All in the Family*'s Jean Stapleton and Carroll O'Connor.[130]

For even if Carter did not care for or about Hollywood, the president's strategists recognized the power of television entertainers to attract audiences and shape media coverage. Aides such as Barry Jagoda and Jerry Rafshoon, like Nixon's advertising men before them, were convinced they could master television. Months into the new presidency, a naïve Jagoda claimed that "Jimmy Carter may be the biggest television star of all time."[131] Only Walter Cronkite and Johnny Carson could compare to what the presumptuous strategist called "the first television President."[132]

Still riding high on the improbable success of the marathon presidential campaign, the strategists seemed to forget how the people around Gerald Ford, Richard Nixon, Lyndon B. Johnson, and John F. Kennedy all, with varying degrees of success, had manipulated both news and entertainment programming. "We're different," an overconfident Jagoda remarked, "because we understand that television is more than journalism."[133] Now, the White House would appreciate both television entertainment and news in its media strategies. Hollywood responded in kind. Only months into the new presidency, Norman Lear called the White House: "I want to do anything I can to help."[134]

In the end, Archie Bunker—and the changes *All in the Family* wrought—outlasted Jimmy Carter in Democratic Party politics. In the brutally frank assessment of journalist Martin Schram, Carter went from using television in the campaign in ways that made him appear "larger than life" to, as president, appearing "smaller than the office."[135] In 1980, the perceived failures of the Carter administration provoked a primary challenge by Edward Kennedy, whose campaign looked, once again, to Carroll O'Connor to entertain and engage. "Friends, Herbert Hoover hid out in the White House too, responding to desperate problems with patriotic pronouncements and we got a hell of a depression," the actor announced in a play on the opening theme of *All in the Family*, "but I'm afraid Jimmy's depression is going to be worse than Herbert's."[136]

Kennedy, of course, had more credibility with the white working class than either Lindsay or McGovern before him. Yet his team recognized, and was open about, the appeal of the character of Archie Bunker. "Archie Bunker is a blue-collar person struggling to make ends meet," an aide told the press. "He makes a very effective messenger for what we're trying to say."[137] The *Washington Post* called it one of the "few well-documented cases were a specific ad made a measurable difference."[138] By 1980, everybody recognized the importance of television—both news and entertainment—and everybody wanted to make the most of it.

Since the days of FDR, liberals had found allies in Hollywood eager to fund, promote, and campaign for their candidates and causes.[139] In the 1960s, John Kennedy was hailed as the "first television president."[140] A decade later, however, the structures of political campaigns and parties had changed. Television had also changed. Together, the transformations provided innovative media strategists with new ways to stand out, attract attention, and connect with voters. The campaigns of liberals such as John Lindsay and George McGovern as well as moderates like Jimmy Carter illustrated the influence of Hollywood and how political campaigns were remade in the image of television entertainment. With the turn to Archie Bunker, a new form of showbiz politics emerged, intentionally blurring the lines between news and entertainment, between show and politics. Hollywood and Washington, DC, each had what the other wanted: Hollywood the fame and fortune, Washington the power. First television entertainment became political, then political campaigns became entertaining.

Act III

FRIENDS AND FOES

Chapter 6

MRS. BUNKER GOES TO WASHINGTON

The convention hall was abuzz with anticipation. Women from all over the United States had gathered at the Sam Houston Coliseum in Houston, Texas, in the middle of November 1977, to partake in the National Women's Conference. Sisterhood was in the air as some 17,000 women joined together to decide on a political plan of action for the feminist movement. Suddenly, the air filled with sounds of excitement: "Look, it's Edith."[1] Cameras flashed and people reached out as the familiar figure of Edith Bunker stepped down from the commissioner's platform and joined the crowds on the convention floor. Only it was not really the beloved character but the actress Jean Stapleton. To the women in the convention hall, however, it was Edith Bunker.[2] And she was their hero.

Both Edith and Stapleton were unlikely idols. Edith, after all, was best known as a "dingbat." Her role, early critics noted, was to be "alternately insulted . . . or patronized or ignored."[3] The *New York Times* called her "the antithesis of women's liberation."[4] And Stapleton, in stark contrast with Carroll O'Connor and Rob Reiner, came to *All in the Family* without strong liberal politics. "I had been quite an apolitical person," she later recalled.[5] *TV Guide* concluded in May 1972 that "she refuses to choose up sides ideologically."[6] Her work on the show, and the people with whom she worked, raised her interest in feminism and liberal politics. It also provided her with a national platform, and over the 1970s Stapleton became deeply involved in political activism.

The women's movement, often called the women's liberation movement (shortened to "women's lib") or second-wave feminism, grew into a mass movement in the late 1960s. While united in their struggle against an oppressive patriarchy, there was no single women's movement but instead a coalition of diverse, at times antagonistic, groups working toward a wide range of aims.[7] Within the mainstream, the liberal National Organization for Women (NOW), formed in 1966 by Betty Friedan, often represented the political face of the women's movement. Yet smaller, more radical, groups such as the Redstockings, the Feminists, and the New York Radical Women attracted mass media attention with political street theater and direct action. Both strands of the movement tended to be treated with a mix of dismissiveness and ridicule by the media.[8] And on prime-time television, men were the main attraction, with women relegated to playing the supporting role. In 1973, for example, no more than six of sixty-two prime-time network shows featured a woman in the lead.[9] Mary Richards (played by Mary Tyler Moore on *The Mary Tyler Moore Show*) and Maude Findlay (Bea Arthur on *Maude*) were the most prominent examples of liberated women on prime time, but it was Edith Bunker who emerged as a feminist icon in the political campaigns of the women's movement.

Stapleton's political use of her character marked a new political environment in which attracting attention was key and the lines between news and entertainment were blurred. Politics itself became more and more of a show over the 1970s as both candidates and public officials developed a more sophisticated appreciation for the potential of television. Media consultants made big bucks by helping politicians craft sound bites and media events to win not only electoral but legislative campaigns.[10] In the mass-mediated attention circus, television entertainment—which held the attention of tens of millions of viewers—constituted the central ring for political interests. And so interest groups and activists turned to the stars of prime time to engage and educate legislators and voters alike.

When *All in the Family* came on the air in January 1971, everybody recognized it was groundbreaking. Yet the gender dynamic on the show was anything but trailblazing. Archie Bunker was the breadwinner, Edith the homemaker. Mike Stivic was in college, Gloria at home. The men came home expecting dinner to be served and in Archie's case, a cold beer delivered to his chair. Whenever Archie lost his temper with his wife, he loudly demanded, "Stifle yourself, dingbat."[11] In short, the patriarchy was alive and well at 704 Hauser Street.

While initial reviews noted the brilliance of Jean Stapleton, Edith was often dismissed as the "dim-witted wife."[12] Gloria was brushed aside in most reviews, often in snide language.[13] "Her mental life consists of affirming whatever her husband says," the *New York Times* observed. "She should have women's lib out after CBS in full cry."[14] Sure enough, within a year, women were writing the production company decrying the portrayal of Gloria. "She doesn't work, nor does she go to school," a group of disappointed women wrote. "Apparently she exists only as Mike's wife."[15] Nor was it only Gloria who elicited protests from women. "With few exceptions all the women are silly, vain, brainless, bitchy, parasitic pains in the ass," one viewer complained.[16] By the second season, that sentiment was—to a degree—shared by the producers and writers. Both Norman Lear and Bud Yorkin were married to committed feminists, Frances Lear and Peggy Yorkin, who were less than comfortable with the early portrayal of women on the show.[17] So when Lear answered complaints, he promised to do better.[18]

Bringing in Virginia Carter, the openly gay feminist leader who left a career in physics for one in television, illustrated the producers' growing interest in the women's movement. Soon, Edith Bunker became more complex. Yes, she remained the naïve and loving wife. But she asserted herself and stood up to Archie more. By the fourth season, in the fall of 1973, Edith actually slapped Archie when she learned that, despite an earlier promise, he was gambling again.[19] The following season, Edith let out a rare "damnit" in frustration when Archie refused to listen to her.[20] Two weeks later, she again defied him and demanded more respect from him. "My mind is made up," Edith declared when refusing to follow her husband's will, "case closed." Confused by her assertiveness, Archie protested: "I'm the only one that closes cases around here."[21] But in the end, Edith—not Archie—emerged victorious. This was a deliberate development on the part of the producers, writers, and cast.

"Edith is growing," writer Bernie West concluded in an interview in 1974. "She is not going to be a doormat."[22] From the beginning, the cast had contributed to the development and writing of the show. While everybody on the show was committed to the mission of ridiculing prejudice, the almost all-male writers' room had some blind spots when it came to the portrayal of women. Whenever a line felt out of place, Stapleton vetoed it. "I've refused to do lines that are obviously dumb-dumb gag lines," she explained in interviews.[23] The idea was, after all, to do a show about real people. Edith, like the rest of the characters, had to be real. "What Edith represents is the housewife who is still in bondage to the male figure, very submissive and restricted to the home," Stapleton remarked.[24]

But there was a purpose to Edith's submissiveness. It was, Stapleton acknowledged, "part of the show's plan to place it all on the table, look at it, recognize it, laugh at it and, maybe, change it."[25] While Mary Richards on *The Mary Tyler Moore Show*, Rhoda Morgenstern (Valerie Harper) on *Rhoda* (CBS, 1974–79), and Maude Findlay on *Maude* represented the modern woman, Edith Bunker served as a symbol of a different age. "You can't put liberated women into every TV show," Stapleton explained. "It just wouldn't be true or honest."[26] Instead, she argued, having a woman gradually grow and learn served the goals of the women's movement. "There's a slow development going on with Edith," she explained, "and that's the way it's really going to happen in this country."[27]

By the later seasons of *All in the Family*, Carter and Stapleton both pushed the writers to develop scripts dealing with issues and situations that the women's movement elevated into the national conversation. Their interest in feminist topics led the writers to explore new story lines. "It gave us a new dimension," writer Larry Rhine later recalled.[28] And so the show dealt with issues such as sexual assault, sex discrimination, birth control, unequal pay, and women's difficulties in securing credit.[29] Even a generally critical report on women and minorities on television by the US Commission on Civil Rights recognized the new turn in which "Edith Bunker stands up to Archie in defining what is right and wrong."[30] "The women's movement caught our awareness, our consciousness, and so caught Edith's," Norman Lear explained.[31] By having beloved characters encounter inequality, discrimination, and sexual violence, the show brought difficult conversations into living rooms across the country. "We are serving the [women's] movement by dramatizing it," Stapleton concluded.[32] Over the years, the feminists at Tandem Productions served the women's movement not only by dramatizing it but by promoting public policy, legislation, and the ratification of the Equal Rights Amendment (ERA).

Virginia Carter pioneered the use of *All in the Family* beyond the actual network broadcast. When she arrived at Tandem Productions in early 1973, she found letters from various organizations and citizens' groups eager to use the show in their work to educate and raise awareness. She immediately recognized that she could work with political interests and activists to maximize the reach and influence of the message on the most popular show on television. This was power she had only dreamed of in her previous position as the leader of the local NOW chapter in Los Angeles: to reach an audience in the tens of millions on a weekly basis. To entertain but also to engage and educate.

Once described as Norman Lear's "right and left hands," Carter developed a keen understanding of the influence of television entertainment.[33] She read the columns, letters, and studies debating the effectiveness of liberal satire and bigotry; she corresponded and collaborated with advocates looking to raise awareness via prime time; and she followed with interest as politicians and candidates turned to Archie Bunker to win elections. When a US senator expressed interest in screening *All in the Family* on Capitol Hill to advance liberal legislation, Carter was eager to collaborate.

The first attempts to use the show to promote a legislative agenda in Congress were not directly about women's rights, yet it started with John Rich's aging mother falling ill. Suddenly, he noticed significant holes in the social safety net. Rich was the director of *All in the Family* and a key creative voice in the development of the show. And because Norman Lear encouraged his writers, director, and cast to bring their own experiences to work, Rich did just that. In the writers' room, the conversation turned to recent reports in the news about the rise of the elderly shoplifting bare necessities. This was an issue of social relevance, and in the hands of the creative team behind *All in the Family* it was the spark needed to light up television screens across the country. An article in the *Washington Post* described it as "a textbook example of how Rich and . . . Lear put together situation comedies with a message."[34]

Broadcast in the fall of 1973, the episode revolved around the experiences of an old man on the run from a retirement home whom Edith Bunker encountered and brought home. Conflict arose when Archie discovered an old man dressed only in pajamas in his living room. Complaining about the strained economy and rising food prices, Archie decried his wife's hospitality: "Let the government take care of him!" In the following argument over welfare, the economy, and the elderly, Mike challenged his father-in-law to consider the fact that Social Security payments were not enough. At the time they only amounted to $180, well short of the official poverty level of $205. "Don't you see, Arch," Mike implored, "the government is just helping old people to starve slower." Flustered, Archie shot back: "Well, maybe when you start working and paying taxes the government can do better."[35]

Throughout the episode, the characters discussed Social Security, Medicare, discrimination in employment, and conditions in nursing homes. It was a stinging rebuke of both political programs and institutions. To viewers at home, in a blurring of entertainment and news, it served as an "exposé."[36] Viewers seemed to love the show and, according to mail received by local stations, CBS, and Tandem Productions, they loved the message.[37] At the time, the aging were either absent or the butt of the joke on prime-time comedy.[38] Johnny Carson's "Aunt Blabby" and Carol Burnett's "The Old Folks" defined the image of the elderly as silly, slow, and senile.[39] On *All in the Family*, however, the old man—and his girlfriend—were portrayed as sharp, witty, and driven. The problem was not the aging; it was how society treated them. "You really got a message across," one viewer remarked, "a much needed message."[40] Other viewers turned to writing their senators and representatives, expressing their hope that public officials were paying attention.[41] Indeed, Congress was.

It was Senator Frank Church (D-ID), the liberal crusader from Idaho, who championed the show on Capitol Hill. Recognizing that public policy relating to the plight of the aging seldom received extended mass media attention, Church made a habit of creating media events to generate publicity.[42] He often visited nursing homes with his wife and once attempted to navigate the halls of the Capitol building in a wheelchair to dramatize the need for investments in accessible public spaces.[43] Now, the most popular show on television was debating public policy on aging. It made, he remarked, "many of the points which the Senate Committee on Aging and I, as its chairman, attempt to make in reports and speeches."[44] Addressing his colleagues, he highlighted the specific policy points addressed on the show, including "the special impact of high food costs upon the elderly, the fact that medicare [sic] covers only 42 percent of the health care costs of older Americans, and the fact that the average social security [sic] benefit is less than the official poverty level."[45] Beyond the discussion on public policy, Church praised it for presenting the life of old people with humor and humanity. Tens of millions of people were watching in their living rooms. The media-savvy Church was determined to make the most of it.

In his role as chairman of the Committee on the Aging, Church turned to Virginia Carter to join forces in framing a conversation among members of Congress, experts, and interest groups.[46] Hosting an evening with *All in the Family*, he invited his colleagues on the committee as well as experts and activists to an advance screening of the show. The guest list included Arthur Flemming, the commissioner on aging who previously had headed the Department of Health, Education, and Welfare under President Dwight Eisenhower; Jack Ossofsky of the National Council on Aging; and Edwin Kaskowitz of the Gerontological Society.[47] This was a venerable who's who of the Beltway elite on the aging. Virginia Carter provided them not only with the advance screening but with copies of the script to circulate among members of the committee and viewer mail for distribution to engaged organizations and activists.[48] Appreciating the power of entertainment to engage, Church used *All in the Family* to attract attention, engage an elite audience, and anchor public policy discussions in the lived experiences of beloved characters. Following the network broadcast, he wrote the producer and the cast. "Once again, Mr. Archie Bunker and company have helped Americans understand themselves a little better."[49]

But while television could help audiences understand issues of social relevance, it could also distort. Many within the women's movement, conscious of the power of mass media to cement harmful stereotypes, viewed television entertainment with deep suspicion.[50] After all, women were often objectified and sexualized in film, television, and the press.[51] This included times when they were victims of violence. "Rape, which is a crime of violence," a representative of NOW told a House of Representatives subcommittee, "all too often is dealt with on a sexual basis in television programing."[52] Television depictions, she remarked, often featured young, attractive, and vulnerable women putting themselves in dangerous situations. Even when detective shows, such as *Baretta* (ABC, 1975–78), *Starsky and Hutch* (ABC, 1975–79), and *Hawaii Five-O* (CBS, 1968–80), dealt with sexual violence, the focus was not on the actual experiences of the victim but instead on the male avengers.[53] The women's movement wanted to change the conventional understanding of sexual violence and, instead, focus on the victims, with speak-outs, demonstrations, support lines, and crisis centers.[54]

Norman Lear and Virginia Carter were eager to contribute to the shift. When they introduced the subject of sexual violence to the *All in the Family* writers' room in the summer of 1977, the idea was to consider it in a way that reflected real-life experiences. They worked closely with antirape advocates to develop the script. Having Edith Bunker attacked by a rapist was a way of participating in the national conversation on the issue. "Edith connects to America like no other person on any of our shows," Lear remarked when introducing the subject in the writers' room with Carter. "We both felt strongly, that if Edith went through an experience . . . [it] makes it okay to take a closer look at it."[55] Liberals on Capitol Hill agreed.

In Congress, Elizabeth Holtzman (D-NY), who in 1972 at age thirty-one became the youngest woman ever elected to the House, introduced legislation providing stronger protections for victims of sexual assault. Cross-examination of victims of rape about their previous relationships and sexual history in open court, which was standard practice at the time, served not only to undermine their testimony but to intimidate them from pursuing charges against their assailants. Holtzman looked to shield victims from such intrusive and unnecessary questioning. Her bill was a part of a larger campaign around the country against sexual violence.[56] NOW hailed Holtzman's proposed congressional action as "an important and critically needed step forward."[57] With the bill under consideration in the judiciary committee, Representatives Herbert Harris (D-VA) and Peter Rodino (D-NJ), cosponsors of the legislation, turned to *All in the Family* and Virginia Carter. Together they organized an advance congressional screening for legislators, advocates, and DC-area rape crisis center volunteers.

Members of Congress and the show's producers wanted to raise awareness and advocate for legislative action with the episode. Gail Abarbanel of the Santa Monica Rape Treatment Center, an activist who had been closely involved in the development of the script, corresponded with Harris's press secretary on how "it can stimulate the kind of open discussion of the true nature and ramifications of rape that we have only recently been able to do with breast cancer and similar hidden major problems."[58] Borrowing this language, at times verbatim, Harris and Rodino invited—and urged—their colleagues to attend the screening. The purpose, according to Harris, was to "help in your understanding of rape and its meaning to the victim, her family, and the community."[59]

The Judiciary Committee room of the Rayburn House Office Building, across the street from the Capitol, was packed. Almost 200 people from Capitol Hill and area rape crisis centers were in attendance. "It is my hope that our meeting tonight will help focus greater public and congressional attention to this problem," Harris said in his opening remarks.[60] Representing Tandem Productions, Virginia Carter presented the show. "We intended to entertain you, to make you laugh, to educate you, and make you cry," she explained.[61] Indeed, both laughter and crying could be heard in the committee room as the audience watched Edith Bunker on the screen.

Following the screening, representatives of rape crisis centers in the District of Columbia as well as nearby Fairfax County, Virginia, and Howard County, Maryland, addressed the room. Speaking on their work and the widespread problems of rape, they called for legislative action. By combining the popular comedy with testimony from advocates and activists, Harris and Rodino wanted to engage fellow legislators. "Norman Lear and 'All in the Family' have shown great courage in utilizing the television medium to sensitize and educate the American public about this horrifying crime," Rodino concluded. "Sometimes it strikes those we least expect, even Edith Bunker."[62]

The following day, liberal stalwart James H. Scheuer (D-NY) praised his colleagues in the *Congressional Record* and called for hearings on research on sexual assault and for a political campaign to end sexual violence.[63] *Broadcasting* reported that "television comedy became part of the legislative process."[64] A version of Elizabeth Holtzman's legislation, incorporated into the Privacy Protection for Rape Victims Act, passed Congress in 1978. But the legislative win was not due to *All in the Family*. The activism of the women's movement and the leadership of Holtzman moved the bill through Congress.[65] "I congratulate Congresswoman Elizabeth Holtzman for her sponsorship of this legislation and for her leadership in this area," President Jimmy Carter remarked when signing the bill into law.[66] The success of Holtzman's bill did not, however, mark a significant change in the criminal justice system—the overwhelming majority of rape cases were prosecuted not in federal court but in state criminal courts—but it did constitute a symbolic win for the women's movement. And by 1978, the movement needed a win as the promises of the early 1970s seemed further and further away. Nothing embodied this more than the struggle over the ERA.

In the early 1970s, it had seemed like the sky was the limit. The burgeoning women's movement went from success to success. "We just kept passing women's rights legislation," remarked Bella Abzug (D-NY), the feminist activist who in 1970 won a seat in Congress with a campaign declaring that a woman's place was in the House of Representatives.[67] With strong bipartisan support for women's rights in Congress, feminists, in particular Martha Griffiths (D-MI) in the House and Birch Bayh (D-IN) in the Senate, turned to the ERA. Since its introduction in 1923, it had been *the* symbol of women's rights yet had, for decades, failed to win enough votes to pass both chambers of Congress. In the early 1970s, it seemed like an idea whose time had come: "Equality of rights under law shall not be denied or abridged by the United States or any state on account of sex."

When the yeas and nays were counted, it was not even close. In October 1971, the House of Representatives approved the amendment with 354 votes for and twenty-four against. In March 1972, the Senate echoed the lopsided vote when it passed the amendment with eighty-four members approving and only eight disapproving.[68] The vote made for some strange bedfellows, with liberal lion Edward Kennedy (D-MA) and conservative champion Strom Thurmond (R-SC) both in favor in the Senate, while segregationist senator Sam Ervin (D-NC) joined civil rights crusader Emanuel Celler (D-NY) in the House in opposition to the amendment.[69] From Congress the amendment was sent out to the states for ratification. Within an hour, Hawaii ratified it without any opposition or debate. The next day, New Hampshire and Delaware followed.[70] Victory seemed certain.[71] On the first anniversary of the amendment passing the Senate, Washington became the thirtieth state to ratify it. Only eight more to go until women's rights were written into the Constitution.

When the amendment went out for ratification in 1972, Jean Stapleton was perhaps the most recognized woman in the country. Yet she was uneasy about her newfound fame. While appreciative of the success of *All in the Family*, she vowed to remain both a private citizen and an actress—not a symbol.[72]

In interviews, she hesitated to speak about her own political views.[73] In part, because, as she later described herself, she was politically naïve when first cast in the role of Edith Bunker.[74] Working on the show, however, broadened her views. "I found myself in this nest of activists out in L.A.," she recalled years later.[75] Virginia Carter was, according to Stapleton, "the first active feminist that I really became friendly with."[76] The first but not the last. In this environment of feminist activists, Stapleton became aware and educated.[77]

A key tool of activism for the women's movement was consciousness-raising—discussion among women about their experiences as women—to appreciate the political, cultural, and economic structures that denied them equal opportunities solely on the basis of their sex.[78] Many women, including Stapleton, became involved in the women's movement as a result of consciousness-raising.[79] For Stapleton, consciousness-raising was not limited to meetings with other women but to the conversations on *All in the Family*. "The social statement that almost every show makes," she explained, "has awakened my own social conscience."[80] By 1974, Stapleton openly embraced feminism, declaring in interviews that she "couldn't be more thrilled with the effects of women's lib."[81] In the following years, she started identifying as a women's rights "activist."[82] It was through Virginia Carter and Frances Lear that she made her way into the activism of the movement.[83]

Frances Lear had a drive and purpose. After reading Betty Friedan's best-selling *The Feminine Mystique* in the mid-1960s, she found her calling in the women's rights movement. "From then on," Norman Lear later wrote, "there was no more vocal and ardent feminist anywhere."[84] She became a leading figure within the Los Angeles chapter of NOW and dedicated most of her time to the movement. "I marched, funded, organized, and lived the movement every moment of the day and most of the night," Frances Lear recalled in her memoir.[85] She frequently hosted dinners and fundraisers in their home. It was at one of these dinners, bringing together women in business, politics, and media, that Stapleton became involved in the fight for the ERA.[86] "We all agreed," she remembered, "that Jean could help by doing some ads in magazines and newspapers."[87] Only they really planned not for Jean Stapleton but Edith Bunker to do the advertisements. While Carroll O'Connor eagerly engaged with the character he played on *All in the Family* at different events, performances, and interviews, Stapleton wanted to keep some professional distance from Edith. When Dick Cavett, during an interview, asked her to do Edith's voice, she politely, but firmly, declined.[88] In fact, *McCall's* reported that she refused any request "to talk like Edith, sing like Edith, [or] walk like Edith."[89] Stapleton viewed the character as distinct from her own identity and refused to merge the two.[90] For the ERA, however, she would make an exception.

By the end of 1974, when the amendment had been ratified in a total of thirty-three states, the momentum stalled as organized opposition grew. In Hollywood, support for the ERA became a cause célèbre. Not since the civil rights movement of the 1960s had liberal Hollywood mobilized as strongly in support of a political grassroots movement as "party-givers, talk-show guests, fund-raisers, lobbyists, and lecturers."[91] To win ratification of the amendment in states such as Illinois, Florida, and Nevada, however, the movement needed to reach beyond committed feminists and secure the support of voters and legislators who viewed both the women's movement and Hollywood liberals with unease. While movie A-listers such as Shirley MacLaine, Jane Fonda, and Robert Redford campaigned for the cause, television actors also played a key role.

Leaders within the women's movement, including Virginia Carter, volunteered to provide stars from such popular shows as *The Mary Tyler Moore Show*, *M*A*S*H*, and *Happy Days* (ABC, 1974–84) with information, talking points, and media preparation on the amendment.[92] "We're going to be asking you to go into the unratified states to speak as high-profile figures and we want you to go in there strong," Carter explained at a California ERA Campaign Fund workshop.[93] Television's favorites, including Carol Burnett (*The Carol Burnett Show*), Karen Grassle (*Little House on the Prairie*), and Susan Blakely (*Rich Man, Poor Man*), rehearsed scenarios such as discussing the ERA on talk shows and news conferences. One of the challenges: how to "cleverly sneak it in" if the talk show host did not want to cover the subject. In one scenario, Valerie Harper shifted the conversation about *Rhoda* to her titular character's growth, her role in the workplace, and the ERA. Harper, already active in the campaign, reassured the other participants that "this today is 20,000 times more difficult [than the real thing]."[94] So, on talk shows or at press conferences, stars such as Marlo Thomas, Mary Tyler Moore, and Cloris Leachman showed a depth of knowledge about the amendment.[95] Linda Lavin (who played the titular character on *Alice*) acknowledged that she brought up the ERA in various interviews "even when they don't ask me."[96] Hollywood film and television activists stoked mass media attention and wide public interest. "When Hollywood stars . . . work to change minds and move votes," the feminist *Ms.* magazine observed, "somehow the world takes notice."[97]

The most important difference between movie stars and television personalities was that while the former symbolized glamour and celebrity, the latter represented beloved characters. Actors such as Alan Alda (*M*A*S*H*), Lorne

Greene (*Bonanza*), Ed Asner (*The Mary Tyler Moore Show*), and Henry Winkler (*Happy Days*) came with a middle American appeal. Television brought them into living rooms across the nation as audiences welcomed them as guests in their homes. Meredith MacRae, whom viewers recognized from her roles on *My Three Sons* (ABC, 1960–65; CBS, 1965–72) and *Petticoat Junction*, noted that she was "pleased that my wholesome, All-American image helps certain kinds of women to listen to me."[98] If any character on television could win them over, it would be Edith Bunker.

Stapleton agreed to use Edith Bunker to advocate for the amendment in print and radio advertisements. She was well aware of her appeal. "So many people approach me with special affection that I know they are doing it because of Edith," she recognized.[99] The ad campaign connected the lived experiences of her beloved character with the status of women in society in a way that engaged readers and listeners. "I'm Jean Stapleton. You know me better as Edith Bunker, Archie's lovable dingbat on 'All in the Family.' It's funny when Archie tells me to stifle myself. But in real life, being treated like a second-class citizen is no laughing matter. I know, because I am. And if you're a woman, you are, too."[100] Listing the inequalities and hardships facing women, ranging from inheritance taxes to insurance rates, Stapleton concluded that "there ought to be a law," before urging the public to write to their legislators.[101] The idea behind the advertisements was, according to Virginia Carter, to persuade opponents of the ERA "to change their votes, and, if not, we want to throw them out of office."[102] By deploying Edith, feminists connected the amendment to one of the most popular women in the nation. After all, most people, *McCall's* recognized, "think she's Edith Bunker."[103] The lines between actress and character were deliberately blurred as the campaign turned her into a prominent spokesperson for the movement.

In the summer of 1976, President Gerald Ford appointed Stapleton to the National Commission on the Observance of International Women's Year.[104] She viewed it as a direct result of the advertisements in Illinois and Florida.[105] "It seems," Stapleton remarked later, "that people listen to the person they've seen come into their home every week."[106] So when the president came calling, the movement had every reason to see Edith Bunker as a winning strategy.

The work of the commission culminated in the National Women's Conference in Houston in late 1977. Stapleton took on her new responsibilities with enthusiasm, studying the issues with care and engaging with other activists ahead of the conference.[107] She recognized that she could bring mass media attention but worried about overshadowing the grassroots activists dedicated to the cause.[108] Stapleton convinced fellow television stars such as Bea Arthur,

Mary Tyler Moore, and Cloris Leachman to commit to a network broadcast production with dance, song, and other performances from Houston.[109] She also personally lobbied President Jimmy Carter and First Lady Rosalynn Carter "to play an active, onstage role" at the convention.[110]

Recognizing the appeal of Edith Bunker, Stapleton used her standing as the most popular homemaker in the nation to publicize and win support for the event. Appearing on talk shows and at press conferences, she turned the conversation to women's rights and equality by using both her own and her character's lived experiences to strengthen her arguments.[111] Connecting the story of women's rights to Edith Bunker served to counter arguments that the commission, and by extension the movement, was under the control of "misfits of society."[112] Stapleton shared with the press the story of a woman whose husband did not approve of her interest in the women's movement. So she ended up sneaking out of the house at four o'clock in the morning to attend a meeting. "Boy, if that isn't Edith Bunker," Stapleton exclaimed, recounting the story.[113] With opponents charging that the women's movement consisted of radicals and lesbians, Edith provided cover for feminist activists.[114] It was harder to charge that a movement with Edith Bunker as its face was out to corrupt the American family.

And so at the conference in Houston, Stapleton was among the most recognized women. Both the press and delegates followed her with excitement. Standing under a giant banner reading "Woman," Stapleton read the Declaration of American Women: "We pledge, with all the strength of our dedication, to form a more perfect union."[115] During the conference, she again blurred the lines between character and actress. At press conferences, she explained that "the image of Edith Bunker is good for the women's movement because Edith is a homemaker."[116] And as a working mother and wife, Stapleton wore a button saying "I'm a housewife for ERA" at the convention.[117] The movement did not lack homemakers in their ranks, but none came with the national profile that Stapleton's Edith enjoyed. Opponents of the ERA wanted to claim the banner of homemakers.[118] Keeping with conservative gender roles, anti-ERA women brought legislators home-baked bread and pies in their campaign against the amendment.[119] The prominent use of Edith Bunker in advertisements and media campaigns, however, signaled the importance of contesting the view of homemakers as inherent opponents of the ERA.

Stapleton not only declared her own support for the ERA but announced that Edith Bunker would endorse it too. "She would support it with all her heart," Stapleton concluded, "because Edith is the soul of justice."[120] Newspapers across the country ran with it. "Edith Will Support ERA," a United Press

Jean Stapleton at the National Women's Conference of 1977. Bettye Lane/David M. Rubenstein Rare Book and Manuscript Library, Duke University.

International article declared.[121] In response, Representative Patricia Schroeder (D-CO) wrote Stapleton a note of appreciation: "How glad I am that you are with us and not against us."[122] With her appointment to the presidential commission, Stapleton developed close relationships on Capitol Hill, and after the convention she wrote members of Congress to advocate for the resolutions passed in Houston.[123] These relationships also contributed to bringing elite attention to her work.

When Stapleton received an honorary doctorate at Emerson College in the spring of 1978, she again addressed the issue of whether Edith Bunker would support the ERA. While noting that the character was developed in collaboration with producers, writers, and her fellow actors, she assumed "the privilege of answering . . . Yes."[124] Again, she highlighted Edith's role as a homemaker. "Contrary to some misconceptions, she will not have to leave her homemaker job unless she chooses," Stapleton observed. "She will not lose the protection of her husband; rather, she will gain more in that her legal rights and standing in the economy, insurance, Social Security, inheritance, divorce, credit, taxes, etc. will be guaranteed."[125] In a signal of the movement's media savvy, activists placed a lengthy excerpt of the address in the *New York Times*.[126] Within weeks,

Elizabeth Holtzman highlighted Stapleton's comments on Capitol Hill by placing the article into the *Congressional Record*.[127]

Stapleton's activism was not, however, an elite campaign. Even after the National Women's Conference, she was out in the street marching, rallying, and speaking for the ERA. "I am not here because of a role that I have played," Stapleton told an ERA march in Chicago. "I am here because, like you, I am a human being who happens to be a woman."[128] Yet she continued to connect the struggle with her character. "As Edith Bunker I don't have equal rights," she declared. "As Jean Stapleton I don't either."[129] In fact, she remarked, "Edith wrestle[s] with many of the issues that are our concern today: the economic status of the homemakers, credit, employment, child care, rape, community property."[130] The use of her character to promote the amendment was not lost on Stapleton, who acknowledged that "Edith Bunker has helped me to communicate with the housewives of America."[131]

Norman Lear also recognized the love people felt for *All in the Family* and Edith Bunker.[132] By the end of the 1970s, Jean Stapleton, Rob Reiner, and Sally Struthers had all left *All in the Family*, though Carroll O'Connor continued under the new title *Archie Bunker's Place* (CBS, 1979–83). Stapleton appeared occasionally over the first season of the new show but did not return for a second season. Edith Bunker faced death. Stapleton was eager to move on, but Lear struggled with losing Edith. Although no longer involved in the day-to-day production, he was the creator of the character. If the show killed Edith Bunker, the producers and network executives would have to convince him first that she would not die in vain.[133]

The network, Lear demanded, would have to honor Edith with a sizable donation in support of the ERA.[134] Through Tandem Productions, CBS donated $500,000, "the largest corporate gift in the history of the women's movement," to NOW for the establishment of the Edith Bunker Memorial Fund.[135] The media stunt, with Lear and NOW holding a press conference on the death of a fictive character, attracted wide media coverage.[136] Lear told the press that "no one was more affected by [the women's movement] than Edith, and in no other woman was the result more apparent."[137] And the fight continued. "We hope that just as people send donations to charities in memory of their loved ones, they will continue to send in donations to build this into a $2-million or a $3-million fund," Lear declared.[138] The production company was barraged by emotional letters from fans hoping to save the character. Save Edith Bunker Committees were formed around the country.[139] Angry correspondence, including letters addressing Lear as "murderer of Edith Bunker," demanded that she live on.[140] Having made a career engaging people on an emotional level, Lear recognized an opportunity. He responded with both an explanation about Stapleton's desire to take on new projects and an appeal: to honor Edith Bunker's legacy. "To lessen our own sadness at dealing with this, and to help make her death more meaningful," he wrote, "it is our hope that people across the country will wish to remember Edith by making a donation, small or large, to the fund which bears her name."[141] Capitalizing on the media moment, and the deep affection for the character, Lear wanted viewers to continue the fight. After all, Lear claimed, the amendment "represents everything Edith believed in and stood for."[142] Stapleton was not involved in the memorial fund but approved of the cause.[143] The way Norman Lear turned the demise of the character into a campaign for the ERA was a publicity stunt, but it followed the example of Stapleton's activism in blurring the lines between entertainment and politics.

Back in Houston in 1977, chants of "ratify the ERA" and "three more states" had echoed in the convention hall.[144] Even then, however, it was already too late. By the time Jean Stapleton became involved in the campaign for the ERA, the opposition was mobilized and organized. "Don't get your legal advice from Mrs. Archie Bunker," Phyllis Schlafly's *Eagle Forum* declared in response to Stapleton's advertisements.[145] The promises of the early 1970s turned into broken dreams as opponents claimed the banner of family values.[146] STOP ERA, under the leadership of Schlafly, lived up to its name. Only after the loss of momentum did proponents turn to innovative new tactics.[147] When Stapleton started using the image of Edith Bunker in her activism for the ERA, a total of thirty-four states had ratified the amendment. Only one more state, Indiana, joined the list, leaving the amendment three short of the required two-thirds majority. Equal rights were not written into the Constitution.

In 1977, Norman Lear suggested that "you could probably trace the whole women's movement just following Edith Bunker."[148] He meant on *All in the Family*. But to really appreciate the role of Edith Bunker in the women's movement requires looking beyond television. Pushed by the movement, the producers and writers of the show wanted to see the character grow. She might not turn into a liberated woman like Maude or Rhoda, but she did learn to stand up for herself on prime time. Yet it was beyond *All in the Family* that Jean Stapleton, influenced by feminists such as Virginia Carter and Frances Lear, turned her beloved character into a champion for women's rights. "Of course," Stapleton recalled later, "I didn't appear as Edith Bunker, but I had played the role, so that was a big part of my welcome there."[149] Indeed, both Jean Stapleton and Edith Bunker emerged as icons of the equal rights movement.

The efforts to use *All in the Family* and Edith Bunker to promote a legislative agenda came about because political interests in the Senate, the House, and the National Organization for Women believed in the value of television. Week in and week out, audiences welcomed prime-time characters into their homes, developing strong connections with them. Norman Lear wanted his show to spark conversation about difficult issues; political activists hoped the conversations would result in votes needed to pass their agenda. In the media age, politicians believed, television entertainment could engage audiences and turn politics into an attraction. Soon, politicians themselves would play leading roles on must-watch television. When Frank Church screened *All in the Family* on Capitol Hill, some of his colleagues missed it due to the newest and most exciting television event in the country: the Senate Watergate hearings.[150] The televised hearings illustrated new ways for ambitious and media-savvy politicians to become the main attraction on television.[151] The shift, however, was the result not of new technologies but of how political interests understood and made use of them.

In the end, even Edith Bunker failed to secure ratification of the ERA. Instead, the attempts to make *All in the Family* a force for women's rights illustrated the potential of prime-time entertainment to mobilize political movements both for and against. Not everybody appreciated the conversations Lear and company were starting across the country. In 1977, a longtime viewer took pen to paper to express her views on *All in the Family*. "In the past year, it has become very offensive in many of the jokes and topics," she complained. "Sex, menopause, homosexuals, etc. are not appropriate subjects for a television show."[152] What some audiences celebrated as honest engagement with issues of social and political relevance, other decried as inappropriate. While liberals and feminists looked to Norman Lear as a key ally, conservatives were "being told Norman Lear is responsible for the filth."[153] In a clash between television and politics, *All in the Family* found itself in the middle of a battle for control over prime time.

Chapter 7
STOPPING IMMORALITY ON TV

Richard E. Wiley was no more than three days into his new job as chairman of the Federal Communications Commission (FCC) on March 12, 1974, when he was badgered in front of an appropriations subcommittee on Capitol Hill. The subject matter was violence on television, and the members wanted the FCC to use its regulatory power to censor prime-time entertainment. Since the early 1970s, the subcommittee had been urging the commission to take action. "Mr. Chairman, I realize you are new but if I do not let you know how strongly I [and] the members of this committee [feel] about this, we are just going to have a plain shootout," Representative Joseph McDade (R-PA) told Wiley.[1] Wiley actually shared their concern over violence but believed it would be unconstitutional for the commission to make decisions on the quality or content of individual broadcasts. "I implore you also to consider the legal issues and, indeed, the constitutional issues involved in this matter," he told them.[2] Patience, however, was wearing thin. "If we need legislative changes," McDade observed, "let's hear about them."[3]

While televised violence was, according to Wiley, "of concern to every American," conservatives such as McDade were also uneasy about sex on television.[4] The two—violence and sex—became linked in conversations about and regulations of prime-time entertainment. Yet while violence was common on television, there was hardly any sex on the air. On crime procedurals such as *Kojak* (CBS, 1973–78), *Hawaii Five-O*, and *Cannon* (CBS, 1971–76), fistfights, stabbings, and shootings held audiences' attention. One study estimated that the average child would witness some 13,000 killings in television entertainment between the ages of five and fifteen.[5] Sex, however, was out of view. "We allow no nudity, frontal, backal or sidal," Herminio Traviesas, the head censor at NBC, declared.[6] In fact, there were already statutes against obscenity and indecency on television.[7] Criticism of sex was really criticism of talk about sex. When one angry viewer wrote CBS to complain about *All in the Family*, she listed "abortion, vasectomy, birth control, homosexuality, [and] transvestites," as unacceptable subject matter.[8] The show featured almost no explicit violence or sex, but the mission of honest engagement with issues of social importance resulted in frequent conversations about sex, sexuality, and women's health care. It was conversations and ideas, not violence or sex, that made *All in the Family* a lightning rod for conservative anger.

In March 1974, Wiley publicly declared that he did not want to serve as "keeper of the nation's morals," yet circumstances forced him to act.[9] Under pressure and eager to avoid a "shootout" with Congress and potential legislation making him the nation's censor in chief, Wiley used his position to pressure broadcasters. Somebody, Wiley reasoned, needed to do something about sex and violence on television and it was better if it was not the government. When Wiley addressed the Illinois Broadcasters Association in October 1974, he wanted to put the burden on broadcasters themselves. "If self-regulation does not work," Wiley remarked in a thinly veiled threat, "governmental action to protect the public may be required—whether you like it or whether I like it."[10]

Six months later, the National Association of Broadcasters voted to adopt a new policy of "self"-regulation championed by Wiley. It read, "Entertainment programming inappropriate for viewing by a general family audience should not be broadcast during the first hour of network entertainment programming in prime time and in the immediately preceding hour."[11] Even though the board offered no definition of what was deemed "inappropriate," it was clear to many that it meant both sex and violence. While violence was the driving factor, the inclusion of sex constituted a win for conservative activists who wanted to package their political campaigns against progressivism as a defense of "family values."[12] In fact, liberals worried about violence finding common cause with conservatives worried about sex was critical to convincing broadcasters to act.[13] The "family viewing hour" represented the most viable attempt to control prime-time entertainment, a key target for the emerging religious right, in the 1970s. Still, the family viewing hour was not only a conservative project but rather the result of demands by a motley crew of politicians, regulators, broadcasters, and activists.[14]

The adoption of the policy, and the subsequent fights over it, was the culmination of decades of growing interest in television. It represented the success of political pressure: Activists pressured members of Congress; Congress pressured the FCC; and the FCC pressured broadcasters. Behind much of the pressure was a countermobilization by conservative activists abhorred by the progressivism of *All in the Family*, *M*A*S*H*, and *The Mary Tyler Moore Show*. The new freedoms writers and producers won with the success of *All in the Family* were met with a conservative movement against television entertainment, which culminated in the most significant policy of government control of television entertainment in decades. Behind it was not a concern for the public interest but rather an effort at political control of television.

"I am writing this letter in protest and disgust in your exceedingly poor taste in selecting this material for your program," an irate woman informed Norman Lear in March 1972.[15] Some weeks earlier, Edith Bunker had suffered from menopausal symptoms on an episode of *All in the Family*.[16] The episode showcased how the producer and writers dealt with issues of real life and was celebrated as an "all time high of excellence" by fans, requested as a teaching tool by nursing schools, and awarded an Emmy Award for the writing.[17] For certain (conservative) audiences, however, it symbolized the problem with prime time: permissiveness. A year later, another episode of *All in the Family* revolved around Gloria's struggle with premenstrual symptoms.[18] Again, conservative viewers protested the subject matter as indecent. An outraged father took to expressing his views by writing on the back of a Kotex box, criticizing the "standard of propriety" at CBS.[19]

Television was unlike any other medium.[20] On the silver screen, audiences in the early 1970s could enjoy sexually explicit content in such films as Mike Nichols's *Carnal Knowledge*, Woody Allen's *Everything You Always Wanted to Know About Sex* (*but Were Afraid to Ask)*, and Robert Altman's *M*A*S*H*. On Broadway, the antiwar rock musical *Hair* featured full-frontal nudity, while *The Hot l Baltimore* and *Last of the Red Hot Lovers* dealt openly with various sexual themes. And bestselling albums were all about sex, drugs, and rock 'n' roll. Television was different.[21] Television brought it into the living room. While you had to seek out and pay for permissive films, plays, or music, you could stumble on sexual conversations on television. And in contrast with ushers at the movies or the theater, the television set did not recognize whether the audience included children. The medium, the FCC recognized, had "uniquely intrusive qualities."[22] Broadcasters also appreciated the added responsibility associated with going into the home.[23] Even network executives conceded that "television clearly has a responsibility in matters of taste different than that of any other medium."[24] As a result, one television executive remarked in the late 1970s, "the sexual breakthrough in TV has probably taken us to where the movies were in 1935."[25]

To avoid government meddling, broadcasters and the networks had long engaged in self-regulation. The censors (or editors, as they called themselves) at the standards and practices department (also called the program practices department) of the networks guaranteed "good taste" in their broadcasts.[26] The editors were, according to Alfred Schneider, the head of ABC's standards and practices department, "judge and jury."[27] For television producers, the department was a thorn in the side. The editors, according to Norman Lear, believed they were the "moral guardians of the nation."[28] There was a constant back-and-forth between the production company and the network over what was acceptable to broadcast.

Left out of these conversations were the affiliate station owners and managers. And yet the affiliate stations were the most vulnerable to activist campaigns, organized boycotts, license challenges, and FCC action. With the proliferation of activist groups eager to reform broadcasting in the early 1970s, affiliates felt exposed. In general, the affiliate owners and managers were local businessmen with conservative political views. Thus, conservative criticism of television entertainment resonated. "There is one subject that I think absolutely must be number one on the list of concerns in the broadcast industry," a committee of affiliates wrote to network executives in 1973, "and that is ... *permissiveness.*"[29] Some, like (future US senator) Jesse Helms of WRAL-TV, the NBC affiliate in Raleigh, North Carolina, badgered network executives over indecent material.[30] Charles Crutchfield of WBTV, the CBS affiliate in Charlotte, North Carolina, went further. Condemning the current "liberalization" of prime time, he encouraged viewers to write the FCC about programs that "offend your sense of decency and taste."[31] He even suggested that Congress should buck the First Amendment to give the courts the opportunity to take action against what he viewed as indecent material.[32]

Conservative anger over permissiveness in the entertainment industry was not exactly anything new. Long before television became a part of everyday life, conservatives worried over the moral standards of the entertainment industry.[33] With the proliferation of television in the 1950s came increased concern. In the heyday of McCarthyism, conservative anticommunists battled television's progressive values on race and sex with blacklists and boycotts. Many women, immigrants, and people of color found themselves targeted for their values. Story lines about race relations or gender roles were off-limits and the talent behind them out of work.[34] Even after the blacklist, along with loyalty oaths at the networks, ended in the late 1950s, many writers shied away from subject matter that might provoke renewed protests.[35] And so television in the 1960s was anodyne not just due to the demands of standards and practices departments at the networks but because writers tended to self-censor to avoid a backlash.

Society in the 1960s, however, was anything but bland. The decade was a period of turmoil as the civil rights movement, student unrest, and the antiwar movement transformed the nation, and conservative activists were determined to fight the change.[36] The media, a broad term that included both news media and prime-time entertainment, became a key target. A wide variety of leaders within the conservative movement portrayed the media as the enemy. Media figures, including William F. Buckley Jr. of *National Review* and Clarence Manion of *Manion Forum*, presented the media as suffering from a liberal bias, attempting to validate their own conservative views as a necessary balance.[37] Religious leaders such as Carl McIntire and Billy James Hargis condemned the immoral influence of the media and claimed that "Satan controls the airwaves."[38] Political strategists, such as Richard Viguerie and Kevin Phillips, suggested that the networks were under the control of liberals.[39] Books on liberal bias proliferated and were embraced with open arms by conservatives eager to undermine the media.[40]

Most significant were President Richard Nixon and Vice President Spiro Agnew, who made an assault on the media a central part of their political campaigns. Intimidating journalists and media executives while also eroding public trust in the media, Nixon understood it as "good politics for us to kick the press around."[41] Following his public condemnation of the television networks and the papers of record, Agnew emerged as the foremost crusader against the so-called liberal media. While his attacks were celebrated in conservative media, they also gained attention in mainstream media. In a cover story in *TV Guide*, Agnew broadened his criticism to entertainment television.[42] His role as media critic turned him into a political rock star on the right.[43] Portraying the media as the enemy, it turned out, was a winning strategy for mobilizing the base.

Ambitious conservative politicians followed Agnew's lead. Having made his name in the entertainment industry, California governor Ronald Reagan blasted broadcasters as irresponsible for "pander[ing] to the drug culture [and] allow[ing] obscenity on the air" in an address to NBC affiliates in 1972.[44]

Conservative constituents concerned about television entertainment found support from their elected officials. "I certainly share your feeling that television shows should reflect high moral standards," Senator Bob Dole (R-KS) wrote in response to a letter calling for the cancellation of *All in the Family*, *Maude*, and *M*A*S*H* because of their "very low moral standard."[45] In another letter, the conservative Kansan described television as "a threat to the fabric of our nation."[46] The same message was amplified in conservative media. "Producers foisting their filth on the American public will go as far as they can," one outlet concluded, ". . . until stopped."[47] Thus, conservative leaders encouraged everyday Americans to apply pressure on political institutions and regulatory agencies.

While angry letters to the production company, the network, members of Congress, the FCC, or sponsors seemed like a grassroots reaction, they were in fact a response to elite signals on the media. When a group of activists, for example, picketed "leftist propaganda" outside Black Rock, the CBS building on West Fifty-Second Street, they claimed that Nixon had inspired them to act.[48] The woman who condemned Norman Lear for dealing with menstruation on *All in the Family* connected her views to Agnew's and potential legislation to restrict the freedom of the press. "I would urge [Congress] to pass the law because the media evidently doesn't have the decency, maturity, honesty, and high enough standards to warrant the freedom they presently enjoy," she concluded.[49] Likewise, the man who used a Kotex box as his stationery referenced public conversations about liberal bias and claimed the lack of network moderation was "inviting" government censorship. "Don't you think that it's time that you and your colleagues put your house in order before big brother does it for you," he asked.[50] To connect the conservative elite's message with grassroots activists, movement leaders organized, and funded, media reform groups to pressure the FCC, the networks, and the legislature.

In December 1972, with Tandem Production's *All in the Family*, *Sanford and Son*, and *Maude* all among the five highest-rated shows, *Broadcasting* reported that "crusades for TV morality [are] on [the] rise."[51] Conservative activist organizations, including white supremacists, antifeminists, and anticommunists, rallied against "permissive" prime-time entertainment.[52] Groups focused on the media, such as Accuracy in Media, Morality in Media, and Stop Immorality on TV, provided the membership, connections, and funds needed to mount significant pressure campaigns.[53] The new right-wing organizations recognized the success of liberals in influencing television entertainment and adopted their tactics of monitoring, picketing, and threatening with court challenges and economic boycotts. These tactics were the same across the ideological divide.

Their stated purpose, however, made it clear they represented something different for conservatives.

John J. O'Connor, the respected television critic at the *New York Times*, recognized this difference and sounded the alarm following the tumult over *Maude* in 1973. "These [conservative] campaigns were not asking for equal time," O'Connor concluded. "They were demanding censorship."[54] There was, liberals concluded, a difference between advocacy groups working with Virginia Carter to deal with issues such as birth control, homosexuality, or race in a responsible and honest way and conservatives looking to banish certain voices and subjects from prime time all together. But conservatives recognized they could not rely on the same elite connections within the creative community in Hollywood and instead turned to building their own networks to "stop immorality on TV."

Stop Immorality on TV grew out of the Society for the Christian Commonwealth, the project of renowned conservative activist L. Brent Bozell Jr., brother-in-law of William Buckley and publisher of *Triumph*, to target television entertainment. Bozell brought to the organization his considerable personal networks within the conservative movement and experience with organizing political campaigns as well as his uncompromising conservatism. The organization's advisory board signaled the extensive conservative networks behind it. Republican Party politicians such as Representative Joel T. Broyhill (R-VA), former governor J. Bracken Lee of Utah, and former representative Katherine St. George (R-NY) appeared alongside an array of clergy (including Rev. Vincent P. Miceli), anticommunist activists (among others Rev. Richard Wurmbrand), community leaders (such as Dr. Ernest L. Wilkinson), and celebrities (for example television icon Red Skelton and baseball legend Phil Rizzuto).[55] In advertising, Stop Immorality on TV warned that "television is hypnotizing the American people—and especially the young—to look with favor upon such abominations as abortion, homosexuality, and extra-marital sex."[56]

Declaring that "God gave all of us a responsibility to fight evil and immorality," the organization launched letter-writing campaigns as a show of strength.[57] Letters, the organization reasoned, "must make it abundantly clear to program sponsors, network officials, local station managers, the Federal Communications Commissioners, and the Congress that this immoral pollution of the airwaves will no longer be tolerated."[58] Pressure, the organization reasoned, would deliver change to prime time. "The pen is one of our greatest weapons," its newsletter proclaimed.[59] Stop Immorality on TV claimed to have mailed over 50,000 letters with a questionnaire on television sex and immorality alongside a form asking for donations between five and fifty dollars and a call to boycott immoral programs and their sponsors.[60] In fact, the work of Stop Immorality on TV lay behind over 50 percent of all complaints about "obscene" material the FCC received in 1973. The campaign achieved such high numbers by mailing out preprinted postcards that people could sign and mail to the commission.[61]

Still, network executives were not impressed. "Part of being responsive to our public," Bob Wood of CBS declared, "is to make sure that we do not allow a small, vocal, and, at times, highly organized minority group to determine what can be seen on your television set."[62] Even when CBS received a total of 24,000 letters condemning the abortion episodes of *Maude* in 1973, Wood called it statistically insignificant in light of the fact that the two episodes enjoyed an audience of some 65 million viewers. Organized letter-writing campaigns were easy for executives to dismiss.[63] Indeed, the presidents of ABC, CBS, and NBC all defended the move to more mature and honest programming that *All in the Family* represented. Television, Wood declared, "must reflect the growing maturity of the audience."[64] In the face of criticism of lower moral standards, Herbert Schlosser, president of NBC Television, protested. "This is not permissiveness," he explained. "It is honesty."[65] Listing issues such as drug abuse, homosexuality, and venereal disease, Walter J. Schwartz, president of ABC Television, called it "inconceivable" for television not to deal with real life.[66]

With the networks determined not to be intimidated, conservative activists recognized a need to apply the pressure in other directions. Congress and the FCC made the rules and became the primary targets in the letter-writing campaigns. In newsletters, Stop Immorality on TV highlighted the efforts of US representatives Harley O. Staggers (D-WV) and Wilmer Mizell (R-NC) to take on permissiveness on entertainment television and encouraged members to "give them some help" by writing to their own representatives.[67] Bombarding members of Congress with letters elevated the issue of television permissiveness on the political agenda and increased pressure on legislators to act. "From our mail and personal contacts," Hugh Scott (R-PA) remarked in the Senate, "all of us in Congress are aware that many parents are deeply concerned."[68]

Political control over prime-time entertainment depended on pressuring members of Congress and the FCC, but conservative activists also understood that sponsors were the soft underbelly of the broadcasting industry. Broadcasting was first and foremost a business.[69] And the business model depended on advertising revenue. While sponsors no longer owned whole shows, they still mattered. "If enough sponsors cancel their advertising," a conservative writer observed, "the network is hit in the pocketbook."[70] To make sponsors listen, conservative activists needed to project strength in numbers. Stop Immorality on TV reported a membership of under 20,000 people yet claimed to speak for "more than 150,000 households nationwide."[71] In newsletters, the organization also claimed that television entertainment defied the moral standards of "most" Americans.[72] In fact, a Roper poll in 1973 found, most Americans believed television treated such issues as sex relations responsibly. Less than a fifth of respondents deemed the treatment offensive.[73] The Nielsen ratings further signaled wide acceptance, even admiration, for shows such as *All in the Family*, *The Carol Burnett Show* (CBS, 1967–78), and *M*A*S*H*, which Stop Immorality on TV described as examples of low morality. All the same, inflating their numbers served an obvious purpose when threatening boycotts of an industry that enjoyed an audience in the tens of millions.[74]

Regardless of actual numbers, advertisers were inherently wary of controversy. In mailings, Stop Immorality on TV asked members to write to the sponsors of *All in the Family*, *Maude*, and *M*A*S*H* to condemn the shows and listed the addresses of Bristol-Myers, Pillsbury, Frito-Lay, and others.[75] Mailings also included a guide on how to formulate the letter and to include strong condemnation, claim to be a regular user of the advertised product, and request an explanation from the company.[76] When representatives of the organization reached out, advertisers proclaimed to share concerns about television programming. "As a matter of policy, we try to see that our advertising runs in programs which are suitable for general family viewing," an advertising vice president for Gillette remarked.[77] And yet, advertising minutes on *All in the Family* went for an all-time high of $120,000.

Norman Lear's shows loomed large in the campaigns of Stop Immorality on TV. According to the organization, only 24 percent of nationwide audiences deemed *All in the Family* suitable for the whole family, making it second only to *Maude* in terms of the least acceptable program.[78] Furthermore, Lear was the most prominent producer in television. Picking a fight with him generated attention. During the controversy over abortion on *Maude*, pickets in New York read "Babies hide in fear / Here comes Norman Lear."[79] When Stop Immorality on TV started awarding a "Shield of Shame" to attract media attention to the worst offenders, Lear was first in line for "assault[ing] the family's basic sense of decency."[80] Defiantly, Lear framed the "award" and displayed it on his office wall.[81] And in the fight over censorship, Lear took center stage. Yet these fights were not, at first, about immorality but about television violence.

In Congress, the most powerful voice when it came to broadcasting in the network era was Senator John O. Pastore. A New Deal Democrat from Rhode Island first elected to the Senate in 1950, Pastore chaired the Senate Communications

Subcommittee of the Commerce Committee and sat on the Senate Appropriations Committee. In charge of both broadcast policy and FCC funding, he was a man feared by network executives.[82] "What Senator Pastore does and will do," the head of CBS once remarked, "was and is a question of daily conversation here."[83] And Pastore's main concern in the 1970s was violence on television.

For over a decade, Pastore, a man once described as "a master of advocacy and prosecution" by an ABC executive, had campaigned against televised violence.[84] As early as 1961, Pastore called on broadcasters to "clean up [their] programs and get away from programs saturated with violence."[85] In 1969, he held hearings on the matter and warned that the networks "ought to get on their toes and they ought to begin doing something about this."[86] Pastore favored self-regulation and suggested that the National Association of Broadcasters (NAB) be empowered to prescreen programming, a proposal that Frank Stanton of CBS vehemently, and successfully, opposed.[87] Instead, Pastore requested a comprehensive study on television violence by the surgeon general. The report, released in 1972, was couched in careful language and devoid of categorical conclusions.[88] In the Senate, however, Pastore badgered the members of the committee behind the report to concede that "something must be done."[89] "There comes a time when the data is sufficient to justify action," the surgeon general acknowledged. "That time has come."[90] Pastore now had the proof he needed to demand action. "I think we have reached the banks of the Rubicon," he concluded.[91] While the FCC acknowledged the need for action, it was unclear what could be done and by whom.[92] Violence was big business.[93] And the only thing that loomed larger than Senator Pastore in the minds of network executives was profits. Unless government action was imminent, the networks would not give up violence.

It was not until Richard Wiley took over as chairman of the FCC in early 1974—and was bombarded in front of Congress—that government action really did seem imminent. Wiley was no crusader. He came to the chairmanship without any intention to assume the role of censor. Addressing the NAB convention in Houston mere weeks after that first congressional grilling as chairman, he promised broadcasters that there would be "no subversion of our basic freedoms under the assumed guise of the public interest."[94] Months later, in a letter to Pastore, Wiley acknowledged the concern about television violence yet still suggested that "the time [for action] is not now."[95] On Capitol Hill, however, waiting around was no longer a viable option. The Senate Appropriations Committee and the House Appropriations Committee both demanded that the FCC produce a report by the end of the year or face possible "punitive action."[96] This was a direct threat with a set deadline. After years of congressional hearings, studies, and delays, "a kind of congressional doomsday clock" was "approaching midnight."[97] Action was now imminent.

Convinced that the FCC had no right to meddle in programming decisions, Wiley initially opted for regulation by raised eyebrow. Since broadcasters were licensed by the commission, suggestions from the chairman were often understood as informal regulatory policy.[98] Instead of adopting new policies, subject to challenges in court, the commission believed it could nudge broadcasters with public statements warning of regulation. In front of Congress, Wiley had described this approach as a "slippery slope" in relation to the First Amendment.[99] Whether or not it was unconstitutional was unclear, but it was a form of government meddling. Compared to direct action, however, Wiley favored suggestions, warnings, and reprimands.[100]

In the fall of 1974, following a spring and summer of pressure, Wiley used an address to the Illinois Broadcasters Association to signal a need for self-regulation. Warning of "some dark clouds" on the horizon, he called for action from broadcasters to avoid commission or government regulation.[101] According to Wiley, broadcasters could take the issue in their own hands with "taste, discretion and decency."[102] The trade press concluded that "Wiley apparently has not quit on jawboning."[103] Following his public call for broadcasters to handle the issue on their own, Wiley summoned network executives for a private meeting at the commission. Recognizing the seriousness of the situation, the executives reluctantly traveled to Washington.[104]

Wiley was now wedded to the idea of self-regulation by the broadcasters, even if he had to use his position of power to force them to do so. There was, according to a CBS executive, a "clear indication" that failure to do so would result in FCC action.[105] In private, according to an NBC executive, Wiley delivered "not very veiled threats" of government interference.[106] Under pressure from Congress, Wiley was now in turn increasing the pressure on the networks. To succeed, he needed an ally among the hesitant network executives on the other side of the negotiating table. Arthur Taylor, president of CBS, emerged as Wiley's "bright hope."[107]

Taylor had come to CBS in 1972, without any experience in broadcasting, news, or entertainment, to succeed the legendary Dr. Frank Stanton. Since the 1940s, Stanton had served as a statesman of the industry in both congressional hearings and broadcasting conventions. His work earned him the moniker "the conscience of broadcasting." Everybody recognized that his were big shoes to fill. Appreciating Stanton's larger-than-life reputation and his standing in Washington, Taylor wanted to make a name for himself not just as a moneymaker but in service of the public good.[108] When Taylor, who at thirty-seven years old was hailed as a "financial whiz" after his work with First Boston Corporation and International Paper Company, arrived at CBS, he was overwhelmed by letters from friends and acquaintances asking him to solve the problems with television.[109] Television was a "sleazy business," and his mentors and friends disapproved of his move to run the network.[110] And so Taylor was never really comfortable with broadcasting. "I was making $400,000 a year," Taylor remarked later, "and I had little respect for the programs."[111] But fighting television violence, he reasoned, would be his moral redemption.[112]

According to his own colleagues, however, Taylor was moved to action by congressional and commission pressure, not by his conscience.[113] With private political ambitions, he appreciated good relationships in Washington.[114] By claiming ownership of the issue of violence on television, which concerned legislators, regulators, and activists, Taylor hoped to win political goodwill. Reading the situation on Capitol Hill, he concluded that television violence was an issue on which he could do well, protecting profits by staving off new regulations, while doing good, serving the public interest by limiting violence on television. Following the network executive summit with the FCC in the fall of 1974, Taylor emerged as the leading voice on the issue.

In a letter to Wayne Kearl, manager of the CBS affiliate in San Antonio, Texas, and the chairman of the NAB code board, Taylor laid out a proposal for what he described as a "family viewing hour."[115] The idea was to amend the NAB code to reserve the first hour of prime time, eight to nine p.m., for programming suitable for "family viewing." Any exception would have to include warnings of the inappropriate content. Yet while it was reported as a CBS proposal and Taylor claimed it as his own, the key components came from Wiley's summit with network executives.[116]

Following another summit meeting between network executives and Wiley, the NAB code board met in Washington with the chief censors of the three networks: Thomas Swafford (CBS), Herminio Traviesas (NBC), and Alfred Schneider (ABC). The board decided to send the family viewing hour to its program standards committee and revisit the matter at the NAB annual convention in April. With considerable sway over both the NAB and the FCC, all three networks claimed to be committed to the policy from the start of the following season.[117] With the power of the networks behind them, not to mention the pressure from Wiley and Congress, the code board voted 12–3 to adopt the "family viewing hour" at the convention.[118] In the new television season beginning in the fall of 1975, programs that were deemed "inappropriate for viewing by a general family audience" would not be allowed before nine o'clock. And yet, nobody seemed to know what exactly they had just banned from prime time.

Ever since the policy had been proposed in public by CBS, broadcasters and regulators alike had asked for a "meaningful and useful definition" of the term "family viewing."[119] The vagueness of the term invited different and at times contradictory definitions. While everybody agreed that excessive violence was now verboten, uncertainty surrounded television comedies. Beyond the abortion story line on *Maude*, one executive remarked, "I don't recall any situation comedy's being criticized as unsuitable for family viewing."[120] Others disagreed. In particular, *All in the Family* was singled out as unsuitable because "it deals with controversial themes week-in and week-out."[121]

Certainly Arthur Taylor did not mean to censor controversial social issues. In February, when the code board was still considering the proposal, Bob Wood promised that CBS would not "retreat from provocative subject matter in favor of bland, insipid programing."[122] When pressed on what exactly would be unsuitable for family viewing, however, Wood deflected and claimed that he, like Justice Potter Stewart once noted about obscenity, would know it when he saw it.[123] Two months later, when the NAB formally adopted the policy, Taylor proudly proclaimed that it would not be "a shield against reality."[124] Taylor was, in fact, an admirer of *All in the Family*. When Thomas Swafford, the chief censor at CBS, in a private meeting suggested that it might not be suitable for family viewing, Taylor protested. To him a family might well enjoy the show together. "Then what, pray tell, is the name of the family?" Swafford inquired. "Taylor," his boss shot back.[125] Regardless of Taylor's intentions, *All in the Family* soon became *the* test case for the new policy.

Even though all networks were committed to the policy, not all executives were excited about it. Meetings between network executives and the code board often became heated. And with Taylor recognized as the man behind family viewing, rivals were determined to make sure CBS would not win a competitive edge with the new policy. For Alfred Schneider, chief censor at ABC, the key question was what CBS intended to do about *All in the Family*.[126] "If the program remains at 8 o'clock," Swafford recognized in private, "it's going to be a long, cold winter."[127] In public, he deflected. In a code board meeting, Schneider finally lost it. "Well, if you are not going to move the goddamn program," he erupted, "we are not going to move the goddamn 'Rookies.'"[128] *The Rookies* (ABC, 1972–76), an Aaron Spelling–produced cop show created by Rita Lakin, was a success at eight on Mondays and ABC's highest-rated show. In conversations about how to implement family viewing, it emerged as a symbol of television violence. And *All in the Family* became a symbol of sex.[129] Refusing to move either show would undermine the new policy and draw criticism from rivals.

With CBS officially committed to the family viewing hour, Wood called Norman Lear in the spring of 1975 demanding "a lot of changes in the show if we want to keep it on at eight o'clock."[130] Lear balked at the request. He certainly did not find *All in the Family* unacceptable for a family. In fact, he wanted it to foster conversation in the family. With Wood now telling him it would need to change to fit into the family viewing hour, Lear grew agitated. Looking for a definition of "family viewing," which Wood could not provide because none existed, Lear asked, "How can you be thinking of moving the show out of the Family Hour unless you know what it is?"[131] It was clear to all that Lear would not change the most popular show on television without a fight. In an internal memorandum, Swafford had recommended moving *All in the Family* to a later hour while acknowledging that it would be hard for Wood.[132] After all, *All in the Family* was a symbol not just of sex but of a new era of television for which Wood was widely celebrated. Still, in conversation with Lear, Wood finally concluded that the show would no longer be broadcast on Saturdays at eight when it returned for the new season. When CBS announced the move, which Wood in public claimed was unrelated to family viewing, the press described it as the biggest surprise of the season.[133] With *All in the Family* out of the family viewing hour, it was clear to all that the policy was no longer about violence but about ideas.

With family viewing the law of the land, tension grew between producers and network executives as the abstract proposal was put into practice. For producers and writers of action shows or police procedurals, it was relatively easy to tone down the violence, or move it offscreen, without having to reconsider the themes, relationships, and ideas of the show. Censoring ideas, talk, and jokes about sexual or social issues was far harder. "We can change an action sequence without diluting the show," Robert Hamner, producer of *S.W.A.T.* (ABC, 1975–76), observed. "People like Lear are dealing with new thoughts, with new ideas. They have a lot more to be concerned about."[134] Indeed, comedy writers and producers were facing new challenges.

Editors deemed story lines about venereal disease and impotency on *M*A*S*H* problematic, along with stories about adultery on *Rhoda* and an episode about a mother's concern over her daughter coming of age on *Phyllis* (CBS, 1975–77). In a meeting between the producers of *Phyllis* and the network, a standards and practices representative described the new standards as meant "not to offend the most up-tight parent you can imagine, watching with his children."[135] The writers and producers protested such an impossible standard. Tension escalated to confrontation. One of the fiercest arguments erupted on the set of *Barney Miller* (ABC, 1975–82), an ABC sitcom starring Hal Linden as the titular police captain, when Alfred Schneider appeared unannounced to make sure that the show followed the new policy. Following a back-and-forth between Schneider and producer Danny Arnold, the latter snapped. "If that's your attitude," he raged, "then you can go fuck yourself!"[136] The creative community in Hollywood would not just argue over the policy; they soon began to fight it.

The family viewing hour marked a key turn in the relationship between politics and television. It depended on a wide belief among various political interests in Washington, DC, and around the country that television entertainment held considerable power. Their conviction that shows influenced values, morals, and attitudes resulted in intense attention to prime time. It had made way for liberal advocates, Democratic candidates, and feminist activists to rely on *All in the Family* in their political campaigns. But it also gave rise to conservative anger and discomfort with honest conversations about race, sexuality, and women's health on television. For liberals, *All in the Family* was a chance to raise awareness and educate while entertaining audiences. For conservatives, however, it was propaganda: "liberal hogwash" disguised as entertainment.[137]

While network executives could shrug off letter-writing campaigns by conservative activists, pressure from Capitol Hill constituted a real threat to the bottom line. Legislation and regulations in the late 1960s and early 1970s, including the ban on cigarette advertisements and the Prime Time Access Rule, had already cost the networks hundreds of millions of dollars in annual revenue. When Richard Wiley, caught between a rock and a hard place, went from promising broadcasters that there would be no undermining of their basic freedoms under his watch to warning of dire consequences unless they would give up their basic freedoms, the networks reacted. Convinced that government action was imminent, broadcasters adopted the family viewing hour under pressure. While it was adopted through NAB, it was self-regulation only in a very limited sense of the term.

Business concerns turned *All in the Family* into the test case of the new policy. The rivals would keep each other honest. If ABC had to move *The Rookies*, then CBS would have to move *All in the Family*. Under the new policy, tension between the networks and the creative community in Hollywood increased. Writers and producers found that standards and practices no longer accepted story lines that had run without controversy in previous seasons. Conflict was inevitable. "It went down their throats like a chicken bone," Bob Wood remarked of the family viewing hour and the Hollywood community.[138] While producers and writers on action shows could tone down violence without compromising on their intentions and visions, comedy writers found their very ideas were being censored. The policy, according to Gene Reynolds of *M*A*S*H*, "is directed not against sex and violence but against ideas."[139] This, the writers and producers concluded, was unacceptable.

Chapter 8

BATTLE ROYALE

"Official war declared by Hollywood on family viewing," the headline in *Broadcasting* announced on November 3, 1975.[1] The Writers Guild of America (WGA), the Screen Actors Guild, and the Directors Guild of America decided to join forces against the family viewing hour.[2] Suing the networks, the National Association of Broadcasters (NAB), and the Federal Communications Commission (FCC) for infringing on their First Amendment rights, they alleged that Richard Wiley had decided "to initiate, foster, encourage and pressure the broadcast industry networks and the NAB to censor prime-time programs."[3] This was a remarkable free speech case. Yet the reporters covering the lawsuit announcement from the offices of the WGA seemed not to appreciate the fundamental rights at stake. Instead, they questioned the alleged censorship and asked for examples of story lines, jokes, or words that had been nixed as a result of the new policy. Writers and producers, including Norman Lear, Allan Burns (*The Mary Tyler Moore Show*), and Susan Harris (*Fay*), tried their best to explain the chilling effect of family viewing. "It's censorship by fear," producer Danny Arnold (*Barney Miller*) proclaimed.[4] Since the family viewing hour was, by design, vague and the censorship opaque, the reporters were looking for concrete examples of forbidden words. But the plaintiffs spoke of ideas. "Those ideas," producer Larry Gelbart (*M*A*S*H*) remarked, "have been very, very restricted."[5]

Considering the family viewing hour an infringement on freedom of expression, the plaintiffs wanted to make clear that the stakes in the case extended beyond the industry. Joining the writers and producers were the stars of the biggest shows on television: Archie Bunker (Carroll O'Connor),

Mary Richards (Mary Tyler Moore), Barney Miller (Hal Linden), and Hawkeye Pierce (Alan Alda) all in the same room fighting for the same cause.[6] A frustrated Carroll O'Connor chided the press for failing to grasp the principle at the heart of the matter. "There seems to be an assumption underlying all of these questions, asking for details and specifics, that the government might be right," he told the roomful of reporters. "They're wrong," he continued. "Congress has no right whatsoever to interfere in the content of the media, whether it's our medium or your medium."[7] With the networks and broadcasters in league with the FCC, the fight fell to the creative community. In the mid-1970s, that community held more power vis-à-vis the networks than ever before. For the first time in history, all three unions formed a coalition in a "nonmoney" political battle—not just over family viewing but over control of prime time.[8] This war, and the fault lines it exposed, defined the relationship between television entertainment and political interests for decades to come.

During conversations between the television code board and network executives about family viewing it became apparent that the policy was intended to address two very different issues: Alfred Schneider of ABC recorded in his notes that "intellectuals" were concerned about violence but not sex while the opposite was true of "fundamentalists."[9] In political terms, it meant liberals wanted to do something about violence and conservatives looked to ban sex.

Censorship was anathema to many liberals, but their worries over violence—especially following the assassinations of President John F. Kennedy, Rev. Martin Luther King Jr., and Senator Robert F. Kennedy in the 1960s—surpassed their concern over government interference. Since Senator Estes Kefauver's (D-TN) hearings on the matter in the 1950s, Democrats had spearheaded efforts to combat television violence. So, when the creative community filed suit over the family viewing hour, Senator John Pastore (D-RI) came down on the side of the networks and the FCC. The producers, writers, directors, and actors challenging the policy were, according to Pastore, only interested in "peddling violence for profit while poisoning the minds of our children and grandchildren with total disregard for the obvious social and psychic costs."[10] This was something of a sleight of hand since the most prominent figures behind the lawsuit were comedy producers such as Lear, Gelbart, and Burns. Yet many leading liberals in the Senate lined up behind their longtime colleague in his crusade against television violence. Old-school liberals such as Warren Magnuson (D-WA), first elected to Congress in 1932, and Hubert H. Humphrey (D-MN), the "Happy Warrior" who had returned to the Senate after his vice presidency and unsuccessful presidential run, praised their fellow New Deal

Democrat for his work on television violence.[11] "It is abundantly clear," Humphrey remarked, "that we must continue to encourage a movement away from repeated scenes of violence in television programs."[12]

The leading voices in the lawsuit in fact shared the concern over excessive violence on television. "I think there is too much violence on television," Allan Burns readily conceded.[13] Similarly, Gene Reynolds, producer of *M*A*S*H*, admitted that "a lot of the violence shown on television *is* gratuitous, and not really necessary."[14] But the family viewing hour ended at nine o'clock every night and almost all police procedurals—shows such as *The Streets of San Francisco* (ABC, 1972–77), *Baretta*, and *Hawaii Five-O*—came on after that. Thus, the censors at the networks leaned not on the producers of *Kojak* or *The Rookies* but on comedy producers such as Lear, Reynolds, and Burns. However, Burns also noted that "I think there is, on the other hand, almost no sex, certainly no explicit sex, on television."[15]

Building a coalition between liberals concerned about violence and conservatives worried about sex had been key to getting the policy on the books, but now it served to rally opposition.[16] "I personally wish they had just addressed themselves to the violence issue," Grant Tinker, the head of MTM Enterprises, which produced *The Mary Tyler Moore Show*, *The Bob Newhart Show* (CBS, 1972–78), and *Rhoda*, concluded.[17] Instead, the policy targeted ideas. Now forbidden, according to Norman Lear, was "asking the public to think while it[']s being entertained."[18] Government interference in which ideas were allowed on prime-time entertainment was unacceptable. "If you censor our jokes," Alan Alda, the star of *M*A*S*H*, remarked later, "then what will keep you from censoring our political jokes."[19] Going after ideas, not violence, provoked the strongest opposition to family viewing.

Dismissing the lawsuit in Los Angeles as "morally bankrupt apologies for a violent status quo which would keep the coins jingling in their pockets at the expense of our youth," Pastore attempted to redefine criticism as self-serving and immoral.[20] Nor was he alone in pointing to the money at stake. Pastore echoed representatives of the FCC who suggested the plaintiffs were "more concerned about . . . their pocketbooks or bank accounts than about the effect of excessive sex, violence or obscenity on the people of this nation."[21] In the business model of broadcasting, however, it was the networks that raked in the big bucks. Production companies often made shows at a deficit. Each episode of *Baretta*, for example, resulted in a loss of $85,000 for the producers. The real money came from the lucrative syndication market: If a show was a success, the producer could expect to sell it into syndication for millions of dollars. The family viewing hour limited syndication possibilities too. "The Mary Tyler

Moore Show consistently loses money in production, and now I don't think it will ever break even in syndication," Grant Tinker complained.[22] "Lear has no market if local stations can't run those programs in [prime-time] access time," a member of the NAB code board acknowledged.[23]

The financial interest of the creative community was not a secret. Tandem Productions, though not the other plaintiffs in the lawsuit, asked for damages due to a reduction in earning potential and fair market value. Lear did not hesitate to admit his business interest in public. "I care very deeply about freedom of speech," he remarked in interviews, "but I'm not ashamed to admit that I also care very deeply about the free-enterprise system."[24] Nor, Lear recognized, was it only the creative community that cared about the bottom line. The networks, after all, ruled the broadcasting industry. "It's their ball park," Lear observed on network dominance, "and you play by their rules."[25] Still, legislators, government officials, and broadcasters used the financial stake to undermine any criticism of family viewing. It resonated with the press and the public who felt disinclined to pity the poor producers. "Is not the mental health of our young people more important than Norman Lear's right to profit from his reruns?" a letter to the *New York Times* asked.[26] On *60 Minutes*, Mike Wallace interviewed Lear on the issue. As long as the policy stood, Lear said, *All in the Family* could not air in syndication due to the stigma of having become a symbol of unsuitable entertainment. Unpersuaded, Wallace pressed for examples of actual censorship, suggesting that Lear's success meant that no problem existed.[27]

With the rise of the independent production companies, and the immense success of Tandem Productions and MTM Enterprises, the creative community wanted more of a voice on broadcasting developments. Los Angeles—Hollywood—was the epicenter of television entertainment, but the real "nerve centers of television" were New York and Washington, DC.[28] Over decades, the networks had invested time and effort to develop close relationships on Capitol Hill, not to mention building the broadcasting lobby into a powerhouse, to make sure they could influence broadcasting policy. Insiders recognized the FCC as a "kept" group.[29] Through regulatory capture—agencies acting in tandem with the very industry they were supposed to regulate—broadcasters had largely defanged the FCC.[30] The family viewing hour was the perfect example of broadcasting policy being developed on the East Coast absent any dialogue with the creative community on the West Coast. In the closed-door summit meetings Wiley convened to address the content on prime-time entertainment, no writer, director, or producer—the people who made prime-time entertainment—was invited. "If the networks were to make a sincere effort, it seems to me they would have called a series of meetings with the creative

Norman Lear in front of monitors. Kathleen Ballard/Los Angeles Times/UCLA.

community to talk about excesses," Norman Lear observed.³¹ Left out in the cold when policy was decided, the producers now wanted to be in the room where it happens.

With many prominent liberals invested in the success of the family viewing hour, the opponents in Hollywood found their champion close to home. Around the time that Richard Wiley called network representatives to Washington to discuss the family viewing hour in early 1975, Henry Waxman (D-CA) arrived in Congress. The mustachioed lawyer had been elected to the House of Representatives in the wake of Nixon's resignation. He was a member of the congressional class of 1974 coming in to reform national politics following the disgrace of Watergate. The Watergate babies, as the new legislators became known, looked askance at the byzantine rules of Congress and were determined to make any changes needed, including bucking the seniority system, to reform the political process.³² Waxman arrived with solid experience out of the California State Assembly and, more important, a close relationship with the "fighting liberal" Phil Burton.³³ Such friendships still mattered in the House and gave Waxman the kind of standing among his colleagues of which most freshmen could only dream.

Media, the Watergate babies recognized, was central to their power. "We were children of television," fellow freshman representative Timothy Wirth

(D-CO) remarked, "not of print."[34] Even with a keen appreciation of television's power to reach the public, the new class of representatives was still not as intimidated by the networks as their older counterparts. The network era, in which William Paley, David Sarnoff, and Leonard Goldenson ruled not just their own networks but the broadcasting industry, was coming to an end with the rise of the cable television industry.[35] Plus, Waxman cared about the creative community. After all, his constituents in California's Twenty-Fourth Congressional District in Los Angeles included television producers, writers, and stars.[36] And so Henry Waxman would become their champion in Congress.

When the creative community filed suit against the networks and the FCC, Waxman requested—and won—a seat on the House Communications Subcommittee. Claiming that the networks and the commission "conspired to impose censorship on TV programing without hearings or opportunity for protest by the industry or the public," he called for congressional hearings on the family viewing hour to investigate "illegitimate attempts" by Congress or the commission to meddle in television programming.[37]

In FCC oversight hearings, Waxman challenged the commission in general and the chairman in particular, asking for a "full airing" on the development of the family viewing hour. When pressed for an answer on how appropriate Wiley's private meetings with the networks were, his fellow commissioners pointed to public criticism and, especially, to congressional pressure. "Indeed, our appropriations were not threatened, but they said they would be in jeopardy if we did not come up . . . with some way of dealing with this overriding question of superviolence on television," commissioner Abbott Washburn remarked.[38] The commissioners claimed that they had acted under direct pressure from Congress and were now, to their surprise, under congressional scrutiny for having done so. Yet, as the crusading liberal representative John E. Moss (D-CA) observed, concern over television violence, and even congressional threats about such violence, had been a part of oversight hearings for decades. "I suppose that it makes good copy to be opposed to violence," he remarked.[39] Moss echoed the criticism of Representative Torbert Macdonald (D-MA), the powerful chairman of the Communications Subcommittee, who viewed the family viewing hour as a public relations effort by the networks and the FCC to ease congressional and public pressure without addressing the root of the problem. "When you say this whole thing depends on [the networks'] reasonableness, their good faith," the liberal Macdonald had observed a year earlier, "that's like writing a letter to Santa Claus."[40]

Waxman, however, focused not on the effects of the policy but on the process behind it, and especially the secret meetings with "those people whose life is affected by licensing of your agency."[41] Wiley dismissed any suggestions of improper pressure and claimed it was more convenient to negotiate in private with the heads of the networks. Astounded, Waxman grilled the chairman in a heated exchange.

> Waxman: Your answer is shocking. What you are saying is "I called the network people in because they knew I had life and death power over their licenses."
>
> Wiley: That is not what I said.
>
> Waxman: You said "We don't regulate the networks in the public interest. I brought in the people whom I regulate to discuss this issue with them."
>
> Wiley: Mr. Taylor swore in open court that he didn't feel he was being coerced, he found nothing threatening in that meeting. You are rewriting history here. That is not what happened. I know you have a feeling about this and you have expressed it many times.
>
> Waxman: Is it a proper process for the FCC to have meetings behind closed doors without other members of the Commission present with people who are licensed present at those meetings to discuss a policy where there is no other input allowed in at those meetings, where there is no public record and there is no input from others?[42]

Under pressure, and in his view misunderstood, Wiley retorted that he believed he was "representing the public" and decried the barrage of criticism: "I have taken nothing but abuse, abuse, abuse when I tried to do something for the public interest."[43] Unmoved by his emotional appeals, Waxman told him that he did not "doubt your motive" but rather "your wisdom."[44] Warning of dangerous precedents and the matters of principle involved, Waxman focused on the actions of the FCC as possible abuses of government power. "This very much concerns me," he remarked soberly, "over and above any matter that might affect you personally."[45] Exasperated, Wiley attempted to correct Waxman's questions and dismiss his accusations, insisting the networks decided on the policy on their own and lamenting the "tightrope" the commission was charged with walking.[46]

Having a congressman take on the chairman of the FCC was important for the creative community fighting the policy both in federal court and in the court of public opinion. Polling suggested broad support for family viewing. But the truth was more complex. A *TV Guide* national poll, the magazine proclaimed, suggested that the answer to whether people wanted the regulatory policy was "a resounding 'YES.'"[47] The actual survey, however, showed that most of the respondents had never heard of family viewing. Still, when given a definition, the overwhelming majority supported a time for "programs that are considered appropriate for viewing by all members of the family, including children."[48] The poll was misleading. "It is hard for people to say they oppose the principle of reducing excessive violence and sex on television," Norman Lear remarked.[49] The policy was intentionally vague in its language in order to secure wide support. "Coming out against it would have been like coming out against motherhood and apple pie," a network executive acknowledged.[50] Even its name, "family viewing hour," gave the policy an air of wholesomeness. Eager to reframe the conversation, the creative community wanted to rename the policy the "prime time censorship rule" to highlight the issue as one not about sex and violence but about free speech and government censorship.

Henry Waxman would provide them with the forum to redefine the conversation surrounding the policy. In May 1976, Torbert Macdonald, the longtime chairman of the House Communications Subcommittee, stepped away from his committee assignments due to health concerns. Within weeks, Macdonald —long recognized as "a man not given to dispense any favors to [the broadcasting] industry"—passed away.[51] His successor as chair of the subcommittee, Lionel Van Deerlin (D-CA), was a former television news director from Southern California. Hearings on the family viewing hour, which Waxman had called for in public, were high on the agenda for the new chairman.[52] Van Deerlin's experience in broadcasting gave him a keen appreciation for the strength of the networks, while his background in California made him aware of the power of the creative community in Los Angeles.[53] He made clear that he would not serve as an "apostle" for congressional meddling in television entertainment.[54] Without Waxman's efforts, however, it is unlikely that Congress would have afforded the creative community a forum. Even Van Deerlin referred to the hearings tongue in cheek as the "Henry Waxman, Henry Waxman Show."[55]

With the family viewing hour lawsuit still pending in federal court, congressional hearings on the policy, held in Los Angeles and Denver in July and August 1976, became a welcomed opportunity for the policy's opponents to convey their dismay to legislators. "They've been beating down the door," staff on the committee said of the television producers and writers, "anxious to testify."[56] Waxman acknowledged that his role was to open the doors. "One of the reasons I was enthusiastic about holding the hearings in Los Angeles," he observed, "was to give the opportunity to the creative community in Hollywood to express their views on this particular subject."[57] The hearings featured representatives of civil rights organizations, academic scholars, representatives from religious establishments, and members of advocacy groups, but the main attraction was the most prominent and respected producers and writers in television.

In a scathing statement condemning the family viewing hour as a public relations gimmick, a "pious, insincere smokescreen," Norman Lear placed the blame for television content on the networks.[58] After all, the networks ordered, bought, and broadcasted shows to make money. "They decide what programs shall be on the air at all, at what times, and with what formats," Larry Gelbart noted. "They see and comment on, and are free to censor or reject, every story premise, every script, every finished program."[59] This was the business of broadcasting. The family viewing hour, however, was, according to Lear, "censorship" and "a deceit."[60] The right of broadcasters to control the content of shows, including standards and practices departments refusing certain subjects, was not the problem. Making a parallel to the world of theater, Grant Tinker remarked that when it comes to television, the networks "do own the theater, and they have every right to have a larger say in what is played in that theater."[61] The problem was government involvement. Such involvement, Lear charged, came with a chilling effect. "It is like smoke that creeps under the doors and through transoms and infects rooms," he remarked. "You can't breathe it in."[62]

Listening to the concerns of the creative community at the hearings, Waxman suggested he was not done with the issue but might, instead, hold future hearings with network executives under subpoena. He also warned the FCC, submitting that Wiley had acted in an improper manner in his secret summit meetings with the networks, and even chided his colleagues in the House for infringing on the First Amendment while "trying to make political points back home."[63] To amplify the voice of the creative community, Waxman also inserted the statements of Norman Lear, Larry Gelbart, Allan Burns, and others into the *Congressional Record*.[64] In his remarks, Gelbart had concluded that "we want the right . . . to be able to discuss mature themes on television, illuminate our concerns and yours."[65] With the help of Henry Waxman, their struggle for that right was recognized on Capitol Hill.

For years, John Pastore in the Senate and Torbert Macdonald in the House had been the most important voices on broadcasting in Congress. Both were tough regulators. But in the middle of the most important fight over control over prime-time entertainment, Macdonald passed away and Pastore retired. The two most vocal and powerful liberal critics of television entertainment were gone. In their absence, the bipartisan consensus on television sex and violence faltered. Waxman, and his cohort of media-savvy marketplace liberals who succeeded the Pastores and Macdonalds, abhorred the idea of Congress, or the chairman of the FCC, as rulers of prime time or stewards of the nation's morals. "No legislative action is planned," Van Deerlin announced, "and I trust that it may never be."[66] Without liberals worried about violence to force the issue, the policy hinged on the conservative mobilization against television entertainment.

Arthur Taylor was not exactly a conservative man. His closest mentors were the kind of GOP liberals more commonly known as "Rockefeller Republicans" after New York governor Nelson Rockefeller. In fact, Rockefeller himself was one of the men Taylor counted among his close friends. Taylor's own politics, however, were even more liberal. His political hero was the late Senator Robert F. Kennedy.[67] Yet his own colleagues described him as "a fanatic" who "believes he's the Messiah."[68] Having made the family viewing hour his legacy-defining crusade, Taylor needed it to succeed. So he claimed that there was wide consensus behind it.[69]

In fact, broadcasters were reluctant to accept any regulations that might hurt the bottom line. Nor did they trust the networks to negotiate policy in closed summit meetings with Wiley.[70] "If broadcasters submit to this," an editorial in *Broadcasting* concluded when the policy was proposed in early 1975, "they will have abandoned all reasonable claims to any independence of action."[71] Still, the networks were determined to have their way—even if that meant steamrolling opposition from the broadcasters. "We mouse trapped the other guys into coming along with us," one CBS executive admitted.[72] Certainly, some broadcasters welcomed the policy. "I don't believe I have ever been as proud or as supportive of anything as I am of your 'family-hour' proposal for prime time," Charles Crutchfield, the conservative head of a CBS affiliate in North Carolina, wrote to Taylor.[73] But he was not exactly representative of the broadcasting community. Even as the NAB code board voted to approve family viewing, there was no consensus on the issue among the members at the convention.[74] By December, a survey of broadcasting executives found that only 55 percent stood behind it.[75] The critics, Arthur Taylor proclaimed in an address to CBS affiliates, were nothing more than "Cassandras who are confusing licensee responsibility with a fatal step toward censorship."[76] Far from uniting broadcasters, family viewing seemed to divide the industry.

With the broadcasting community split and the creative community united in opposition, Taylor found allies in the emergent religious right. Taylor's crusade against television violence aligned him with the conservative broadcasters and activists who were concerned about sex, profanity, and progressive values on television. In the process, he grew increasingly "messianic" in his defense of the family viewing hour.[77]

Conservative Christians had long viewed television, and before that film, with deep suspicion.[78] By the end of the 1960s, the fierce evangelical pastor W. A. Criswell warned of the corrosive influence of the "idiot box" and "the disintegration and decay of a civilization."[79] Over the following decade, conservative church leaders increasingly voiced their dismay with Hollywood.[80] Fervent right-wing evangelicals such as Billy James Hargis warned that prime-time entertainment was "anti-God, antichrist, anti-moral [and] anti-American."[81] Even the mainstream evangelical leader Billy Graham revealed his antisemitic resentment toward the producers of television entertainment in private conversations.[82] While the criticism was growing louder, television became more and more permissive with the success of shows such as *All in the Family*, *M*A*S*H*, and *The Mary Tyler Moore Show*.

The very same treatment of race, gender, and sexuality that executives, critics, and audiences celebrated as honest and sophisticated, disgusted many conservative Christians. They believed television brought dangerous "anti-family themes" into living rooms across the country.[83] Condemning television entertainment, the Assemblies of God (with over a million members, the largest Pentecostal body) singled out "morally offensive material such as raw sex, homosexuality, nudity, profanity, and ruthless violence."[84] Prominent evangelists such as Bill Bright believed that Hollywood was mainstreaming feminism and homosexuality.[85] And the very nature of television, bringing prime-time entertainment into the home, heightened the concern for conservative Christians. "The world itself," one evangelical magazine lamented, "has invaded the sanctum of the home through television."[86] Instead of keeping the actual television out of the home, they wanted to keep real life out of television entertainment.

Conservative media reform organizations were often connected to churches or other religious organizations. The Catholic Church played a key role in conservative campaigns against the abortion episodes on *Maude*, and Stop Immorality on TV was an outgrowth of the Society for the Christian Commonwealth. In Catholic newspapers, editorials and letters to the editor endorsed the efforts of Stop Immorality on TV.[87] Protestant clergy and publications also celebrated the campaign against prime-time entertainment. Highlighting the organization, Adventist magazine *These Times* denounced "dirty and sick jokes about religion, decency, and family."[88] This marked a turn in conservative campaigns.

Conservative movements in the 1970s were moving toward a focus on moral and cultural conflicts.[89] In particular, the decade marked the emergence of an interfaith religious right made up of conservative Protestants, Catholics, and Mormons willing to set aside internal conflicts to win political influence.[90] Stop Immorality on TV was an example of this trend. On the organization's letterhead, Phyllis Schlafly, the anticommunist and antifeminist Catholic activist, and Dr. Fred Schwarz, the anticommunist Protestant activist, appeared side by side.[91] Two decades earlier, the Schlaflys had been rebuffed by Schwarz in their efforts to join forces over denominational divides in their conservative crusade.[92] In the 1970s, however, conservative activists came together in their campaigns against permissiveness on television.

Convinced that the family was under attack by prime-time entertainment, conservative Christians embraced family viewing hour. Churches, the president of the Southern Baptist Radio and Television Commission concluded, "have as much an obligation to make our influence felt on this television prime time family viewing concept as any other group in this country."[93] A force to reckon with, the Southern Baptist Convention had around 12 million members.[94] Some leaders within the church were critical of the policy for allowing "abnormal presentations of sex, sadistic depictions of violence, dirty jokes and gross profanity" to continue after nine o'clock.[95] Flawed as it might have been, however, they still viewed it as a necessary first step in fighting violence, sex, and profanity on television.[96] Even before the policy was adopted by the NAB, Richard Wiley in an address to the Southern Baptist Convention had warned of broadcasting "driv[ing] the American home down into the gutter."[97]

When Pastore, Wiley, or Taylor looked to convince liberals of the dangers of violence on television they relied on social science research, but their appeals to conservative audiences were often couched in language of morality and "family values."[98] At a communion breakfast in Washington in May 1976, for example, Wiley shared his belief that "the time has come for a moral and spiritual reawakening in this country."[99] Pastore embraced this rhetoric, placing Wiley's address into the *Congressional Record*.[100] "In my opinion," Wiley wrote Pastore to praise him for his steadfast support of the family viewing hour, "your efforts very much serve the public interest."[101] The public interest was increasingly being read as a moral interest. Such a reading appealed to religious leaders and activists who connected their conservative politics with a defense of "family values."

Eager to build relationships with broadcasters and gain a voice in conversations on entertainment, many conservative religious leaders embraced the architects of the family viewing hour. The Southern Baptist Radio and Television Commission, for example, awarded Arthur Taylor its Abe Lincoln Award for his leadership on the issue.[102] Recognizing the value of an ally willing to fight for the policy, Taylor in an address to the commission spoke not only of violence but of a responsibility to "develop humor that is not only appealing, but responsible."[103] Committed to the policy, Taylor actively courted evangelical support. Appearing on televangelist Robert Schuller's *Hour of Power* broadcast, Taylor spoke of his own faith and the need to defend the family viewing hour.[104] Echoing Wiley's rhetoric of victimhood under questioning from Henry Waxman, Taylor lamented that both the policy and he personally were being "attacked."[105] His appeals to victimhood were dismissed as "pratt[ling] about morality" by television critics.[106] Yet weaponizing victimhood mobilized activists on the right.[107] So Taylor urged the mass audience of evangelicals viewing *Hour of Power* to support the family viewing hour.

With the bipartisan congressional consensus for stronger regulation of television entertainment gone, Taylor's and Wiley's courting of the emerging religious right achieved nothing more than strengthening conservative mobilization against television. Conservative televangelists, such as Jerry Falwell, James Dobson, and Tim and Beverly LaHaye, rose to prominence via savvy use of broadcasting yet at the same time condemned the permissiveness of the medium.[108] The fight over the family viewing hour made it clear that crusades against television entertainment could mobilize grassroots activists. In the wake of the fight, conservative activist campaigns increasingly focused on television to engage supporters. The Southern Baptist Convention sent mailings to over 50,000 community leaders with instructions on how to campaign against "immoral" television. The National Religious Broadcasters organized campaigns against television entertainment dealing with issues such as homosexuality.[109] Leaders such as Donald Wildmon, a United Methodist minister who founded the National Federation for Decency, made a name for himself in the fight against prime time *after* the family viewing hour struggle was already over.[110] These movements used the church to mobilize a coalition against so-called immorality on television. And yet, the fate of the family viewing hour would be decided not in the churches but in the courts.

"Censorship by government or privately created review boards cannot be tolerated," read district court judge Warren J. Ferguson's opinion finding the family viewing hour unconstitutional in November 1976.[111] The 223-page opinion was a stinging and thorough repudiation of Richard Wiley and Arthur Taylor. "The Commission's pressure in this case was persistent, pronounced, and unmistakable," the decision concluded, describing the threat of government action as "a crucial, necessary, and indispensable cause."[112] Regulation, Ferguson declared, should not be the result of "informal pressure accompanied by self-serving and unconvincing denials of responsibility."[113] While Ferguson acknowledged the FCC's interest in television programming, he noted that threats or coercion "involve *per se* violations of the First Amendment."[114]

Even though the decision concluded that family viewing was unconstitutional, it offered no immediate relief or remedy. "This court," Ferguson acknowledged, "has no authority to declare an end to the family hour."[115] Nor could he order CBS to move *All in the Family* back to the Saturday time slot it had enjoyed for years before family viewing hour, even if "a stigma has attached" to the show and "the damage involved is potentially large."[116] This was a landmark decision for broadcasting. According to the *Washington Post*, the case was "the strongest test" of the limits of government regulation of broadcasting.[117] Thus, the decision was a repudiation not only of the family viewing hour policy and the men behind it but also of the idea of political control over prime time.

It was a clear win for the creative community.[118] Yet even in defeat, Wiley, broadcasters, and grassroots activists had reason to rejoice. In public, both the commission and network executives denounced the decision and vowed to appeal.[119] But in private, Wiley never wanted government control of prime time.[120] And behind closed doors network executives admitted the policy had not had "as good an effect as we had hoped it would have" in easing congressional hostility toward the broadcasting industry.[121] Broadcasters were rumored to secretly nurture hope that the court would side with the creative community and send a message to Washington that "television programing is not to be toyed with."[122] Thus, the trade press recognized the decision as a victory for broadcasters.[123]

Everybody involved in the lawsuit, the commission, the networks, the NAB, and the trade guilds were eager to move on from the family viewing hour. Having aligned his own future with the policy, Arthur Taylor was abruptly fired just weeks before the decision came down in a move widely understood as William Paley rejecting family viewing.[124] The other architect of the policy, Richard Wiley, left the FCC the following year. His successor, Charles Ferris, who had been on Pastore's staff yet identified with the new liberalism of the Watergate babies, rejected the family viewing hour as inappropriate involvement in television programming.[125] Instead, the commission moved toward deregulation as technological advances, including pay-per-view, cable, and satellite television, rendered regulation of violence and sex to protect the public moot.[126] Signaling the deregulatory philosophy of the commission in the following decade, Mark Fowler, Ferris's Reagan-appointed successor, described television as "just another appliance—it's a toaster with pictures."[127]

Without the threat of a "shootout" with Congress hanging over their heads, network executives returned to sex and violence to boost ratings while paying lip service to family viewing. A year after the court struck down the policy, *All in the Family* was in afternoon reruns; in the evening television viewers in New York could catch a repeat of *The Rookies* at seven and Alfred Hitchcock's *Psycho* an hour later.[128] Business remained good. In 1975, television became a $5 billion industry, and the following year, in the middle of the legal and political wrangling over the policy, it surpassed the $6 billion mark. Industry insiders concluded that the "failure-proof business" overcame the family viewing hour "without financial hardship."[129]

In March 1977, Lionel Van Deerlin held final hearings in Washington, DC, on television sex and violence. While Henry Waxman and Timothy Wirth pressed nonchalant network heads, suggesting that their claims of addressing the problem were "insulting," the executives appeared cool and unmoved.[130] The final report of Van Deerlin's hearings placed the blame "largely" on the networks, with Waxman, Wirth, Barbara Mikulski (D-MD), John M. Murphy (D-NY), Ed Markey (D-MA), and Al Gore (D-TN) issuing a "blistering dissent" calling for stronger condemnation of the networks.[131] Still, the networks were in the clear. The Watergate babies, with their market-friendly liberalism, did not share their older colleagues' concern over morality. In short, the fever had broken in Congress, and campaigns over television content moved from Capitol Hill to Madison Avenue.

While Congress and the FCC were burned by Judge Ferguson's decision, grassroots activists were energized by the fight. Without action in Washington, they would turn to the Achilles' heel of broadcasting and focus on the sponsors. Following the fall of the family viewing hour, a wide array of activist campaigns turned to the corporations that made television entertainment possible. Norman Lear encouraged viewers to make their voices heard. "The government is now precluded from interfering," he observed, "but the public has the full right—in fact obligation—to interfere."[132] The best way of doing so was to pressure the advertisers. Liberal media reform organizations, including the National Citizens' Committee for Broadcasting led by media activist and former FCC commissioner Nicholas Johnson, monitored not only which shows included the most violence but also listed the advertisers most associated with such shows. "The mere publication of that," Johnson remarked on *The MacNeil/Lehrer Report*, "does tend to have an impact on what programs they want to sponsor."[133]

Indeed, while a 1976 survey found that only around 5 percent of the public had considered not buying products advertised on violent shows, the advertising insiders were alarmed.[134] A representative of the trade paper *Advertising Age* described boycotts as a "realistic threat."[135] Big advertisers such as General Foods, Miracle White, and Best Foods all avoided violent shows.[136] A study by advertising agency J. Walter Thompson warned that the campaigns of activists were not just "a minor bit of noise from a few crusading reformers, [but] this issue should be recognized as a genuine threat."[137] But while liberals were eager to pressure advertisers in their campaigns against television violence, they were disturbed by similar tactics by conservatives looking to stop permissiveness on television.

Conservative Christians were disappointed with Judge Ferguson. Calling the decision "unacceptable and odorous," conservative Southern Baptist broadcasters from across the country denounced both the ruling and the Hollywood producers behind the lawsuit.[138] While the religious campaigns in support of family viewing proved unable to save the policy, they established a keen interest in television entertainment, large networks of grassroots activists, and an appreciation of ways to make themselves heard about the values broadcast into homes. "Hit them in the billfold," a speaker at a Southern Baptist Convention event suggested. "You can't get any closer to their hearts."[139] Conservatives organized letter-writing campaigns over issues related to sex and gender, including homosexuality, contraception, women's health care, and adultery. "Networks and sponsors have the right to put out any kind of programs they want," Wildmon of the newly founded National Federation for Decency declared, "but we have an equal right to say we're not going to buy your products."[140] Conservatives, just like liberals, recognized that television was a business and going after the bottom line was the best way to make your voice heard.

Still, while violence decreased following the campaigns of activist media reform organizations, sex continued to sell.[141] The sophisticated comedy about real life in *All in the Family*, *M*A*S*H*, and *The Mary Tyler Moore Show* was replaced at the top of the ratings by the nostalgic pap of *Happy Days* and the risqué jiggle of *Three's Company* (ABC, 1977–84).[142] And so the conservative campaigns against prime-time entertainment continued to mobilize activists and elevate leaders into kingmakers on the right. While these campaigns, driven by leaders that Larry Gelbart termed "the far righteous," failed to "clean up" television from cleavage, legs, and sexual innuendo, they did succeed in making certain ideas around sexuality and sexual health more controversial.[143] And network executives, always concerned about the bottom line, were inherently disinclined to court controversy.

The fight over the family viewing hour marked the culmination of the increasing political interest in television entertainment that *All in the Family* sparked in the 1970s. It was a struggle that engaged network executives in New York, the creative community in Los Angeles, politicians in Washington, and grassroots activists around the country. Everybody recognized the political relevance of prime-time entertainment.

When Judge Ferguson ruled the policy unconstitutional, the networks committed themselves to appeal the decision and continue the policy on their own.[144] In fact, family viewing hour "went the way of the dodo" long before an appellate court overturned Ferguson's ruling in 1979, on jurisdiction rather than the merits, and the Supreme Court declined to hear it the following year.[145] The fight over family viewing was not really about the policy but about the relationship between television entertainment and political interests. It was a fight over who had the right to determine what goes over the airwaves and into homes. Following the district court ruling in November 1976 it was clear that neither congressional committees nor the chairman of the FCC had that right. Nor was it the right of the writers and producers who made the shows. The networks assumed it was their right, yet activists pressuring advertisers over violence and sex wanted to claim it for their own. This was the new terror balance—everybody wanted to shape prime time according to their political needs.

In the process, political interests realized the value of television to, in the words of Bud Yorkin, "raise money, to have a power base and . . . to use it as a political pawn to get what they want."[146] The fight over the family viewing hour made clear to politicians, broadcasters, producers, advertisers, and activists alike that skirmishes over prime time, sometimes described as culture wars, were actually battles over political power. The battle lines were drawn for decades to come: the liberal creative community, the moralistic conservative movement, broadcasters putting profits over the public interest, a Federal Communications Commission turning to deregulation, and the rise of political showmanship over popular entertainment. "This is a political battle," media journalist Jeff Greenfield remarked, "because television, whether it meant to be or not, is a political institution."[147]

CONCLUSION

ARCHIE BUNKER IN THE WHITE HOUSE

Following the election of Donald Trump in 2016, it seemed like a fragmented media environment provided viewers across the political spectrum with content that confirmed, rather than challenged, their beliefs and values. "Echo chambers," "filter bubbles," and "information cocoons" came into vogue as the election results signaled a political divide extending to the "balkanized" media environment.[1] And the divide wasn't limited to news media. Republican viewers tuned in to watch *Last Man Standing* (ABC, 2011–17; FOX, 2018–21), starring Tim Allen as a conservative father of three daughters. Democratic viewers preferred *The Good Place* (NBC, 2016–20), in which Kristen Bell, William Jackson Harper, Jameela Jamil, and Manny Jacinto navigated moral philosophy in the afterlife with the help of Ted Danson.[2]

From the White House, Trump sharpened the division with tweets condemning ABC's decision to fire Roseanne Barr from *Roseanne* over racist comments while also calling for NBC to dismiss Debra Messing from *Will & Grace* over her criticism of conservative donors.[3] After ABC censored a 2018 episode of *Black-ish* addressing NFL quarterback Colin Kaepernick's kneeling before football games to protest police brutality, a practice criticized by Trump and fellow conservatives, showrunner Kenya Barris left the network for Netflix.[4] It all looked like a story of political polarization and media fragmentation. Instead, it was the result of decisions made by entertainers, executives, politicians, and activists grappling with the impact of *All in the Family* some five decades earlier in the network era.

When Norman Lear announced his exit from television in the spring of 1978, he wasn't just walking away from a prime-time juggernaut. He turned his back on a forum for political conversation. Though past its prime, when over half of all households with a television in use were tuned to *All in the Family*, it still commanded a rating of 24.4 (more than double that of the most watched shows today). Although Sally Struthers and Rob Reiner also left *All in the Family* after the eighth season, it ran for one more year with Jean Stapleton, before turning into Carroll O'Connor's solo adventure *Archie Bunker's Place*. And yet the show's run over the 1970s catapulted television entertainment into American political life. "Only television," Lear recognized when he left day-to-day television production behind him, "offers the excitement of having an idea the first week in September that will be on the air in the second week of November getting across to 90 million people."[5] This was the wonder of television in the 1970s: the biggest, and most immediate, soap box in the country.

It's unclear whether *All in the Family* actually changed anybody's mind; whether Archie Bunker won any votes for George McGovern; whether Edith Bunker converted anyone to the women's movement; whether Gloria and Mike Stivic convinced anyone about liberal policies. Certainly, McGovern never reached the White House; the Equal Rights Amendment never won ratification; and the 1970s marked a long turn toward conservatism in the United States. Perhaps, as Norman Lear concluded in his memoirs, the show's main effect on the audience was getting families to talk.[6] There is reason to believe it did more than that.[7]

First, it changed prime time, opening it up for new themes and new voices. "Television can be broken into two parts," Phil Rosenthal, producer of *Everybody Loves Raymond* (CBS, 1996–2005), remarked, "BN and AN, before Norman [Lear] and after Norman [Lear]."[8] Lear's expectation that the writers bring their own experiences and relations to the scripts gave the wider creative community permission to address issues that mattered to them. Comedy writers started exploring the human condition in all forms—including regarding sexuality and sexual health. The writers on *The Golden Girls*, for example, featured story lines about Dorothy Zbornak (Bea Arthur) hosting a lesbian friend at their house; Blanche Devereaux (Rue McClanahan) accepting her gay younger brother; and Rose Nylund (Betty White) having to reflect on AIDS following a blood transfusion.[9] While the sympathetic treatment of homosexuality on *The Golden Girls* was met with approval from gay rights activists, conservative activists were "diametrically opposed" to such portrayals.[10]

Advanced by the pioneering work of Virginia Carter at Tandem Productions, activists and advocates recognized the value of collaboration and connections in Hollywood. By the 1990s, representatives of the Environmental Media Association, formed with support from Norman Lear, Robert Redford, and the talent agent Michael Ovitz, claimed that they fielded calls "every day from writers and directors and producers looking for briefings or research."[11] The strongest campaigns often followed the same strategy of building elite consensus around an issue that David Poindexter modeled at the Population Institute. When the Harvard Alcohol Project battled driving under the influence by trying to normalize the practice of a designated driver, the initial plan was to ask for free network time for public service announcements. Frank Stanton, the former president of CBS who gave the green light for advocates and producers to collaborate on abortion topics on prime time in the 1970s, served on the organization's advisory board and suggested that story lines on popular shows would have more impact.[12] And so Norm Peterson (played by George Wendt) became the designated driver, staying sober and making sure everyone got home safe from the bar on an episode of *Cheers* (NBC, 1982–93).[13] Over the 1980s and 1990s, television's didactic attempts to address—and resolve within half an hour—issues such as the dangers of hitchhiking, drug use, or suicide sometimes resulted in maudlin "very special episodes."[14] Still, they drew audiences and raised awareness for important issues. When Ellen Morgan (played by Ellen DeGeneres) came out as gay in a 1997 episode of *Ellen* (ABC, 1994–98), the Human Rights Campaign and Gay and Lesbian Alliance Against Defamation celebrated with "coming out" house parties. But Jerry Falwell condemned her as "Ellen Degenerate."[15] "What Ellen does in her personal life is her business," Falwell concluded. "What she does on prime-time television over publicly owned airways is the business of all American families."[16]

Television executives remained averse to risk, working hard to protect their business from backlash over political activism on the left and the right. Yes, Bob Wood of CBS took a chance on *All in the Family*, a gamble that might have ended his career. No, Wood did not change the conservative corporate culture at the networks. Profits still ruled every decision. The executive class viewed the activists that people such as Norman Lear and Virginia Carter wanted to bring into the development and production process of television shows as an introduction of risk into the system. And so executives reestablished their control by restructuring their own departments of standards and practices, recognizing the need for defensive mechanisms to undermine and overcome outside pressure.[17] Moving to institutionalize relationships with outside interest groups, the networks granted certain moderate groups favored status and relied on them for feedback and credibility on political or controversial themes.

At the same time, the return on decades of investment in deregulatory broadcasting policies made the networks even stronger in relation to media activists toward the end of the twentieth century. Controversy could still lead to action, such as Puerto Rican activism over an episode of *Seinfeld* (NBC, 1989–97) that forced NBC to apologize and pull it from summer reruns.[18] But the most important lesson of the fight over the family viewing hour in the 1970s was that targeting prime-time entertainment with accusations of "liberal bias" and "immorality on television" resulted in fundraising, attention, and political clout. "Television is the most destructive instrument in our society," Donald Wildmon concluded in the early 1990s, having made a career out of assailing "permissiveness" on television.[19] The weakest link, activists recognized, was corporate America sponsoring the shows with advertisement dollars.

When Terry Rakolta, a Michigan mother concerned about indecency on television, wrote corporate executives to complain about their sponsorship of the "soft pornography" of *Married . . . with Children* (FOX, 1987–97) in the late 1980s, the president of Coca-Cola offered an apology, saying he was "corporately, professionally and personally embarrassed."[20] The protest propelled Rakolta to the front page of the *New York Times* and onto prime time for interviews with Larry King, Ted Koppel, and Phil Donahue, but *Married . . . with Children* continued to sell out the advertisement slots (including to Coca-Cola).[21] Advertisers were eager to placate critics but less willing to follow through. After all, an audience in the tens of millions eclipsed even the most impressive boycott campaigns.

By the twenty-first century, media fragmentation resulted in success being measured in millions of viewers rather than tens of millions. As a result, activists found it easier to mobilize but much harder to successfully pressure the networks, cable companies, and streaming services. Online campaigns could still mobilize enough viewers to save shows after initial cancellation, including the conservative favorite *Last Man Standing* and the liberal darling *Brooklyn Nine-Nine* (FOX, 2013–18; NBC, 2019–21).[22] But the same fragmentation, along with media deregulation, made it impossible for activists to dictate or censor content with threats of pickets, letter-writing campaigns, or advertising boycotts because the television networks, cable channels, and streaming services increasingly were narrowcasting to a specific audience niche.

In the monolithic media environment of broadcasting in the network era, turning television entertainment into a political force was hard. It required boldness in a business known for its blandness. For activists and politicians, however, prime-time shows were irresistible. The audience was simply too large and the perceived influence too big to ignore. At the same time, the very size of the audience, coupled with the profit interests of network executives and production companies, tempered the political appeals. *All in the Family* had considerable leeway to engage in political controversy because of its immense popularity. But while it broke new ground on prime time, it still stayed within the political mainstream. With the fragmentation of the media landscape from the 1980s on, it became easier to use entertainment for political purposes as new networks, cable, and eventually streaming changed the business model of broadcasting. Shows no longer needed an audience in the tens of millions to stay on the air. Instead, shows—even channels—catered to specific audiences.

Second, the political potential of entertainment television continued to captivate political elites, remaking modern American political history in lasting ways. "The power of the media," sociologist Michael Schudson recognized, "resides in the perception of experts and decision makers that the general public is influenced by the mass media."[23] Nowhere is that conviction stronger than in politics. The belief that *All in the Family* both entertained audiences and engaged voters transformed political campaigns, institutions, and movements.

It elevated the political prominence of television stars, and over the next decades successful producers and actors used their entertainment fame to advance their political interests outside of prime time. Rob Reiner, who in the 1970s campaigned for George McGovern and joined Jean Stapleton in the campaign for the Equal Rights Amendment, spent decades as a leading figure in a variety of liberal causes, including initiatives for the environment, against tobacco, and for marriage equality. He endorsed, fundraised for, and even advised presidential candidates while continuing his career in film and television.[24] By the early 2000s, his own name was mentioned in serious conversation as a challenger to the incumbent California governor and fellow actor Arnold Schwarzenegger.[25] Reiner declined to run for office, but in 2012 another, far more controversial, prime-time celebrity announced her candidacy for the White House. "I ran a successful TV show," Roseanne Barr offered as qualification. "I know how to produce stories for the public that the public likes."[26] Her campaign failed, but her remark served as a harbinger of a new political era.

In Washington, politicians continued experimenting with different strategies for using television entertainment to their advantage. Appearing on popular sitcoms provided a way for politicians to polish their image, such as Speaker Thomas "Tip" O'Neill, who visited *Cheers* for a drink and a laugh with Sam Malone (played by Ted Danson) in 1983; Speaker Newt Gingrich, who traded some light barbs with the titular character (Candice Bergen) on *Murphy Brown* in 1996; and Vice President Joe Biden, who charmed Leslie Knope (Amy Poehler) on *Parks and Recreation* in 2012.[27] The concept was straight out of Richard Nixon's playbook: using television entertainment to come off as cool and "with it." Some, such as Democratic Party presidential hopefuls Jesse Jackson in 1988, Jerry Brown in 1992, and Joe Biden in 2020, followed McGovern's example and recorded advertisements with television stars, who endorsed them more or less in character: Cliff Huxtable (Bill Cosby) of *The Cosby Show* (NBC, 1984–92), Archie Bunker and Mike Stivic of *All in the Family*, and Newman (Wayne Knight) of *Seinfeld*, respectively.[28]

At the same time, politicians also turned to Nixon's more confrontational strategies to generate attention and boost their profile as culture warriors. Vice President Dan Quayle, for example, used prime time as a foil in the 1992 presidential campaign by criticizing Murphy Brown for "mocking the importance of fathers" by having a child out of wedlock. In response, producer Diane English challenged the vice president to debate her "anytime, anywhere."[29] When he refused, English addressed the criticism on prime time. "We could choose to blame the media, the Congress, or an administration that has been in power for twelve years," Brown remarked on the show, "or we could blame me."[30] The lines between television entertainment and political reality were blurred beyond recognition. This was the world that *All in the Family* wrought.

The family debates from the Bunker household permeated political discourse in unanticipated ways as well. With the rise of the 24/7 news cycle, cable news turned to confrontation, opinion, and entertainment to keep audiences watching.[31] The blueprints, it seemed, were the arguments at 704 Hauser Street.[32] "There are nights when I wonder," one reporter noted, "whether 'Crossfire' and 'McLaughlin Group' aren't the 90's version of 'All in the Family.'"[33] Television entertainment, media theorist Neil Postman warned in the 1980s, corrupted not only news and public affairs programming but turned "our culture into one vast arena for show business."[34] The outrage on television "news" was followed by entertainment shows such as *Politically Incorrect* (Comedy Central, 1993–2002), which deliberately brought political strategists and provocateurs into conversation with comedians, celebrities, and journalists in an effort to "ma[ke] controversy funny."[35] Suddenly, entertainers were an unavoidable part of political conversations. While Fox News repackaged C-listers such as Scott Baio of *Happy Days* into political surrogates for conservative audiences, MSNBC gave its liberal viewers familiar figures from Hollywood as political commentators. "The show part of [news] is getting bigger and bigger," Rob Reiner remarked with some bite when invited onto MSNBC to talk about the 2016 presidential campaign, "[to the point] where showbusiness and news have blurred."[36]

Out of the merging of television entertainment, news, and politics, which *All in the Family* accelerated decades earlier, emerged Donald Trump. The New York real estate developer embraced television entertainment's capacity to shape reality. Trump learned to master the mix of entertainment and outrage that Fox News packaged as politics for the Republican base.[37] During the Obama years, he became a staple on *Fox & Friends*, the morning show then hosted by Gretchen Carlson, Steve Doocy, and Brian Kilmeade, leveraging his success on reality TV into political clout.[38] From 2004 onward, after television producer Mark Burnett signed him as the figurehead of *The Apprentice*, a reality competition where contestants vie for an executive position in the Trump Organization, television producers had sold the American people fiction under the label of reality.[39] They turned Trump into "an icon of American success."[40] Without *The Apprentice*, Burnett concluded—and even Trump himself seemed to agree—Trump would not have run for and won the presidency.[41] But even before that, Trump recognized that the appearance of success was as important as, if not more important than, actual accomplishment. Throughout the 1990s, Trump appeared on a variety of sitcoms, including *The Fresh Prince of Bel-Air* (NBC, 1990–96), *The Nanny* (CBS, 1993–99), and *Spin City* (ABC, 1996–2002), as the epitome of a successful businessman.[42] He was, for all intents and purposes, a man made for television and a man made by television.

And so from the moment Trump announced his candidacy for the White House in June 2015, he ran as the personification of politics as television entertainment. He was, it seemed, the new incarnation of Archie Bunker: outspoken and outrageous, beloved, bigoted, and a buffoon.[43] Most of all, he was a television character.[44] The result was a total domination of the attention of both the news and entertainment media. "I go on one of these shows and the ratings double, they triple," Trump boasted.[45] Like a deer in the headlights, television was unable—and unwilling—to look away as Trump assaulted the foundation of American democracy with lies and misinformation. Television and cable executives could not believe the numbers Trump delivered to cable news in the 2016 race and kept the cameras fixated on the "ratings machine."[46] This meant profits. "It may not be good for America," Les Moonves, president of CBS, remarked, "but it's damn good for CBS."[47]

"Television brings people together, but television can also tear us apart," Jimmy Kimmel reflected on the candidacy of Donald Trump at the Emmy Awards in September 2016.[48] More than a half a century earlier, the legendary news anchor Edward R. Murrow talked about television's potential to fight "ignorance, intolerance and indifference." But, he stressed, it worked "only to the extent that humans are determined to use it to those ends."[49] The people behind *All in the Family* wanted to use television entertainment to combat ignorance, intolerance, and indifference. They wanted to address bigotry and prejudice; they wanted to raise awareness about women's rights, sexual assault, and birth control; they wanted to educate viewers about residential segregation, gun control, and economic inequality. The writers wanted to address real issues and concerns. The producers wanted to spark conversation and action. The cast wanted to work for electoral, legislative, and judicial campaigns.

Television was supposed to serve a master looking for political change. Since the 1970s, when political interests—ranging from the president to grassroots activists—started to appreciate the potential of television entertainment to win elections, enact legislation, and advance an agenda, they sought to master television. But the business model of television entertainment was in fact the real master and would turn anything it touched—including democracy—into "entertainment packages."[50] The result: President Donald Trump. "We've got Archie in the White House," an outraged Rob Reiner exclaimed on a late-night talk show.[51] Norman Lear also recognized the similarities between the two television characters, calling Trump "a thorough fool" and "the middle finger of the American right hand."[52] The political success and enduring popularity of Donald Trump, not unlike other television characters, was due to his entertainment value. His remarkable hold over a significant part of the American electorate, a hold that survived two impeachments, an electoral defeat, an insurrection, a criminal conviction, and numerous criminal indictments, was never rooted only in ideology, partisanship, or politics but rather in entertainment, celebrity, and performance. Some five decades before Trump announced his candidacy for the White House, graffiti in the New York City subway read "Archie Bunker for President." Beneath it, somebody had scrawled: "He is."[53]

ACKNOWLEDGMENTS

At the end of a television show, the end credits roll, highlighting how many people it takes to transform an idea into an actual broadcast. This book comes with only my name on the cover, but it was made possible with the encouragement, advice, and assistance of a large crew. Cue the end theme of your favorite show and settle in, for this is the book version of the end credits.

None of this would exist if it wasn't for *All in the Family*. Long after it went off the air, I discovered it in afternoon reruns and it became my introduction course to the political history of the modern United States. The producers, writers, and cast were my first professors, and I remain grateful for all the lessons and all the laughter. While conducting the research, I had the privilege of connecting with some of the key figures behind it. Generously, Virginia Carter answered all of my questions about her work at Tandem Productions. In 2017, a nonagenarian Norman Lear, still working in television production, took time to sit down with me on two occasions. Even more incredible, he kindly gave me access to his private archives. Unfortunately, he died before this book was finished, but I still like to think he would have enjoyed the read.

Archivists are the best. I want to express my appreciation for all, far too many to name here, who have assisted me in locating the material that made it possible for me to tell this story. At the Nixon Library, Ryan Pettigrew helped me navigate the Nixon tapes and locate images while Carla Braswell answered every question, found every letter and memo I needed, and even sent me material I didn't realize existed. Hilary Swett at the Writers Guild Foundation was incredibly helpful. Jean Anderson, Norman Lear's personal archivist, went above and beyond in making sure I had all the relevant material at my disposal. I have listened to over 100 hours of interviews collected by the Archive of American Television, read *Broadcasting* magazine for another 100 hours online at the World Radio History archive, and scrolled through books for even more hundreds of hours online at the Internet Archive—these online resources have made it possible for me to be transported from Helsinki to sound stages in Studio City and executive suites at Black Rock. Libraries are indeed wonders.

I'm grateful for the people at Photofest, the Rubenstein Library, the Richard Nixon Library, the Jimmy Carter Library, and Gary O'Neil who assisted me in securing the rights for the images. I love how Sage Goodwin turned dry stats on ratings and awards into visually striking illustrations.

Working on American history from the other side of the Atlantic is not without costs. The Åbo Akademi University Foundation, the Society of Swedish Literature in Finland, the Waldemar von Frenckell Foundation, the Oskar Öflund Foundation, the Otto A. Malm Foundation, the TOP-Foundation, the Turku University Foundation, the Finnish Society of Sciences and Letters, and the European Association for American Studies provided the funding necessary to conduct the research.

This project started as a dissertation, and I'm grateful to Margaret O'Mara and Emilie Raymond for serving as preliminary examiners and Heather Hendershot for taking on the role of opponent at the public defense. Most of all, Katie Brownell deserves an executive producer credit on this book for her role as my adviser, her ability to find my argument in every first draft, her mentorship, and her friendship.

Over the years, I have been welcomed into many communities and remain grateful to everybody, too numerous to name here, who have read my work and provided encouragement and new perspectives at research seminars and symposia at the history department at Åbo Akademi University, the American Political History Institute at Boston University,, the John Morton Center for North American Studies at the University of Turku, and the Turku Institute for Advanced Studies. In particular, Martin Cloonan, Outi Hakola, Benita Heiskanen, and Bruce Schulman have provided support and opportunities.

I have enjoyed conversations about *All in the Family* and political history with fellow historians, American studies scholars, and the occasional political scientist at a variety of conferences on both sides of the Atlantic. I can't possibly name all of them here, but I do want to highlight the support and friendship of Patrick Andelic, Aniko Bodroghkozy, Patrick T. J. Browne, Kellie Carter Jackson, Seth Cotlar, David Greenberg, Niki Hemmer, Kate Jewell, Mike Koncewicz, Kevin Kruse, Lauren Lassabe Shepherd, Kathryn McGarr, Natalia Mehlman-Petrzela, Allison Perlman, Paul Renfro, Daniel Rowe, Danielle Seid, Henry Tonks, Neil Young, Ben Zdencanovic, and Thomas Zimmer. This is very much a book formed by the American Political History Conference, and Katie, Niki, and Leah Wright Rigueur deserve immense credit for building that community. Thanks to Margaret, Natalia, Lauren, Mike, Blake Scott Ball, Matthew Pressman, Brian Rosenwald, and Randall Stephens for talking presses and proposals with me.

My writers' room when working on this manuscript was the BOS-HEL-OX writing group Zoom, a space full of laughs and encouragement. Cari Babitzke and Sage Goodwin have read every single chapter, they have tracked down archival material an ocean away, they have organized panels and roundtables with me, and they have been there whenever I needed a laugh. Lauren Lassabe Shepherd joined the writing group during the revisions stage and has helped me navigate the publication process with great insight and unfailing encouragement.

From my first meeting with Andrew Winters, I recognized his enthusiasm for this project. He has been everything a first-time author could ask for in an editor, and the book is better because of him. I also want to express my gratitude to everybody else at UNC Press, including Mary Carley Caviness, Lindsay Starr, Iza Wojciechowska, and Jenny Volvovski. I am forever grateful to the two anonymous readers who provided clear and insightful suggestions that improved the manuscript. Any and all mistakes are, of course, mine and mine alone.

It has been the privilege of my life to write this book with the support of all in *my* family. Like the end credits of *All in the Family*, which concluded with "A Bud Yorkin–Norman Lear Tandem Production," I want to recognize this as tandem production. This book would not have been possible without the tandem pedaling, unwavering support, and love of Jutta Rosenberg (or without her telling me in no uncertain terms to stop diving into new archives and to just finish the damn manuscript). My most trusted research assistant, Charlie, provided joy, warmth, and walks when rewriting and editing was too ruff.

Finally, my children, Vincent, Liv, Vivan, and Will, probably cannot remember a time when I wasn't working on this book. And yet I cannot recall them complaining about my preoccupation with such an old show (though to be honest, to them even *Seinfeld* is an *old* show). I realize that it must be taxing to watch shows with a father who is—literally—writing a book on the history of television entertainment. And still, sharing the (modern) classics, in particular *The Good Place*, *Brooklyn Nine-Nine*, and *Superstore*, with the kids is one of my favorite pastimes. *Fortsätt titta på tv och fortsätt läsa*. This, like everything I do, is for them.

Oscar Winberg, Helsinki, Finland
December 2024

NOTES

Abbreviations

- AAT   Archive of American Television, Television Academy Foundation, North Hollywood, CA
- JSP   Jean Stapleton Papers, Archives Center, National Museum of American History, Washington, DC
- LHP   Laura Keane Zametkin Hobson Papers, 1930–86, Rare Book and Manuscript Library, Columbia University, New York, NY
- NLP   Norman Lear Papers, private collection
- PC-CA   Paley Center for Media, Beverly Hills, CA
- PC-NY   Paley Center for Media, New York, NY
- SL   Schlesinger Library, Radcliffe Institute, Harvard University, Cambridge, MA
- WHSF   White House Special Files Collection, Richard Nixon Presidential Library and Museum, National Archives, Yorba Linda, CA
- WHT   White House Tapes, Richard Nixon Presidential Library and Museum, National Archives, Yorba Linda, CA

Introduction

1. Ted Johnson, "Hollywood Alarm Grows over Prospect of Donald Trump Victory," *Variety*, November 2, 2016, https://variety.com/2016/biz/news/donald-trump-hillary-clinton-hollywood-panic-fear-1201907750.

2. Brooks Barnes, "*Will & Grace* Is Back: Will Its Portrait of Gay Life Hold Up?," *New York Times*, September 14, 2017, www.nytimes.com/2017/09/14/arts/television/will-grace-debra-messing-eric-mccormack.html.

3. While television often is divided into two robust categories, news and entertainment, "television entertainment" is such a wide term that it can, depending on the definition, encompass most, if not all, scripted and unscripted broadcasting, cable, and streaming content. The focus of this book is television situation comedies, and I use the term "television entertainment" primarily, but not exclusively, as a shorthand for scripted television comedies.

4. Burrows and Friedfeld, *Directed by James Burrows*, 322–23.

5. Barnes, "*Will & Grace* Is Back."

6. Lesley Goldberg, "*Will & Grace*'s Debra Messing, Eric McCormack on Clinton-Themed Reunion and a Possible Revival," *Hollywood Reporter*, September 27, 2016, www.hollywoodreporter.com/tv/tv-news/will-grace-reunion-debra-messing-932915.

7. Megan Garber, "Will & Grace & Donald," *Atlantic*, September 29, 2017, www.theatlantic.com/entertainment/archive/2017/09/will-and-grace-revival-review/541362.

8. Jeffrey Fleishman and Yvonne Villarreal, "From Panic to Possibility: A Reeling Entertainment Industry Regroups after Trump's Win," *Los Angeles Times*, December 6, 2016, www.latimes.com/entertainment/movies/la-ca-trump-hollywood-20161126-story.html.

9. Caroline Framke, "How the People Who Make TV Are Reacting to President Trump," *Vox*, January 18, 2017, www.vox.com/culture/2017/1/18/14296880/tv-donald-trump-pop-culture-reaction.

10. Joanna Weiss, "How Trump Inspired the *Roseanne* Reboot," *Politico*, March 26, 2018, www.politico.com/magazine/story/2018/03/26/roseanne-reboot-trump-voters-217711. The show was later reworked as *The Conners* (ABC, 2018–25) after Roseanne Barr was let go and *Roseanne* was canceled over Barr's racist remarks on social media.

11. Fleishman and Villarreal, "From Panic to Possibility."

12. Gary Levin, "How *Murphy Brown* Revival Finds New Targets in the Trump Era," *USA Today*, September 26, 2018, https://eu.usatoday.com/story/life/tv/2018/09/26/murphy-brown-returns-cbs-candice-bergen-trump-era-revival/1415726002.

13. Emily St. James, "*Superstore*'s Finale Changes Everything: Showrunner Justin Spitzer Explains," *Vox*, May 16, 2019, www.vox.com/culture/2019/5/16/18628224/superstore-season-4-finale-employee-appreciation-day-recap-mateo.

14. Barnes, "*Will & Grace* Is Back." This is not to suggest that all members of the LGBTQ+ community were against Trump. See Neil J. Young, *Coming Out Republican*.

15. Raul A. Reyes, "*One Day at a Time* Is the Sitcom America Needs Right Now," *HuffPost*, March 27, 2018, www.huffpost.com/entry/opinion-reyes-one-day-time_n_5aba68e6e4b0decad04e760f. The Latinx community is not a monolith and includes many conservatives. See Cadava, *Hispanic Republican*; and Márquez, *Making the Latino South*.

16. "Fake News," season 11, episode 1, *Murphy Brown* (CBS, September 27, 2018), written by Diane English.

17. "That's What Friends Are For," season 8, episode 1, *Black-ish* (ABC, January 4, 2022), written by Laura Gutin.

18. Maggie Haberman and Patrick Healy, "Trump Rings Up Roseanne Barr after Her Show Is a Ratings Winner," *New York Times*, March 28, 2018, www.nytimes.com/2018/03/28/us/politics/trump-roseanne-barr-ratings.html.

19. Caitlin Oprysko, "Trump Attacks Actress Debra Messing after She Pushed to Out His Donors," *Politico*, September 5, 2019, www.politico.com/story/2019/09/05/trump-debra-messing-1481987.

20. Poniewozik, *Audience of One*, xix.

21. Adler, *"All in the Family,"* xxvi.

22. Adler, *"All in the Family,"* xxxiv.

23. Quoted in Adler, *"All in the Family,"* xv.

24. Historians, media scholars, and journalists have studied the cultural influence of *All in the Family* at length since the 1970s. The foremost source remains Richard Adler's critical appraisal, which collects scripts, reviews, audience research, essays, articles, and interviews in one edition. For a wide-ranging popular biography of the show, see McCrohan, *Archie & Edith*. The best synthesis on the show's cultural importance can be found in Cullen, *Those Were the Days*. For an insightful transnational look at *All in the Family*, the BBC show *Till Death Us Do Part*, which inspired *All in the Family*, and the

West German version, *Ein Herz und eine Seele*, see von Hodenberg, *Television's Moment*. L. Benjamin Rolsky provides a religious studies approach to the show and to Norman Lear's career, in Rolsky, *Rise and Fall*. One of the most influential modern texts on the show is Emily Nussbaum, "The Great Divide: Norman Lear, Archie Bunker, and the Rise of the Bad Fan," *New Yorker*, April 7, 2014, which is reprinted in Nussbaum, *I Like to Watch*, 36–47. See also Brownstein, *Rock Me*; Ozersky, *Archie Bunker's America*; Campbell, *Sitcoms of Norman Lear*; and Whetsell, *Norman Lear*. For reflections on the archival challenges of studying *All in the Family*, see Kathleen Collins, "Trouble with Archie"; and Kimberly Springer, "What're Youse Lookin' at, Meathead? Locating Archie Bunker across Archives," *Flow*, May 21, 2010, www.flowjournal.org/2010/05/whatre-youse-lookin-at-meathead.

25. A look at historical overviews of the United States in the 1970s illustrates both the importance of *All in the Family* and the way historians have struggled to appreciate the connections between television entertainment and political life without relying on technological determinist suggestions that the show was an inevitable reaction to the turmoil of the 1960s and a reflection of the "popular mood." See, for example, Sandbrook, *Mad as Hell*; Berkowitz, *Something Happened*; Jenkins, *Decade of Nightmares*; Kruse and Zelizer, *Fault Lines*; Bailey and Farber, *America in the Seventies*; Schulman, *Seventies*; and Carroll, *It Seemed*.

26. This is not to suggest that no television show had engaged controversial subject matter before *All in the Family*. The scholarship on the various attempts to include political themes such as civil rights, civil liberties, class, anticommunism, gender, and counterculture on shows throughout the 1950s and 1960s is considerable. While earlier shows occasionally addressed controversy, however, *All in the Family* made political and social turmoil an inherent and ever-present part of the show. Furthermore, the immense popularity of *All in the Family* contributed to an understanding of it as something new. See, for example, Boddy, *Fifties Television*; Brook, "Checks and Imbalances"; Schneider, *Gold Dust*; Murphy, "Black Panthers"; Bogle, *Primetime Blues*; Nadel, *Television in Black-and-White America*; Calhoun, *Only the Names*; Spigel and Curtin, *Revolution Wasn't Televised*; Stabile, *Broadcast 41*; Bodroghkozy, *Groove Tube*; MacDonald, *Television and the Red*; MacDonald, *Blacks and White TV*; and Watson, *Expanding Vista*.

27. Norman Lear, "On My 100th Birthday, Reflections on Archie Bunker and Donald Trump," *New York Times*, July 27, 2022, www.nytimes.com/2022/07/27/opinion/archie-bunker-donald-trump-norman-lear.html.

28. "Meet the Bunkers," season 1, episode 1, *All in the Family* (CBS, January 12, 1971), written by Norman Lear. The script is reprinted in its entirety in Adler, *"All in the Family,"* 3–26.

29. Norman Lear, *Even This*, 251.

30. "Success Story," season 1, episode 12, *All in the Family* (CBS, March 30, 1971), written by Burt Styler.

31. "Gloria Has a Belly Full," season 1, episode 6, *All in the Family* (CBS, February 16, 1971), written by Jerry Mayer.

32. "Archie Is Worried about His Job," season 1, episode 10, *All in the Family* (CBS, March 16, 1971), story by William Bickley Jr., teleplay by Norman Lear, Don Nicholl, and Bryan Joseph.

33. Norman Lear, *Even This*, 246.

34. This quote is from a famed address by legendary broadcast journalist Edward R. Murrow. See Brian Stelter, "'Wires and Lights in a Box,' 50 Years Later," *New York Times*, October 15, 2008, https://archive.nytimes.com/mediadecoder.blogs.nytimes.com/2008/10/15/wires-and-lights-in-a-box-fifty-years-later.

35. Stelter, "'Wires and Lights.'"

36. Recent work by historians shows that the development of new modes of political communication is not inevitable but instead the result of work and investment by ambitious political, media, and business interests. See, in particular, the political history of cable television, talk radio, and the internet in Brownell, *24/7 Politics*; Rosenwald, *Talk Radio's America*; and O'Mara, *Code*. See also Hemmer, *Partisans*.

37. For more on the way television became a political force in the 1960s, see Bodroghkozy, *Equal Time*; Brownell, *24/7 Politics*; Greenberg, *Republic of Spin*; Greenberg, "Do Historians Watch"; Goodwin, "Making the News"; Delmont, *Why Busing Failed*; Hallin, *Uncensored War*; Hendershot, *Open to Debate*; Hendershot, *When the News Broke*; Quail, "Propaganda and the Presidency"; Raphael, *Investigated Reporting*; Gitlin, *Whole World Is Watching*; Ponce De Leon, *That's the Way*; and Conway, *Contested Ground*.

Chapter 1

1. "Meet the Bunkers," season 1, episode 1, *All in the Family* (CBS, January 12, 1971), written by Norman Lear.

2. Bedell, *Up the Tube*, 44.

3. Quoted in "TV: Speaking about the Unspeakable," *Newsweek*, November 29, 1971, 59.

4. For more on the new shows of the late 1960s, see Bodroghkozy, *Groove Tube*.

5. Advertisement, *Variety*, December 30, 1970, 12–13.

6. Brown, *Televi$ion*, 125.

7. Gitlin, *Inside Prime Time*, 206.

8. Among the casualties of Wood's housecleaning were *Mayberry R.F.D.*, *Petticoat Junction* (CBS, 1963–70), and *Green Acres* (CBS, 1965–71). For more on the rural comedies on CBS in the 1960s and the "rural purge," see Eskridge, *Rube Tube*.

9. Dann quoted in Metz, *CBS*, 332.

10. Silverman quoted in Neuwirth, *They'll Never Put That*, 134.

11. Schneider is quoted in Paper, *Empire*, 265.

12. Brown, *Televi$ion*, 254.

13. Brown, *Televi$ion*, 210. The rights of the affiliate were acknowledged in the FCC's chain broadcasting rule from 1941 and affirmed by the Supreme Court. See National Broadcasting Co. v. United States 319 US 190 (1943).

14. Brown, *Televi$ion*, 218.

15. Brown, *Televi$ion*, 214.

16. For more on Wood's conservatism, see Bedell, *Up the Tube*, 44; and Brown, *Televi$ion*, 220.

17. For examples of conservative mistrust of television networks, see Efron, *News Twisters*; and Spiro T. Agnew, "Television News Coverage," speech given November 13, 1969, Des Moines, IA, in Porter, *Assault on the Media*, 255–62. For an analysis of two

controversies in which this distrust played a role, see Barrett, *Survey of Broadcast Journalism, 1969–1970*, 31–45; and Barrett, *Survey of Broadcast Journalism, 1970–1971*, 32–49. For a history of the conservative distrust of the networks, see Greenberg, "Idea"; Hemmer, *Messengers of the Right*; and Hendershot, *When the News Broke*.

18. Classen, *Watching Jim Crow*, 108, 118–22. See also MacDonald, *Blacks and White TV*. On public television, the FCC as late as 1970 approved of Alabama stations refusing to air shows offered by PBS, even if it meant removing most if not all broadcasts featuring Black Americans. See Barrett, *Survey of Broadcast Journalism, 1969–1970*, 78–79.

19. The Communications Act of 1934 stipulated the demand to act in the public interest. For more on the concept of the public interest and how it featured in struggles over broadcasting, see Perlman, *Public Interests*.

20. Baughman, *Television's Guardians*, 54–69.

21. Brown, *Keeping Your Eye*, 1.

22. The decision is quoted in Mills, *Changing Channels*, 104.

23. Johnson quoted in "Multiple Ownerships Now up for Grabs," *Broadcasting*, January 27, 1969, 25–26.

24. Barnouw, *Tube of Plenty*, 299–300, 356–57. For more on the concept of regulation by raised eyebrow, see Zarkin and Zarkin, *Federal Communications Commission*, 146. For more on the struggles of the FCC to take on the broadcasting industry in the 1960s, see Baughman, *Television's Guardians*.

25. Hilmes, *Only Connect*, 258.

26. MacDonald, *One Nation under Television*, 185–86.

27. Norman Lear, interview by Margot Hardenbergh, March 16, 2005, TV Oral History Project, Donald McGannon Communication Research Center, Fordham University Libraries, New York, NY.

28. Hilmes, *Only Connect*, 258.

29. Bedell, *Up the Tube*, 52; MacDonald, *One Nation under Television*, 185.

30. Burch's description of the rule can be found in Brown, *Televi$ion*, 233.

31. Hilmes, *Only Connect*, 259.

32. The Supreme Court had articulated the scarcity rationale decades earlier. See *National Broadcasting Co.* 319 US 190.

33. *Red Lion Broadcasting Co. v. Federal Communications Commission*, 395 US 367 (1969), www.oyez.org/cases/1968/2.

34. "A Bleak Benchmark in Regulation," *Broadcasting*, June 16, 1969, 21.

35. "Highest Court, Lowest Blow," *Broadcasting*, June 16, 1969, 86. In fact, the decision did not mark a new turn toward stricter FCC regulation of programming, and soon the Supreme Court limited the impact of the decision. See *Columbia Broadcasting System v. Democratic National Committee* 412 US 94 (1973).

36. The description can be found in Brown, *Televi$ion*, 158.

37. Brown, *Televi$ion*, 180–81.

38. Brownell, *24/7 Politics*, 31–33.

39. For more on the efforts of broadcasters to use connections in Washington to hamstring competing business models, see Brownell, *24/7 Politics*, 15–59.

40. For more on Nixon and cable, see Brownell, *24/7 Politics*, 84–105; and Brownell, "'Ideological Plugola.'"

41. The final report of the National Commission on the Causes and Prevention of Violence is quoted in Rowland, *Politics of TV Violence*, 130–32.

42. Milov, *Cigarette*, 118–59.

43. Brown, *Televi$ion*, 163. The lost cigarette advertising constituted 10 percent of broadcasters' billings in 1970. See Barrett, *Survey of Broadcast Journalism, 1970–1971*, 83.

44. Barrett, *Survey of Broadcast Journalism, 1970–1971*, 5.

45. Brown, *Televi$ion*, viii.

46. For more insight into *Till Death Us Do Part*, see von Hodenberg, *Television's Moment*, 19–29, 108–28.

47. Norman Lear, interview by Barbara Cady, *Playboy*, March 1976, 62.

48. Bud Yorkin, interview by Morrie Gelman, December 2, 1997, AAT.

49. Leonard H. Goldenson, interview by Marvin Wolf, May 14, 1996, AAT; Alfred Schneider, interview by Karen Herman, July 22, 2004, AAT. See also Neuwirth, *They'll Never Put That*, 125–33.

50. Neuwirth, *They'll Never Put That*, 130.

51. Gitlin, *Inside Prime Time*, 43–44.

52. There were other companies that offered rating services, but the Nielsen ratings were the closest to official ratings in the broadcasting industry. The company calculated the rating through a selection of 2,200 representative homes across the nation participating in the effort by keeping daily viewing diaries and 1,200 homes with a small box, the Nielsen audiometer, attached to their television sets that recorded the exact use of the TV. The information was then broken down for the advertisers into ratings, which represented the percentage of the total possible national audience households, and shares, which consisted of the part of the actual audience watching television at the time, and demographic categories of both. Insiders recognized the ratings as "the Bible of TV Management." Barrett, *Survey of Broadcast Journalism, 1971–1972*, 10. For more on the Nielsen ratings, see Brown, *Televi$ion*, 15, 32–35.

53. Brown, *Televi$ion*, 287.

54. For more on the concept of the "consumers' republic," see Lizabeth Cohen, *Consumers' Republic*. For more on the importance of the young generation to broadcasters, see Brown, *Televi$ion*, 262–66.

55. For more on the development of rural comedies on CBS as a response to the Red Scare, see Eskridge, *Rube Tube*.

56. Gitlin, *Inside Prime Time*, 208–11.

57. William Grimes, "Michael Dann, TV Programmer, Dies at 94," *New York Times*, May 30, 2016, www.nytimes.com/2016/05/31/business/media/michael-dann-tv-programmer-who-scheduled-horowitz-and-hillbillies-dies-at-94.html.

58. Metz, *CBS*, 337.

59. Brown, *Televi$ion*, 56.

60. Paper, *Empire*, vii.

61. Brown, *Televi$ion*, 361.

62. Rich, *Warm Up the Snake*, 3.

63. Gitlin, *Inside Prime Time*, 213.

64. "CBS-TV Affiliates Strike a Harmonious Chord," *Broadcasting*, May 11, 1970, 38.

65. "CBS-TV Affiliates," 38.

66. According to Perry Lafferty of CBS, only a few affiliates opted out, "not too many, but there's always a few." Lafferty quoted in Neuwirth, *They'll Never Put That*, 136. According to Carroll O'Connor, no more than 8 of 197 affiliates rejected the show. Dick Adler, "He's the Bigot Next Door," *Los Angeles Times*, June 13, 1971.

67. Wood to CBS affiliate stations, wire, January 1971, box S-212, NLP. I was generously given access by Norman Lear to his vast private archive—an invaluable source for this project—at the Beverly Hills offices of Act III Productions in December 2017. In order to protect the privacy and integrity of private individuals, we reached an understanding that I would not publish the names of any nonpublic figures that appear in the archive. As such, all references to audience members from the Lear Papers are anonymized.

68. Wood to CBS affiliate stations, January 1971.

69. Emery Wister, "New Series on CBS Delivers Message," *Charlotte News*, January 13, 1971; and Walter Saunder, "*All in the Family* to Jolt Viewers," *Rocky Mountain News*, January 13, 1971, both in folder 3, box 15, LHP.

70. Neuwirth, *They'll Never Put That*, 136. Emphasis in the original.

71. Alan Wagner, quoted in Neuwirth, *They'll Never Put That*, 135.

72. Bedell, *Up the Tube*, 45.

73. William Tankersley, the head of the standards and practices department at CBS, later insisted the disclaimer did not come from his people and suggested it originated in the law department. Tankersley quoted in Neuwirth, *They'll Never Put That*, 138.

74. For an engaging account of the exchanges before the premiere, see Norman Lear, *Even This*, 233–39.

75. "Most Liked *Family*, CBS-TV Survey Claims," *Broadcasting*, January 18, 1971, 44.

76. Rowland Barber, "Bellowing, Half-Baked, Fire-Breathing Bigotry," *TV Guide*, May 29, 1971, reprinted in Harris, "*TV Guide*," 183–85.

77. Metz, *CBS*, 334.

78. Quoted in Gitlin, *Inside Prime Time*, 213.

79. Bedell, *Up the Tube*, 46.

80. Dwight Newton, "Introduction to a Bigot," *San Francisco Examiner*, January 12, 1971, reprinted in Adler, "*All in the Family*," 81–82.

81. "'Pearl Bailey' Scores High in NY Ratings," *Broadcasting*, February 1, 1971, 49.

82. A good sample of reviews can be found in Adler, "*All in the Family*." The most comprehensive collection of reviews and articles about *All in the Family* that I have located was prepared by CBS for Laura Hobson and can be found in folders 3 and 4, box 15, LHP.

83. Cleveland Amory, review of *All in the Family*, *TV Guide*, February 27, 1971, reprinted in Adler, "*All in the Family*," 89–90.

84. Cynthia Lowry, Associated Press, "Writer Finds Series Offensive, Vulgar," *Hamlet News-Messenger*, January 13, 1971, 10.

85. Review of *All in the Family*, *Variety*, January 13, 1971; and review of *All in the Family*, *Daily Variety*, January 13, 1971, both reprinted in Adler, "*All in the Family*," 69–71.

86. Tim Gray, "Looking Back on the Legacy of *All in the Family* 50 Years Later," *Variety*, January 12, 2021, https://variety.com/2021/tv/spotlight/all-in-the-family-50-year-anniversary-1234878168.

87. Kay Gardella, "John Wayne Is Needled in *All in the Family* TVer," *New York Daily News*, January 20, 1971, 82.

88. For more on the role of television critics in elevating conversations about the medium in the 1970s, see Petruska, "Critical Eye," 192. For contemporary books on television, see McGinniss, *Selling of the President*; Johnson, *How to Talk Back*; Brown, *Televi$ion*; and Mayer, *About Television*.

89. McChesney, *Communication Revolution*, 30–34. See also Bodroghkozy, introduction to *Companion to the History*, 2–4; and Newcomb, *TV*, 1–24.

90. Ouellette, *Viewers Like You*, 65.

91. Fred Ferretti, "TV: Are Racism and Bigotry Funny?," *New York Times*, January 12, 1971, reprinted in Adler, *"All in the Family,"* 71–73.

92. Stephanie Harrington, "The Message Sounds Like 'Hate Thy Neighbor,'" *New York Times*, January 24, 1971, reprinted in Adler, *"All in the Family,"* 76–77.

93. Jack Gould, "Can Bigotry Be Laughed Away? It's Worth a Try," *New York Times*, February 21, 1971, reprinted in Adler, *"All in the Family,"* 73–75. Adler, however, mistakes the date for January instead of February.

94. See, for example, Barrett, *Survey of Broadcast Journalism, 1971–1972*, 3.

95. Norman Lear, "Laughing While We Face Our Prejudices," *New York Times*, April 11, 1971, D22.

96. Alan Bunce, "*All in the Family*: TV Social Departure," *Christian Science Monitor*, January 18, 1971, reprinted in Adler, *"All in the Family,"* 82–83.

97. Pamela Haynes, "New TV Comedy Takes Hard, Realistic Poke at Bigotry," *Los Angeles Sentinel*, January 28, 1971, reprinted in Adler, *"All in the Family,"* 84–85.

98. Don Freeman, review of *All in the Family*, *San Diego Union*, January 14, 1971, reprinted in Adler, *"All in the Family,"* 79–81.

99. Newton, "Introduction to a Bigot," 81–82.

100. "Family Fun," *Newsweek*, March 15, 1971, 64–68.

101. Norman Mark, "*All in the Family* Gets Better as Weeks Go By," *Chicago Daily News*, February 23, 1971, reprinted in Adler, *"All in the Family,"* 87–88.

102. Cynthia Lowry, Associated Press, "TV Racist 'Strong Medicine,'" *Lockport Union-Sun and Journal*, March 3, 1971, 24.

103. George Gent, "*All in the Family* Takes First Place in Nielsen Ratings," *New York Times*, May 25, 1971, 79.

104. Laura Z. Hobson, "As I Listened to Archie Say 'Hebe' . . . ," *New York Times*, September 12, 1971, D1, reprinted in Adler, *"All in the Family,"* 97–106.

105. Hobson's article was distributed through the New York Times News Service and appeared in papers across the country. See, for example, *Kansas City Star*, September 26, 1971; *New Orleans States-Item*, October 16, 1971; *Missoula Missoulian*, September 12, 1971; *Grand Rapids Press*, September 19, 1971; *Fort Lauderdale News-Sun-Sentinel*, September 12, 1971; and *Anchorage News*, October 4, 1971, all in folder 4, box 15, LHP.

106. John J. O'Connor, review of *All in the Family*, *New York Times*, September 20, 1971, 53.

107. Furthermore, the editor claimed to have received a number of phone calls on the matter. Seymour Peck to Hobson, September 15, 1971, folder 1, box 15, LHP.

108. "Archie, Lovable or Lamentable?," *New York Times*, October 3, 1971, D17.

109. "Archie, Lovable or Lamentable?"

110. "Archie, Lovable or Lamentable?"

111. Norman Lear, "As I Read How Laura Saw Archie . . . ," *New York Times*, October 10, 1971, reprinted in Adler, *"All in the Family,"* 106–11.

112. Norman Lear, "As I Read," 106–11.

113. Joseph Morgenstern, "Can Bigotry Be Funny?," *Newsweek*, November 29, 1971, 59–60.

114. Arnold Hano, "Can Archie Bunker Give Bigotry a Bad Name?," *New York Times*, March 12, 1972, SM32.

115. Perry Lafferty, interview by Morrie Gelman, December 4, 1997, AAT.

116. Quoted in Brownstein, *Rock Me*, 281.

117. Carroll O'Connor, interview by Dick Cavett, *Dick Cavett Show*, ABC, December 7, 1971, PC-CA.

118. Carroll O'Connor, interview by Johnny Carson, *Tonight Show Starring Johnny Carson*, NBC, October 5, 1972, PC-CA.

119. Norman Lear, interview by David Frost, *David Frost Show*, Westinghouse Broadcasting Company, March 15, 1971.

120. Norman Lear and cast of *All in the Family*, interview by Merv Griffin, *Merv Griffin Show*, CBS, March 31, 1971. For Griffin's view of the visit, see Griffin and Barsocchini, *Merv*, 265.

121. Percy Shain, *"All in the Family*: A TV Phenomenon, Indeed!," *Boston Globe*, May 21, 1972, 7.

Chapter 2

1. Hubbell Robinson, "The Pursuit of Excellence," *Television Quarterly*, Fall 1972, 9–10.

2. Branch, *Pillar of Fire*, 394. For a personal narrative written by Lelyveld's son, see Joseph Lelyveld, *Omaha Blues*, 177–94.

3. Arthur J. Lelyveld, "Archie Bunker Creates New Freedom to Be Offensive," *Congress Bi-Weekly*, April 28, 1972, reprinted in *National Observer*, May 27, 1972, in box S-212, NLP. Following publication in *Congress Bi-Weekly*, the article was picked up by the Associated Press and appeared in papers across the country. See American Jewish Congress, memorandum, May 5, 1972, container 8, folder 138, MS 4639, Lelyveld Papers, Western Reserve Historical Society, Cleveland, OH. Bound volumes of *Congress Bi-Weekly* are available at the American Jewish Historical Society, New York, NY.

4. Contemporary studies actually showed that even young children viewed television with a heavy dose of cynicism. See Barrett, *Survey of Broadcast Journalism, 1971–1972*, 7.

5. The concept was developed by sociologist W. Phillips Davison and articulated in 1983. See Davison, "Third-Person Effect."

6. Victor M. Bienstock, "'Likable Bigot' on TV Perturbs Ethnic Leaders," *Jewish Week*, February 25, 1971, in folder 3, box 15, LHP.

7. Ernie Santosuosso, "Seriously, Folks, Here's Jerry Lewis," *Boston Globe*, November 23, 1972, 99.

8. J. J. Fishbein, "It's Not Funny," *Jewish Sentinel*, April 22, 1971, 7, in folder 3, box 15, LHP.

9. Petersen, *How Machines*.

10. For examples of the new approach to television, see Johnson, *How to Talk Back*; Brown, *Televi$ion*; Efron, *News Twisters*; and Mayer, *About Television*. While very different in content, they all suggested that television was a political force to reckon with in modern society.

11. Newcomb, *TV*, 19–20. See also Jeff Levine, "Television," *New York Times*, June 27, 1971, D21.

12. The number is from Johnson, *How to Talk Back*, 11. By 1972, that had grown to over seven hours, according to Barrett, *Survey of Broadcast Journalism, 1971–1972*, 5.

13. Levine, "Television."

14. Mayer, *About Television*, xi.

15. Arthur J. Lelyveld, "Archie Bunker Creates."

16. Hy Gardner, Glad You Asked That!, *Record Newspapers*, August 12, 1972, B7.

17. Sidney Harris, cartoon, *Broadcasting*, September 18, 1972, 76.

18. Hazel Garland, "Video Vignettes," *New Pittsburgh Courier*, February 13, 1971, 13.

19. Pamela Haynes, "New TV Comedy Takes Hard, Realistic Poke at Bigotry," *Los Angeles Sentinel*, January 28, 1971, reprinted in Adler, *"All in the Family,"* 84–85.

20. Jack Gould, for example, makes a direct reference to the *Los Angeles Sentinel* review to bolster his own argument in the *New York Times*. See Jack Gould, "Can Bigotry Be Laughed Away? It's Worth a Try," *New York Times*, February 21, 1971, reprinted in Adler, *"All in the Family,"* 73–75.

21. Whitney M. Young Jr., "Irresponsible Television Production Aids Racism," *Los Angeles Sentinel*, February 4, 1971.

22. For more on *Amos 'n' Andy*, the reactions to the show, and the campaigns against it, see Cripps, "*Amos 'n' Andy*"; Ely, *Adventures*; and MacDonald, *Blacks and White TV*.

23. Quoted in Charles L. Sanders, "Is Archie Bunker the Real White America?," *Ebony*, June 1972, 190.

24. "Producing and Directing: Conversations with Bud Yorkin," pt. 1, October 10, 1989, Museum of Broadcasting Seminar Series, PC-NY. See also Bud Yorkin, interview by Morrie Gelman, December 2, 1997, AAT.

25. Sanders, "Is Archie Bunker," 192.

26. Sanders, "Is Archie Bunker," 188; George Friedman, "AJCommittee's *Family* Plan: Weighing Bigotry in the Balances," *JTA Daily News Bulletin*, June 22, 1971, in box S-212, NLP.

27. Bienstock, "'Likable Bigot.'"

28. Friedman, "AJCommittee's *Family* Plan."

29. Laura Z. Hobson, "As I Listened to Archie Say 'Hebe' . . . ," *New York Times*, September 12, 1971, reprinted in Adler, *"All in the Family,"* 97–106.

30. American Jewish Committee, memorandum, August 4, 1971, box S-212, NLP.

31. Benjamin R. Epstein, letter to the editor, in "Archie, Lovable or Lamentable?," *New York Times*, October 3, 1971, D17.

32. Abbot Rosen to Cohen, March 31, 1971, folder 3, box 15, LHP.

33. Kaufman to Epstein, April 15, 1971, folder 3, box 15, LHP.

34. Epstein to Kaufman, April 19, 1971, folder 3, box 15, LHP.

35. Justin J. Finger to Lily Edelman, July 6, 1971, folder 3, box 15, LHP.

36. In private, Hobson was fuming over Epstein's misleading suggestion that the Anti-Defamation League was committed against *All in the Family* when letters he had shared with her told a different story. She had, however, promised not to quote publicly from the correspondence. "I can never correct the impression your letter to the Times creates," Hobson wrote him, "but I think you did me a disservice in it." Hobson to Epstein, September 30, 1971, folder 1, box 15, LHP.

37. Epstein, letter to the editor.

38. Fact sheet, n.d. [ca. 1971], box S-212, NLP.

39. Robert E. Segal, "Archie Bunker under Fire," *Jewish Advocate*, September 21, 1972, 2.

40. "Archie Gets B'nai B'rith Award," *Jewish Post and Opinion*, October 6, 1972, 7.

41. Memorandum, n.d. [ca. 1972], Field Staff Regional Directors, Region 1: West Coast, Leonard H. Carter, Image Awards, 1971–72, NAACP Papers, Library of Congress, Washington, DC.

42. Morsell to Epstein, November 30, 1972, NAACP Papers, Library of Congress, Washington, DC.

43. McCrohan, *Archie & Edith*, 32–33.

44. Letter to Lelyveld, April 27, 1972, container 8, folder 138, MS 4639, Lelyveld Papers, Western Reserve Historical Society, Cleveland, OH.

45. Because the archival records of CBS are unavailable, earlier scholarship has failed to appreciate the intense consideration, and sometimes conflict, over which lines were appropriate. There is, one scholar observed, "no known instance in which CBS executives objected to the use of ethnic epithets and antiminority remarks in the sitcom." This is due not to a lack of objections but rather to a lack of insight into the conversations between the network and the production company. In fact, the archival record makes clear that the network frequently raised objections to the language related to ethnic minorities. Von Hodenberg, *Television's Moment*, 237.

46. The episode was "Mike's Problem," season 2, episode 9, *All in the Family* (CBS, November 20, 1971), story by Alan J. Levitt, teleplay by Alan J. Levitt and Philip Mishkin.

47. Norman Lear, *Even This*, 255.

48. Memorandum, September 17, 1971, box S-212, NLP.

49. Norman Lear, *Even This*, 228.

50. Norman Lear, *Even This*, 237–39.

51. Quoted in Neuwirth, *They'll Never Put That*, 137.

52. McCrohan, *Archie & Edith*, 150.

53. Neuwirth, *They'll Never Put That*, 144.

54. Neuwirth, *They'll Never Put That*, 144.

55. Norman Lear, interview by Morrie Gelman, February 26, 1998, AAT.

56. Rich, *Warm Up the Snake*, 117.

57. Arnold Hano, "Can Archie Bunker Give Bigotry a Bad Name?," *New York Times*, March 12, 1972, SM32.

58. John Brady, "Keeping Archie Engaging and Enraging," *New York Times*, February 24, 1974, 15.

59. For more, see Norman Lear, *Even This*; Rich, *Warm Up the Snake*; and the oral history interviews with the writers of the show, found at AAT.

60. See, for example, memoranda, August 3, September 30, November 5, December 13, 1971, box S-212, NLP.

61. See, for example, memoranda, October 29, 1971, February 11, 1972, box S-212, NLP.

62. Memorandum, November 10, 1970, box S-212, NLP.

63. Norman Lear, "As I Read How Laura Saw Archie . . . ," *New York Times*, October 10, 1971, reprinted in Adler, *"All in the Family,"* 106–11.

64. Hano, "Can Archie Bunker."

65. The episode in question is "The Saga of Cousin Oscar," season 2, episode 1, *All in the Family* (CBS, September 18, 1971), story by Burt Styler, teleplay by Burt Styler and Norman Lear.

66. Rich, *Warm Up the Snake*, 128–29.

67. Memorandum, September 30, 1971, box S-212, NLP.

68. "The Insurance Is Cancelled," season 2, episode 10, *All in the Family* (CBS, November 27, 1971), written by Lee Kalcheim.

69. "Edith Writes a Song," season 2, episode 4, *All in the Family* (CBS, October 9, 1971), written by Lee Kalcheim.

70. Memorandum, August 17, 1971, box S-212, NLP.

71. For more on earlier portrayals of minorities on television, see MacDonald, *Blacks and White TV*.

72. Montgomery, *Target: Prime Time*, 25.

73. "Flashback: Mike Meets Archie," season 2, episode 5, *All in the Family* (CBS, October 16, 1971), written by Philip Mishkin and Rob Reiner.

74. Letter to Lelyveld, April 26, 1972, container 8, folder 138, MS 4639, Lelyveld Papers, Western Reserve Historical Society, Cleveland, OH.

75. Richard K. Shull, "'Archie' Popular with All," *Lockport Union-Sun and Journal*, June 29, 1971, 20.

76. Carroll O'Connor, interview by Johnny Carson, *Tonight Show Starring Johnny Carson*, NBC, October 5, 1972, PC-CA; Arthur Bell, "What Would Archie Bunker Say?," *New York Times*, October 29, 1972, D15.

77. Hano, "Can Archie Bunker."

78. von Hodenberg, *Television's Moment*, 265.

79. 90 Cong. Rec. 21505 (1968).

80. For the definitive account of the Television Code, see Jaramillo, *Television Code*.

81. National Association of Broadcasters, *Television Code*.

82. For more on the WLBT case and the United Church of Christ challenge, see Classen, *Watching Jim Crow*.

83. For more on earlier campaigns, see Montgomery, *Target: Prime Time*, 21–26.

84. FCC to Jarzab, September 1971, box S-212, NLP.

85. Stockton Helffrich to Jarzab, October 28, 1971, box S-212, NLP.

86. Polish-American Guardian Society to Stockton Helffrich, November 2, 1971, box S-212, NLP.

87. Stockton Helffrich to Jarzab, November 10, 1971, box S-212, NLP.

88. See, for example, letter, August 13, 1972, box S-212, NLP.

89. Eugene Kusielewicz, letter to the editor, *New York Times*, April 9, 1972, SM20.

90. 92 Cong. Rec. 11185 (1972).

91. *Sex and Violence on TV: Hearings Before the Subcommittee on Communications of the Committee on Interstate and Foreign Commerce of the US House of Representatives*, 94th Cong. 4–5 (1976).

92. McCrohan, *Archie & Edith*, 151.

93. Montgomery, *Target: Prime Time*, 25.

94. "Archie, Lovable or Lamentable?," D36.

95. Joseph Morgenstern, "Can Bigotry Be Funny?," *Newsweek*, November 29, 1971, reprinted in Adler, *"All in the Family,"* 111–14. Most contemporary work about television agreed that its influence was both enormous and impossible to accurately measure. See, for example, MacNeil, *People Machine*, ix; Johnson, *How to Talk Back*, 11–35; and Martin, *About Television*, ix–xii.

96. Lawrence Laurent, "Archie Bunker Has Two Kinds of Viewers," *Washington Post*, December 19, 1971, 5. See also *Look Up and Live*, CBS, September 24, 1972, PC-NY.

97. McCrohan, *Archie & Edith*, 194.

98. Columnist Leonard Lyons suggests they were motivated by fear, while Sally Bedell Smith claims it was hope. Lyons quoted in Sanders, "Is Archie Bunker," 188; Smith, *In All His Glory*, 494.

99. Smith, *In All His Glory*, 494; Bogle, *Primetime Blues*, 187.

100. Christina von Hodenberg rediscovered a total of twenty-two empirical studies on audience response, including the elusive CBS report, in her work on *All in the Family*. See von Hodenberg, *Television's Moment*, 238–39.

101. Rosen to Cohen, March 31, 1971.

102. John Slawson, "How Funny Can Bigotry Be?," *Educational Broadcasting Review*, April 1972, reprinted in Adler, *"All in the Family,"* 114–20.

103. Vidmar and Rokeach, "Archie Bunker's Bigotry." The paper is also reprinted in Adler, *"All in the Family,"* 123–38.

104. It remains the most cited study on *All in the Family* and is often the only social science study referenced in work on the show. To this day, it dominates—and distorts—understandings of *All in the Family*.

105. Staiger, *Blockbuster TV*, 109.

106. von Hodenberg, *Television's Moment*, 238–41.

107. Research suggests that conservatives are less inclined to appreciate satire than liberals. For more, see Dannagal Goldthwaite Young, *Irony and Outrage*.

108. Rich, *Warm Up the Snake*, 117.

109. "TV: Speaking about the Unspeakable," *Newsweek*, November 29, 1971, 53.

110. Vernon Scott, "The Real 'Rhoda' and 'Archie' Stand Up," *Washington Post*, December 24, 1972, TC10.

111. Rich, *Warm Up the Snake*, 117.

112. Norman Lear, *Even This*, 245. Lear made the same argument five decades earlier when talking about *All in the Family* on public affairs television. See *Look Up and Live*, CBS, September 24, 1972, PC-NY.

113. McCrohan, *Archie & Edith*, 187.

114. The sermon is reprinted in full in 93 Cong. Rec. 13451–53 (1973).

115. Letter, June 12, 1972, box S-212, NLP.

116. Letters, February 17, March 1, April 8, 1971, box S-212, NLP.

117. See, for example, John Clare, "All Kinds of Reactions to *All in the Family*," *Catholic Transcript*, March 5, 1971, 14; Robert E. Segal, "'Archie' Reveals Built-in Prejudices," *Jewish Advocate*, May 27, 1971, A2; and "Good Is Evil," *American Baptist*, July-August 1971, 30.

118. Letters, August 10, 1971, August 7, 1973, box S-212, NLP. See also Dan Lewis, "*Family* Popular with All," *Lockport Union-Sun and Journal*, August 18, 1971, 24.

119. Letters, June 12, 1972, November 2, 1971, box S-212, NLP.

120. Letter from Tandem Productions, December 11, 1973, box S-212, NLP.

121. Letter to Lelyveld, April 28, 1972, container 8, folder 138, MS 4639, Lelyveld Papers, Western Reserve Historical Society, Cleveland, OH.

122. Brown, *Keeping Your Eye*, 1.

123. Norman Lear, "As I Read," 106–11.

124. 95 Cong. Rec. 29973 (1978).

125. Norman Lear, interview by Barbara Cady, *Playboy*, March 1976, 62.

126. The quote is Lear's from *Look Up and Live*, CBS, September 24, 1972, PC-NY.

127. Letter, April 8, 1971, box S-212, NLP.

128. *Look Up and Live*, CBS, September 24, 1972, PC-NY.

129. Marian Rees, interview by Karen Herman, September 3 and November 5, 2004, AAT.

Chapter 3

1. Alley and Brown, *Women Television Producers*, 80–81.

2. Jean Murphy, "NOW President Tells Her Goals for Feminists," *Los Angeles Times*, March 27, 1972, F1.

3. Virginia Carter, interview by the author, February 16, 2016. In a telling quote, one of the men who found success in the booming 1950s noted, "If you had a college diploma, a dark suit, and anything between your ears, it was like an escalator; you just stood there and you moved up." Diggins, *Proud Decades*, 219.

4. Elaine Markoutsas, "A Physicist Reaches the Stars—via TV," *Chicago Tribune*, April 16, 1978, D5.

5. Carter interview.

6. Norman Lear, interview by the author, December 13, 2017.

7. "Advancing the Story: The Next Chapter in Media Impact," panel discussion, November 2, 2016, PC-NY, www.paleycenter.org/events/2016-advancing-the-story-2.

8. For a short overview of the influence of television in the network era, see Lotz, *Television Will Be Revolutionized*, 31–35.

9. Unnamed studio executive quoted in Brown, *Televi$ion*, 218.

10. For the origins of the Television Code as a way for the National Association of Broadcasters to protect the interests of the networks and broadcasters, see Jaramillo, *Television Code*.

11. Sheldon Leonard, interview by Sam Denoff, July 11, 1996, AAT.

12. James L. Brooks, interview by Karen Herman, January 17 and February 12, 2003, AAT; Allan Burns, interview by Dan Pasternack, February 18, 2004, AAT.

13. Brown, *Televi$ion*, 60–61, 293–96.

14. MacDonald, *Blacks and White TV*, 89–90.

15. Austin Kalish and Irma Kalish, interview by Amy Harrington, December 21, 2012, AAT.

16. During the blacklist of the 1950s, both progressive talent, including an inordinate number of women, and progressive values, including on race and gender, were removed from the air. The shadow of the lost careers and abandoned stories lingered throughout the network era. See Stabile, *Broadcast 41*.

17. Brown, *Keeping Your Eye*, 83.

18. See "Judging Books by Covers," season 1, episode 5, *All in the Family* (CBS, February 9, 1971), written by Burt Styler and Norman Lear; "Mike's Hippie Friends Come to Visit," season 1, episode 7, *All in the Family* (CBS, February 23, 1971), story by Philip Mishkin and Rob Reiner, teleplay by Philip Mishkin, Rob Reiner, Don Nicholl, and Bryan Joseph; "Lionel Moves into the Neighborhood," season 1, episode 8, *All in the Family* (CBS, March 2, 1971), written by Don Nicholl and Bryan Joseph; "Gloria Discovers Women's Lib," season 1, episode 11, *All in the Family* (CBS, March 23, 1971), written by Norman Lear and Sandy Stern; and "The First and Last Supper," season 1, episode 13, *All in the Family* (CBS, April 6, 1971), written by Jerry Mayer.19. For a short oral history on the tension between *All in the Family* and the program practices department at CBS, see Neuwirth, *They'll Never Put That*, 123–55.

20. The best, though not without flaws, study of *Maude* and the controversy surrounding the show can be found in Montgomery, *Target: Prime Time*, 27–50.

21. "Cousin Maude's Visit," season 2, episode 12, *All in the Family* (CBS, December 11, 1971), teleplay by Philip Mishkin, Michael Ross, and Bernie West, story by Philip Mishkin.

22. Fred Silverman, interview by Dan Pasternack, March 16, 29, 2001, AAT. See also Norman Lear, *Even This*, 259–60.

23. "The Team behind Archie Bunker and Co.," *Time*, September 25, 1972, 50.

24. Dow, *Prime-Time Feminism*, 61. See also Norman Lear, *Even This*, 264.

25. "Maude's Dilemma: Part 1," season 1, episode 9, *Maude* (CBS, November 14, 1972), teleplay by Susan Harris, story by Austin Kalish and Irma Kalish; "Maude's Dilemma: Part 2," season 1, episode 10, *Maude* (CBS, November 21, 1972), teleplay by Susan Harris, story by Austin Kalish and Irma Kalish, story editors Bob Schiller, Bob Weiskopf, and Alan J. Levitt.

26. For more on abortion rights in New York state, see Taranto, *Kitchen Table Politics*, 78.

27. For Poindexter's own account of his campaigns to change television, see Poindexter, *Out of the Darkness*, 31–45.

28. "In Memoriam: David Poindexter," Population Media Center, February 10, 2018, www.populationmedia.org/the-latest/in-memoriam-david-poindexter.

29. While politically liberal, Poindexter was strongly influenced by Paul Ehrlich, the biologist, author of *The Population Bomb*, and prominent voice on population control. Despite alliances with liberal or progressive groups on specific issues such as birth control and women's health, population control movements also included racist and reactionary coalitions and rhetoric on immigration and race. For more context on population control movements, see Connelly, *Fatal Misconception*; and Hoff, *State and the Stork*. For more on Ehrlich, see Sabin, *Bet*. On the racist and anti-immigration activists coming out of the population control movement, see Goodman, "Unmaking the Nation"; and Goodman, *Dreamland*.

30. David Poindexter, speech at Everett M. Rogers Colloquium, October 2, 2008, given at Norman Lear Center, USC Annenberg School of Communications, Los Angeles, CA, online at www.youtube.com/watch?v=QpkBDUQ68Qg&ab_channel=USCAnnenberg (accessed April 16, 2025).

31. Kathryn Montgomery mistakenly claims that Norman Lear attended the luncheon. Both Poindexter's memoirs and his correspondence with Lear contradict the claim. Montgomery, *Target: Prime Time*, 30; Poindexter, *Out of the Darkness*, 45.

32. John D. Rockefeller III was the oldest of the Rockefeller brothers; his younger brothers were Nelson (governor of New York), David (chairman of Chase Manhattan), Laurence (a prominent conservationist), and Winthrop (governor of Arkansas). All of the brothers were prominent members of high society in New York. Both William Paley, chairman of CBS, and David Sarnoff, chairman of NBC's parent company RCA, were close friends with the brothers. Smith, *In All His Glory*, 202, 322; Lyons, *David Sarnoff*, 171.

33. Packwood's career unraveled in the 1990s following substantial evidence of a pattern of sexual harassment, sexual abuse, and sexual violence.

34. Poindexter to Harry Ackerman, November 16, 1970, folder 55, box 5, ML-81, Ackerman Papers, Rauner Library Archives and Manuscripts, Dartmouth College, Hanover, NH.

35. Montgomery, *Target: Prime Time*, 30.

36. Poindexter, speech at Everett M. Rogers Colloquium.

37. Ackerman to Poindexter, February 26, 1971, folder 55, box 5, ML-81, Ackerman Papers, Rauner Library Archives and Manuscripts, Dartmouth College, Hanover, NH. In his address years later, Poindexter recalled the line as "There is very little that any writer or producer in Hollywood can accomplish on your subject until you can achieve a climate of support and approval at the networks," but the archival record makes clear that quote is not verbatim. See Poindexter, speech at Everett M. Rogers Colloquium.

38. Montgomery, *Target: Prime Time*, 30.

39. Montgomery, *Target: Prime Time*, 30–31.

40. Poindexter, speech at Everett M. Rogers Colloquium.

41. Poindexter to Lear, November 3, 1971, box S-212, NLP.

42. Montgomery, *Target: Prime Time*, 30–31.

43. Manon Perry, *Broadcasting Birth Control*.

44. Aljean Harmetz, "Maude Didn't Leave 'Em All Laughing," *New York Times*, December 10, 1972, D3.

45. Kalish and Kalish interview.

46. Harmetz, "Maude Didn't Leave 'Em."

47. Bob Schiller and Bob Weiskopf, interview by Karen Herman, April 4, 2000, AAT.

48. Harmetz, "Maude Didn't Leave 'Em"; Cecil Smith, "Maude's Abortion Evokes Protests," *Los Angeles Times*, November 29, 1972, D25.

49. WCIA-TV in Champaign and WMBD-TV in Peoria, both in Illinois, held to their decision, while WJBK in Detroit reconsidered. Harmetz, "Maude Didn't Leave 'Em."

50. "NOW Suit over Maude Abortion Show Denied," *Los Angeles Times*, November 25, 1972, A3; Montgomery, *Target: Prime Time*, 36–37.

51. For insightful studies of antiabortion grassroots activist mobilization before and after *Roe v. Wade*, see Taranto, *Kitchen Table Politics*; Gillian Frank, "Colour of the Unborn"; and Holland, *Tiny You*.

52. "Without the Catholic Church, there would have been no pro-life movement," historian Neil Young remarks. Neil J. Young, *We Gather Together*, 118.

53. Norman Lear, *Even This*, 265.

54. Poindexter to Lear, July 31, 1973, box S-212, NLP. See also Montgomery, *Target: Prime Time*, 43; and Staggenborg, *Pro-Choice Movement*, 71.

55. Lee Gidding to NARAL directors and organization supporters, January 1973, carton 7 "Maude Correspondence," MC 313, NARAL Records, SL.

56. Lawrence Lader, memorandum, August 17, 1973, carton 7 "Maude Correspondence," MC 313, NARAL Records, SL.

57. Albin Krebs, "25 C.B.S. Affiliates Won't Show *Maude* Episodes on Abortion," *New York Times*, August 14, 1973, 67.

58. Poindexter describes a second meeting with Stanton ahead of the reruns asking him to honor his promise. Poindexter, *Out of the Darkness*, 44.

59. Fred Silverman, the head of programming at CBS in the early 1970s, claims *Maude* was "Paley's favorite show." Silverman interview.

60. Carter interview.

61. Carter interview.

62. Patricia de Luna, "Rides Tandem to the Top," *Long Beach Independent*, February 14, 1979, B8.

63. Tia Gindick, "Feminist Flees Physics Role for TV Comedies," *Los Angeles Times*, September 5, 1974, CS1.

64. For a detailed account of the production process on *All in the Family*, see James E. Lynch, "Seven Days with *All in the Family*: Case Study of the Taped TV Drama," *Journal of Broadcasting*, Summer 1973, reprinted in Adler, *"All in the Family,"* 217–30.

65. See the Television Academy Foundation's interviews with writers and directors on the show, for example, Tolkin, interview by Bob Claster, November 4, 1997; Mort Lachman, interview by Jeff Abraham, January 26, 2004; Schiller and Weiskopf interview; Ben Starr, interview by Don Harrison, November 9, 2009; Stanley Ralph Ross, interview by Dan Pasternack, February 11, 1998; Bill Dana, interview by Jeff Abraham, February 10, 2007; John Rich, interview by Henry Colman, August 3, 1999; Paul Bogart, interview by Michael Rosen, May 19, 2001; and H. Wesley Kenney, interview by Gary Rutkowski, April 30, 2008, all in AAT. See also Bill Davidson, "Trouble in Paradise," *TV Guide*, April 6, 1974, 5.

66. Don Shirley, "'Archie and the Kiss': One Episode with the Bunkers," *Washington Post*, September 30, 1973, K2.

67. "Team behind Archie Bunker," 50.

68. Rob Reiner, interview by Karen Herman, November 29, 2004, AAT. Decrying *All in the Family* as "the worst type of program," television legend Red Skelton went even further: "It's out and out Communism from start to finish." Nesteroff, *Outrageous*, 99.

69. At times she also convinced Lear to change his mind on pitches he initially had rejected and would then find her office "filled with flowers" from the writers. Clark, *Producing Feminism*, 107–8.

70. Geoffrey Wolff, "Shortcuts to the Heart," *Esquire*, August 1981.

71. Norman Lear, *Even This*, 262.

72. Larry Rhine, interview by Gary Rutkowski, February 24, 2000, AAT; Rob Reiner interview; Kalish and Kalish interview.

73. Tom Shales, "Tonight: Edith Bunker's Ordeal," *Washington Post*, October 16, 1977, G1–G2.

74. "Conversation With: Norman Lear," live discussion moderated by Steve Levitan at LA 2014, December 15, 2014, Producers Guild of America, www.youtube.com/watch?v=RyuGSGGufzQ&ab_channel=ProducersGuildofAmerica.

75. Barbara Isenberg, "Sex Education via Entertainment," *Los Angeles Times*, January 24, 1980, F1.

76. "Gloria's False Alarm," season 7, episode 14, *All in the Family* (CBS, December 18, 1976), written by Phil Doran and Douglas Arango, story editors Lou Derman and Bill Davenport.

77. Marina Dundjerski, "Her Life's Work: Changing Society's Views of Rape and How Its Victims Are Treated," *UCLA Newsroom*, August 19, 2015, https://newsroom.ucla.edu/stories/her-life-s-work:-changing-society-s-views-of-rape-and-how-its-victims-are-treated.

78. See Virginia Carter's correspondence with Newt Deiter, box 39, folder 5, Kanter Papers, Wisconsin Historical Society Archives, Wisconsin Center for Film and Theater Research, University of Wisconsin, Madison.

79. Isenberg, "Sex Education via Entertainment."

80. Story conference transcript, June 3, 1977, in *All in the Family* mss., Lilly Library Manuscript Collections, Indiana University Libraries, Bloomington. See also staff meeting transcript, June 6, 1977, ser. 2 "Development Materials, 1966–1978," box 7, Tolkin Papers, Writers Guild Foundation Archive, Los Angeles, CA.

81. Story conference transcript, June 9, 1977, in *All in the Family* mss., Lilly Library Manuscript Collections, Indiana University Libraries, Bloomington.

82. Staff meeting transcript, August 11, 1977, in *All in the Family* mss., Lilly Library Manuscript Collections, Indiana University Libraries, Bloomington.

83. "Edith's 50th Birthday: Part 1," season 8, episode 4, *All in the Family* (CBS, October 16, 1977), written by Bob Weiskopf and Bob Schiller.

84. Montgomery, *Target: Prime Time*, 72–73.

85. Carter interview.

86. Harry F. Waters, "TV: Do Minorities Rule?," *Newsweek*, June 2, 1975, 79.

87. Bill O'Hallaren, "Nobody (in TV) Loves You When You're Old and Gray," *New York Times*, July 24, 1977, D21.

88. For more on the women's movement's distrust of television and on the media campaigns of NOW, see Perlman, *Public Interests*, 65–93. See also Bradley, *Mass Media*; and Dow, *Watching Women's Liberation*.

89. The historiography on the women's movement tends to portray *All in the Family* as reinforcing traditional gender roles rather than contesting them. See, for example, Rosen, *World Split Open*, 320–21.

90. Arthur Bell, "What Would Archie Bunker Say?," *New York Times*, October 29, 1972, D15.

91. Lear to viewer, February 11, 1972, box S-212, NLP.

92. "Advancing the Story." Neither Lear nor Tandem were, however, always viewed as feminist. "Working with Norman," writer Ann Marcus recalled, "was very difficult because at first he was very chauvinistic." Another woman working at Tandem, producer Fern

Field, remembered telling Lear, "You're very comfortable with women, but not all the executives here are." Gregory, *Women Who Run*, 30–32.

93. "Mike and Gloria Mix It Up," season 4, episode 16, *All in the Family* (CBS, January 5, 1974), written by Michael Ross and Bernie West.

94. Carter to friend, December 14, 1973, box S-212, NLP.

95. Friend to Carter, December 28, 1973, box S-212, NLP.

96. Tandem memoranda, n.d., box S-212, NLP.

97. Gindick, "Feminist Flees Physics Role"; Alley and Brown, *Women Television Producers*, 81.

98. Dick Adler, "Just One Big Happy Family," *Los Angeles Times*, January 23, 1975, G1.

99. "Gloria the Victim," season 3, episode 23, *All in the Family* (CBS, March 17, 1973), written by Austin Kalish, Irma Kalish, and Don Nicholl, story editors Michael Ross and Bernie West.

100. Women's Coalition on Rape Prevention to Carroll O'Connor, March 25, 1973, box S-212, NLP.

101. Carter to Women's Coalition on Rape Prevention, June 11, 1973, box S-212, NLP.

102. Carter to Women's Coalition on Rape Prevention, August 7, 1973, box S-212, NLP.

103. To be sure, it was not the first time a television show was used in law enforcement and judicial training. Years earlier, the 1950s police procedural *Dragnet* (NBC, 1951–59), the product of close collaboration between producers and the Los Angeles Police Department, was used by various law enforcement agencies across the country. See Calhoun, *Only the Names*, 86.

104. Criminal Justice Training and Education Center to Carter, November 5, 1974, box S-212, NLP.

105. McCrohan, *Archie & Edith*, 75.

106. Robert McLean, "Edith Raises Rape Issue," *Boston Globe*, October 12, 1977, 35.

107. Monica Corcoran Harel, "Taking Back the Night," *Los Angeles Magazine*, November 27, 2013, www.lamag.com/longform/taking-back-the-night/3.

108. The quote is often, mistakenly, attributed to Samuel Goldwyn, the legendary studio mogul in early Hollywood. Berg, *Goldwyn*, 219.

109. Newcomb and Alley, *Producer's Medium*, 177. See also *Look Up and Live*, CBS, September 24, 1972, PC-NY.

110. Norman Lear, *Even This*, 266.

111. Martin Kasindorf, "A TV Dynasty: Archie and Maude and Fred and Norman and Alan," *New York Times Magazine*, June 24, 1973, 19.

112. "TV Sales for New Season Go through the Roof," *Broadcasting*, July 16, 1973, 17.

113. "The Weight Lear Swings at CBS," *Broadcasting*, August 6, 1973, 18.

114. Carl Reiner, interview by Morrie Gelman, March 23, 1998, AAT.

115. Montgomery, *Target: Prime Time*, 31.

116. For an insightful conversation on television as a producer's medium, see Newcomb and Alley, *Producer's Medium*, 3–45.

117. John Brady, "Keeping Archie Engaging and Enraging," *New York Times*, February 24, 1974, 15.

118. See, for example, Lachman interview; Schiller and Weiskopf interview; and Kalish and Kalish interview. See also staff writer Mel Tolkin's unpublished memoir "Where Did

I Go Right: My Days from the Czar to the Kings of Comedy," chap. 27, ser. 3, subseries C, box 6, Tolkin Papers, Writers Guild Foundation Archive, Los Angeles, CA.

119. Brady, "Keeping Archie Engaging," 15.

120. Gene Reynolds, interview by Henry Colman, August 22, 2000, AAT; Larry Gelbart, interview by Dan Harrison, May 26, 1998, AAT.

121. Feuer, "MTM Enterprises," 7.

122. Komack quoted in Adler, *"All in the Family,"* 266. Not everyone rejoiced in Lear opening the doors. "The citizen's groups are getting to be like Frankenstein's monster," David Gerber, producer of *Police Woman* (NBC, 1974–78), lamented in the press. Waters, "Do Minorities Rule?," 78.

123. For alcoholism, see, for example, "The Consultant," season 3, episode 17, *M*A*S*H* (CBS, January 21, 1975), teleplay by Robert Klane, story by Larry Gelbart; and "Walter's Problem: Part 1," season 2, episode 1, *Maude* (CBS, September 11, 1973), written by Bob Weiskopf and Bob Schiller. For homosexuality, see, for example, "My Brother's Keeper," season 3, episode 17, *Mary Tyler Moore Show* (CBS, January 13, 1973), written by Dick Clair and Jenna McMahon; "George," season 2, episode 22, *M*A*S*H* (CBS, February 16, 1974), written by John W. Regier and Gary Markowitz; and "Experience," season 1, episode 2, *Barney Miller* (ABC, January 30, 1975), written by Steve Gordon. For equal pay, see "The Good-Time News," season 3, episode 1, *Mary Tyler Moore Show* (CBS, September 16, 1972), written by Allan Burns and James L. Brooks.

124. See, for example, Liz Roberts, memorandum, April 28, 1975, folder 403, box 31, Dunlop Papers, Rockefeller Papers, Rockefeller Archive Center, Sleepy Hollow, NY. See also reports of Senator William Hathaway's 1976 meeting with television producers regarding battling alcohol abuse, which both Bud Yorkin and a representative of Norman Lear's attended in "Can TV Do Something about Alcoholism?," *Broadcasting*, June 7, 1976, 39.

125. See, for example, Gray Panthers Records, documents, ser. 1, subseries 1.12, box 146, and subseries 1.4, box 80, Gray Panther Records, Special Collections Research Center, Temple University Libraries, Temple University, Philadelphia, PA; and correspondence in box 31, ser. 5 and 5.4.2.5., Dunlop Papers, Rockefeller Papers, Rockefeller Archive Center, Sleepy Hollow, NY.

126. See, for example, "Population Group Presents TV Awards," *Los Angeles Times*, May 12, 1975, E16.

127. "It Takes Two for Tandem: Bud Yorkin, Norman Lear," *Broadcasting*, July 3, 1972, 51.

128. Waters, "Do Minorities Rule?"

129. "Team behind Archie Bunker," 50.

130. Kasindorf, "TV Dynasty."

131. "King Lear," *Time*, April 5, 1976; Richard Levine, "Norman Lear—Daring the Sitcom Audience," *New York Times*, May 18, 1975, D1.

132. Brown, *Televi$ion*, 179–81.

133. For a look at the power of the networks in relation to the regulatory system and politics, see Brownell, *24/7 Politics*, 15–41.

134. Brownell, *24/7 Politics*, 109–10. That is not to say that the networks did not make money on the news department, even if they often claimed news was a money-losing

commitment to public service, in the network era. For more on the news department and network profits, see Socolow, "Commercial Television's Secret Goldmine."

135. Robert Wood to Norman Lear, December 9, 1975, ser. 1, box 91, folder "CBS: Executives," Crutchfield Papers, Southern Historical Collection, Wilson Library, University of North Carolina, Chapel Hill. See also Schneider and Pullen, *Gatekeeper*, 39.

136. Waters, "Do Minorities Rule?," 79.

137. Spiro T. Agnew, "Television News Coverage," speech given November 13, 1969, Des Moines, IA, reprinted in Porter, *Assault on the Media*, 255–62.

138. Wood to Lear, December 9, 1975.

139. Tom Shales, "TV Creating Stereotypes?," *Boston Globe*, October 2, 1977, F12.

140. Clark, *Producing Feminism*, 103.

Chapter 4

1. "Nixon Never Watches Himself on Television," *New York Times*, January 24, 1971, 49. See also Colson, *Born Again*, 112; and Ehrlichman, *Witness to Power*, 68.

2. For descriptions of his predecessors as television presidents, see Bodroghkozy, "Media"; Mitchell, *Harry S. Truman*; Allen, *Eisenhower*; Berry, *John F. Kennedy*; Quail, "Propaganda and the Presidency"; and Greenberg, *Republic of Spin*.

3. OVAL 498-5, May 13, 1971, WHT. The White House tapes as source material are not without controversy. Nixon's own advisers have suggested that the tapes consist of private conversations to let off steam and that such private moments should not dominate our understanding of the president. Historian Michael Koncewicz, however, makes a compelling case for historians to rely *more* on the rich source material, calling the tapes "a valuable resource that further informs us on Nixon's worldview." Koncewicz, *They Said No*, 19–22.

4. "Judging Books by Covers," season 1, episode 5, *All in the Family* (CBS, February 9, 1971), written by Burt Styler and Norman Lear.

5. The episode was "Writing the President," season 1, episode 2, *All in the Family* (CBS, January 19, 1971), teleplay by Paul Harrison, Lennie Weinrib, and Norman Lear, story by Lee Erwin and Fred Freiberger.

6. OVAL 498-5, May 13, 1971, WHT. For more on the concept of the hard hats as the embodiment of Nixon's conservative, white, male, working-class supporters, see Cowie, *Stayin' Alive*; Freeman, "Hardhats"; Penny Lewis, *Hardhats, Hippies, and Hawks*; and Kuhn, *Hardhat Riot*.

7. OVAL 498-5, May 13, 1971, WHT.

8. OVAL 498-8, May 13, 1971, WHT.

9. For more on the Republican Party's history with television, see Critchlow, *When Hollywood Was Right*; Brownell, *Showbiz Politics*; Kruse, "'Why Don't You'"; Greenberg, "New Way of Campaigning"; and Greenberg, *Nixon's Shadow*, 1–35.

10. Reeves, *President Nixon*, 12. See also Drew, *Richard M. Nixon*, 1; and Wicker, *One of Us*, 24–25.

11. The description of the two White House advisers as a Berlin Wall stuck in public memory to the degree that it appears in their obituaries some two decades after Nixon resigned in disgrace. See, for example, J. Y. Smith, "H. R. Haldeman Dies," *Washington*

Post, November 13, 1993, A12; and David Stout, "John D. Ehrlichman, Nixon Aide Jailed for Watergate, Dies at 73," *New York Times*, February 16, 1999, A1.

12. Critchlow, *When Hollywood Was Right*, 109–33.
13. Farrell, *Richard Nixon*, 190–91.
14. Quoted in Farrell, *Richard Nixon*, 208.
15. Farrell, *Richard Nixon*, 283–86.
16. Nixon, *Six Crises*, 293–426.
17. Brownell, *Showbiz Politics*, 201–2.
18. Hess, *Bit Player*, 66; Maxine Cheshire, "No Time to Quit," *Washington Post*, March 18, 1969, B1.
19. Nixon to H. R. Haldeman, memorandum, July 25, 1962, folder 35, box 62, WHSF.
20. Keyes to H. R. Haldeman, memorandum, October 13, 1962, folder 1, box 63, WHSF.
21. Keyes to Nixon, memorandum, August 27, 1962, folder 2, box 63, WHSF; and Keyes to Haldeman, October 13, 1962.
22. The campaign recognized that such a move would hurt the campaign if it was leaked to the press, so it sent a memorandum to Keyes rejecting the suggestion in strong terms. Mary Rose Woods to Keyes, memorandum, August 6, 1962, folder 3, box 63, WHSF. Keyes himself, however, scribbled a note on his personal copy of the memo saying it was a fake memo written only for the purpose of defending the campaign against any charges of planting questions. Keyes's papers were sold at auction in 2011 and are not available to researchers, but a photo of the memo in question is available online at "Sale 2444—Lot 259," Swann Auction Galleries, accessed December 1, 2024, https://catalogue.swanngalleries.com/Lots/auction-lot/(PRESIDENTS—1968)-Papers-of-Nixon-publicist-and-speechwrite?saleno=2444&lotNo=259&refNo=728685.
23. Witcover, *Resurrection of Richard Nixon*, 40.
24. Brownell, *Showbiz Politics*, 197–98.
25. Jeffrey Frank, *Ike and Dick*, 242–43.
26. Jeffrey Frank, *Ike and Dick*, 243.
27. *Jack Paar Program*, NBC, March 8, 1963. The joke was apparently a reference to President Harry S. Truman, who was a talented pianist.
28. McLuhan, *Understanding Media*, 309.
29. Quoted in Brownell, *Showbiz Politics*, 198.
30. *Tonight Show Starring Johnny Carson*, NBC, November 22, 1967, www.youtube.com/watch?v=BsxFyCVlSXo&ab_channel=JohnnyCarson.
31. Perlstein, *Nixonland*, 86.
32. *Tonight Show Starring Johnny Carson*, November 22, 1967.
33. For a firsthand account of the guest turn, see McMahon and Fisher, *When Television Was Young*, 212.
34. Witcover, *Resurrection of Richard Nixon*, 374.
35. Ailes quoted in McGinniss, *Selling of the President*, 149.
36. For Gleason's remarks, see McGinniss, *Selling of the President*, 151. Keyes had suggested the general outline of the remarks as early as 1962, during the California race. Keyes to Haldeman, October 13, 1962.
37. The colorful description is by one of the writers on the show, quoted in Miller, "What Closes," 199.

38. Brownell, *Showbiz Politics*, 188–89.
39. George Schlatter, interview by Dan Pasternack, March 6, 2002, AAT.
40. Neuwirth, *They'll Never Put That*, 74.
41. Elizabeth Kolbert, "Stooping to Conquer," *New Yorker*, April 19, 2004; Neuwirth, *They'll Never Put That*, 75–76.
42. Judy Bachrach, "From One Schtick to Another," *Washington Post*, August 7, 1974, E1.
43. Neuwirth, *They'll Never Put That*, 76.
44. For contemporary accounts of the election, see Theodore H. White, *Making of the President, 1968*; Chester et al., *American Melodrama*; and Witcover, *Resurrection of Richard Nixon*. For later scholarly accounts, see Gould, *1968*; Michael A. Cohen, *American Maelstrom*; Nelson, *Resilient America*; Schumacher, *Contest*; Goudsouzian, *Men and the Moment*; and O'Mara, *Pivotal Tuesdays*.
45. Rowland Evans and Robert Novak, "The Archie Bunker Vote," *Washington Post*, March 17, 1972, A27. See also *CBS Evening News*, CBS, April 4, 1972, Vanderbilt Television News Archive, Jean and Alexander Heard Libraries, Vanderbilt University, Nashville, TN.
46. William S. White, Associated Press, "The 'Bunker Vote,'" 92 Cong. Rec. 11230.
47. OVAL 655-003, January 25, 1972, White House Tapes, Nixon Library.
48. OVAL 655-003, January 25, 1972, WHT.
49. Nixon quoted in Ambrose, *Nixon*, 150.
50. EOB 301-007, November 3, 1971, WHT.
51. EOB 301-007, November 3, 1971, WHT.
52. EOB 301-007, November 3, 1971, WHT.
53. See, for example, OVAL 518-008, June 12, 1971; and EOB 301-007, November 3, 1971, both in WHT.
54. OVAL 662-004, February 1, 1972, WHT.
55. OVAL 662-004, February 1, 1972, WHT. Parts of the conversation are transcribed in Brinkley and Nichter, *Nixon Tapes*, 359–60.
56. OVAL 662-004, February 1, 1972, WHT.
57. For examples of Nixon's antisemitic views and remarks, see Small, *Presidency of Richard Nixon*, 182–83; and Farrell, *Richard Nixon*, 426. For the long roots of antisemitism and Hollywood, see Carr, *Hollywood & Anti-Semitism*.
58. Quoted in Small, *Presidency of Richard Nixon*, 227.
59. Frank Mankiewicz and Tom Braden, "Agnew Unintentionally Triggers Renewed Round of Anti-Semitism," *Washington Post*, December 30, 1969, A15.
60. Brown, *Televi$ion*, 214–16.
61. "Mike's Problem," season 2, episode 9, *All in the Family* (CBS, November 20, 1971), story and teleplay by Austin Kalish and Irma Kalish, teleplay by Michael Ross and Bernie West.
62. Thomas W. Downer Jr. to Norman Lear, memorandum, September 16, 1971, box S-212, NLP.
63. Lear to Thomas W. Downer Jr., memorandum, September 17, 1971, box S-212, NLP.
64. CBS Program Practices memorandum, September 17, 1971; and W. H. Tankersley to Lear, memorandum, September 28, 1971, both in box S-212, NLP.
65. Lear to Perry Lafferty, memorandum, October 13, 1971, box S-212, NLP.
66. Norman Lear, *Even This*, 255–56.

67. OVAL 655-003, January 25, 1972, WHT.

68. Rich, *Warm Up the Snake*, 117.

69. Henry C. Cashen II to Bruce Kehrli, memorandum, July 9, 1971, in Richard Nixon Presidential Library (website), accessed December 1, 2024, www.nixonlibrary.gov/sites/default/files/virtuallibrary/documents/contested/contested_box_46/Contested-46-23.pdf.

70. Nixon to Rose Mary Woods and H. R. Haldeman, memorandum, January 31, 1970, in Richard Nixon Presidential Library (website), accessed December 1, 2024, www.nixonlibrary.gov/sites/default/files/virtuallibrary/documents/jan10/043.pdf.

71. For more on New Hollywood, see Kirshner, *Hollywood's Last Golden Age*; Biskind, *Easy Riders, Raging Bulls*; and Jon Lewis, *Road Trip to Nowhere*.

72. Charles W. Colson to H. R. Haldeman, memorandum, November 6, 1970, in Richard Nixon Presidential Library (website), accessed December 1, 2024, www.nixonlibrary.gov/sites/default/files/virtuallibrary/documents/contested/contested_box_06/Contested-06-64.pdf.

73. Nixon aide Ray Caldiero quoted in Brownell, *Showbiz Politics*, 218–19.

74. Bruck, *When Hollywood*, 289; McDougal, *Last Mogul*, 344; Brownstein, *Power and the Glitter*, 187.

75. McDougal, *Last Mogul*, 331–33; Cannon, *Reagan*, 92–93, 121.

76. Bruck, *When Hollywood*, 268–69.

77. Bruck, *When Hollywood*, 308–10. Still, Nixon sometimes turned to remarks tinged with antisemitism tropes when frustrated by Schreiber. See Bruck, *When Hollywood*, 292–93.

78. Jon A. Foust to John N. Mitchell, memorandum, May 5, 1972, in Richard Nixon Presidential Library (website), accessed December 1, 2024, www.nixonlibrary.gov/sites/default/files/virtuallibrary/documents/contested/contested_box_31/Contested-31-01.pdf.

79. Brownell, *Showbiz Politics*, 212.

80. Bruck, *When Hollywood*, 270–74.

81. "Party Favor," *Broadcasting*, September 18, 1972, 5.

82. The letter, dated September 12, 1972, was reprinted in "The President Takes Sides against Network Reruns," *Broadcasting*, September 18, 1972, 13.

83. "How Lone Crusade by Unknown Editor Led to Rerun Fuss," *Broadcasting*, September 25, 1972, 39.

84. See, for example, OVAL 771-005, September 6, 1972; and OVAL 780-015, September 16, 1972, both in WHT.

85. "Party Favor," 5.

86. Foust to Mitchell, May 5, 1972.

87. Magruder, *American Life*, 258–59. While the evening described in Magruder was billed as including Kissinger, he bowed out due to his dislike of Martha Mitchell and was replaced by the First Lady. See White, *Breach of Faith*, 208.

88. Magruder, *American Life*, 258.

89. Bruck, *When Hollywood*.

90. Brownell, *Showbiz Politics*, 207–18.

91. For more on Nixon's relationship with Davis, see Haygood, *In Black and White*, 422–34.

92. For more on Nixon's relationship with Sinatra, see Summers and Swan, *Sinatra*, 350–54. See also Charles W. Colson to H. R. Haldeman, memorandum, February 1, 1971, in Oudes, *From the President*, 211.

93. CD 213-031, September 24, 1972, WHT.

94. Dwight Chapin to H. R. Haldeman, memorandum, June 12, 1972, folder 9, box 16, Contested Materials Collection, Richard Nixon Presidential Library and Museum, National Archives, Yorba Linda, CA.

95. Irving Wallace, "Archie's Vote to Astonish Millions," *Corpus Christi Times*, November 1, 1972, 7F.

96. Wallace, "Archie's Vote."

97. Peter H. Dailey to Dwight Chapin, memorandum, June 20, 1972, in Richard Nixon Presidential Library (website), accessed December 1, 2024, www.nixonlibrary.gov/sites/default/files/virtuallibrary/documents/contested/contested_box_46/Contested-46-23.pdf.

98. Gordon Strachan to H. R. Haldeman, memorandum, July 21, 1972, in Richard Nixon Presidential Library (website), accessed December 1, 2024, www.nixonlibrary.gov/sites/default/files/virtuallibrary/documents/contested/contested_box_14/Contested-14-08.pdf.

99. Haldeman, *Haldeman Diaries*, 505.

100. Klein, *Making It Perfectly Clear*, 278–79.

101. Price, *With Nixon*, 30. See also Klein, *Making It Perfectly Clear*, 278–79.

102. Len Garment quoted in Farrell, *Richard Nixon*, 421.

103. Magruder, *American Life*, 75; Haldeman and DiMona, *Ends of Power*, 5; Safire, *Before the Fall*, 17.

104. Colson, *Born Again*, 59.

105. Haldeman and DiMona, *Ends of Power*, 5–6; Ehrlichman, *Witness to Power*, 78–79.

106. Crouse, *Boys on the Bus*, 214–42.

107. Witcover, *Resurrection of Richard Nixon*, 379.

108. Rather and Gates, *Palace Guard*, 247; Haldeman and DiMona, *Ends of Power*, 54–55.

109. Ehrlichman, *Witness to Power*, 78.

110. The description of Ziegler is James Naughton's of the *New York Times*. See Wise, *Politics of Lying*, 278.

111. Magruder, *American Life*, 2–3.

112. Spear, *Presidents and the Press*, 44.

113. The memorandum is known as the "Shot-gun vs. Rifle" memo. Jeb Magruder to H. R. Haldeman, memorandum, October 17, 1969, in Porter, *Assault on the Media*, 244–49.

114. Halberstam, *Powers That Be*, 597.

115. The speech was written by Patrick Buchanan but reviewed and edited by Nixon himself. Despite Nixon's later claims to have "toned down" and "moderated" the rhetoric, it seems he did the opposite. In his diary, Haldeman noted that Nixon could not "contain his mirth" when working on the speech. William Safire, speechwriter in the White House, also recalled an excited Nixon "toughening it up." Nixon, *RN*, 411; Haldeman, *Haldeman Diaries*, 107–9; Safire, *Before the Fall*, 352. For more on Agnew's thinking on the speech, see Holden et al., *Republican Populist*, 109–13.

116. Spiro T. Agnew, "Television News Coverage," speech given November 13, 1969, Des Moines, IA, reprinted in Porter, *Assault on the Media*, 255–62.

117. Brinkley, *Cronkite*, 442–43. For statements by the heads of all three networks, see Barrett, *Survey of Broadcast Journalism, 1969–1970*, 139.

118. OVAL 771-5A, September 6, 1972, WHT.

119. Porter, *Assault on the Media*, 158–59.

120. See, for example, OVAL 771-005, September 6, 1972, WHT; Magruder to Haldeman, October 17, 1969; John J. O'Connor, "The TV Antitrust Suits," *New York Times*, April 17, 1972, 67; Eileen Shanahan, "The Nation," *New York Times*, April 16, 1972, E4; and Eileen Shanahan, "Antitrust or Distrust?," *New York Times*, April 18, 1972, 46. An editorial in *Broadcasting* raised concern about political motivations yet noted that it could not, at the time, find evidence to support such a conclusion. "Fumble," *Broadcasting*, April 24, 1972, 66.

121. OVAL 780-15, September 16, 1972, WHT.

122. OVAL 780-15, September 16, 1972, WHT.

123. Brownell, *24/7 Politics*, 98–105.

124. OVAL 848-010, February 5, 1973, WHT.

125. Pat Buchanan to Charles Colson, memorandum, December 6, 1972, folder "CBS 1 of 5," box 44, Colson Subject Files, Richard Nixon Presidential Library and Museum, National Archives, Yorba Linda, CA.

126. White, *Making of the President, 1972*, 255. See also Porter, *Assault on the Media*, 202. Cronkite, Rather, and Schorr were all victims of the various tactics of intimidation favored by the White House, and Schorr was among a select group of only twenty names on the first enemies list compiled by Nixon's men.

127. See Bianculli, *Dangerously Funny*; and Bodroghkozy, *Groove Tube*, 123–63. See also the account of a CBS programming executive in Dann, *As I Saw It*, 131–43. Many of the writers, as well as Tom and Dick Smothers, are interviewed for the oral history collections of the Archive of American Television. See, for example, Tom Smothers and Dick Smothers, interview by Karen Herman, October 14, 2000; Allan Blye, interview by Adrienne Faillace, April 24, 2019; Sam Bobrick, interview by Amy Harrington, December 12, 2016; Ron Clark, interview by Stephen J. Abramson, November 23, 2015; and Carl Gottlieb, interview by Dan Pasternack, October 24, 2018, all in AAT.

128. Bianculli, *Dangerously Funny*, 132–34.

129. Dann, *As I Saw It*, 136.

130. Nixon to John Ehrlichman, memorandum, March 11, 1969, folder "Memos—March 1969," box 1, President's Personal Files, Staff Member and Office Files, WHSF. The memo is reprinted in Stuart, *Never Trust a Local*, 71–72.

131. Nixon to Ehrlichman, March 11, 1969.

132. Nixon to Ehrlichman, March 11, 1969.

133. Greenberg, *Republic of Spin*, 400; Perlstein, *Nixonland*, 363.

134. Jeb S. Magruder to H. R. Haldeman and Herbert Klein, memorandum, July 17, 1970, in Porter, *Assault on the Media*, 270–73.

135. Bianculli, *Dangerously Funny*, 325–26. For more on how Nixon abused the IRS to hurt his enemies, see Koncewicz, *They Said No*.

136. Smothers and Smothers interview.

137. Ozersky, *Archie Bunker's America*, 38–39.

138. Thrift, *Conservative Bias*, 149.

139. Dann, *As I Saw It*, 136–42.

140. Oudes, *From the President*, 356–57.

141. Bruck, *When Hollywood Had*, 309.

142. *Dick Cavett Show*, ABC, June 30, 1971. Some three decades later, when Senator John Kerry became the Democratic Party nominee for president, O'Neill cofounded the activist organization Swift Boat Veterans for Truth, which gained national prominence by tarring Kerry with baseless claims about his service in Vietnam.

143. Colson to Haldeman, memorandum, June 11, 1971, in Richard Nixon Presidential Library (website), accessed December 1, 2024, www.nixonlibrary.gov/sites/default/files/virtuallibrary/documents/jan10/045.pdf.

144. OVAL 518-008, June 12, 1971, WHT.

145. OVAL 521-004, June 15, 1971, WHT.

146. In various books and documentary films, the two separate conversations Nixon had on June 12 and June 15 about Cavett are edited together. See, for example, *Dick Cavett's Watergate*, special, PBS, August 8, 2014; and Nesteroff, *Comedians*, 240–41. In fact, the conversations are three days apart. The conversation from June 15 is transcribed in Cavett, *Talk Show*, 62. A short recording of the conversation is also available online. See "Nixon's Secret Revenge on Dick Cavett," Pioneers of Television, June 29, 2007, YouTube video, 0:25, www.youtube.com/watch?v=PxwXBS8AM6M&list=WL&index=84&ab_channel=PioneersofTelevision.

147. OVAL 520-003, June 15, 1971, WHT.

148. Cavett, *Talk Show*, xvi; "Fairness Creates Strange Alliance," *Broadcasting*, November 15, 1971, 48.

149. Cavett himself mentions his inclusion on the list with pride. However, the archival record does not confirm his inclusion on the actual enemies list. Cavett, *Talk Show*, 176.

150. WHT 011-163, October 20, 1971, WHT.

151. "ABC's Cavett Coup," *Broadcasting*, November 8, 1971, 23.

152. "Archie and the Editorial," season 3, episode 1, *All in the Family* (CBS, September 16, 1972), story and teleplay by George Bloom, teleplay by Don Nicholl.

153. "Archie's Fraud," season 3, episode 2, *All in the Family* (CBS, September 23, 1972), written by Michael Ross and Bernie West.

154. Letter, October 2, 1972, box S-357, NLP.

155. Letter, September 23, 1972, box S-357, NLP.

156. Dorsey Short, "Debunking Bunker," *Ridgewood Times*, September 28, 1972, 1.

157. The equal-time rule stipulated that a broadcaster must provide equal opportunities, at the same price, for political candidates and would not have been relevant to protest the political comedy on *All in the Family*. Neither would the fairness doctrine, often confused with the equal-time rule, provide relief for anybody outraged by the show, because it only required broadcasters to provide balanced coverage of all sides of subjects of public importance, such as a presidential election, in their programming as a whole, not on each individual show. For more on *All in the Family*, FCC regulations, and the Communications Act of 1934, see Bethea, "Fairness Doctrine." See also Pickard, *America's Battle*.

158. Short, "Debunking Bunker," 1.

159. Ken W. Clawson, letter to the editor, *Ridgewood Times*, October 12, 1972, 5.

160. Victor Gold, letter to the editor, *Ridgewood Times*, December 28, 1972, 5.

161. Letters from activists in Agnew's papers attest to his status as *the* standard-bearer on charges of liberal bias in the media. See, for example, letter to Agnew, November 20, 1972, folder 1, box 145, subseries 3.5 "Subject Files: White House Central Files System, 1968–1974," Agnew Papers, Special Collections and University Archives, University of Maryland, College Park.

162. "Mike Comes into Money," season 3, episode 8, *All in the Family* (CBS, November 4, 1972), written by Michael Ross and Bernie West.

163. "Mike Comes into Money."

164. Letter, November 6, 1972, box S-357, NLP.

165. Tandem Productions, fan mail report memorandum, December 2, 1972, box S-212, NLP.

166. Letters, November 4, 5, 6, 1972, box S-357, NLP.

167. Letter, November 4, 1972, box S-357, NLP.

168. Letter, November 5, 1972, box S-357, NLP.

169. Letter, November 6, 1972, box S-357, NLP.

170. Since the emergence of television as a mass medium in the 1950s, journalists and scholars had warned about its persuasive influence. See, for example, Packard, *Hidden Persuaders*; Mayer, *Madison Avenue, USA*; Boorstin, *Image*; McLuhan, *Understanding Media*; MacNeil, *People Machine*; and Mayer, *About Television*. For media activists on the left, the must-read book was Johnson, *How to Talk Back*. On the right, it was Efron, *News Twisters*.

171. Letter, November 5, 1972, box S-357, NLP.

172. Letter, November 6, 1972, box S-357, NLP.

173. Letter, November 5, 1972, box S-357, NLP.

174. Letter, November [n.d.] 1972, box S-357, NLP.

175. Letter, November 5, 1972, box S-357, NLP.

176. Letters, November [n.d.], November [n.d.], November 5, 6, 1972, box S-357, NLP.

177. Letter, November [n.d.] 1972, box S-357, NLP.

178. *CBS Evening News with Walter Cronkite*, CBS, October 27, 1972.

179. Schorr, *Clearing the Air*, 35.

180. For a deeply reported account by a former CBS News correspondent, see Schorr, *Clearing the Air*, 53–58. For accounts by the men who compromised journalistic integrity under political pressure, see Paley, *As It Happened*, 317–27; and Buzenberg and Buzenberg, *Salant*, 100–110. See also Halberstam, *Powers That Be*, 652–63. For later accounts, see Brinkley, *Cronkite*, 474–80; and Greenberg, *Nixon's Shadow*, 160–62.

181. *Tonight Show Starring Johnny Carson*, NBC, November 9, 1972, PC-CA.

182. Klein, *Making It Perfectly Clear*, 173, 207, 212–13.

183. Though popular memory often connects Lear's inclusion on the list to Nixon's dislike of *All in the Family*, it remains unclear why the producer was on it. The list included both entertainers using their celebrity for liberal campaigns, such as Paul Newman or Shirley MacLaine, and big-time Democratic donors, such as Lear's friend Stanley Sheinbaum. While it is probable that Lear was on the list as the producer of *All in the Family*, it is plausible that it was rather because of his campaign donations to Democratic candidates. Lear mentions the list only in passing in his autobiography. Norman Lear, *Even This*, xiv.

184. For examples of such action, see Clay T. Whitehead, speech on communications policy, December 18, 1972, reprinted in Porter, *Assault on the Media*, 300–304. The proposals in the speech were described as "the most dangerous thing to come along in fifty years of broadcasting" by Fred Friendly in Spear, *Presidents and the Press*, 152. For a list of other proposed actions by the Nixon administration, see Schorr, *Clearing the Air*, 57.

185. Halberstam, *Powers That Be*, 656.

186. For an analysis of Colson's tendency to exaggerate his own achievements in regard to the networks, see Porter, *Assault on the Media*, 70–73.

187. While entertainment was critical to the business, the idea that the networks never made any money on news is a myth. See Socolow, "'We Should Make Money.'"

188. The archival record, however, is limited because the corporate papers of CBS are unavailable. Furthermore, censors working for the standards and practices department did not rely on written rules but rather on their own good judgment.

189. Norman Lear, interview by the author, March 18, 2017.

190. Schorr, *Clearing the Air*, 57.

191. Ernie Kreiling, "Network News Presidents Take a Look at Their Producers and Their Critics," *Los Angeles Times*, June 14, 1972.

192. Lawrence Glickman has written about the concept of "elite victimization" in the context of free enterprise advocates portraying themselves as vulnerable or injured and suggests it "shaped the nature of American conservatism." The concept is also useful when exploring conservatives and the media in the last half century. Glickman, *Free Enterprise*, 4.

Chapter 5

1. O'Connor telethon, VTR 6, Dup, October 27, 1972, V4480/R2, ser. 20 "Audiovisual Items," mss. 217, Sheinbaum Collection, Department of Special Collections, Davidson Library, University of California, Santa Barbara.

2. The best account of the history of showbiz politics is Brownell, *Showbiz Politics*. For an engaging history of the politics of entertainers, including liberals such as Charlie Chaplin, Edward G. Robinson, and Warren Beatty, see Ross, *Hollywood Left and Right*. For the definitive study of liberal entertainers and the civil rights movement, see Raymond, *Stars for Freedom*.

3. For more on the McGovern-Fraser Commission, see Hilton, "Path to Polarization." While the commission restructured the party's presidential nomination process, Jaime Sánchez Jr. challenges the understanding of the reform as an insurgency against the establishment and instead presents it as a part of a nationalization of the Democratic Party driven by national party leaders. Sánchez, "Revisiting McGovern-Fraser."

4. Viteritti, "'Times A-Changin','" 17.

5. Kabaservice, *Rule and Ruin*, 147–55.

6. Kabaservice, *Rule and Ruin*, 155.

7. Cannato, *Ungovernable City*, 63–68.

8. In explaining his party move, Lindsay accused the GOP under Nixon of having "stifled dissent and driven progressives from its ranks." Kabaservice, *Rule and Ruin*, 328.

9. Roessner, *Jimmy Carter*, 29.

10. For more on the collapse of the old system in which party leaders picked the nominee at the convention, see Hendershot, *When the News Broke*.

11. Quoted in Cannato, *Ungovernable City*, 516.

12. Theodore H. White, *Making of the President, 1972*, 87–93.

13. For examples of the conservatism Archie represented, see Taranto, *Kitchen Table Politics*; Cowie, *Stayin' Alive*; Self, *All in the Family*; and Phillips-Fein, *Fear City*. For a challenge to the narrative of all white ethnics as a conservative monolith, see Merton, "Rethinking the Politics."

14. Lombardo, *Blue-Collar Conservatism*; Delmont, *Why Busing Failed*; Rieder, *Canarsie*; Formisano, *Boston against Busing*.

15. Holden et al., *Republican Populist*.

16. See, for example, Clayton Fritchey, "Mrs. Dayton, Meet Mr. Bunker," *Washington Post*, April 22, 1972, A15. In a sly sign of contrarianism, Jim Naughton of the *New York Times* traveled on the 1972 campaign trail with a "Dingbat for President" sticker on his typewriter. Crouse, *Boys on the Bus*, 58.

17. William S. White, "The 'Bunker Vote,'" *Washington Post*, March 25, 1972, A19. The column is reprinted in 92 Cong. Rec. 11230.

18. Nussbaum, *I Like to Watch*, 42.

19. William S. White, "'Bunker Vote.'"

20. Cannato, *Ungovernable City*, 67–68.

21. For a longer list of entertainers lining up behind Lindsay, see list of entertainers, folder 476, box 158, pt. 2, ser. 7, Lindsay Papers, Yale University Library, New Haven, CT.

22. Campaign manager quoted in Hirshon, "One More Miracle," 5.

23. Caro, *Power Broker*, 1118.

24. Cannato, *Ungovernable City*, 405.

25. Lindsay, *City*, 41.

26. James M. Perry, *Us & Them*, 53.

27. Racism and Lindsay's strong support for civil rights were key components in his difficulties with white working-class voters. In Brooklyn, the mayor was met by protesters calling for him to "go back to Africa with the niggers." Rieder, *Canarsie*, 24. For more on the white backlash of the 1969 race, see also Lizzi, "'My Heart.'"

28. Hirshon, "One More Miracle."

29. Deveney, *Fun City*, 279.

30. For examples of the correspondence, see Mansfield to O'Connor, September 29, 1970, folder 2, box 181; March 6, 1963, folder 4, box 84; June 28, 1961, folder 4, box 65; February 10, 1956, folder 3, box 16; and Peggy DeMichele to O'Connor, September 30, 1960, folder 1, box 57, all in ser. 15, Mansfield Papers, Mansfield Library, University of Montana, Missoula.

31. Rob Reiner, interview by Karen Herman, November 29, 2004, AAT.

32. Norman Lear, interview by Morrie Gelman, February 26, 1998, AAT. See also O'Connor, *I Think*, 166–68; and Carroll O'Connor, interview by Charles Davis, August 13, 1999, AAT. See also Carroll O'Connor, interview by Dick Cavett, *Dick Cavett Show*, ABC, December 7, 1971, PC-CA.

33. Vernon Scott, "The Real 'Rhoda' and 'Archie' Stand Up," *Washington Post*, December 24, 1972, TC10. In his memoir, O'Connor, surprisingly perhaps, spends very little time on

All in the Family. He makes no mention at all of his campaigning for liberal candidates. O'Connor, *I Think*.

34. "Carroll O'Connor, Tops on TV, Says Lindsay's Tops with Him," press release, March 8, 1972, MS 592, folder 65, box 173, pt. 2, ser. 8, Lindsay Papers, Yale University Library, New Haven, CT.

35. "Carroll O'Connor, Tops on TV."

36. Fundraising was especially important to Lindsay following his break with the Republican Party, as his most important contributors in previous races had been the scions of wealthy Republican families such as the Rockefellers and the Whitneys. Kabaservice, *Rule and Ruin*, 328.

37. John van Gieson, "Dem Candidates Spend More Than $1 Million for TV Spots," *Daytona Beach Morning Journal*, March 13, 1972, 15.

38. John V. Lindsay, "8 Listen," March 6, 1972, Julian P. Kanter Political Commercial Archive, University of Oklahoma, Norman.

39. Advertisement transcripts, MS 592, folder 65, box 173, pt. 2, ser. 8, Lindsay Papers, Yale University Library, New Haven, CT.

40. Martin F. Nolan, "Archie Bunker for Lindsay," *Boston Globe*, March 10, 1972, 14.

41. Don Oberdorfer, "Wisconsin Voters Target of TV Blitz," *Washington Post*, March 31, 1972, A1.

42. Nolan, "Archie Bunker for Lindsay," 14.

43. Thompson, *Fear and Loathing*, 117–18.

44. Theodore H. White, *Making of the President, 1972*, 89–92.

45. James M. Perry, *Us & Them*, 52.

46. Cannato, *Ungovernable City*, 515.

47. Historians have failed to appreciate the importance of Lindsay's media strategies in the 1972 primaries, perhaps blinded by the swift collapse of his campaign. In his biography of Lindsay, Vincent Cannato brushes aside O'Connor's endorsement and the Archie Bunker advertisements. Cannato concludes that "it was unlikely liberals would listen to the political advice of America's favorite bigot, nor would conservatives be fooled into voting for the liberal Lindsay." Echoing Cannato's dismissive attitude, Rick Perlstein remarks of the Archie Bunker ads, "What the point was supposed to be, no one was sure." Both overestimate the ideological commitment of voters while underestimating the popularity—across the ideological divide—of the character and the strong emotional connection television audiences had developed with the Bunkers. Neither acknowledges the fact that following the implosion of the Lindsay run, both Democrats and Republicans remained convinced of the political influence of Archie Bunker. Cannato, *Ungovernable City*, 519; Perlstein, *Nixonland*, 633.

48. Thomas Oliphant, "Alone before the Cameras, McGovern Feels Right at Home," *Boston Globe*, October 31, 1972, 16. The political reporters for *Newsweek* disagreed: "His eyes go flat and lifeless on television. His voice struggles for passion." Historian Ernest R. May was even harsher: "On the screen his tense smile seemed that of a man holding fast to false teeth." Even media adviser Charles Guggenheim acknowledged that "McGovern would not be my first choice of a person to use on television." In any case, McGovern enjoyed being in front of the cameras for telethons. "The Senator enjoyed doing them more than giving rally speeches," Gary Hart noted. *Newsweek* reporters quoted in Dougherty,

Goodbye, Mr. Christian, 245; and May, introduction to *Campaign '72*, 4. Guggenheim quoted in Jamieson, *Packaging the Presidency*, 324. See also Hart, *Right from the Start*, 363.

49. Thompson, *Fear and Loathing*, 273.

50. Anson, *McGovern*, 267.

51. Weil, *Long Shot*, 33.

52. May, introduction to *Campaign '72*, 4; Theodore H. White, *Making of the President, 1972*, 78.

53. Brownstein, *Power and the Glitter*, 205. Mankiewicz, the son of screenwriter Herman J. Mankiewicz and nephew of director Joseph L. Mankiewicz, himself grew up surrounded by the glamour of Hollywood.

54. Brownstein, *Power and the Glitter*, 237.

55. Brownell, *Showbiz Politics*, 190. For an insightful introduction to the studio system in Hollywood, including the move from "Old Hollywood" to the 1970s' "New Hollywood," see Gomery, *Hollywood Studio System*.

56. "Show Biz in Politics," *Newsweek*, September 25, 1972, 38.

57. Brownell, *Showbiz Politics*, 221.

58. Brownstein, *Power and the Glitter*, 243.

59. McGovern press and scheduling memorandum, [n.d.] 1972, folder "Staff: re television & radio, 1972," box 175, Public Policy Papers, McGovern Papers, Special Collections, Princeton University Library, Princeton, NJ.

60. Brownell, *Showbiz Politics*, 221.

61. Part of section 315 of the Communications Act of 1934, the equal-time provision guaranteed candidates for political office the same access to the airwaves. For equal time as a political tool, see Hemmer, *Messengers of the Right*, 65–67, 118–20.

62. Johnson, *How to Talk Back*, 209.

63. See campaign documents in folders "Staff: re media monitoring, 1972" and folder "Staff: re television & radio, 1972," box 175, Public Policy Papers, McGovern Papers, Special Collections, Princeton University Library, Princeton, NJ.

64. Robert Squier, Muskie's media man in his 1970 Senate reelection and the 1972 nomination race, claimed his candidate was "perfectly tuned to [television]." Lippman and Hansen, *Muskie*, 226–27. For a look at Muskie's failure to run a modern campaign, see James M. Naughton, "The Taste of Defeat," *New York Times*, May 14, 1972, SM13.

65. Theodore H. White, *Making of the President, 1972*, 86.

66. James M. Perry, *Us & Them*, 26. Behind the demise of Muskie's campaign was not only the media coverage but Richard Nixon. The front-runner was the primary target of the dirty tricks that Carl Bernstein and Bob Woodward discovered were referred to as "ratfucking" among the president's staff. In particular, a fake letter published in the right-wing *Manchester Union Leader* claiming that Muskie had used a derogatory term for Americans of French Canadian ancestry was understood as "the beginning of the end of the Muskie campaign." When Muskie appeared to break down in tears in public while answering the charge, he later concluded, "It changed people's minds about me." The disappointing results in New Hampshire, home to tens of thousands of French Canadian Americans, "hit the Muskie bandwagon like a front-wheel blowout" and derailed the campaign. The crude term describing murine copulation was popularized in Bernstein and Woodward, *All the President's Men*. For more on the origins of the "Canuck letter" in

the office of Ken W. Clawson at the White House, see Bernstein and Woodward, *All the President's Men*, 127–48. For Muskie's comment, see Theodore H. White, *Making of the President, 1972*, 85–86. See also Thompson, *Fear and Loathing*, 117. For a reflection on the whole affair, see David Broder, "The Story That Still Nags at Me," *Washington Monthly*, February 1, 1987.

67. "McGovern Dominating Coast Media Coverage," *New York Times*, June 6, 1972, 27.

68. Crouse, *Boys on the Bus*, 26.

69. For more on this transformation, see Crouse, *Boys on the Bus*; James M. Perry, *Us & Them*; and Roessner, *Jimmy Carter*.

70. "McGovern Dominating."

71. Eden Lispon to R. H. Nolte (Institute of Current World Affairs), September 22, 1972, folder "Sparklies," White Papers, John F. Kennedy Presidential Library and Museum, Boston, MA. Kathryn Cramer Brownell generously shared this letter with me.

72. "Show Biz in Politics," 34.

73. Guggenheim memo quoted in Cowie, *Stayin' Alive*, 90.

74. Hart, *Right from the Start*, 144.

75. The sociodemographic construction of hawks and doves, as Penny Lewis has argued, is "a falsehood." Yet the constructed understanding of the antiwar movement as a coalition of liberals and students and the ardent supporters of the war as representatives of blue-collar "middle America" shaped political perceptions at the time. Archie Bunker emerged as the most popular representative of the middle-aged, working-class hawks. Penny Lewis, *Hardhats, Hippies, and Hawks*, 5. See also Kuhn, *Hardhat Riot*.

76. Political scientists recognize a key difference in the parties: While the Republican Party is an ideological movement, the Democratic Party is "fundamentally a group coalition." Grossman and Hopkins, *Asymmetric Politics*, 3. For more on the influence of labor, as well as other political movements, within the Democratic Party in the post–New Deal era, see Schlozman, *When Movements Anchor Parties*; and Hilton, "Path to Polarization." For efforts to strengthen partisanship in the same age, see Rosenfeld, *Polarizers*. For more on the waning power of organized labor within the Democratic Party in the 1970s, see Cowie, *Stayin' Alive*. For a comprehensive study of parties as political institutions, see Schlozman and Rosenfeld, *Hollow Parties*.

77. Cowie, *Stayin' Alive*, 116.

78. According to opinion polls, around a quarter of the electorate viewed McGovern as "radical" or "very liberal." Jack Rosenthal, "McGovern Is Radical or Very Liberal to Many in Polls," *New York Times*, August 27, 1972, 34.

79. Miroff, *Liberals' Moment*, 171–72.

80. The advertisement is available on YouTube through the Carl Albert Congressional Research and Studies Center at the University of Oklahoma, accessed December 1, 2024, www.youtube.com/watch?v=y-bS1-mKY-4&ab_channel=CongressionalArchivesCarlAlbertCenter.

81. Warren Weaver Jr., "McGovern Talks Tougher in Latest TV Commercials," *New York Times*, October 10, 1972, 35.

82. The way *All in the Family* portrayed the white working class as representative of bigotry was not without controversy. Bob Kasen, editor of the Teamster's magazine *Focus*, lamented the distortion of the American worker in the press and entertainment media.

"For some reason, the writers of those shows decided the average worker is a dingbat—fat, more than a little dumb, a committed racist and most of all, very comical." Others noted that the working class in media and arts is "portrayed as a hard-hat Archie Bunker or a brainless pawn." Some liberals, such as Representative Michael Harrington (D-MA), called Archie Bunker "symptomatic" of a "bemused condescension" with which elites looked at workers outraged over a political and economic system that favored the wealthy. The consequence of such distortions was, argued Kasen, that the powers that be "have no idea of what a working person is like and what he needs." In fact, the politics of the white working class were far more heterogenous than the image of Archie Bunker suggested. For example, even before *All in the Family* came on the air, almost half of the Northern white working class favored immediate withdrawal from Vietnam. That number was higher than among the white middle class. Similarly, the liberal George McGovern won a larger share of blue-collar workers than he did of white-collar professionals. Workers understood Archie Bunker as "a fool." Kasen's quotes are from "Unions: Archie Is a Fink," *Time*, April 24, 1972; and Jim Wright, *Dallas Morning News*, July 13, 1973, reprinted in 93 Cong. Rec. 24148. Harrington's comments are from 92 Cong. Rec. 13093. The numbers on the white working class are from Appy, *Working-Class War*, 41; and Andrew Levison, "The Blue-Collar Majority—or, Shattering the 'Hard Hat' Myths," *Washington Post*, September 29, 1974. The final quote is from autoworker Dewey Burton in Cowie, *Stayin' Alive*, 9–10, 192–98.

83. "Carroll O'Connor doing McGovern commercials," an aide cautioned the Nixon campaign, "is not an impossibility." Dwight Chapin to H. R. Haldeman, memorandum, June 12, 1972, folder 9, box 16, Contested Materials Collection, Richard Nixon Presidential Library and Museum, National Archives, Yorba Linda, CA.

84. For more on the struggle of the McGovern campaign to convince labor, see Cowie, *Stayin' Alive*, 95–105.

85. Irving Wallace, "Archie's Vote to Astonish Millions," *Corpus Christi Times*, November 1, 1972, 7F.

86. Lindsay had developed a friendship with O'Connor that lasted. He continued to associate himself with the actor and character, including awarding O'Connor the key to the city of New York on April 23, 1973, and participating in a roast of O'Connor on *The Dean Martin Show*, NBC, December 7, 1973.

87. Wallace, "Archie's Vote."

88. Associated Press, "Archie Bunker Backs McGovern," *Indiana Evening Gazette*, October 28, 1972, 3.

89. Walter R. Mears, Associated Press, "Archie, HHH Assist George in Trying to Erase 'Radicalism' Image," *Mitchell Daily Republic*, October 28, 1972, 1.

90. [Carroll] O'Connor, VTR 5, master, October 26, 1972, V4477/R2, ser. 20 "Audiovisual Items," mss. 217, Sheinbaum Collection, Department of Special Collections, Davidson Library, University of California, Santa Barbara.

91. O'Connor telethon, VTR 6, Dup, October 27, 1972, V4480/R2, ser. 20 "Audiovisual Items," mss. 217, Sheinbaum Collection, Department of Special Collections, Davidson Library, University of California, Santa Barbara.

92. Wallace, "Archie's Vote."

93. Peter Greenberg, "A New Political Beat to Follow: Rock and Roll," *Detroit Free Press*, April 23, 1972.

94. Associated Press, "Archie Bunker Backs McGovern."

95. When O'Connor used the persona of Archie Bunker to support Lindsay in the primaries in the spring of 1972, there was concern at the production company. In the middle of contract negotiations with the actor, the producers were hesitant to grant him permission to use the character in his personal ventures. With a new contract signed by the end of May, however, O'Connor conceded he would agree to no further political uses of his character without the approval of Tandem Productions. The liberal producers Norman Lear and Bud Yorkin both supported McGovern over Nixon, with Lear even ending up on the president's enemies list. Whether Tandem approved of O'Connor returning to Archie Bunker in political appearances for George McGovern or not, the producers were eager to tackle political themes on the show in the middle of the campaign. I have found no evidence in the historical record of conversations between the producers and O'Connor regarding the use of Archie Bunker for the McGovern campaign. Tandem Productions memorandum, May 8, 1972, box S-212, NLP. For Lear's politics, see Norman Lear, *Even This*, xiv. For Yorkin's politics, see Martin Kasindorf, "A TV Dynasty: Archie and Maude and Fred and Norman and Alan," *New York Times Magazine*, June 24, 1973, 15.

96. "Archie Will Spout Off about Politics," *Richmond County Daily Journal*, May 30, 1972, 6.

97. "Archie Will Spout Off."

98. For more on Nixon and the show, see chap. 4.

99. Letter, December 4, 1971, box S-351, NLP.

100. "Archie's Fraud," season 3, episode 2, *All in the Family* (CBS, September 23, 1972), written by Michael Ross and Bernie West.

101. "Mike Comes into Money," season 3, episode 8, *All in the Family* (CBS, November 4, 1972), written by Michael Ross and Bernie West.

102. Letter, November 5, 1972, box S-357, NLP.

103. Letter, November 10, 1972, box S-357, NLP.

104. Letter, November [n.d.] 1972, box S-357, NLP.

105. R. W. Apple Jr., "McGovern's Campaign: Candidate's Heavy Use of Television Is Raising Doubt about His Strategy," *New York Times*, September 9, 1972, 10.

106. Roessner, *Jimmy Carter*.

107. For examples of conservatives developing their own institutions and networks, see Hemmer, *Messengers of the Right*; Stahl, *Right Moves*; Decker, *Other Rights Revolution*; and Shepherd, *Resistance from the Right*.

108. Jamieson, *Packaging the Presidency*, 340–41.

109. Anderson, *Electing Jimmy Carter*, 16.

110. Roessner, *Jimmy Carter*, 33.

111. Roessner, *Jimmy Carter*, 67–75.

112. Witcover, *Marathon*, 15.

113. For the assessments of some journalists and historians, see Brown, *Keeping Your Eye*, 6; Carroll, *It Seemed*, 189; Witcover, *Marathon*, 13; Roessner, *Jimmy Carter*; Kalman, *Right Star Rising*, 153; and Schram, *Great American Video Game*, 28. Carter himself acknowledged the role of television in his campaign. See Witcover, *Marathon*, 14.

114. Brownstein, *Power and the Glitter*, 264.

115. Roessner, *Jimmy Carter*, 34.

116. Roessner, *Jimmy Carter*, 70, 80–83.

117. Brownstein, *Power and the Glitter*, 207–8, 234.

118. Witcover, *Marathon*, 144. For a study of Harris's populist politics, see Bloodworth, *Losing the Center*, 57–74. See also Lowitt, *Fred Harris*.

119. Lowitt, *Fred Harris*, 129.

120. Mimi to Frank Greer, memorandum, n.d., box 288, folder 13, Presidential Campaign 1956–76, Harris Collection, Carl Albert Center Congressional and Political Collections, University of Oklahoma, Norman.

121. Harris to Jim Hightower, memorandum, December 28, 1975, box 290, folder 25, Presidential Campaign 1956–76, Harris Collection, Carl Albert Center Congressional and Political Collections, University of Oklahoma, Norman.

122. J. J. Huthmacher to Jim Hightower, Frank Greer, and Al Shulman, memorandum, July 23, 1975, box 291, folder 21, Presidential Campaign 1956–76, Harris Collection, Carl Albert Center Congressional and Political Collections, University of Oklahoma, Norman.

123. The campaign won O'Connor's support and an endorsement from producer Norman Lear. While the Harris camp appreciated that a star's endorsement was "much more valuable than his money," they never made full use of the blue-collar appeal of Archie Bunker. Lear represented more traditional showbiz politics. The campaign hoped Lear would serve as a gateway to fundraising "biggies," including moguls Ted Ashley and Lew Wasserman, actor Henry Fonda, music producer Barry Gordy, and television producers and writers Carl Reiner and David Rintels. Judy Cohen to Jim Hightower, September 5, 1975, box 292, folder 24, Presidential Campaign 1956–76, Harris Collection, Carl Albert Center Congressional and Political Collections, University of Oklahoma, Norman.

124. Witcover, *Marathon*, 301.

125. Anderson, *Electing Jimmy Carter*, 90.

126. "Carter Tells Film Stars about Poverty in South," *New York Times*, August 24, 1976, 17.

127. Helen Dewar, "Neo-Populist Theme: The Plains Farmer Stages a March across Movieland," *Washington Post*, August 24, 1976, A1.

128. Dewar, "Neo-Populist Theme."

129. Christopher Lydon, "Most Reagan Aides Are Saying 'No' to Job Offers from Ford Camp," *New York Times*, August 30, 1976, 11.

130. Clive Barnes, "'A New Spirit' Is a National Celebration of Togetherness in TV Inaugural Concert," *New York Times*, January 20, 1977, 33.

131. Richard Reeves, "Maestro of the Media," *New York Times*, May 15, 1977, 203.

132. Reeves, "Maestro of the Media."

133. Reeves, "Maestro of the Media."

134. Reeves, "Maestro of the Media."

135. Schram, *Great American Video Game*, 28.

136. Advertisement, Kennedy Spots from 1980, ser. 5., Clymer Personal Papers, John F. Kennedy Presidential Library and Museum, Boston, MA. Hoover, as historian Bruce Schulman notes, "remained the bogeyman of American politics," and Edward Kennedy at several times portrayed the president as the reincarnation of the Republican behind the Great Depression. Schulman, *Seventies*, 132. See also Jacobs, *Panic at the Pump*, 262; and Leuchtenburg, *In the Shadow*, 203. In the opening theme of *All in the Family*, "Those Were

the Days," written by Lee Adams and Charles Strouse, Archie and Edith Bunker wax nostalgic about Glenn Miller and old LaSalles while concluding, "Mister, we could use a man like Herbert Hoover again."

137. Bernard Weinraub, "Archie Bunker Adds Clout to Kennedy's TV Message," *New York Times*, April 9, 1980, 24. Playing on the attention garnered by the spot, a Kennedy aide claimed the campaign "received a letter from the [Herbert Hoover Presidential] library asking us not to be so tough on Herbert Hoover." "Inside Washington," *San Bernardino Sun*, September 28, 1980, 12.

138. Nicholas Lemann, "The Storcks," *Washington Post Magazine*, December 7, 1980, 38.

139. Brownell, *Showbiz Politics*.

140. Bodroghkozy, "Media." See also Berry, *John F. Kennedy*.

Chapter 6

1. Judy Klemesrud, "A Reporter's Notebook: Symbolic Attire," *New York Times*, November 21, 1977, 44.

2. Even *TV Guide* acknowledged that "it is hard to tell where Edith leaves off and Jean Stapleton begins." Dwight Whitney, "For the Dingbat, These Are the Days," *TV Guide*, May 27, 1972, 22.

3. Stephanie Harrington, "The Message Sounds Like 'Hate Thy Neighbor,'" *New York Times*, January 24, 1971, reprinted in Adler, *"All in the Family,"* 76–77.

4. Judy Klemesrud, "Jean Stapleton Hopes Most Wives Aren't Like Edith," *New York Times*, May 17, 1972, 36.

5. Jean Stapleton, interview by Karen Herman, November 28, 2000, AAT.

6. Whitney, "For the Dingbat," 25.

7. Among the most engaging accounts on modern feminism are Rosen, *World Split Open*; Evans, *Tidal Wave*; Freedman, *No Turning Back*; Gail Collins, *When Everything Changed*; Cobble et al., *Feminism Unfinished*; and Spruill, *Divided We Stand*.

8. See Douglas, *Where the Girls Are*; Dow, *Watching Women's Liberation*; and Bradley, *Mass Media*.

9. Wandersee, *On the Move*, 170.

10. See, for example, Roessner, *Jimmy Carter*; Greenberg, *Republic of Spin*; and Brownell, *24/7 Politics*.

11. For character studies of Edith Bunker, see McCrohan, *Archie & Edith*, 61–76; and Cullen, *Those Were the Days*, 85–104.

12. Kay Gardella, "CBS Gambles on Reality with New Comedy Series," *New York Daily News*, January 13, 1971, reprinted in Adler, *"All in the Family,"* 78–79.

13. See, for example, Don Freeman, review of *All in the Family*, *San Diego Union*, January 14, 1971, reprinted in Adler, *"All in the Family,"* 79–81.

14. Harrington, "Message Sounds Like."

15. Letter, December 26, 1971, box S-354, NLP.

16. Letter, January 20, 1972, box S-212, NLP.

17. Jaqueline Trescott, "For Frances Lear, Life Is Not All in the Family," *Washington Post*, March 13, 1976, B1.

18. Lear to audience member, February 11, 1972, box S-212, NLP.

19. "Archie the Gambler," season 4, episode 5, *All in the Family* (CBS, October 13, 1973), story by Steve Zacharias and Michael Leeson, teleplay by Michael Ross and Bernie West.

20. "Prisoner in the House," season 5, episode 17, *All in the Family* (CBS, January 4, 1975), teleplay by Bud Wiser, Lou Derman, and Bill Davenport.

21. "All's Fair," season 5, episode 19, *All in the Family* (CBS, January 18, 1975), written by Lloyd Turner and Gordon Mitchell.

22. John Brady, "Keeping Archie Engaging and Enraging," *New York Times*, February 24, 1974, 15.

23. Klemesrud, "Jean Stapleton Hopes," 36. See also Jean Stapleton, interview by Dick Cavett, *Dick Cavett Show*, ABC, April 24, 1972, www.youtube.com/watch?v=oyW_YfBQ4-g&t=286s&ab_channel=TelevisionVanguard.

24. Klemesrud, "Jean Stapleton Hopes," 36.

25. Arthur Unger, "Those Bunkers of *All in the Family*," *Christian Science Monitor*, September 9, 1974, 12.

26. Unger, "Those Bunkers."

27. Unger, "Those Bunkers."

28. Larry Rhine, interview by Gary Rutkowski, February 24, 2000, AAT.

29. See "Edith's 50th Birthday," season 8, episode 4, *All in the Family* (CBS, October 16, 1977), written by Bob Weiskopf and Bob Schiller; "Mike Faces Life," season 6, episode 7, *All in the Family* (CBS, October 27, 1975), written by Mel Tolkin and Larry Rhine; "Gloria's False Alarm," season 7, episode 14, *All in the Family* (CBS, December 18, 1976), written by Phil Doran and Douglas Arango; "Edith Breaks Out," season 6, episode 8, *All in the Family* (CBS, November 3, 1975), written by Lou Derman and Bill Davenport; and "Edith vs. the Bank," season 9, episode 8, *All in the Family* (CBS, November 19, 1978), written by Mel Tolkin and Larry Rhine.

30. US Commission on Civil Rights, *Window Dressing*, 23.

31. McCrohan, *Archie & Edith*, 67.

32. Unger, "Those Bunkers."

33. The description is by a moderator for a National Association of Broadcasters workshop. See "Minority Programing Fails to Capture Majority's Attention at NAB Workshop," *Broadcasting*, March 29, 1976, 56.

34. John Carmody, "Getting a Message across with the Laughs," *Washington Post*, September 29, 1973.

35. "Edith Finds an Old Man," season 4, episode 3, *All in the Family* (CBS, September 29, 1973), story by Susan Harris, teleplay by Michael Ross and Bernie West.

36. Letter, September 29, 1973, box S-212, NLP.

37. See, for example, letters, September 29, October 1, 16, 1973, box S-212, NLP.

38. Kuhn et al., *No Stone Unturned*, 159–62.

39. Bill O'Hallaren, "Nobody (in TV) Loves You when You're Old and Gray," *New York Times*, July 24, 1977, D21.

40. Letter, September 29, 1973, box S-212, NLP.

41. Letters, September 29, October 1, 1973, box S-212, NLP.

42. Ashby and Gramer, *Fighting the Odds*, 355.

43. Tim Woodward, "Frank Church: Ten Years after His Death, His Profile Continues to Grow," *Lewiston Tribune*, April 10, 1994.

44. 93 Cong. Rec. 32700.
45. 93 Cong. Rec. 32700.
46. William Oriol to Carter, October 9, 1973, box S-212, NLP.
47. Letter from Church, September 21, 1973, box S-212, NLP.
48. Rogers, Cowan & Brenner to David Steinberg Public Relations, September 26, 1973; Carter to William Oriol, September 27, 1973; and Oriol to Carter, October 9, 1973, all in box S-212, NLP.
49. Church to Norman Lear, October 9, 1973, box 4, folder 1, Church Papers, Boise State University Library, Boise, ID.
50. See, for example, Perlman, *Public Interests*, 65–93; Dow, *Watching Women's Liberation*; and Bradley, *Mass Media*.
51. Freedman, *No Turning Back*, 222.
52. *Sex and Violence on TV: Hearings Before the Subcommittee on Communications of the Committee on Interstate and Foreign Commerce of the House of Representatives*, 94th Cong. 27 (1976).
53. Cuklanz, *Rape on Prime Time*, 6. For a study of rape on daytime soap operas, see Levine, *Wallowing in Sex*, 208–52.
54. Gordon, "Women's Liberation Movement," 120.
55. Story conference, June 3, 1977, in *All in the Family* mss., Lilly Library Manuscript Collections, Indiana University Libraries, Bloomington.
56. See, in particular, Brownmiller, *Against Our Will*.
57. "Groups Dispute Parts of Rape-Trial Evidence Bill," *Philadelphia Inquirer*, July 30, 1976, in clippings file "New York and Washington, DC, offices, 1957, 1970–1980 [Washington, DC]: rape bill (1975–1976), March 1976–August 1976," folder E.269, Holtzman Papers MC 793, SL.
58. Abarbanel to Jack Sweeney, October 3, 1977, box 4, folder "All in the Family taping," Harris Papers, Albert and Shirley Small Special Collections Library, University of Virginia, Charlottesville.
59. "The Crisis of Rape," box 4, folder "All in the Family taping," Harris Papers, Albert and Shirley Small Special Collections Library, University of Virginia, Charlottesville.
60. Herbert Harris remarks, transcript, October 12, 1977, box 4, folder "All in the Family taping," Harris Papers, Albert and Shirley Small Special Collections Library, University of Virginia, Charlottesville.
61. Ruth Dean, "TV 2: And Sympathizing with a Frightened Edith Bunker," *Washington Star*, October 14, 1977, F5.
62. Peter Rodino remarks, transcript, October 12, 1977, box 18, folder 14, Rodino Papers, Peter W. Rodino Jr. Law Library, Seton Hall University, Newark, NJ.
63. 95 Cong. Rec. 33721.
64. "Art Imitating Life, and Vice Versa," *Broadcasting*, October 17, 1977, 23.
65. Freedman, *Redefining Rape*, 280–81.
66. Jimmy Carter, "Protection for the Privacy of Rape Victims Statement on Signing H.R. 4727 into Law," October 30, 1978, American Presidency Project, accessed December 1, 2024, www.presidency.ucsb.edu/node/243718.
67. Abzug quoted in Spruill, *Divided We Stand*, 30.
68. Spruill, *Divided We Stand*, 31–32.

69. Spruill, *Divided We Stand*, 31–32; Davis, *Moving the Mountain*, 129–34.
70. Spruill, *Divided We Stand*, 32.
71. Gail Collins, *When Everything Changed*, 214.
72. Lawrence Laurent, "Edith Meets All with a Simple Act of Love," *Washington Post*, May 7, 1972, TC5.
73. Klemesrud, "Jean Stapleton Hopes," 36; "The Prime of Mrs. William H. Putch," *McCall's*, September 1972, 42.
74. Transcript of Jean Stapleton address, Los Angeles, March 30, 1980, box 19, folder 4, JSP.
75. Stapleton interview by Herman.
76. Jean Stapleton, interview by Constance Ashton Myers, 1977, 1977 International Women's Year Oral History Collection, Department of Oral History, University of South Carolina, Columbia.
77. Stapleton interview by Myers.
78. Gail Collins, *When Everything Changed*, 186–88.
79. Gordon, "Women's Liberation Movement."
80. "Dinah Shore—Bette Davis, All in the Family Cast, Jean Stapleton Sings, 1978 TV," posted by Alan Eichler, January 16, 2022, YouTube video, 27:11, www.youtube.com/watch?v=Ww8p_YNNlYs&ab_channel=AlanEichler.
81. Unger, "Those Bunkers."
82. "Dinah Shore."
83. Transcript of Jean Stapleton address, Los Angeles.
84. Norman Lear, *Even This*, 204.
85. Frances Lear, *Second Seduction*, 127–28.
86. In her account of *All in the Family*, Christina von Hodenberg claims Jean Stapleton took an active role in the leadership of the Los Angeles chapter of NOW, including serving as communications officer and vice president. Indeed, a Jean Stapleton did hold the positions. It was, however, not the actress but rather a namesake journalism professor at East L.A. College. Virginia Carter confirmed the misunderstanding in an interview with the author. See von Hodenberg, *Television's Moment*, 147. For more on the other Jean Stapleton, see Turk, *Women of NOW*.
87. Stapleton interview by Myers.
88. Stapleton interview by Cavett.
89. "Prime of Mrs. William H. Putch," 45.
90. Stapleton, foreword to *Edith the Good*, viii.
91. Letty Cottin Pogrebin, "Hollywood Mobilizes for the ERA," *Ms.*, June 1978, 53.
92. Pogrebin, "Hollywood Mobilizes," 78; Beverly Beyette, "Stars Prep for Final Push on ERA," *Los Angeles Times*, May 16, 1978, G1.
93. Beyette, "Stars Prep."
94. Beyette, "Stars Prep."
95. Pogrebin, "Hollywood Mobilizes," 53–78.
96. Pogrebin, "Hollywood Mobilizes," 54.
97. Pogrebin, "Hollywood Mobilizes," 53.
98. Pogrebin, "Hollywood Mobilizes," 55.

99. Unger, "Those Bunkers."

100. "We're Advertising for Equality," ca. 1977, box 31, folder 398, Dunlop Papers, Rockefeller Papers, Rockefeller Archive Center, Sleepy Hollow, NY.

101. "We're Advertising for Equality."

102. Carter quoted in Brock, "Religion, Sex & Politics," 133.

103. "Prime of Mrs. William H. Putch," 40.

104. White House press release, July 1, 1976, box 28, White House Press Releases, Gerald R. Ford Presidential Library, Ann Arbor, MI; also accessed online April 1, 2025, www.fordlibrarymuseum.gov/sites/default/files/pdf_documents/library/document/0248/whpr19760701-018.pdf.

105. Stapleton interview by Myers.

106. Aimee Lee Ball, "How Jean Stapleton Became a Fighter," *Boston Globe*, January 15, 1984, SMA18.

107. Stapleton to Judy Frie, September 15, 1976, box 18, folder 10, ser. 6 "National Commission on the Observance of International Women's Year," East Papers, SL; Stapleton to Gen. Jeanne Holm, September 11, 1976, FG399, White House Central Files, Gerald R. Ford Presidential Library, Ann Arbor, MI.

108. Stapleton to Alan Alda, August 13, 1982, box 19, folder 4, JSP.

109. Due to limited funds, however, the broadcast event never came about. Leader and Hyatt, *American Women*, 33–34, 38.

110. Mattingly, *Feminist*, 154.

111. Spruill, *Divided We Stand*, 206. For examples, see Jean Stapleton, interview by Dinah Shore, *Dinah!*, 20th Century Fox Television, April 1, 1977; and Jean Stapleton, interview by Bill Carlson, *Midday*, WCCO-TV, 1976, www.youtube.com/watch?v=sWEok9WS8os&ab_channel=tcmedianow.

112. National Commission on the Observance of International Women's Year, *Spirit of Houston*, 113.

113. Spruill, *Divided We Stand*, 207.

114. Critchlow, *Phyllis Schlafly*, 245.

115. *A Simple Matter of Justice*, Keller Barron (dir.), 1978, Texas Archive of the Moving Image, accessed December 1, 2024, https://texasarchive.org/2017_03286.

116. Quoted in McCrohan, *Archie & Edith*, 67.

117. "Jean Stapleton Wearing a Lei, Diana Henry Mara Collection, University of Massachusetts Amherst, accessed online April 1, 2025, www.digitalcommonwealth.org/search/commonwealth-oai:or96bp50b.

118. Mansbridge, *Why We Lost*, 98–110.

119. Spruill, *Divided We Stand*, 97–99.

120. Bird, *What Women Want*, 35.

121. United Press International, "Edith Will Support ERA," *Times-News*, October 27, 1977, 6.

122. Schroeder to Stapleton, November 7, 1977, box 17, folder 11, JSP.

123. Stapleton to Anthony C. Beilenson, February 2, 1978, box 17, folder 11, JSP.

124. Transcript of Jean Stapleton address, Emerson College, May 1978, box 19, folder 4, JSP.

125. Transcript of Jean Stapleton address, Emerson College.

126. Mary Lou Shields to Jean Stapleton, May 11, 1978, box 19, folder 4, JSP. See also Jean Stapleton, "'Edith Bunker' on the E.R.A.," *New York Times*, May 12, 1978, A29.

127. Holtzman to Stapleton, July 12, 1978, box 19, folder 4, JSP; 95 Cong. Rec. 15156.

128. Transcript of Jean Stapleton address, Chicago, May 10, 1980, box 19, folder 4, JSP.

129. Carroll, *It Seemed*, 271.

130. Transcript of Jean Stapleton address, ca. 1979, box 19, folder 4, JSP.

131. Joseph McLellan, "Reaching a New Stage," *Washington Post*, November 18, 1979.

132. Pogrebin, "Hollywood Mobilizes," 57.

133. Norman Lear, *Even This*, 317.

134. Norman Lear, *Even This*, 317.

135. Enid Nemy, "Archie Bunker's Loss Is NOW's Gain," *New York Times*, April 11, 1980, A16.

136. See clippings, folder 8, box 87, MC 496, National Organization for Women Records, SL.

137. See news release, 1980, folder 8, box 87, MC 496, National Organization for Women Records, SL.

138. Ellen Hume, "Lears to Donate $500,000 to ERA," *Los Angeles Times*, April 10, 1980, 1.

139. Tom Shales, "A Death in the Family; Dirge for the Dingbat," *Washington Post*, April 23, 1980.

140. Correspondence, box S-355, NLP.

141. Lear to viewer, June 24, 1980, box S-355, NLP.

142. Shales, "Death in the Family."

143. Arthur Unger, "Jean Stapleton: A Life after Edith Bunker," *Christian Science Monitor*, December 11, 1981. See also Shales, "Death in the Family."

144. Spruill, *Divided We Stand*, 8.

145. The article from the May 1976 issue of the *Eagle Forum* is reprinted in "A Marketing Blitz to Sell ERA," *Woman Constitutionalist*, June 12, 1976, 3.

146. Self, *All in the Family*, 291.

147. Pleck, "Failed Strategies; Renewed Hope," 109.

148. Tom Shales, "Stereotypes in Videoland," *Washington Post*, August 17, 1977.

149. Stapleton interview by Herman.

150. Letters, September 26, 27, 1973, box S-212, NLP.

151. Brownell, "Watergate."

152. Letter, February 26, 1977, box S-352, NLP.

153. Letter, February 26, 1977, box S-352, NLP.

Chapter 7

1. Cowan, *See No Evil*, 88.
2. Cowan, *See No Evil*, 85.
3. Cowan, *See No Evil*, 85.
4. Cowan, *See No Evil*, 84.
5. Les Brown, "F.C.C. Head Has TV 'Family' Time," *New York Times*, February 11, 1975, 79.

6. Edith Efron, "TV's Sex Crisis," *TV Guide*, October 18, 1975, 6.

7. The Communications Act of 1934 granted the commission the mandate to regulate "obscene, indecent, or profane language." This was later confirmed in the landmark Supreme Court decision *Federal Communications Commission v. Pacifica Foundation*. In a challenge of the commission's declaratory order concerning the 1973 broadcast of comedian George Carlin's monologue "Seven Words You Can Never Say on Television," the court sided with the FCC. "When the Commission finds that a pig has entered the parlor," Justice John Paul Stevens held, "the exercise of its regulatory power does not depend on proof that the pig is obscene." See Federal Communications Commission v. Pacifica Foundation, 438 US 726 (1978), www.oyez.org/cases/1977/77-528.

8. Letter, September 30, 1975, box S-352, NLP.

9. "Wiley Puts the Burden on Broadcasters While Taking One On for Himself," *Broadcasting*, March 25, 1974, 32.

10. Quoted in Cowan, *See No Evil*, 93.

11. "'Family Time' Is Chiseled in NAB Code," *Broadcasting*, April 14, 1975, 24.

12. The conservative understanding of "family values," as historian Robert Self has argued, combined "gender and sexual orthodoxy with the neoliberal agenda of shrinking the welfare state and its social contract." Self, *All in the Family*, 10–11.

13. Writers Guild of America, West v. Federal Communications Commission, Nos. CV 75-3641-F, CV 75-3719-F, 423 F. Supp. 1064, 1110 (C.D. Cal. 1976).

14. For years, historians and cultural scholars have tended to portray the family viewing hour as the result only of right-wing anger. See, for example, Ozersky, *Archie Bunker's America*, 108; and Rolsky, *Rise and Fall*, 84. With increasing calls for less focus on polarization and more attention to issues that have fostered a form of consensus, historians are today challenging frameworks that rely on simplistic dichotomies of liberal versus conservative. See Schulman, "Post-1968 US History"; Cebul et al., "Beyond Red and Blue"; and Zimmer, "Reflections on the Challenges."

15. Letter, March 20, 1973, box S-354, NLP.

16. "Edith's Problem," season 2, episode 15, *All in the Family* (CBS, January 8, 1972), story by Steve Zacharias and Burt Styler, teleplay by Burt Styler.

17. Letter, January 9, 1972, box S-351, NLP. See also letter to Virginia Carter, November 2, 1973, box S-212, NLP.

18. "Battle of the Month," season 3, episode 24, *All in the Family* (CBS, March 24, 1973), written by Michael Ross and Bernie West.

19. Letter, [n.d.] 1973, box S-212, NLP.

20. Efron, "TV's Sex Crisis," 6.

21. Alley, *Television*, 43.

22. Harry F. Waters, Martin Kasindorf, and Betsy Carter, "Sex and TV," *Newsweek*, February 20, 1978, 54.

23. Chauncey and Sabine, *Tom Chauncey*, 69. See also Waters et al., "Sex and TV," 55.

24. "CBS Affirms Network Editorial Control," *Broadcasting*, May 26, 1969, 56.

25. Waters et al., "Sex and TV," 54.

26. Pondillo, *America's First*, 2–3.

27. Schneider and Pullen, *Gatekeeper*, xiv.

28. Norman Lear, *Even This*, 289.

29. Schneider and Pullen, *Gatekeeper*, 30. Emphasis in the original.

30. Schneider and Pullen, *Gatekeeper*, 138.

31. Cowan, *See No Evil*, 61–62.

32. "Broadcaster Says Free Speech Shouldn't Be So Free," *Broadcasting*, April 14, 1969, 53.

33. Ross, *Hollywood Left and Right*. See also Doherty, *Hollywood's Censor*.

34. For an account of how the television blacklist targeted entertainers dealing with race and gender in their work, see Stabile, *Broadcast 41*.

35. Stabile, *Broadcast 41*.

36. The literature on conservative mobilization against changing norms in education, legislation, media, and society is extensive. See, in particular, McGirr, *Suburban Warriors*; Hemmer, *Messengers of the Right*; Petrzela, *Classroom Wars*; Neil J. Young, *We Gather Together*; Shepherd, *Resistance from the Right*; Hinton, *From the War*; Lassiter, *Silent Majority*; Lassiter, *Suburban Crisis*; Huntington, *Far-Right Vanguard*; Delmont, *Why Busing Failed*; McRae, *Mothers of Massive Resistance*; Kuhn, *Hardhat Riot*; Hendershot, *When the News Broke*; and Walsh, *Taking America Back*.

37. Hemmer, *Messengers of the Right*.

38. Hargis quoted in Gillis, "Say No," 196. For more, see Hendershot, *What's Fair*.

39. Kalman, *Right Star Rising*, 26.

40. See, for example, Efron, *News Twisters*; Coyne, *Impudent Snobs*; and Keeley, *Left-Leaning Antenna*.

41. Feldstein, *Poisoning the Press*, 129.

42. Spiro T. Agnew, "Another Challenge to the Television Industry," *TV Guide*, May 16, 1970, 6. See also Bodroghkozy, *Groove Tube*, 43–45.

43. Hemmer, *Messengers of the Right*, 218–22.

44. "No Return," *Broadcasting*, May 29, 1972, 66.

45. Constituent to Dole, August 9, 1974; and Dole to constituent, August 15, 1974, both in box 286, folder 4, ser. 4 "Issue Mail, 1967–1996," Constituent Relations, 1969–96, Dole Senate Papers, Robert and Elizabeth Dole Archive and Special Collections, University of Kansas, Lawrence.

46. Dole to constituent, April 30, 1973, box 286, folder 4, ser. 4 "Issue Mail, 1967–1996," Constituent Relations, 1969–96, Dole Senate Papers, Robert and Elizabeth Dole Archive and Special Collections, University of Kansas, Lawrence.

47. Gerald S. Pope, "Revolution in Television," *Christian Crusade Weekly*, December 31, 1972, 3.

48. "Silent Majority Pickets CBS," *Broadcasting*, August 30, 1971, 38.

49. Letter, March 20, 1973, box S-354, NLP.

50. Letter, [n.d.] 1973, box S-212, NLP.

51. "Silent Majority Pickets CBS," 37.

52. Gillis, "Say No."

53. For more on conservative organizing against popular culture and the connections between right-wing movements such as the John Birch Society and campaigns to defeat immoral comedy, see Nesteroff, *Outrageous*.

54. John J. O'Connor, "These Little Pressure Groups Went to Market—with a Club," *New York Times*, September 2, 1973, 97.

55. Stop Immorality on TV newsletter, n.d., folder 8, box 8, Subject Files, Yoakum Papers, Wisconsin Historical Society Archives, Wisconsin Center for Film and Theater Research, University of Wisconsin, Madison.

56. See Albert Walsh, "Toward a Christian Social Order," *Triumph*, May 1973, 19.

57. Stop Immorality on TV newsletter, n.d., Stop Immorality on TV, Society for the Christian Commonwealth, box 54, FC-06-0054-04, Benedict Polemical Literature, University Archives and Special Collections, California State University, Fullerton.

58. Walsh, "Toward a Christian Social Order," 19.

59. Stop Immorality on TV newsletter, n.d., Stop Immorality on TV, Society for the Christian Commonwealth, box 54, FC-06-0054-04, Benedict Polemical Literature, University Archives and Special Collections, California State University, Fullerton.

60. "Crusades for TV Morality on Rise," *Broadcasting*, December 18, 1972, 37.

61. "Fifteen-Fold Increase in Obscenity Complaints to FCC in Fiscal '73," *Broadcasting*, August 13, 1973, 33.

62. "Double Barrels for Freedom in TV Programs," *Broadcasting*, October 22, 1973, 27.

63. "'Permissive' TV Still Far Short of Going All the Way," *Broadcasting*, December 10, 1973, 34.

64. "Double Barrels for Freedom."

65. "Double Barrels for Freedom."

66. "ABC Affiliates Convention More of a Celebration," *Broadcasting*, May 28, 1973, 54.

67. Stop Immorality on TV newsletter, n.d., folder 8, box 8, Subject Files, Yoakum Papers, Wisconsin Historical Society Archives, Wisconsin Center for Film and Theater Research, University of Wisconsin, Madison.

68. 94 Cong. Rec. 2059 (1976). Not everybody recognized the constituent pressure Scott described, as Senator John Tunney (D-CA) told Grant Tinker he had seen no letters of complaints during his years in Congress. See "TV Producers: All in the Family Hour," *Broadcasting*, September 15, 1975, 30.

69. Brown, *Televi$ion*, 173.

70. David S. Binnings, "Stop Immorality on TV," *Friar*, December 1973, 29–32.

71. The first number is from Jack Allen, "Letters from 'Stop' Groups Swells Christmas Mail Bag," *Buffalo Courier Express*, December 21, 1972, 6. The latter number is from "More against *Maude*," *Broadcasting*, August 27, 1973, 10. Stop Immorality on TV made a habit of buying mailing lists "of any group we think would be interested in us." Apparently, it resulted in even Hugh Hefner, the libertine founder and editor in chief of *Playboy*, being added to its mailing list. "Boob-Tube Blues," *Playboy*, December 1973, 94.

72. Stop Immorality on TV newsletter, n.d., Society for the Christian Commonwealth, Stop Immorality on TV, RH WL Eph 1050, Wilcox Collection of Contemporary Political Movements, Spencer Library, University of Kansas, Lawrence.

73. "Public Again Gives High Marks to TV," *Broadcasting*, April 2, 1973, 74.

74. For more on the need for different conservative activist movements to inflate their membership numbers, see Shepherd, *Resistance on the Right*, 187.

75. Stop Immorality on TV brochure, n.d., Society for the Christian Commonwealth, Stop Immorality on TV, RH WL Eph 1050, Wilcox Collection of Contemporary Political Movements, Spencer Library, University of Kansas, Lawrence.

76. Stop Immorality on TV brochure, n.d., Stop Immorality on TV, Society for the Christian Commonwealth, box 54, FC-06-0054-04, Benedict Polemical Literature, University Archives and Special Collections, California State University, Fullerton.

77. "Advertisers Wary of Buying Time on 'Dirty' TV Shows," *Variety*, November 28, 1973, 1. The story was reprinted in religious newspapers and newsletters. See, for example, "Advertisers Wary of Objectionable Shows," *Catholic News*, December 20, 1973, 4.

78. Stop Immorality on TV press release, March 7, 1974, Society for the Christian Commonwealth, Stop Immorality on TV, RH WL Eph 1050, Wilcox Collection of Contemporary Political Movements, Spencer Library, University of Kansas, Lawrence.

79. "*Sticks* and *Maude* Run the Gauntlet," *Broadcasting*, August 27, 1973, 40.

80. Stop Immorality on TV press release, March 7, 1974.

81. Tom Shales, "Lear Quitting TV," *Washington Post*, February 28, 1978.

82. Morgenthau, *Pride without Prejudice*, 163.

83. Cowan, *See No Evil*, 54.

84. Schneider and Pullen, *Gatekeeper*, 14–15.

85. Morgenthau, *Pride without Prejudice*, 163.

86. "Is TV Guilty 'til Proved Innocent?," *Broadcasting*, March 10, 1969, 28.

87. "Code Office to Be Television Censor?," *Broadcasting*, March 17, 1969, 27–30. For Stanton's account, see Frank Stanton, interview by Don West, May 22, 2000, AAT.

88. See Murray et al., *Television and Social Behavior*. The understanding of the surgeon general's report as inconclusive was cemented by early reports in the *New York Times*, where the front-page headline read "TV Violence Held Unharmful to Youth." The article, by the grand old man of the television beat, Jack Gould, was based on leaked segments of the report and mistakenly misrepresented it. Jack Gould, "TV Violence Held Unharmful to Youth," *New York Times*, January 11, 1972, 1. See also Lewis L. Gould, *Watching Television*, 21.

89. "Where the Buck Should Stop," *Broadcasting*, April 3, 1972, 144.

90. Schneider and Pullen, *Gatekeeper*, 15.

91. Rowland, *Politics of TV Violence*, 187.

92. "Downhold on Television Violence," *Broadcasting*, March 27, 1972, 25–27.

93. Brown, *Televi$ion*, 31.

94. "Wiley Puts the Burden," 32–34.

95. Wiley to Pastore, June 7, 1974, reprinted in *Violence on Television: Hearings Before the Subcommittee on Communications of the Committee of Commerce of the United States Senate*, 93rd Cong. 191–92 (1974).

96. *Writers Guild of America*, 423 F. Supp. 1095.

97. "Wiley Feels Heat from TV's Screen," *Broadcasting*, October 21, 1974, 41.

98. For more on the concept of the raised eyebrow and the FCC, see Zarkin and Zarkin, *Federal Communications Commission*, 146–47.

99. "Same Old Act up on the Hill for the New Chairman down at the FCC," *Broadcasting*, March 18, 1974, 38.

100. *Writers Guild of America*, 423 F. Supp. 1097–98.

101. "Wiley Feels Heat," 41.

102. "Chairman Wiley Raises an FCC Eyebrow over Violence, Obscenity in TV Programing," *Broadcasting*, October 14, 1974, 4.

103. "Wiley Feels Heat," 41.

104. Cowan, *See No Evil*, 94.

105. Richard Jencks, CBS vice president in Washington, quoted in *Writers Guild of America*, 423 F. Supp. 1099.

106. David Adams, vice chairman of NBC, quoted in *Writers Guild of America*, 423 F. Supp. 1100.

107. *Writers Guild of America*, 423 F. Supp. 1064.

108. Smith, *In All His Glory*, 497.

109. Cowan, *See No Evil*, 65–66. See also Halberstam, *Powers That Be*, 732–33.

110. Arthur R. Taylor, interview by John T. Mason Jr., January 23, 1985, George D. Woods Oral History Project, Rare Books and Manuscript Library, Columbia University, New York, NY.

111. Smith, *In All His Glory*, 497. Taylor's 1974 salary equals approximately $2.5 million in 2024.

112. Bedell, *Up the Tube*, 100.

113. Thomas Swafford, vice president of standards and practices at CBS, quoted in *Writers Guild of America*, 423 F. Supp. 1109.

114. Bedell, *Up the Tube*, 190. Both Halberstam and Smith note that Taylor had dreams of becoming president not only of the network but of the United States. See Halberstam, *Powers That Be*, 732; and Smith, *In All His Glory*, 501.

115. The letter is reprinted in Cowan, *See No Evil*, 110–12.

116. A CBS memo noted that it was representatives of the commission that suggested that "all programming before 9 PM (New York Time) would be of a type that parents could generally rely on as being suitable for viewing by the young audience." The memo went on to say it "presumably" applied to violence, sex, and profanity and noted the need for a disclaimer in case of exceptions and the option of NAB adoption of the rule. Gene Mater, memorandum, December 10, 1974, quoted in *Writers Guild of America*, 423 F. Supp. 1103.

117. "Networks Ban Sex, Violence in Prime-Time 'Family Hour,'" *Broadcasting*, January 13, 1975, 16.

118. "'Family Time' Is Chiseled in NAB Code," *Broadcasting*, 24.

119. "Another Wiley Summit Meeting Called as Movement Starts toward Standards for 'Family Viewing' Prime-Time Hour," *Broadcasting*, January 6, 1975, 6.

120. "What Programs Get the Bounce when 'Family Hour' Goes into Effect?," *Broadcasting*, January 13, 1975, 16–17.

121. "What Programs Get the Bounce," 16–17.

122. "Network Heads Cite Realities of 'Family' Life," *Broadcasting*, February 17, 1975, 34.

123. "Affiliates Air Their Concerns at Atlanta Sessions," *Broadcasting*, February 17, 1975, 26. Stewart's famous remark on pornography is from Jacobellis v. Ohio, 378 US 184 (1964), www.oyez.org/cases/1963/11.

124. "'Family Time' Is Chiseled," 24–25.

125. Cowan, *See No Evil*, 33–34.

126. Cowan, *See No Evil*, 32–33.

127. Cowan, *See No Evil*, 37.

128. *Writers Guild of America*, 423 F. Supp. 1111. In his memoir, Schneider contests the coarse language yet concedes that the meeting "disintegrated into a shouting match." Schneider and Pullen, *Gatekeeper*, 103.

129. Schneider and Pullen, *Gatekeeper*, 103.
130. Cowan, *See No Evil*, 19.
131. Cowan, *See No Evil*, 19–21.
132. Swafford to Wood, memorandum, April 23, 1975, in Cowan, *See No Evil*, 37–39.
133. "CBS Doesn't Plan to Rest on Its Laurels," *Broadcasting*, May 5, 1975, 26.
134. Peter Schrag, "TV's New Chastity Belt," *More*, August 1975, 6.
135. "Producers Talk of Frustrations of Family Hours," *Broadcasting*, May 3, 1976, 26. For a longer account of the meeting, see Cowan, *See No Evil*, 138–39.
136. Cowan, *See No Evil*, 147.
137. Victor Lasky, "Entertainment or Propaganda," *Santa Ana Register*, October 14, 1973. Occasionally, Lasky functioned as an outside surrogate for Richard Nixon, agreeing to White House suggestions on targets for his columns. See Spear, *Presidents and the Press*, 101–2.
138. Bedell, *Up the Tube*, 102.
139. "TV Producers: All in the Family Hour," *Broadcasting*, 30.

Chapter 8

1. "Official War Declared by Hollywood on Family Viewing," *Broadcasting*, November 3, 1975, 25.
2. The plaintiffs in the case also included Concept Plus II Productions, Four D Productions, Danny Arnold, Allan Burns, Sam Denoff, Larry Gelbart, Susan Harris, Norman Lear, Bill Persky, Paul Witt, and Edwin Weinberger. Tandem Productions filed a separate lawsuit. The two lawsuits were combined in the US District Court in California. See Writers Guild of America, West v. Federal Communications Commission, Nos. CV 75-3641-F, CV 75-3710-F. 423 F. Supp. 1064 (C.D. Cal., 1976).
3. "Official War Declared," 25.
4. Jon Nordheimer, "3 Unions Join in Suit to Halt Television Family Hour," *New York Times*, October 31, 1975, 67.
5. Cowan, *See No Evil*, 177.
6. The star power was enough to have the lawsuit announcement make the network evening news on both NBC and ABC, though not on CBS. *NBC Evening News*, NBC, October 31, 1975; and *ABC Evening News*, ABC, October 31, 1975, both in Vanderbilt Television News Archive, Jean and Alexander Heard Libraries, Vanderbilt University, Nashville, TN.
7. Cowan, *See No Evil*, 179.
8. Nordheimer, "3 Unions Join," 67.
9. Cowan, *See No Evil*, 79.
10. 94 Cong. Rec. 41497 (1975).
11. 94 Cong. Rec. 41616 (1975).
12. 94 Cong. Rec. 42442 (1975).
13. Robert Scheer, "Race for Ratings Determines TV's Content," *Los Angeles Times*, June 27, 1977, 3.
14. "TV Producers: All in the Family Hour," *Broadcasting*, September 15, 1975, 29–30.
15. Scheer, "Race for Ratings," 3.

16. Thomas Swafford of CBS admitted that the alliance between opponents of violence and sex was critical in passing the family viewing hour policy. See *Writers Guild of America*, 423 F. Supp. 1110.
17. Kay Gardella, "The Cry of 'Censorship' over the 'Family Hour,'" *New York Daily News*, July 1, 1975, 78.
18. Alley, *Television*, 54.
19. Alan Alda, interview by Michael Rosen, November 17, 2000, AAT.
20. 94 Cong. Rec. 41498 (1975).
21. "Hardy Shoots Back at FCC Snipers," *Broadcasting*, November 17, 1975, 29.
22. Karl Fleming, "Pity the Poor Producers of TV Series," *New York Times*, August 31, 1975, 89.
23. Steve Hoffman, "Family Hour Maybe TV's Miranda Decision—Gordon," *Cincinnati Enquirer*, February 8, 1976, G13.
24. Norman Lear, interview by Barbara Cady, *Playboy*, March 1976, 57.
25. Fleming, "Pity the Poor Producers."
26. Letter to the editor, *New York Times*, November 23, 1976, 25.
27. *60 Minutes*, CBS, April 11, 1976, PC-NY.
28. Scheer, "Race for Ratings," 3.
29. Alley, *Television*, 43–44. See also Brown, *Televi$ion*.
30. Pickard, *America's Battle*, 38.
31. David Black, "Inside TV's 'Family Hour' Feud," *New York Times*, December 7, 1975, 169.
32. Lawrence, *Class of '74*.
33. Andelic, *Donkey Work*, 186.
34. Lawrence, *Class of '74*, 57.
35. For more on the rise of cable and the way the industry appealed to young and media-savvy legislators, see Brownell, *24/7 Politics*.
36. Rowland, *Politics of TV Violence*, 257.
37. "Family-Viewing Fire in His Eye, Waxman Heads for Macdonald Subcommittee," *Broadcasting*, November 24, 1975, 43–44.
38. *Regulatory Reform: Hearings Before the Subcommittee on Oversight and Investigations of the Committee on Interstate and Foreign Commerce of the US House of Representatives*, 94th Cong. 324 (1976).
39. *Regulatory Reform*, 324.
40. "Macdonald Doubts Family Viewing Will Do the Job," *Broadcasting*, March 17, 1975, 23.
41. *Regulatory Reform*, 325.
42. *Regulatory Reform*, 327.
43. *Regulatory Reform*, 327.
44. *Regulatory Reform*, 327.
45. *Regulatory Reform*, 327.
46. *Regulatory Reform*, 327.
47. *TV Guide* advertisement, *New York Times*, December 8, 1975.
48. *TV Guide* advertisement, *New York Times*, December 8, 1975.

49. Les Brown, "Lear Assails FCC on Family Viewing," *New York Times*, February 24, 1976, 71.

50. "Corporate Candor," *Broadcasting*, April 21, 1975, 8.

51. "Torbert Macdonald, 'a Tough Act to Follow,'" *Broadcasting*, May 31, 1976, 48.

52. "Macdonald Retirement Changes the Line-Up," *Broadcasting*, May 3, 1976, 42.

53. Rowland, *Politics of TV Violence*, 256–57.

54. "Family Viewing Hearings Are Still On, Says Van Deerlin," *Broadcasting*, June 7, 1976, 40.

55. The joke referenced Norman Lear's latest comedy success, *Mary Hartman, Mary Hartman* (syndication, 1976–77). *Sex and Violence on TV: Hearings Before the Subcommittee on Communications of the Committee on Interstate and Foreign Commerce of the House of Representatives*, 94th Cong. 259 (1976).

56. Gary Grossman, "Questioning Hollywood about Violence on TV," *Boston Globe*, August 15, 1976.

57. *Sex and Violence on TV*, 134.

58. *Sex and Violence on TV*, 260.

59. *Sex and Violence on TV*, 140.

60. *Sex and Violence on TV*, 262.

61. *Sex and Violence on TV*, 92.

62. *Sex and Violence on TV*, 266.

63. *Sex and Violence on TV*, 265–69.

64. 94 Cong. Rec. 35460, 35472, 35475, 35481, 35505.

65. *Sex and Violence on TV*, 141.

66. *Sex and Violence on TV*, 71.

67. Paper, *Empire*, 288.

68. Cowan, *See No Evil*, 196.

69. Paper, *Empire*, 289.

70. "Family Viewing Gets a Going-Over from the Troops," *Broadcasting*, April 14, 1975, 25–26.

71. "Not This Time," *Broadcasting*, January 13, 1975, 58.

72. "Corporate Candor," 8.

73. Crutchfield to Taylor, January 24, 1975, ser. 1, box 91, folder "CBS: Arthur Taylor," Crutchfield Papers, Southern Historical Collection, Wilson Library, University of North Carolina, Chapel Hill.

74. "The Action's on the Strip for Broadcasters This Week," *Broadcasting*, April 7, 1975, 42.

75. "TV Chiefs Think Medium Is Going to Be Around for Quite a While," *Broadcasting*, December 15, 1975, 40.

76. "Taylor Copyrights Family Viewing," *Broadcasting*, May 19, 1975, 34–35.

77. Smith, *In All His Glory*, 498.

78. See Doherty, *Hollywood's Censor*; Kruse, *One Nation under God*, and Dochuk, *From Bible Belt*.

79. W. A. Criswell, "The Illusion of Progress," February 11, 1968, W. A. Criswell Sermon Library, Dallas, TX.

80. Flippen, *Jimmy Carter*, 52.

81. Quoted in Gillis, "Say No," 196.

82. OVAL 662-004, February 1, 1972. The conversation with President Nixon is transcribed in Brinkley and Nichter, *Nixon Tapes*, 359.

83. Stephens and Giberson, *Anointed*, 106.

84. Minutes, revised constitution, and bylaws of the General Council of the Assemblies of God, Thirty-Fifth General Council, August 16–21, 1973, Flower Pentecostal Heritage Center, Springfield, MO. For membership numbers, see Mead, *Handbook of Denominations*, 32.

85. Flippen, *Jimmy Carter*, 52.

86. "Why Have a Family Altar?," *KB Biola Broadcaster*, April 1971, 36–37, https://digitalcommons.biola.edu/biola-broadcaster-1971/10.

87. See, for example, "We Make the Wars," *Catholic Transcript*, February 9, 1973, 2; and "'Air' Pollution," *Pittsburgh Catholic*, November 17, 1972, 4.

88. "'Stop Immorality on TV' Raps Several Programs," *These Times*, December 1973, 15. See also "Catholic Lay Organization Fights TV Immorality," *These Times*, October 1973, 7.

89. See, for example, Neil J. Young, *We Gather Together*; Self, *All in the Family*; Spruill, *Divided We Stand*; Hartman, *War for the Soul*; and Offenbach, *Conservative Movement*.

90. Neil J. Young, *We Gather Together*.

91. Montgomery, *Target: Prime Time*, 39.

92. Neil J. Young, *We Gather Together*, 155–57.

93. "Baptist Broadcast Chief Praises 'Family Viewing,'" *Baptist Press*, October 17, 1975, in Southern Baptist Historical Library and Archives, Nashville, TN.

94. Mead, *Handbook of Denominations*, 42.

95. "Family Viewing Time Concept Said Inadequate," *Baptist Press*, November 10, 1975.

96. "Illinois Baptists Support 'Family Viewing' on Television," *Baptist Press*, November 3, 1975; "W. Va. Baptists Call Family Viewing 'Inadequate,'" *Baptist Press*, November 19, 1975.

97. "Wiley Plan to Clean Up Television Goes to Hill," *Broadcasting*, February 24, 1975, 25.

98. Over the 1960s and 1970s, the political right increasingly embraced the political concept of the family and family values. See, for example, Self, *All in the Family*; Spruill, *Divided We Stand*; Taranto, *Kitchen Table Politics*; Zaretsky, *No Direction Home*; Du Mez, *Jesus and John Wayne*; and Renfro, *Stranger Danger*.

99. "'Family Plan' Would Tune Out Violence for Children," *Catholic Transcript*, May 30, 1975.

100. 94 Cong. Rec. 15561–62.

101. Wiley to Pastore, December 19, 1975, folder "Communications 1970–1975," box 6, Subject Files, Pastore Papers, Special and Archival Collections, Phillips Memorial Library, Providence College, Providence, RI.

102. "CBS President to Address Abe Lincoln Awards Banquet," *Baptist News*, December 4, 1975, in Southern Baptist Historical Library and Archives, Nashville, TN.

103. "CBS President Lauds Baptist Broadcasting," *Baptist News*, February 17, 1976, in Southern Baptist Historical Library and Archives, Nashville, TN.

104. Stanton, *Daniel Dilemma*, 118–19.

105. Cowan, *See No Evil*, 185.

106. Gary Deeb, "'Penny-Pinching' Taylor Fired from CBS," *Times Record*, October 23, 1976, B8.

107. For more on the concept of weaponizing victimhood, see Bebout, "Weaponizing Victimhood."

108. For more on the rise of the religious right, see Williams, *God's Own Party*; Dowland, *Family Values*; Stephens, *Family Matters*; Sutton, *Jerry Falwell*; and Du Mez, *Jesus and John Wayne*.

109. Harry F. Waters, Martin Kasindorf, and Betsy Carter, "Sex and TV," *Newsweek*, February 20, 1978, 55.

110. Waters et al., "Sex and TV," 58. See also Montgomery, *Target: Prime Time*, 154–56.

111. *Writers Guild of America*, 423 F. Supp. 1073.

112. *Writers Guild of America*, 423 F. Supp. 1094.

113. *Writers Guild of America*, 423 F. Supp. 1073.

114. *Writers Guild of America*, 423 F. Supp. 1073–74. The Supreme Court held in *Mutual Film Corporation v. Industrial Commission of Ohio* (1915) that First Amendment protections of free speech did not extend to motion pictures and approved of the concept of government censorship of films. Almost four decades later the court overturned the decision in *Joseph Burstyn, Inc. v. Wilson* (1952). "It cannot be doubted," the court concluded, "that motion pictures are a significant medium for the communication of ideas." Further, the decision held, "their importance as an organ of public opinion is not lessened by the fact that they are designed to entertain as well as to inform." In the landmark decision *Red Lion Broadcasting Co. v. Federal Communications Commission* the Supreme Court strongly suggested broadcasters enjoyed First Amendment rights. "The First Amendment is relevant to public broadcasting," the decision concluded, "but it is the right of the viewing and listening public, and not the right of the broadcasters, which is paramount." Ferguson cited *Red Lion* several times in his legal reasoning that the FCC restricted the freedom of speech of the public with the family viewing policy. Joseph Burstyn, Inc. v. Wilson, 343 US 495 (1952); Red Lion Broadcasting Co. v. Federal Communications Commission, 395 US 367 (1969). For more on freedom of speech and mass media, see Petersen, *How Machines*.

115. *Writers Guild of America*, 423 F. Supp. 1072.

116. *Writers Guild of America*, 423 F. Supp. 1128.

117. Bill Richards, "'Family Hour': In the Networks' Court," *Washington Post*, November 5, 1976, B1.

118. *CBS Evening News*, CBS, November 4, 1976, in Vanderbilt Television News Archive, Jean and Alexander Heard Libraries, Vanderbilt University, Nashville, TN; "TV's 'Family Hour' Ruled Unconstitutional," *Los Angeles Times*, November 5, 1976, 7; Robert Lindsey, "US Judge Rules TV 'Family Hour' Constitutes Federal Censorship," *New York Times*, November 5, 1976, 12.

119. "Judge Says Networks, NAB, FCC All Acted Illegally on Family Viewing," *Broadcasting*, November 8, 1976, 20–21,120. Looking back on the whole affair years later, Wiley concluded it was "inconsistent with my philosophy." See Richard Wiley, interview by Margot Hardenbergh, January 27, 2005, TV Oral History Project, Donald McGannon Communication Research Center, Fordham University Libraries, New York, NY.

121. Minutes of the meeting of the board of directors of CBS Television Network Affiliates, November 3, 1975, ser. 1, box 91, folder "CBS: Affiliates Advisory Board," Crutchfield

Papers, Southern Historical Collection, Wilson Library, University of North Carolina, Chapel Hill. In the weeks and months before the decision came down, CBS cleaned house. Out were the architects of the new and relevant entertainment of the 1970s: Bob Wood, president of CBS Television; Fred Silverman, vice president in charge of the programming department; and Thomas Swafford, vice president of the standards and practices department. But out was also the man who claimed credit for the family viewing hour: Arthur Taylor.

122. "No Fireworks Expected at NAB Board Meet in Florida," *Broadcasting*, January 19, 1976, 34.

123. "First Principles," *Broadcasting*, November 8, 1976, 106.

124. According to Taylor, Paley viewed the policy as an indictment of his life work. See Arthur R. Taylor, interview by John T. Mason Jr., January 23, 1985, George D. Woods Oral History Project, Rare Books and Manuscript Library, Columbia University, New York, NY.

125. Cowan, *See No Evil*, 297.

126. Rowland, *Politics of TV Violence*, 274–75. For the political history of cable television, see Brownell, *24/7 Politics*.

127. Quoted in Engelhardt, "Children's Television," 76. For more on Fowler's "marketplace approach to regulation," see Perlman, *Public Interests*, 97–98.

128. "Televisions," *New York Times*, October 14, 1977, 76.

129. Les Brown, "Television Becomes the 'Failure-Proof Business,'" *New York Times*, March 15, 1976, 59.

130. Rowland, *Politics of TV Violence*, 278–80.

131. Rowland, *Politics of TV Violence*, 282–84. Wirth even reprimanded his colleagues and suggested Congress should not "absolve ourselves entirely of blame for the way Mr. Wiley handled the matter [with family viewing]," recognizing that the pressure on the chairman to act might have been unconstitutional. Rowland, *Politics of TV Violence*, 268–69.

132. Arthur Unger, "Lear Wages Campaign against 'Family Hour,'" *Albuquerque Journal*, November 28, 1976, 50.

133. *MacNeil/Lehrer Report*, PBS, November 11, 1976 in American Archive of Public Broadcasting (WGBH and the Library of Congress), Boston, MA, and Washington, DC. Also available online, accessed April 1, 2025, https://americanarchive.org/catalog/cpb-aacip_507-k06ww77p8d.

134. Montgomery, *Target: Prime Time*, 110.

135. *MacNeil/Lehrer Report*, PBS, November 11, 1976, in American Archive of Public Broadcasting (WGBH and the Library of Congress), Boston, MA, and Washington, DC.

136. Gary Grossman, "Questioning Hollywood about Violence on TV," *Boston Globe*, August 15, 1976.

137. Quoted in Bedell, *Up the Tube*, 206.

138. "Leaders Dismayed at Family Viewing Ruling," *Word and Way*, November 18, 1976.

139. Toby Druin, "Hit Sponsors' Billfold TV Hearing Testimony Declares," *Baptist News*, November 17, 1976, in Southern Baptist Historical Library and Archives, Nashville, TN.

140. Waters et al., "Sex and TV," 58.

141. "Those of a more cynical bent note that police/detective shows, chief offenders in the violence category, had proliferated to the point of diminishing ratings returns

anyway," John J. O'Connor remarked in an attempt to provide depth to the conversation. John J. O'Connor, "TV Is Getting Tough on Violence and Loose with Sex," *New York Times*, September 11, 1977. See also Brown, *Keeping Your Eye*, 67.

142. Levine, *Wallowing in Sex*, 37. Behind *Three's Company* were the trio Don Nicholl, Michael Ross, and Bernie West, who made their name as staff writers on *All in the Family*.

143. Gitlin, *Inside Prime Time*, 247–64.

144. "Judge Says Networks," 20.

145. Joan Hanauer, "Family Viewing Hour Misses Mark, Is Ignored," *Leader-Telegram*, August 11, 1979.

146. Lee Margulies, "Proliferation of Pressure Groups in Primetime Symposium 1981," *Emmy Magazine*, Summer 1981, A23.

147. Margulies, "Proliferation of Pressure Groups," A30.

Conclusion

1. As political scientists and communication scholars have shown, the academic works on the subject "frequently contradict or at least complicate" the narratives of selective exposure and echo chambers. Guess et al., *Avoiding the Echo Chamber*, 3.

2. Anjelica Oswald, "The 27 Most Politically Divisive Shows on TV," *Business Insider*, December 6, 2018. At the same time, the most popular shows, including *The Big Bang Theory* (CBS, 2007–19) and *Modern Family* (ABC, 2009–20), enjoyed large audiences across the political spectrum. "Study Finds Republicans Favor Popular 'Non-Conservative' TV Shows," *ABC News*, November 11, 2010, accessed April 1, 2025, https://abcnews.go.com/Entertainment/study-finds-republicans-modern-family-democrats-dexter/story?id=12117179.

3. Katie Rogers and Emily Cochrane, "Trump Responds to Fury over *Roseanne*, but Not Her Racist Remarks," *New York Times*, May 30, 2018; Christie D'Zurilla, "Trump Calls *Will & Grace* Star Debra Messing a 'McCarthy Style Racist,'" *Los Angeles Times*, September 5, 2019.

4. The episode was eventually released two years later, following the racial reckoning of the summer of 2020. "Please, Baby, Please," season 4, episode 24, *Black-ish* (ABC, August 10, 2020), written by Kenya Barris and Peter Saji; Yohana Desta, "*Black-ish*: What Was So Controversial about That Shelved Episode?," *Vanity Fair*, August 11, 2020.

5. Les Brown, "Norman Lear Dreams Up a Twist in the Plot for Himself," *New York Times*, April 9, 1978.

6. Norman Lear, *Even This*, 245.

7. For experimental work on the issue of television entertainment and political attitudes, see Chattoo and Feldman, *Comedian and an Activist*; Dannagal Goldthwaite Young, *Irony and Outrage*; and Mutz and Nir, "Not Necessarily the News."

8. "Norman Lear: Just Another Version of You," *American Masters*, PBS, October 25, 2016.

9. "Isn't It Romantic?," season 2, episode 5, *Golden Girls* (NBC, November 8, 1986), written by Jeffrey Duteil; "Scared Straight," season 4, episode 9, *Golden Girls* (NBC, December 10, 1988), written by Christopher Lloyd; "72 Hours," season 5, episode 19, *Golden Girls* (NBC, February 17, 1990), written by Tracy Gamble and Richard Vaczy.

10. John J. O'Connor, "Gay Image: TV's Mixed Signals," *New York Times*, May 19, 1991, H1.

11. Richard W. Stevenson, ". . . And Now a Message from an Advocacy Group," *New York Times*, May 27, 1990, H21.

12. Bill Carter, "A Message on Drinking Is Seen and Heard," *New York Times*, September 11, 1989, D11.

13. "Loverboyd," season 8, episode 22, *Cheers* (NBC, March 29, 1990), written by Brian Pollack and Mert Rich.

14. Emily Nussbaum, "When Episodes Could Still Be Very Special," *New York Times*, April 13, 2003. See also Cohn and Porst, *Very Special Episodes*.

15. Bruce Handy, "He Called Me Ellen DeGenerate?," *Time*, April 14, 1997.

16. John Carmody, "*Ellen* Draws a Crowd to Her Coming Out," *Washington Post*, May 1, 1997.

17. Montgomery, *Target: Prime Time*, 217.

18. The episode in question included a scene in which Kramer (Michael Richards) accidentally burns a Puerto Rican flag and then stomps on it to extinguish the flames. "The Puerto Rican Day Parade," season 9, episode 20, *Seinfeld* (NBC, May 7, 1998), written by Alec Berg, Jennifer Crittenden, Spike Feresten, Bruce Eric Kaplan, Gregg Kavet, Steve Koren, et al.; "NBC Apologizes for *Seinfeld* Episode on the Puerto Rican Day Parade," *New York Times*, May 9, 1998.

19. Quoted in Tim Stafford, "Taking On TV's Bad Boys," *Christianity Today*, August 19, 1991. For more on Wildmon, see Mendelhall, "Responses to Television."

20. Paula Span, "The Mother Who Took On Trash TV," *Washington Post*, October 9, 1989.

21. "The Media Business: A Mother Is Heard as Sponsors Abandon a TV Hit," *New York Times*, March 2, 1989, A1.

22. Stephen Battaglio, "Tim Allen's *Last Man Standing* Returns—This Time on Fox's Fall Schedule," *Los Angeles Times*, May 14, 2018; Joe Otterson, "*Brooklyn Nine-Nine* to Continue on NBC," *Variety*, May 11, 2018.

23. Schudson, *Power of News*, 121.

24. Eric Alterman, "The Hollywood Campaign," *Atlantic*, September 2004.

25. Tina Daunt, "Reiner Says He Won't Run for Governor Next Year," *Los Angeles Times*, December 5, 2008.

26. Josh Rottenberg, "Is Roseanne Barr Fit to Be President of the United States? Well, if You Ask Her . . . ," *Los Angeles Times*, June 29, 2016.

27. "No Contest," season 1, episode 18, *Cheers* (NBC, February 17, 1983), written by Heide Perlman; Tom Shales, "Hey Bartender, Here's Your Tip," *Washington Post*, January 18, 1983; "All Singing! All Dancing! All Miserable!," season 8, episode 19, *Murphy Brown* (CBS, March 4, 1996), written by Adolphus Spriggs; Sharon Waxman, "Murphy Brown's Soft Spot: Sitcom Goes Easy on Guest Newt Gingrich," *Washington Post*, February 7, 1996; "Leslie vs. April," season 5, episode 7, *Parks and Recreation* (NBC, November 15, 2012), written by Harris Wittels; Sean Sullivan, "Vice President Biden's *Parks and Recreation* Cameo," *Washington Post*, November 16, 2012.

28. "Cosby for Jackson," Jesse Jackson 1988 campaign ad, P-349-15368; and "Archie and Meathead," Jerry Brown 1992 campaign ad, P-1013-40756, both online through Carl Albert

Congressional Research and Studies Center, Julian P. Kanter Political Commercial Collection, University of Oklahoma, Norman, www.youtube.com/watch?v=p69opqcuwmo&ab_channel=CongressionalArchivesCarlAlbertCenter and www.youtube.com/watch?v=vFKPti7SOiI&ab_channel=CongressionalArchivesCarlAlbertCenter; Robin Toner, "Clinton and Brown Make Last Appeal for New York Vote," *New York Times*, April 7, 1992; Joe Concha, "*Seinfeld*'s Newman Accuses Trump of 'Premeditated Assault on the US Mail' in New Democratic Ad," *Hill*, October 9, 2020, https://thehill.com/blogs/in-the-know/in-the-know/520430-seinfelds-newman-accuses-trump-of-premeditated-assault-on-the/-.

29. Bill Carter, "Back Talk from *Murphy Brown* to Dan Quayle," *New York Times*, July 20, 1992, C14.

30. "You Say Potatoe, I Say Potato," season 5, episode 1, *Murphy Brown* (CBS, September 21, 1992), story by Steven Peterman, Gary Dontzig, and Korby Siamis, teleplay by Gary Dontzig and Steven Peterman.

31. Brownell, *24/7 Politics*, 305–11. See also Hemmer, *Partisans*; and Rosenwald, *Talk Radio's America*.

32. Historian Nicole Hemmer instead traces the origin of news shows that were "loud, opinionated, full of shouting and laughter" to the *60 Minutes* segment Point/Counterpoint. Notably, the segment, which pitted conservative James J. Kilpatrick against liberal Nicholas von Hoffman, debuted in 1971—the same year that *All in the Family* came on the air. Hemmer, *Partisans*, 72–73.

33. Anna Quindlen, "Talking about the Media Circus," *New York Times Magazine*, June 26, 1994.

34. Postman, *Amusing Ourselves to Death*, 80.

35. Hemmer, *Partisans*, 196–97.

36. *Morning Joe*, MSNBC, May 5, 2016, www.youtube.com/watch?v=EFz4YbxTfG4&ab_channel=MSNBC.

37. Stelter, *Hoax*, 43–55.

38. Poniewozik, *Audience of One*, 142–72.

39. See Patrick Radden Keefe, "How Mark Burnett Resurrected Donald Trump as an Icon of American Success," *New Yorker*, December 27, 2018; and Marc Fisher, "Donald Trump, Remade by Reality TV," *Washington Post*, January 27, 2017.

40. Keefe, "How Mark Burnett Resurrected." For more on *The Apprentice* as key to Trump's political success, see Poniewozik, *Audience of One*, 85–172. See also Conor Friedersdorf, "The People behind *The Apprentice* Owe America the Truth about Donald Trump," *Atlantic*, September 19, 2016; Nancy Benac, "In Trump's *Apprentice* Run, Reality Wasn't What It Seemed," Associated Press, October 15, 2016, https://apnews.com/article/entertainment-arts-and-entertainment-election-2020-campaign-2016-events-1ab9c6b8ebd444bdbcfc3fbf0a424765; and Jay Newton-Small, "How Reality TV Took Over US Politics," *Time*, March 23, 2016.

41. Setoodeh, *Apprentice in Wonderland*, 18.

42. "For Sale by Owner," season 4, episode 25, *Fresh Prince of Bel-Air* (NBC, May 16, 1994), written by Harrison Boyd; "The Rosie Show," season 4, episode 4, *Nanny* (CBS, October 9, 1996), written by Nastaran Dibai and Jeffrey B. Hodes; "The Paul Lassiter Story," season 2, episode 14, *Spin City* (ABC, January 21, 1998), written by Bill Lawrence.

43. Even Steve Bannon, chief strategist in the first Trump White House, viewed the president as Archie Bunker. See Woodward, *Fear*, 3.

44. Poniewozik, *Audience of One*, xix.

45. Newton-Small, "How Reality TV."

46. Jim Rutenberg, "The Mutual Dependence of Donald Trump and the News Media," *New York Times*, March 20, 2016. Donald Trump described himself as "a ratings machine" in interviews. See Setoodeh, *Apprentice in Wonderland*, 221.

47. Paul Bond, "Leslie Moonves on Donald Trump: 'It May Not Be Good for America, but It's Damn Good for CBS,'" *Hollywood Reporter*, February 29, 2016.

48. Keefe, "How Mark Burnett Resurrected."

49. Brian Stelter, "'Wires and Lights in a Box,' 50 Years Later," *New York Times*, October 15, 2008.

50. While Neil Postman seems to find this turn the natural result of the medium, it was not an outcome determined by the technology but instead the result of the business model of television entertainment and American politics. See Postman, *Amusing Ourselves to Death*, 159.

51. *Late Show with Stephen Colbert*, CBS, August 4, 2018, www.youtube.com/watch?v=PjhLpMWBdVk&ab_channel=TheLateShowwithStephenColbert.

52. Nolan D. McCaskill, "Norman Lear: Trump Is a Real-Life Archie Bunker," *Politico*, June 3, 2016; James Poniewozik, "A TV Master, A Celebrity President and the End of a Political Cease-Fire," *New York Times*, August 3, 2017.

53. Castleman and Podrazik, *Watching TV*, 211.

BIBLIOGRAPHY

Primary Sources

ARCHIVAL COLLECTIONS

Albert and Shirley Small Special Collections Library, University of Virginia, Charlottesville
    Herbert Harris Papers
American Archive of Public Broadcasting (WGBH and the Library of Congress), Boston and Washington, DC
American Jewish Historical Society, New York, NY
Archives Center, National Museum of American History, Washington, DC
    Jean Stapleton Papers
Boise State University Library, Boise, ID
    Frank Church Papers
Carl Albert Center Congressional and Political Collections, University of Oklahoma, Norman
    Fred R. Harris Collection
    Julian P. Kanter Political Commercial Collection
Department of Special Collections, Davidson Library, University of California, Santa Barbara
    Stanley K. Sheinbaum Collection
Flower Pentecostal Heritage Center, Springfield, MO
Gerald R. Ford Presidential Library, Ann Arbor, MI
    White House Central Files
    White House Press Releases
Jimmy Carter Presidential Library and Museum, Atlanta, GA
John F. Kennedy Presidential Library and Museum, Boston, MA
    Adam Clymer Personal Papers
    Theodore White Papers
Library of Congress, Washington, DC
    NAACP Papers
Lilly Library Manuscript Collections, Indiana University Libraries, Bloomington
    All in the Family mss., 1977–78
Mansfield Library, University of Montana, Missoula
    Mike Mansfield Papers
Paley Center for Media, Beverly Hills, CA
Paley Center for Media, New York, NY
Peter W. Rodino Jr. Law Library, Seton Hall University, Newark, NJ
    Peter W. Rodino Jr. Papers

Private collection
   Norman Lear Papers
Rare Book and Manuscript Library, Columbia University, New York, NY
   Laura Keane Zametkin Hobson Papers, 1930–86
Rauner Library Archives and Manuscripts, Dartmouth College, Hanover, NH
   Harry Ackerman Papers
Richard Nixon Presidential Library and Museum, National Archives, Yorba Linda, CA
   Charles W. Colson Subject Files
   Contested Materials Collection
   White House Special Files Collection
   White House Tapes
Robert and Elizabeth Dole Archive and Special Collections, University of Kansas, Lawrence
   Robert J. Dole Senate Papers
Rockefeller Archive Center, Sleepy Hollow, NY
   John D. Rockefeller 3rd Papers, Associates
      Joan Dunlop Papers
Schlesinger Library, Radcliffe Institute, Harvard University, Cambridge, MA
   Elizabeth Holtzman Papers, 1945–81
   NARAL Records
   National Organization for Women Records, 1959–2002
   Papers of Catherine Shipe East
Southern Baptist Historical Library and Archives, Nashville, TN
Southern Historical Collection, Wilson Library, University of North Carolina, Chapel Hill
   Charles Harvey Crutchfield Papers
Special and Archival Collections, Phillips Memorial Library, Providence College, Providence, RI
   John O. Pastore Papers
Special Collections, Princeton University Library, Princeton, NJ
   George S. McGovern Papers
Special Collections and University Archives, University of Maryland, College Park
   Spiro T. Agnew Papers
Special Collections Research Center, Temple University Libraries, Temple University, Philadelphia, PA
   Gray Panther Records
Spencer Library, University of Kansas, Lawrence
   Wilcox Collection of Contemporary Political Movements
Texas Archive of the Moving Image, Austin, TX
University Archives and Special Collections, California State University, Fullerton
   Russell G. Benedict Polemical Literature
Vanderbilt Television News Archive, Jean and Alexander Heard Libraries, Vanderbilt University, Nashville, TN
W. A. Criswell Sermon Library, Dallas, TX
Western Reserve Historical Society, Cleveland, OH
   Arthur J. Lelyveld Papers

Wisconsin Historical Society Archives, Wisconsin Center for Film and Theater Research, University of Wisconsin, Madison
    Hal Kanter Papers
    Robert Yoakum Papers
Writers Guild Foundation Archive, Los Angeles, CA
    Mel Tolkin Papers, 1932–97
Yale University Library, New Haven, CT
    John Vliet Lindsay Papers

NEWSPAPERS, MAGAZINES, AND SERIAL PUBLICATIONS

Albuquerque (NM) Journal
American Baptist
Atlantic
Baptist Press
Boston Globe
Broadcasting
Buffalo (NY) Courier Express
Business Insider
Catholic News
Catholic Transcript
Chicago Daily News
Chicago Tribune
Christian Crusade Weekly
Christianity Today
Christian Science Monitor
Cincinnati (OH) Enquirer
Congressional Record
Corpus Christi (TX) Times
Daily Variety
Dallas Morning News
Daytona Beach (FL) Morning Journal
Detroit Free Press
Ebony
Educational Broadcasting Review
Emmy Magazine
Esquire
Flow
Friar
Hamlet (NC) News-Messenger
Hill
Hollywood Reporter
HuffPost
Indiana (PA) Evening Gazette
Jewish Advocate
Jewish Post and Opinion
Journal of Broadcasting
KB Biola Broadcaster
Leader-Telegram (Eau Claire, WI)
Lewiston (ID) Tribune
Lockport (NY) Union-Sun and Journal
Long Beach (CA) Independent
Los Angeles Magazine
Los Angeles Sentinel
Los Angeles Times
McCall's
Mitchell (SD) Daily Republic
More
Ms.
New Pittsburgh (PA) Courier
Newsweek
New York Daily News
New Yorker
New York Times
New York Times Magazine
Pittsburgh (PA) Catholic
Playboy
Politico
Record Newspapers
Richmond County Daily Journal (Rockingham, NC)
Ridgewood (NY) Times
San Bernardino (CA) Sun
San Diego (CA) Union
San Francisco Examiner
Santa Ana (CA) Register
Television Quarterly
These Times
Time
Times-News (Twin Falls, ID)
Times Record (Troy, NY)

Triumph
TV Guide
UCLA Newsroom
USA Today
Vanity Fair
Variety
Vox

Washington Monthly
Washington Post
Washington Post Magazine
Washington Star
Woman Constitutionalist
Word and Way

INTERVIEWS

Archive of American Television, Television Academy Foundation, North Hollywood, CA
    Alan Alda, interview by Michael Rosen, November 17, 2000, New York, NY
    Allan Blye, interview by Adrienne Faillace, April 24, 2019, Cathedral City, CA
    Sam Bobrick, interview by Amy Harrington, December 12, 2016, Los Angeles, CA
    Paul Bogart, interview by Michael Rosen, May 19, 2001, Chapel Hill, NC
    James L. Brooks, interview by Karen Herman, January 17 and February 12, 2003, Bel Air, CA
    Allan Burns, interview by Dan Pasternack, February 18, 2004, Brentwood, CA
    Ron Clark, interview by Stephen J. Abramson, November 23, 2015, Los Angeles, CA
    Bill Dana, interview by Jeff Abraham, February 10, 2007, Los Angeles, CA
    Larry Gelbart, interview by Dan Harrison, May 26, 1998, Los Angeles, CA
    Leonard H. Goldenson, interview by Marvin Wolf, May 14, 1996, Long Boat Key, FL
    Carl Gottlieb, interview by Dan Pasternack, October 24, 2018, North Hollywood, CA
    Austin Kalish and Irma Kalish, interview by Amy Harrington, December 21, 2012, Los Angeles, CA
    H. Wesley Kenney, interview by Gary Rutkowski, April 30, 2008, North Hollywood, CA
    Mort Lachman, interview by Jeff Abraham, January 26, 2004, Los Angeles, CA
    Perry Lafferty, interview by Morrie Gelman, December 4, 1997, Brentwood, CA
    Norman Lear, interview by Morrie Gelman, February 26, 1998, Brentwood, CA
    Sheldon Leonard, interview by Sam Denoff, July 11, 1996, Beverly Hills, CA
    Carroll O'Connor, interview by Charles Davis, August 13, 1999, Malibu, CA
    Marian Rees, interview by Karen Herman, September 3 and November 5, 2004, Studio City, CA
    Carl Reiner, interview by Morrie Gelman, March 23, 1998, Los Angeles, CA
    Rob Reiner, interview by Karen Herman, November 29, 2004, Beverly Hills, CA
    Gene Reynolds, interview by Henry Colman, August 22, 2000, Los Angeles, CA
    Larry Rhine, interview by Gary Rutkowski, February 24, 2000, Brentwood, CA
    John Rich, interview by Henry Colman, August 3, 1999, Beverly Hills, CA
    Stanley Ralph Ross, interview by Dan Pasternack, February 11, 1998, Beverly Hills, CA
    Bob Schiller and Bob Weiskopf, interview by Karen Herman, April 4, 2000, Santa Monica, CA
    George Schlatter, interview by Dan Pasternack, March 6, 2002, Los Angeles, CA
    Alfred Schneider, interview by Karen Herman, July 22, 2004, New York, NY
    Fred Silverman, interview by Dan Pasternack, March 16 and March 29, 2001, Westwood, CA
    Tom Smothers and Dick Smothers, interview by Karen Herman, October 14, 2000, Las Vegas, NV

Frank Stanton, interview by Don West, May 22, 2000, New York, NY
Jean Stapleton, interview by Karen Herman, November 28, 2000, Brentwood, CA
Ben Starr, interview by Dan Harrison, November 9, 2009, Los Angeles, CA
William Tankersley, interview by Don Carleton, May 17, 2001, Wharton, VA
Mel Tolkin, interview by Bob Claster, November 4, 1997, Beverly Hills, CA
Bud Yorkin, interview by Morrie Gelman, December 2, 1997, Beverly Hills, CA
Author Interviews
Virginia Carter, February 16, 2016, videoconference
Norman Lear, March 18, 2017, videoconference
Norman Lear, December 13, 2017, Beverly Hills, CA
George D. Woods Oral History Project, Rare Books and Manuscript
    Library, Columbia University, New York, NY
Arthur R. Taylor, interview by John T. Mason Jr., January 23, 1985, New York, NY
1977 International Women's Year Oral History Collection, Department
    of Oral History, University of South Carolina, Columbia
Jean Stapleton, interview by Constance Ashton Myers, n.d. 1977, Houston, TX
TV Oral History Project, Donald McGannon Communication Research
    Center, Fordham University Libraries, New York, NY
Norman Lear, interview by Margot Hardenbergh, March 16, 2005, Beverly Hills, CA
Richard Wiley, interview by Margot Hardenbergh, January 27, 2005, Washington, DC

TELEVISION SHOWS

ABC Evening News
All in the Family
Barney Miller
Black-ish
CBS Evening News with Walter Cronkite
Cheers
The David Frost Show
The Dean Martin Show
The Dick Cavett Show
Dick Cavett's Watergate
Dinah!
The Fresh Prince of Bel-Air
The Golden Girls
The Jack Paar Program
The Late Show with Stephen Colbert
Look Up and Live
The MacNeil/Lehrer Report
The Mary Tyler Moore Show
M*A*S*H
Maude
The Merv Griffin Show
Midday
Morning Joe
Murphy Brown
The Nanny
NBC Evening News
Parks and Recreation
Seinfeld
60 Minutes
Spin City
The Tonight Show Starring Johnny Carson
Tonight Starring Jack Paar

Published Primary Sources

Burrows, James, and Eddy Friedfeld. *Directed by James Burrows: Five Decades of Stories from the Legendary Director of "Taxi," "Cheers," "Frasier," "Friends," "Will & Grace," and More.* New York: Ballantine Books, 2022.
Cavett, Dick. *Talk Show: Confrontations, Pointed Commentary, and Off-Screen Secrets.* New York: Times Books, 2010.

Chauncey, Tom, and Gordon A. Sabine. *Tom Chauncey: A Memoir*. Tempe: Arizona State University Libraries, 1989.
Colson, Charles W. *Born Again*. New York: Bantam Books, 1977.
Dann, Mike. *As I Saw It: The Inside Story of the Golden Years of Television*. El Prado, New Mexico: Levine Mesa, 2009.
Dougherty, Richard. *Goodbye, Mr. Christian: A Personal Account of McGovern's Rise and Fall*. New York: Doubleday, 1973.
Ehrlichman, John. *Witness to Power: The Nixon Years*. New York: Simon and Schuster, 1982.
Griffin, Merv, and Peter Barsocchini. *Merv: An Autobiography*. New York: Simon and Schuster, 1980.
Haldeman, H. R. *The Haldeman Diaries: Inside the Nixon White House*. New York: G. P. Putnam's Sons, 1994.
Haldeman, H. R., and Joseph DiMona. *The Ends of Power*. New York: Times Books, 1978.
Hart, Gary Warren. *Right from the Start: A Chronicle of the McGovern Campaign*. New York: Quadrangle, 1973.
Hess, Stephen. *Bit Player: My Life with Presidents and Ideas*. Washington, DC: Brookings Institution Press, 2018.
Klein, Herbert G. *Making It Perfectly Clear*. New York: Doubleday, 1980.
Kuhn, Maggie, Christina Long, and Laura Quinn. *No Stone Unturned: The Life and Times of Maggie Kuhn*. New York: Ballantine Books, 1991.
Lear, Frances. *The Second Seduction*. New York: Alfred A. Knopf, 1992.
Lear, Norman. *Even This I Get to Experience*. New York: Penguin Books, 2014.
Lindsay, John V. *The City*. New York: W. W. Norton, 1970.
Magruder, Jeb Stuart. *An American Life: One Man's Road to Watergate*. New York: Pocket Books, 1975.
McMahon, Ed, and David Fisher. *When Television Was Young: The Inside Story with Memories by Legends of the Small Screen*. Nashville: Thomas Nelson, 2007.
Nixon, Richard. *RN: The Memoirs of Richard Nixon*. New York: Simon and Schuster, 1990.
Nixon, Richard. *Six Crises*. Garden City: Doubleday, 1962.
O'Connor, Carroll. *I Think I'm Outta Here: A Memoir of All My Families*. New York: Pocket Books, 1998.
Paley, William S. *As It Happened: A Memoir*. Garden City, NY: Doubleday, 1979.
Poindexter, David O. *Out of the Darkness of Centuries*. Charleston, SC: BookSurge, 2009.
Price, Raymond. *With Nixon*. New York: Viking, 1977.
Rich, John. *Warm Up the Snake: A Hollywood Memoir*. Ann Arbor: University of Michigan Press, 2006.
Safire, William. *Before the Fall: An Inside View of the Pre-Watergate White House*. New York: Doubleday, 1975.
Schneider, Alfred R., and Kaye Pullen. *The Gatekeeper: My 30 Years as a TV Censor*. Syracuse, NY: Syracuse University Press, 2002.
Stapleton, Jean. Foreword to *Edith the Good: The Transformation of Edith Bunker from Total Woman to Whole Person*, by Spencer Marsh. New York: Harper and Row, 1977.
Stuart, Charles. *Never Trust a Local: Inside the Nixon White House*. New York: Algora, 2005.
Thompson, Hunter S. *Fear and Loathing on the Campaign Trail '72*. New York: Popular Library, 1973.

Secondary Sources

Adler, Richard P., ed. *"All in the Family": A Critical Appraisal*. New York: Praeger, 1979.
Allen, Craig. *Eisenhower and the Mass Media: Peace, Prosperity, and Prime-Time TV*. Chapel Hill: University of North Carolina Press, 1993.
Alley, Robert S. *Television: Ethics for Hire?* Nashville: Abingdon, 1977.
Alley, Robert, and Irby Brown. *Women Television Producers, 1948–2000*. Rochester, NY: University of Rochester Press, 2001.
Ambrose, Stephen E. *Nixon: The Education of a Politician, 1913–1962*. New York: Simon and Schuster, 1987.
Andelic, Patrick. *Donkey Work: Congressional Democrats in Conservative America, 1974–1994*. Lawrence: University Press of Kansas, 2019.
Anderson, Patrick. *Electing Jimmy Carter: The Campaign of 1976*. Baton Rouge: Louisiana State University Press, 1994.
Anson, Robert Sam. *McGovern: A Biography*. New York: Holt, Rinehart and Winston, 1972.
Appy, Christian G. *Working-Class War: American Combat Soldiers and Vietnam*. Chapel Hill: University of North Carolina Press, 1993.
Ashby, LeRoy, and Rod Gramer. *Fighting the Odds: The Life of Senator Frank Church*. Pullman: Washington State University Press, 1994.
Bailey, Beth, and David Farber, eds. *America in the Seventies*. Lawrence: University Press of Kansas, 2004.
Barnouw, Erik. *Tube of Plenty: The Evolution of American Television*. New York: Oxford University Press, 1990.
Barrett, Marvin, ed. *Survey of Broadcast Journalism, 1969–1970: Year of Challenge, Year of Crisis*. New York: Grosset and Dunlap, 1970.
Barrett, Marvin, ed. *Survey of Broadcast Journalism, 1970–1971: A State of Siege*. New York: Grosset and Dunlap, 1971.
Barrett, Marvin, ed. *Survey of Broadcast Journalism, 1971–1972: The Politics of Broadcasting*. New York: Thomas Y. Crowell, 1973.
Baughman, James L. *Television's Guardians: The FCC and the Politics of Programming, 1958–1967*. Knoxville: University of Tennessee Press, 1985.
Bebout, Lee. "Weaponizing Victimhood: Discourses of Oppression and the Maintenance of Supremacy on the Right." In *News on the Right: Studying Conservative News Cultures*, edited by Anthony Nadler and A. J. Bauer, 64–83. New York: Oxford University Press, 2020.
Bedell, Sally. *Up the Tube: Prime-Time TV and the Silverman Years*. New York: Viking, 1981.
Berg, A. Scott *Goldwyn: A Biography*. New York: Riverhead Books, 1989.
Berkowitz, Edward D. *Something Happened: A Political and Cultural Overview of the Seventies*. New York: Columbia University Press, 2007.
Bernstein, Carl, and Bob Woodward. *All the President's Men*. New York: Simon and Schuster, 1974.
Berry, Joseph P. *John F. Kennedy and the Media: The First Television President*. Lanham, MD: University Press of America, 1987.
Bethea, Charles G. "The Fairness Doctrine and Entertainment Programming: *All in the Family*." *Georgia Law Review* 7, no. 3 (1973): 554–70.

Bianculli, David. *Dangerously Funny: The Uncensored Story of "The Smothers Brothers Comedy Hour."* New York: Simon and Schuster, 2009.

Bird, Caroline. *What Women Want: From the Official Report to the President, the Congress and the People of the United States.* New York: Simon and Schuster, 1979.

Biskind, Peter. *Easy Riders, Raging Bulls: How the Sex-Drugs-and-Rock 'n' Roll Generation Saved Hollywood.* New York: Simon and Schuster, 1999.

Bloodworth, Jeffrey. *Losing the Center: The Decline of American Liberalism, 1968–1992.* Lexington: University Press of Kentucky, 2013.

Boddy, William. *Fifties Television: The Industry and Its Critics.* Urbana: University of Illinois Press, 1990.

Bodroghkozy, Aniko. *Equal Time: Television and the Civil Rights Movement.* Champaign: University of Illinois Press, 2013.

Bodroghkozy, Aniko. *Groove Tube: Sixties Television and the Youth Rebellion.* Durham, NC: Duke University Press, 2001.

Bodroghkozy, Aniko. Introduction to *A Companion to the History of American Broadcasting*, edited by Aniko Bodroghkozy, 1–23. Hoboken, NJ: Wiley Blackwell, 2018.

Bodroghkozy, Aniko. "The Media." In *A Companion to John F. Kennedy*, edited by Marc J. Selverstone, 187–206. Oxford, UK: Wiley Blackwell, 2014.

Bogle, Donald. *Primetime Blues: African Americans on Network Television.* New York: Farrar, Straus and Giroux, 2001.

Boorstin, Daniel J. *The Image: A Guide to Pseudo-Events in America.* New York: Harper Colophon, 1964.

Bradley, Patricia. *Mass Media and the Shaping of American Feminism, 1963–1975.* Jackson: University Press of Mississippi, 2004.

Branch, Taylor. *Pillar of Fire: America in the King Years, 1963–65.* New York: Simon and Schuster, 1998.

Brinkley, Douglas. *Cronkite.* New York: HarperCollins, 2012.

Brinkley, Douglas, and Luke A. Nichter, eds. *The Nixon Tapes, 1971–1972.* New York: Mariner Books, 2015.

Brock, Laura E. "Religion, Sex & Politics: The Story of the Equal Rights Amendment in Florida." PhD diss., Florida State University, 2013.

Brook, Vincent. "Checks and Imbalances: Political Economy and the Rise and Fall of *East Side/West Side*." *Journal of Film and Video* 50, no. 3 (1998): 24–39.

Brown, Les. *Keeping Your Eye on Television.* New York: Pilgrim, 1979.

Brown, Les. *Televi$ion: The Business behind the Box.* New York: Harcourt Brace Jovanovich, 1971.

Brownell, Kathryn Cramer. "'Ideological Plugola,' 'Elitist Gossip,' and the Need for Cable Television." In *Media Nation: The Political History of News in Modern America*, edited by Bruce J. Schulman and Julian E. Zelizer, 160–75. Philadelphia: University of Pennsylvania Press, 2017.

Brownell, Kathryn Cramer. *Showbiz Politics: Hollywood in American Political Life.* Chapel Hill: University of North Carolina Press, 2014.

Brownell, Kathryn Cramer. *24/7 Politics: Cable Television and the Fragmenting of America from Watergate to Fox News.* Princeton, NJ: Princeton University Press, 2023.

Brownell, Kathryn Cramer. "Watergate, the Bipartisan Struggle for Media Access, and the Growth of Cable Television." *Modern American History* 3, no. 3 (2020): 175–98.

Brownmiller, Susan. *Against Our Will: Men, Women, and Rape*. New York: Ballantine Books, 1993.

Brownstein, Ronald. *The Power and the Glitter: The Hollywood-Washington Connection*. New York: Pantheon Books, 1990.

Brownstein, Ronald. *Rock Me on the Water: 1974, the Year Los Angeles Transformed Movies, Music, Television, and Politics*. New York: Harper, 2021.

Bruck, Connie. *When Hollywood Had a King: The Reign of Lew Wasserman, Who Leveraged Talent into Power and Influence*. New York: Random House, 2003.

Buzenberg, Susan, and Bill Buzenberg, eds. *Salant, CBS, and the Battle for the Soul of Broadcast Journalism: The Memoirs of Richard S. Salant*. Boulder, CO: Westview, 1999.

Cadava, Geraldo. *The Hispanic Republican: The Shaping of an American Political Identity, from Nixon to Trump*. New York: Ecco, 2020.

Calhoun, Claudia. *Only the Names Have Been Changed: "Dragnet," the Police Procedural, and Postwar Culture*. Austin: University of Texas Press, 2022.

Campbell, Sean. *The Sitcoms of Norman Lear*. Jefferson, NC: McFarland, 2007.

Cannato, Vincent J. *The Ungovernable City: John Lindsay and His Struggle to Save New York*. New York: Basic Books, 2002.

Cannon, Lou. *Reagan*. New York: G. P. Putnam's Sons, 1982.

Caro, Robert A. *The Power Broker: Robert Moses and the Fall of New York*. New York: Vintage Books, 1975.

Carr, Steven. *Hollywood and Anti-Semitism: A Cultural History up to World War II*. Cambridge: Cambridge University Press, 2001.

Carroll, Peter N. *It Seemed Like Nothing Happened: The Tragedy and Promise of America in the 1970s*. New York: Holt, Rinehart and Winston, 1982.

Castleman, Harry, and Walter J. Podrazik. *Watching TV: Six Decades of American Television*. Syracuse, NY: Syracuse University Press, 2010.

Cebul, Brent, Lily Geismer, and Mason B. Williams. "Beyond Red and Blue: Crisis and Continuity in Twentieth-Century US Political History." In *Shaped by the State: Toward a New Political History of the Twentieth Century*, edited by Brent Cebul, Lily Geismer, and Mason B. Williams, 3–17. Chicago: University of Chicago Press, 2019.

Chattoo, Caty Borum, and Lauren Feldman. *A Comedian and an Activist Walk into a Bar: The Serious Role of Comedy in Social Justice*. Oakland: University of California Press, 2020.

Chester, Lewis, Godfrey Hodgson, and Bruce Page. *An American Melodrama: The Presidential Campaign of 1968*. New York: Viking, 1969.

Clark, Jennifer S. *Producing Feminism: Television Work in the Age of Women's Liberation*. Oakland: University of California Press, 2024.

Classen, Steven D. *Watching Jim Crow: The Struggles over Mississippi TV, 1955–1969*. Durham, NC: Duke University Press, 2004.

Cobble, Dorothy Sue, Linda Gordon, and Astrid Henry. *Feminism Unfinished: A Short, Surprising History of American Women's Movements*. New York: Liveright, 2014.

Cohen, Lizabeth. *A Consumers' Republic: The Politics of Mass Consumption in Postwar America*. New York: Vintage Books, 2003.

Cohen, Michael A. *American Maelstrom: The 1968 Election and the Politics of Division*. New York: Oxford University Press, 2016.

Cohn, Jonathan, and Jennifer Porst, eds. *Very Special Episodes: Televising Industrial and Social Change*. New Brunswick, NJ: Rutgers University Press, 2021.

Collins, Gail. *When Everything Changed: The Amazing Journey of American Women from 1960 to the Present*. Boston: Little, Brown, 2009.

Collins, Kathleen. "The Trouble with Archie: Locating and Accessing Primary Sources for the Study of the 1970s US Sitcom, *All in the Family*." *Critical Studies in Television* 5, no. 2 (2010): 118–32.

Connelly, Matthew. *Fatal Misconception: The Struggle to Control World Population*. Cambridge, MA: Belknap Press of Harvard University Press, 2008.

Conway, Mike. *Contested Ground: "The Tunnel" and the Struggle over Television News in Cold War America*. Amherst: University of Massachusetts Press, 2019.

Cowan, Geoffrey. *See No Evil: The Backstage Battle over Sex and Violence on Television*. New York: Simon and Schuster, 1979.

Cowie, Jefferson. *Stayin' Alive: The 1970s and the Last Days of the Working Class*. New York: New Press, 2010.

Coyne, John R., Jr. *The Impudent Snobs: Agnew vs. the Intellectual Establishment*. New Rochelle, NY: Arlington House, 1972.

Cripps, Thomas. "*Amos 'n' Andy* and the Debate over American Racial Integration." In *American History/American Television: Interpreting the Video Past*, edited by John E. O'Connor, 33–54. New York: Frederick Ungar, 1983.

Critchlow, Donald T. *Phyllis Schlafly and Grassroots Conservatism: A Woman's Crusade*. Princeton, NJ: Princeton University Press, 2005.

Critchlow, Donald T. *When Hollywood Was Right: How Movie Stars, Studio Moguls, and Big Business Remade American Politics*. Cambridge: Cambridge University Press, 2013.

Crouse, Timothy. *The Boys on the Bus*. New York: Random House, 2003.

Cuklanz, Lisa M. *Rape on Prime Time: Television, Masculinity, and Sexual Violence*. Philadelphia: University of Pennsylvania Press, 1999.

Cullen, Jim. *Those Were the Days: Why "All in the Family" Still Matters*. New Brunswick, NJ: Rutgers University Press, 2020.

Davis, Flora. *Moving the Mountain: The Women's Movement in America since 1960*. New York: Simon and Schuster, 1991.

Davison, W. Phillips. "The Third-Person Effect in Communication." *Public Opinion Quarterly* 47, no. 1 (1983): 1–15.

Decker, Jefferson. *The Other Rights Revolution: Conservative Lawyers and the Remaking of American Government*. New York: Oxford University Press, 2016.

Delmont, Matthew F. *Why Busing Failed: Race, Media, and the National Resistance to School Desegregation*. Berkeley: University of California Press, 2016.

Deveney, Sean. *Fun City: John Lindsay, Joe Namath, and How Sports Saved New York in the 1960s*. New York: Sports Publishing, 2015.

Diggins, John P. *The Proud Decades: America in War and Peace, 1941–1960*. New York: W. W. Norton, 1989.

Dochuk, Darren. *From Bible Belt to Sun Belt: Plain-Folk Religion, Grassroots Politics, and the Rise of Evangelical Conservatism*. New York: W. W. Norton, 2011.

Doherty, Thomas. *Cold War, Cool Medium: Television, McCarthyism, and American Culture*. New York: Columbia University Press, 2005.

Doherty, Thomas. *Hollywood's Censor: Joseph I. Breen and the Production Code Administration*. New York: Columbia University Press, 2007.

Douglas, Susan. *Where the Girls Are: Growing Up Female with the Mass Media*. New York: Penguin, 1995.

Dow, Bonnie J. *Prime-Time Feminism: Television, Media Culture, and the Women's Movement since 1970*. Philadelphia: University of Pennsylvania, 1996.

Dow, Bonnie J. *Watching Women's Liberation, 1970: Feminism's Pivotal Year on the Network News*. Champaign: University of Illinois Press, 2014.

Dowland, Seth. *Family Values and the Rise of the Christian Right*. Philadelphia: University of Pennsylvania Press, 2018.

Drew, Elizabeth. *Richard M. Nixon*. New York: Times Books, 2007.

Du Mez, Kristin Kobes. *Jesus and John Wayne: How White Evangelicals Corrupted a Faith and Fractured a Nation*. New York: W. W. Norton, 2020.

Efron, Edith. *The News Twisters*. Los Angeles: Nash, 1971.

Ely, Melvyn Patrick. *The Adventures of Amos 'n' Andy: A Social History of an American Phenomenon*. Charlottesville: University of Virginia Press, 2001.

Engelhardt, Tom. "Children's Television: The Shortcake Strategy." In *Watching Television: A Pantheon Guide to Popular Culture*, edited by Todd Gitlin, 68–110. New York: Pantheon Books, 1986.

Eskridge, Sara K. *Rube Tube: CBS and Rural Comedy in the Sixties*. Columbia: University of Missouri Press, 2018.

Evans, Sara M. *Tidal Wave: How Women Changed America at Century's End*. New York: Free Press, 2004.

Farrell, John A. *Richard Nixon: The Life*. New York: Penguin, 2018.

Feldstein, Mark. *Poisoning the Press: Richard Nixon, Jack Anderson, and the Rise of Washington's Scandal Culture*. New York: Farrar, Straus and Giroux, 2010.

Feuer, Jane. "MTM Enterprises: An Overview." In *MTM: Quality Television*, edited by Jane Feuer, Paul Kerr, and Tise Vahimagi, 1–31. London: British Film Institute, 1984.

Flippen, J. Brooks. *Jimmy Carter, the Politics of Family, and the Rise of the Religious Right*. Athens: University of Georgia Press, 2011.

Formisano, Ronald P. *Boston against Busing: Race, Class, and Ethnicity in the 1960s and 1970s*. Chapel Hill: University of North Carolina Press, 1991.

Frank, Gillian. "The Colour of the Unborn: Anti-Abortion and Anti-Bussing Politics in Michigan, United States, 1967–1973." *Gender and History* 26, no. 2 (2014): 351–78.

Frank, Jeffrey. *Ike and Dick: Portrait of a Strange Political Marriage*. New York: Simon and Schuster, 2013.

Freedman, Estelle B. *No Turning Back: The History of Feminism and the Future of Women*. New York: Ballantine Books, 2002.

Freedman, Estelle B. *Redefining Rape: Sexual Violence in the Era of Suffrage and Segregation*. Cambridge, MA: Harvard University Press, 2013.

Freeman, Joshua B. "Hardhats: Construction Workers, Manliness, and the 1970 Pro-War Demonstrations." *Journal of Social History* 26, no. 4 (1993): 725–44.
Gillis, William. "Say No to the Liberal Media: Conservatives and Criticism of the News Media in the 1970s." PhD diss., Indiana University, 2013.
Gitlin, Todd. *Inside Prime Time*. New York: Pantheon Books, 1985.
Gitlin, Todd. *The Whole World Is Watching: Mass Media in the Making and Unmaking of the New Left*. Berkeley: University of California Press, 2003.
Glickman, Lawrence B. *Free Enterprise: An American History*. New Haven, CT: Yale University Press, 2019.
Gomery, Douglas. *The Hollywood Studio System: A History*. London: British Film Institute, 2005.
Goodman, Carly. *Dreamland: America's Immigration Lottery in an Age of Restriction*. Chapel Hill: University of North Carolina Press, 2023.
Goodman, Carly. "Unmaking the Nation of Immigrants: How John Tanton's Network of Organizations Transformed Policy and Politics." In *A Field Guide to White Supremacy*, edited by Kathleen Belew and Ramón Gutiérrez, 203–19. Berkeley: University of California Press, 2021.
Goodwin, Sage. "Making the News: The Development of Network Television News and the Struggle for Black Freedom in the 1950s and 1960s." PhD diss., University of Oxford, 2022.
Gordon, Linda. "The Women's Liberation Movement." In *Feminism Unfinished: A Short, Surprising History of American Women's Movements*, edited by Dorothy Sue Cobble, Linda Gordon, and Astrid Henry, 69–146. New York: Liveright, 2014.
Goudsouzian, Aram. *The Men and the Moment: The Election of 1968 and the Rise of Partisan Politics in America*. Chapel Hill: University of North Carolina Press, 2019.
Gould, Lewis L. *1968: The Election That Changed America*. Chicago: Ivan R. Dee, 2010.
Gould, Lewis L., ed. *Watching Television Come of Age: "The New York Times" Reviews of Jack Gould*. Austin: University of Texas Press, 2002.
Greenberg, David. "Do Historians Watch Enough TV? Broadcast News as a Primary Source." In *Doing Recent History: On Privacy, Copyright, Video Games, Institutional Review Boards, Activist Scholarship, and History That Talks Back*, edited by Claire Bond Potter and Renee C. Romano, 185–200. Athens: University of Georgia Press, 2012.
Greenberg, David. "The Idea of 'the Liberal Media' and Its Roots in the Civil Rights Movement." *Sixties* 1, no. 2 (2008): 167–86.
Greenberg, David. "A New Way of Campaigning: Eisenhower, Stevenson, and the Anxieties of Television Politics." In *Liberty and Justice for All: Rethinking Politics in Cold War America, 1945–1965*, edited by Kathleen Donohue, 185–212. Amherst: University of Massachusetts Press, 2012.
Greenberg, David. *Nixon's Shadow: The History of an Image*. New York: W. W. Norton, 2003.
Greenberg, David. *The Republic of Spin: An Inside History of the American Presidency*. New York: W. W. Norton, 2016.
Gregory, Mollie. *Women Who Run the Show: How a Brilliant and Creative New Generation of Women Stormed Hollywood*. New York: St. Martin's, 2002.

Grossman, Matt, and David A. Hopkins. *Asymmetric Politics: Ideological Republicans and Group Interest Democrats*. New York: Oxford University Press, 2016.

Guess, Andrew, Benjamin Lyons, Brendan Nyhan, and Jason Reifler. *Avoiding the Echo Chamber about Echo Chambers: Why Selective Exposure to Like-Minded Political News Is Less Prevalent Than You Think*. Miami, FL: Knight Foundation, 2018.

Halberstam, David. *The Powers That Be*. New York: Knopf, 1979.

Hallin, Daniel C. *The Uncensored War: The Media and Vietnam*. Berkeley: University of California Press, 1989.

Harris, Jay S. *"TV Guide": The First 25 Years*. New York: Simon and Schuster, 1978.

Hartman, Andrew. *A War for the Soul of America: A History of the Culture Wars*. Chicago: University of Chicago Press, 2019.

Haygood, Wil. *In Black and White: The Life of Sammy Davis, Jr.* New York: Billboard Books, 2003.

Hemmer, Nicole. *Messengers of the Right: Conservative Media and the Transformation of American Politics*. Philadelphia: University of Pennsylvania Press, 2016.

Hemmer, Nicole. *Partisans: The Conservative Revolutionaries Who Remade American Politics in the 1990s*. New York: Basic Books, 2022.

Hendershot, Heather. *Open to Debate: How William F. Buckley Put Liberal America on the Firing Line*. New York: Broadside Books, 2016.

Hendershot, Heather. *What's Fair on the Air? Cold War Right-Wing Broadcasting and the Public Interest*. Chicago: University of Chicago Press, 2011.

Hendershot, Heather. *When the News Broke: Chicago 1968 and the Polarizing of America*. Chicago: University of Chicago Press, 2022.

Hess, Stephen, and David Broder. *The Republican Establishment: The Present and Future of the G.O.P.* New York: Harper and Row, 1967.

Hilmes, Michele. *Only Connect: A Cultural History of Broadcasting in the United States*. Boston: Wadsworth, 2014.

Hilton, Adam. "The Path to Polarization: McGovern-Fraser, Counter-Reformers, and the Rise of the Advocacy Party." *Studies in American Political Development* 33, no. 1 (2019): 87–109.

Hinton, Elizabeth. *From the War on Poverty to the War on Crime: The Making of Mass Incarceration in America*. Cambridge, MA: Harvard University Press, 2016.

Hirshon, Nicholas. "One More Miracle: The Groundbreaking Media Campaign of John 'Mets' Lindsay." *American Journalism* 34, no. 1 (2017): 2–25.

Hoff, Derek S. *The State and the Stork: The Population Debate and Policy Making in US History*. Chicago: University of Chicago Press, 2012.

Holden, Charles J., Zach Messitte, and Jerald Podair. *Republican Populist: Spiro Agnew and the Origins of Donald Trump's America*. Charlottesville: University of Virginia, 2019.

Holland, Jennifer L. *Tiny You: A Western History of the Anti-Abortion Movement*. Oakland: University of California Press, 2020.

Huntington, John S. *Far-Right Vanguard: The Radical Roots of Modern Conservatism*. Philadelphia: University of Pennsylvania Press, 2021.

Jacobs, Meg. *Panic at the Pump: The Energy Crisis and the Transformation of American Politics in the 1970s*. New York: Hill and Wang, 2016.

Jamieson, Kathleen Hall. *Packaging the Presidency: A History and Criticism of Presidential Campaign Advertising*. New York: Oxford University Press, 1996.

Jaramillo, Deborah L. *The Television Code: Regulating the Screen to Safeguard the Industry*. Austin: University of Texas Press, 2018.

Jenkins, Philip. *Decade of Nightmares: The End of the Sixties and the Making of Eighties America*. New York: Oxford University Press, 2006.

Johnson, Nicholas. *How to Talk Back to Your Television Set*. Boston: Little, Brown, 1970.

Kabaservice, Geoffrey. *Rule and Ruin: The Downfall of Moderation and the Destruction of the Republican Party, from Eisenhower to the Tea Party*. New York: Oxford University Press, 2012.

Kalman, Laura. *Right Star Rising: A New Politics, 1974–1980*. New York: W. W. Norton, 2010.

Keeley, Joseph. *The Left-Leaning Antenna: Political Bias in Television*. New Rochelle, NY: Arlington House, 1971.

Kirshner, Jonathan. *Hollywood's Last Golden Age: Politics, Society, and the Seventies Film in America*. Ithaca, NY: Cornell University Press, 2013.

Koncewicz, Michael. *They Said No to Nixon: Republicans Who Stood Up to the President's Abuses of Power*. Berkeley: University of California Press, 2018.

Kruse, Kevin M. *One Nation under God: How Corporate America Invented Christian America*. New York: Basic Books, 2015.

Kruse, Kevin M. "'Why Don't You Just Get an Actor?' The Advent of Television in the 1952 Campaign." In *America at the Ballot Box: Elections and Political History*, edited by Gareth Davies and Julian E. Zelizer, 167–83. Philadelphia: University of Pennsylvania Press, 2015.

Kruse, Kevin M., and Julian E. Zelizer. *Fault Lines: A History of the United States since 1974*. New York: W. W. Norton, 2019.

Kuhn, David Paul. *Hardhat Riot: Nixon, New York, and the Dawn of the White Working-Class Revolution*. New York: Oxford University Press, 2020.

Lassiter, Matthew D. *The Silent Majority: Suburban Politics in the Sunbelt South*. Princeton, NJ: Princeton University Press, 2006.

Lassiter, Matthew D. *The Suburban Crisis: White America and the War on Drugs*. Princeton, NJ: Princeton University Press, 2023.

Lawrence, John A. *Class of '74: Congress after Watergate and the Roots of Partisanship*. Baltimore: Johns Hopkins University Press, 2018.

Leader, Shelah Gilbert, and Patricia Rusch Hyatt. *American Women on the Move: The Inside History of the National Women's Conference, 1977*. Lanham, MD: Lexington Books, 2016.

Lelyveld, Joseph. *Omaha Blues: A Memory Loop*. New York: Farrar, Straus and Giroux, 2005.

Leuchtenburg, William E. *In the Shadow of FDR: From Harry Truman to Barack Obama*. Ithaca, NY: Cornell University Press, 2009.

Levine, Elana. *Wallowing in Sex: The New Sexual Culture of 1970s American Television*. Durham, NC: Duke University Press, 2007.

Lewis, Jon. *Road Trip to Nowhere: Hollywood Encounters the Counterculture*. Oakland: University of California Press, 2022.

Lewis, Penny. *Hardhats, Hippies, and Hawks: The Vietnam Antiwar Movement as Myth and Memory*. Ithaca, NY: ILR Press, 2013.
Lippman, Theo, Jr., and Donald C. Hansen. *Muskie*. New York: W. W. Norton, 1971.
Lizzi, Maria C. "'My Heart Is as Black as Yours': White Backlash, Racial Identity, and Italian American Stereotypes in New York City's 1969 Mayoral Campaign." *Journal of American Ethnic History* 27, no. 3 (2008): 43–80.
Lombardo, Timothy J. *Blue-Collar Conservatism: Frank Rizzo's Philadelphia and Populist Politics*. Philadelphia: University of Pennsylvania Press, 2018.
Lotz, Amanda D. *The Television Will Be Revolutionized*. New York: New York University Press, 2007.
Lowitt, Richard. *Fred Harris: His Journey from Liberalism to Populism*. Lanham, MD: Rowman and Littlefield, 2002.
Lyons, Eugene. *David Sarnoff: A Biography*. New York: Harper and Row, 1966.
MacDonald, J. Fred. *Blacks and White TV: African Americans in Television since 1948*. Chicago: Nelson-Hall, 1992.
MacDonald, J. Fred. *One Nation under Television: The Rise and Decline of Network TV*. New York: Pantheon Books, 1990.
MacDonald, J. Fred. *Television and the Red Menace: The Video Road to Vietnam*. New York: Praeger, 1985.
MacNeil, Robert. *The People Machine: The Influence of Television on American Politics*. New York: Harper and Row, 1968.
Mansbridge, Jane J. *Why We Lost the ERA*. Chicago: University of Chicago Press, 1986.
Márquez, Cecilia. *Making the Latino South: A History of Racial Formation*. Chapel Hill: University of North Carolina Press, 2023.
Mattingly, Doreen J. *A Feminist in the White House: Midge Costanza, the Carter Years, and America's Culture Wars*. New York: Oxford University Press, 2016.
May, Ernest R. Introduction to *Campaign '72: The Managers Speak*, edited by Ernest R. May and Janet Fraser, 1–29. Cambridge, MA: Harvard University Press, 1973.
Mayer, Martin. *About Television*. New York: Harper and Row, 1972.
Mayer, Martin. *Madison Avenue, USA*. New York: Harper and Brothers, 1958.
McChesney, Robert W. *Communication Revolution: Critical Junctures and the Future of Media*. New York: New Press, 2007.
McCrohan, Donna. *Archie & Edith, Mike & Gloria: The Tumultuous History of "All in the Family."* New York: Workman, 1987.
McDougal, Dennis. *The Last Mogul: Lew Wasserman, MCA, and the Hidden History of Hollywood*. New York: Crown, 1998.
McGinniss, Joe. *The Selling of the President, 1968*. New York: Trident, 1969.
McGirr, Lisa. *Suburban Warriors: The Origins of the New American Right*. Princeton, NJ: Princeton University Press, 2001.
McLuhan, Marshall. *Understanding Media: The Extensions of Man*. Cambridge, MA: MIT Press, 1994.
McRae, Elizabeth Gillespie. *Mothers of Massive Resistance: White Women and the Politics of White Supremacy*. New York: Oxford University Press, 2018.
Mead, Frank S. *Handbook of Denominations in the United States*. Nashville, TN: Abingdon, 1975.

Mendelhall, Robert Roy. "Responses to Television from the New Christian Right: The Don Wildmon Organizations." PhD diss., University of Texas at Austin, 1994.

Merton, Joe. "Rethinking the Politics of White Ethnicity in 1970s America." *Historical Journal* 55, no. 3 (2012): 731–56.

Metz, Robert. *CBS: Reflections in a Bloodshot Eye*. Chicago: Playboy, 1975.

Miller, Jeffrey S. "What Closes on Saturday Night." In *NBC: America's Network*, edited by Michele Hilmes, 192–208. Berkeley: University of California Press, 2007.

Mills, Kay. *Changing Channels: The Civil Rights Case That Transformed Television*. Jackson: University Press of Mississippi, 2004.

Milov, Sarah. *The Cigarette: A Political History*. Cambridge, MA: Harvard University Press, 2019.

Miroff, Bruce. *The Liberals' Moment: The McGovern Insurgency and the Identity Crisis of the Democratic Party*. Lawrence: University Press of Kansas, 2007.

Mitchell, Franklin D. *Harry S. Truman and the News Media: Contentious Relations, Belated Respect*. Columbia: University of Missouri Press, 1998.

Montgomery, Kathryn C. *Target: Prime Time: Advocacy Groups and the Struggles over Television Entertainment*. Oxford: Oxford University Press, 1989.

Morgenthau, Ruth S. *Pride without Prejudice: The Life of John O. Pastore*. Providence: Rhode Island Historical Society, 1989.

Murphy, Caryn. "Black Panthers in *Peyton Place*: Integrating the Prime-Time Serial." *Media History* 26, no. 2 (2020): 185–98.

Murray, John P., Eli A. Rubinstein, and George A. Comstock, eds. *Television and Social Behavior: A Technical Report to the Surgeon General's Advisory Committee on Television and Social Behavior*. Washington, DC: Government Printing Office, 1972.

Mutz, Diana C., and Lilach Nir. "Not Necessarily the News: Does Fictional Television Influence Real-World Policy Preferences?" *Mass Communication and Society* 13, no. 2 (2010): 196–217.

Nadel, Alan. *Television in Black-and-White America: Race and National Identity*. Lawrence: University Press of Kansas, 2005.

National Association of Broadcasters. *The Television Code*. 14th ed. Washington, DC: National Association of Broadcasters, 1969.

National Commission on the Observance of International Women's Year. *The Spirit of Houston: The First National Women's Conference*. Washington, DC: National Commission on the Observance of International Women's Year, 1978.

Nelson, Michael. *Resilient America: Electing Nixon in 1968, Challenging Dissent, and Dividing Government*. Lawrence: University Press of Kansas, 2017.

Nesteroff, Kliph. *The Comedians: Drunks, Thieves, Scoundrels and the History of American Comedy*. New York: Grove, 2015.

Nesteroff, Kliph. *Outrageous: A History of Showbiz and the Culture Wars*. New York: Abrams, 2023.

Neuwirth, Allan. *They'll Never Put That on the Air: An Oral History of Taboo-Breaking TV Comedy*. New York: Allworth, 2006.

Newcomb, Horace. *TV: The Most Popular Art*. Garden City, NY: Anchor Books, 1975.

Newcomb, Horace, and Robert S. Alley. *The Producer's Medium: Conversations with Creators of American TV*. New York: Oxford University Press, 1983.

Nussbaum, Emily. *I Like to Watch: Arguing My Way through the TV Revolution*. New York: Random House, 2019.
Offenbach, Seth. *The Conservative Movement and the Vietnam War: The Other Side of Vietnam*. New York: Routledge, 2019.
O'Mara, Margaret. *The Code: Silicon Valley and the Remaking of America*. New York: Penguin, 2019.
O'Mara, Margaret. *Pivotal Tuesdays: Four Elections That Shaped the Twentieth Century*. Philadelphia: University of Pennsylvania Press, 2015.
Oudes, Bruce, ed. *From the President: Richard Nixon's Secret Files*. New York: Harper and Row, 1989.
Ouellette, Laurie. *Viewers Like You: How Public TV Failed the People*. New York: Columbia University Press, 2002.
Ozersky, Josh. *Archie Bunker's America: TV in an Era of Change, 1968–1978*. Carbondale: Southern Illinois University Press, 2003.
Packard, Vance. *The Hidden Persuaders*. London: Longmans, Green, 1957.
Paper, Lewis J. *Empire: William S. Paley and the Making of CBS*. New York: St. Martin's, 1987.
Perlman, Allison. *Public Interests: Media Advocacy and Struggles over US Television*. New Brunswick, NJ: Rutgers University Press, 2016.
Perlstein, Rick. *Nixonland: The Rise of a President and the Fracturing of America*. New York: Scribner, 2008.
Perry, James M. *Us & Them: How the Press Covered the 1972 Election*. New York: Clarkson N. Potter, 1973.
Perry, Manon. *Broadcasting Birth Control: Mass Media and Family Planning*. New Brunswick, NJ: Rutgers University Press, 2013.
Petersen, Jennifer. *How Machines Came to Speak: Media Technologies and Freedom of Speech*. Durham, NC: Duke University Press, 2022.
Petruska, Karen C. "The Critical Eye: Re-Viewing 1970s Television." PhD diss., Georgia State University, 2012.
Petrzela, Natalia Mehlman. *Classroom Wars: Language, Sex, and the Making of Modern Political Culture*. New York: Oxford University Press, 2015.
Phillips-Fein, Kim. *Fear City: New York's Fiscal Crisis and the Rise of Austerity Politics*. New York: Metropolitan Books, 2017.
Pickard, Victor. *America's Battle for Media Democracy: The Triumph of Corporate Libertarianism and the Future of Media Reform*. New York: Cambridge University Press, 2015.
Pleck, Elizabeth. "Failed Strategies; Renewed Hope." In *Rights of Passage: The Past and Future of the ERA*, edited by Joan Hoff-Wilson, 106–20. Bloomington: Indiana University Press, 1986.
Ponce De Leon, Charles L. *That's the Way It Is: A History of Television News in America*. Chicago: University of Chicago Press, 2015.
Pondillo, Robert. *America's First Network TV Censor: The Work of NBC's Stockton Helffrich*. Carbondale: Southern Illinois University Press, 2010.
Poniewozik, James. *Audience of One: Donald Trump, Television, and the Fracturing of America*. New York: Liveright, 2019.

Porter, William E. *Assault on the Media: The Nixon Years*. Ann Arbor: University of Michigan Press, 1976.
Postman, Neil. *Amusing Ourselves to Death: Public Discourse in the Age of Show Business*. New York: Penguin, 2005.
Quail, Ben. "Propaganda and the Presidency: An Analysis of Lyndon B. Johnson's Media Relations, 1963–1968." PhD diss., University of Strathclyde, 2018.
Raphael, Chad. *Investigated Reporting: Muckrakers, Regulators, and the Struggle over Television Documentary*. Champaign: University of Illinois Press, 2005.
Rather, Dan, and Gary Paul Gates. *The Palace Guard*. New York: Harper and Row, 1974.
Raymond, Emilie. *Stars for Freedom: Hollywood, Black Celebrities, and the Civil Rights Movement*. Seattle: University of Washington Press, 2015.
Reeves, Richard. *President Nixon: Alone in the White House*. New York: Simon and Schuster, 2002.
Renfro, Paul. *Stranger Danger: Family Values, Childhood, and the American Carceral State*. New York: Oxford University Press, 2020.
Rieder, Jonathan. *Canarsie: The Jews and Italians of Brooklyn against Liberalism*. Cambridge, MA: Harvard University Press, 1985.
Roessner, Amber. *Jimmy Carter and the Birth of the Marathon Media Campaign*. Baton Rouge: Louisiana State University Press, 2020.
Rolsky, L. Benjamin. *The Rise and Fall of the Religious Left: Politics, Television, and Popular Culture in the 1970s and Beyond*. New York: Columbia University Press, 2019.
Rosen, Ruth. *The World Split Open: How the Modern Women's Movement Changed America*. New York: Penguin, 2000.
Rosenfeld, Sam. *The Polarizers: Postwar Architects of Our Partisan Era*. Chicago: University of Chicago Press, 2017.
Rosenwald, Brian. *Talk Radio's America: How an Industry Took Over a Political Party That Took Over the United States*. Cambridge, MA: Harvard University Press, 2019.
Ross, Steven J. *Hollywood Left and Right: How Movie Stars Shaped American Politics*. New York: Oxford University Press, 2011.
Rowland, Willard D., Jr. *The Politics of TV Violence: Policy Uses of Communications Research*. Beverly Hills, CA: Sage, 1983.
Sabin, Paul. *The Bet: Paul Ehrlich, Julian Simon, and Our Gamble over Earth's Future*. New Haven, CT: Yale University Press, 2013.
Sánchez, Jaime, Jr. "Revisiting McGovern-Fraser: Party Nationalization and the Rhetoric of Reform." *Journal of Policy History* 32, no. 1 (2020): 1–24.
Sandbrook, Dominic. *Mad as Hell: The Crisis of the 1970s and the Rise of the Populist Right*. New York: Alfred A. Knopf, 2011.
Schlozman, Daniel. *When Movements Anchor Parties: Electoral Alignments in American History*. Princeton, NJ: Princeton University Press, 2016.
Schlozman, Daniel, and Sam Rosenfeld. *The Hollow Parties: The Many Pasts and Disordered Present of American Party Politics*. Princeton, NJ: Princeton University Press, 2024.
Schneider, Molly A. *Gold Dust on the Air: Television Anthology Drama and Midcentury American Culture*. Austin: University of Texas Press, 2024.
Schorr, Daniel. *Clearing the Air*. Boston: Houghton Mifflin, 1977.

Schram, Martin. *The Great American Video Game: Presidential Politics in the Television Age.* New York: William Morrow, 1987.

Schudson, Michael. *The Power of News.* Cambridge, MA: Harvard University Press, 1995.

Schulman, Bruce J. "Post-1968 US History: Neo-Consensus History for the Age of Polarization." *Reviews in American History* 47, no. 3 (2019): 479–99.

Schulman, Bruce J. *The Seventies: The Great Shift in American Culture, Society, and Politics.* Boston: Da Capo, 2001.

Schumacher, Michael. *The Contest: The 1968 Election and the War for America's Soul.* Minneapolis: University of Minnesota Press, 2018.

Self, Robert O. *All in the Family: The Realignment of American Democracy since the 1960s.* New York: Hill and Wang, 2012.

Setoodeh, Ramin. *Apprentice in Wonderland: How Donald Trump and Mark Burnett Took America through the Looking Glass.* New York: HarperCollins, 2024.

Shepherd, Lauren Lassabe. *Resistance from the Right: Conservatives and the Campus Wars in Modern America.* Chapel Hill: University of North Carolina Press, 2023.

Small, Melvin. *The Presidency of Richard Nixon.* Lawrence: University Press of Kansas, 1999.

Smith, Sally Bedell. *In All His Glory: The Life and Times of William S. Paley, the Legendary Tycoon and His Brilliant Circle.* New York: Random House, 2002.

Socolow, Michael J. "Commercial Television's Secret Goldmine: The Hidden Riches Generated by US Network TV News, 1960–1970." *Journalism History* 49, no. 2 (2023): 91–94.

Socolow, Michael J. "'We Should Make Money on Our News': The Problem of Profitability in Network Broadcast Journalism History." *Journalism* 11, no. 6 (2010): 675–91.

Spear, Joseph C. *Presidents and the Press: The Nixon Legacy.* Cambridge, MA: MIT Press, 1984.

Spigel, Lynn, and Michael Curtin, eds. *The Revolution Wasn't Televised: Sixties Television and Social Conflict.* New York: Routledge, 1997.

Spruill, Marjorie J. *Divided We Stand: The Battle over Women's Rights and Family Values That Polarized American Politics.* New York: Bloomsbury, 2017.

Stabile, Carol A. *The Broadcast 41: Women and the Anti-Communist Blacklist.* London: Goldsmiths, 2018.

Staggenborg, Suzanne. *The Pro-Choice Movement: Organizations and Activism in the Abortion Conflict.* Oxford: Oxford University Press, 1995.

Stahl, Jason. *Right Moves: The Conservative Think Tank in American Political Culture since 1945.* Chapel Hill: University of North Carolina Press, 2016.

Staiger, Janet. *Blockbuster TV: Must-See Sitcoms in the Network Era.* New York: New York University Press, 2000.

Stanton, Peggy. *The Daniel Dilemma: The Moral Man in the Public Arena.* Waco, TX: Word Books, 1978.

Stelter, Brian. *Hoax: Donald Trump, Fox News, and the Dangerous Distortion of Truth.* New York: One Signal, 2020.

Stephens, Hilde Løvdal. *Family Matters: James Dobson and Focus on the Family's Crusade for the Christian Home.* Tuscaloosa: University of Alabama Press, 2019.

Stephens, Randall J., and Karl W. Giberson, *The Anointed: Evangelical Truth in a Secular Age.* Cambridge, MA: Harvard University Press, 2011.

Summers, Anthony, and Robbyn Swan. *Sinatra: The Life*. New York: Alfred A. Knopf, 2005.
Sutton, Matthew Avery. *Jerry Falwell and the Rise of the Religious Right: A Brief History with Documents*. Boston: Bedford/St. Martin's, 2012.
Taranto, Stacie. *Kitchen Table Politics: Conservative Women and Family Values in New York*. Philadelphia: University of Pennsylvania Press, 2017.
Thrift, Bryan Hardin. *Conservative Bias: How Jesse Helms Pioneered the Rise of Right-Wing Media and Realigned the Republican Party*. Gainesville: University Press of Florida, 2014.
Turk, Katherine. *The Women of NOW: How Feminists Built an Organization That Transformed America*. New York: Farrar, Straus and Giroux, 2023.
US Commission on Civil Rights. *Window Dressing on the Set: Women and Minorities in Television*. Washington, DC: Government Printing Office, 1977.
Vidmar, Neil, and Milton Rokeach. "Archie Bunker's Bigotry: A Study in Selective Perception and Exposure." *Journal of Communication* 24, no. 1 (1974): 36–47.
Viteritti, Joseph P. "'Times A-Changin': A Mayor for the Great Society." In *Summer in the City: John Lindsay, New York, and the American Dream*, edited by Joseph P. Viteritti, 1–26. Baltimore: Johns Hopkins University Press, 2014.
von Hodenberg, Christina. *Television's Moment: Sitcom Audiences and the Sixties Cultural Revolution*. New York: Berghahn, 2015.
Walsh, David Austin. *Taking America Back: The Conservative Movement and the Far Right*. New Haven, CT: Yale University Press, 2024.
Wandersee, Winifred D. *On the Move: American Women in the 1970s*. Boston: Twayne, 1988.
Watson, Mary Ann. *The Expanding Vista: American Television in the Kennedy Years*. New York: University of Oxford Press, 1990.
Weil, Gordon L. *The Long Shot: George McGovern Runs for President*. New York: W. W. Norton, 1973.
Whetsell, Tripp. *Norman Lear: His Life and Times*. New York: Applause, 2024.
White, Theodore H. *Breach of Faith*. New York: Laurel, 1975.
White, Theodore H. *The Making of the President, 1968*. New York: Atheneum, 1969.
White, Theodore H. *The Making of the President, 1972*. New York: Atheneum, 1973.
Wicker, Tom. *One of Us: Richard Nixon and the American Dream*. New York: Random House, 1991.
Williams, Daniel K. *God's Own Party: The Making of the Christian Right*. New York: Oxford University Press, 2012.
Wise, David. *The Politics of Lying: Government Deception, Secrecy, and Power*. New York: Random House, 1973.
Witcover, Jules. *Marathon: The Pursuit of the Presidency, 1972–1976*. New York: Viking, 1977.
Witcover, Jules. *The Resurrection of Richard Nixon*. New York: G. P. Putnam's Sons, 1970.
Woodward, Bob. *Fear: Trump in the White House*. New York: Simon and Schuster, 2018.
Young, Dannagal Goldthwaite. *Irony and Outrage: The Polarized Landscape of Rage, Fear, and Laughter in the United States*. New York: Oxford University Press, 2020.
Young, Neil J. *Coming Out Republican: A History of the Gay Right*. Chicago: University of Chicago Press, 2024.
Young, Neil J. *We Gather Together: The Religious Right and the Problems of Interfaith Politics*. Oxford: Oxford University Press, 2016.

Zaretsky, Natasha. *No Direction Home: The American Family and the Fear of National Decline, 1968–1980*. Chapel Hill: University of North Carolina Press, 2007.

Zarkin, Kimberly A., and Michael J. Zarkin. *Federal Communications Commission: Front Line in the Culture and Regulations Wars*. Westport, CT: Greenwood, 2006.

Zimmer, Thomas. "Reflections on the Challenges of Writing a (Pre-)History of the 'Polarized' Present." *Modern American History* 2, no. 3 (2019): 403–8.

INDEX

Abarbanel, Gail, 116
abortion, 49, 51–53, 127, 132–33, 134, 138, 152
Abourezk, James, 44
Abzug, Bella, 117
Academy of Television Arts and Sciences, 15, 50, 51
Accuracy in Media, 131
Ackerman, Harry, 50–51
affiliates, 14, 18–20, 23, 24–25, 26, 52–53, 129, 130, 137, 151
Agnew, Spiro, 62, 74, 79–80, 82, 84, 86, 92, 130, 131
Ailes, Roger, 71
Alda, Alan, 119–20, 143, 144
Allen, Tim, 3, 159
All in the Family, 4–7, 8–9, 53–54, 57–58, 93, 112–14, 123, 159, 163–66; criticism of, 26–27, 28–29, 32–36, 36–37, 39–42, 56, 110–11, 127, 128, 134; "Edith Finds an Old Man" episode, 113–14; "Edith's 50th Birthday" episode, 55–58, 115–17; and family viewing hour, 128, 131, 133–34, 138–41, 155–56, 158; "Judging Books by Covers" episode, 68–69; "Mike Comes into Money" episode, 84–86, 100–101; and Richard Nixon, 68, 72–73, 74–75, 77–78, 83–85, 87–88; origins of, 13–18, 23–25; reception of, 7, 15, 26–30, 42–45, 58–59, 60, 92; success of, 4, 15, 33, 58–60, 134; themes on, 5–7, 48, 54–55, 60; and women's movement, 117–18, 124–25
American Broadcasting Company (ABC), 18, 19, 48, 83, 133, 159; and *All in the Family*, 23, 24, 37; and family viewing hour, 138, 140
American Jewish Committee, 34–35
American Jewish Congress, 32, 36
Americans of Italian Descent, 40
Amos 'n' Andy, 33
Annunzio, Frank, 41

Anti-Defamation League of B'nai B'rith, 34, 35, 181n36
antisemitism, 13, 19, 28, 73–74, 152
A. Philip Randolph Institute, 34
Apple, R. W. "Johnny," 101
The Apprentice, 3, 165
Archie Bunker's Place, 123, 160
Arnaz, Desi, 96
Arnold, Danny, 140, 142
Arthur, Bea, 49, 110, 120–21, 160
Ashley, Ted, 76
Asner, Ed, 120

Baio, Scott, 3, 164
Ball, Lucille, 15, 24, 48, 75
Barbeau, Adrienne, 49
Baretta, 144
Barney Miller, 140, 142–43
Barr, Roseanne, 2, 3, 159, 163
Barris, Kenya, 2, 158
Bayh, Birch, 103, 117
Beame, Abraham, 91
Beatty, Warren, 76, 95, 96, 103
Belafonte, Harry, 92
Bell, Kristen, 159
Benny, Jack, 54
Bergen, Candice, 163–64
Berle, Milton, 36, 54
Biden, Joe, 3, 164
Black-ish, 2, 3, 159
Blakely, Susan, 119
The Bob Newhart Show, 30
Bobst, Elmer, 74
Bozell, L. Brent, Jr., 132
Bright, Bill, 152
Brooklyn Nine-Nine, 162
Brown, Jerry, 102, 103, 164
Brown, Les, 48
Brown, Tony, 34
Broyhill, Joel T., 132

Buckley, William F., Jr., 91, 130, 132
Bunker, Archie, 4–7, 13, 113–14, 142–43, 165–66; and bigotry, 15, 17, 27–29, 31–32, 33, 36, 37–41, 42–44, 73, 75; and Jerry Brown, 164; and Jimmy Carter, 104–5; and Fred Harris, 102–3, and Edward Kennedy, 105; and John Lindsay, 92–95; and George McGovern, 89–90, 98–101, 160; and Richard Nixon, 8, 67–68, 72–73, 74–75, 77–78, 83–85; and Donald Trump, 165–66; and women's movement, 110, 111–12, 120
Bunker, Edith, 5, 54–55, 57–58, 110–12, 113, 115–16, 128; and Equal Rights Amendment, 9, 112, 118–25, 160
Burch, Dean, 21
Burnett, Carol, 113, 119
Burnett, Mark, 165
Burns, Allan, 142, 143, 144, 150
Burrows, James, 1
Burton, Phil, 146

cable news, 164–65
Carmichael, Stokely. *See* Ture, Kwame
The Carol Burnett Show, 30, 134
Carson, Johnny, 29, 67, 71, 75, 77, 78, 86, 105, 113
Carter, Jimmy, 101–6, 117, 121
Carter, Rosalynn, 121
Carter, Virginia, 46–47, 60, 62–63, 112–14, 115–16, 124, 132, 160, 161; and *All in the Family*, 53–58, 111–112, 115; and Equal Rights Amendment, 118–20; and *Maude*, 52–53
Cavett, Dick, 74, 82–83, 96, 118
CBS News, 79, 80, 86, 87–88, 123
Celler, Emanuel, 117
censorship, 35, 48, 129–34, 134–35, 159, 162, 222n114; and *All in the Family*, 25, 37, 40–41, 131, 134, 138–140, 145; and family viewing hour, 9, 126–27, 137–41, 142–45, 147, 149, 150, 154; and Nixon administration, 74, 82, 86, 132
Cheers, 161, 163
Chisholm, Shirley, 91, 92, 95
Church, Frank, 103, 114, 125
City Commission on Human Rights, 34
Clawson, Ken, 84, 87

Clinton, Bill, 3
Clinton, Hillary Rodham, 1–2, 3
Coalition of Italian-American Societies, 34
Cohen, Oscar, 35
Cole, Nat King, 19
Colson, Charles "Chuck," 79, 80, 82–83, 86–88
Columbia Broadcasting System (CBS), 14–15, 17–19, 22–23, 30, 41, 50–52, 62, 133, 135, 165; and *All in the Family*, 13, 23–26, 36–37, 42, 48, 59; and family viewing hour, 136–139, 140, 151, 155; and Nixon administration, 74, 80, 82, 85–86, 87–88, 131
Cosby, Bill, 34, 164
Cowan, Lou, 50
Cranston, Alan, 44
Criswell, W. A., 152
Cronkite, Walter, 59, 67, 80, 87, 105, 196n126
Crutchfield, Charles, 129, 151

Dann, Michael, 17, 23, 24
Danson, Ted, 159, 163
Davies, Ossie, 92
Davis, Sammy, Jr., 19, 77, 92
Dee, Ruby, 92
DeGeneres, Ellen, 161
Derwinski, Edward J., 41
The Dick Van Dyke Show, 48, 59
Directors Guild of America, 142
Dobson, James, 154
Dole, Bob, 131
Donovan, Garrett, 2
Douglas, Mike, 75

Ehrlichman, John, 68, 69
Eisenhower, Dwight D., 15, 83, 85, 114
Ellen, 161
English, Diane, 2, 164
Epstein, Benjamin R., 35, 36, 181n36
Equal Rights Amendment (ERA), 9, 112, 117–25, 160, 163
equal-time rule, 52, 84, 97, 132, 197n157
Ervin, Sam, 117
Evans, Mike, 5, 38
Evans, Rowland, 72

fairness doctrine, 21, 197n157
Falwell, Jerry, 154, 161

family viewing hour, 9, 127–28, 137–41, 142–58, 162
Federal Communications Commission (FCC), 14, 18, 19–22, 40–42, 52, 61, 97, 158; and family viewing, 9, 126–28, 129–31, 133, 135–37, 142–45, 147–49, 150–51, 155–56; and Nixon administration, 76–77, 79, 83. *See also* Wiley, Richard E.
Ferguson, Warren J., 154–55, 156, 157, 158, 222n114
Ferris, Charles, 155
Financial Interest and Syndication Rules, 20–21, 48
Flemming, Arthur, 114
Fonda, Jane, 82, 101, 119
Ford, Gerald, 105, 120
Forster, Arnold, 35
Fowler, Mark, 156
Foxx, Redd, 104
Friedan, Betty, 110, 118

Gabor, Zsa Zsa, 77
Gardenia, Vincent, 5
Garrett, Betty, 5
Gelbart, Larry, 142, 143, 150, 157
Gingrich, Newt, 163
Glazer, Ilana, 3
Gleason, Jackie, 14, 24, 71, 75
Goldberg, Leonard, 20
The Golden Girls, 49, 160
Goldenson, Leonard, 18, 19, 74, 83, 147
Goldwyn, Samuel, 76
The Good Place, 159
Gore, Al, 156
Gould, Jack, 27
Graham, Billy, 74, 78, 152
Grassle, Karen, 119
Greene, Lorne, 119–20
Griffin, Merv, 29, 75, 78, 96,
Griffiths, Martha, 117
Guggenheim, Charles, 97, 98

Hagerty, James, 83
Haldeman, H. R., 68, 69, 72, 73, 74–75, 77, 79, 80, 82–83, 195n115
Hamner, Robert, 139
Happy Days, 119, 157

Hargis, Billy James, 130, 152
Harper, Valerie, 112, 119
Harper, William Jackson, 159
Harris, Fred, 102–3, 206n123
Harris, Herbert, 115–16
Harris, Susan, 49, 142
Hart, Gary, 98, 201n48
Hawn, Goldie, 76, 96
Hayes, Sean, 1
Helford, Bruce, 2
Helms, Jesse, 129
Hemsley, Sherman, 5
Heston, Charlton, 76
Hicks, Louise Day, 92
Hobson, Laura Z., 28–29, 32, 35, 37, 38, 42, 181n36
Hoffman, Dustin, 92
Holtzman, Elizabeth, 115, 116–17, 122–23
Hoover, Herbert, 105, 206n136, 207n137
Hoover, J. Edgar, 71
Hope, Bob, 54, 60, 75
The Hot l Baltimore, 128
Humphrey, Hubert H., 72, 82, 90, 91, 95, 98, 99, 143–44

Jacinto, Manny, 159
Jackson, Henry, 91
Jackson, Jesse, 164
Jacobson, Abbi, 3
Jagoda, Barry, 104–5
Jamil, Jameela, 159
Jarzab, Leonard, 40–41
Javits, Jacob, 91
Jefferson, Henry, 75
Jefferson, Lionel, 38–39
The Jeffersons, 59
Jewish Centers Association, 36
Jewish Community Relations Council, 36
Johnson, Lyndon B., 22, 81, 105
Johnson, Nicholas, 20, 42, 97, 156–57
Julia, 7, 14

Kaepernick, Colin, 159
Kalish, Austin "Rocky" and Irma, 48, 49, 51, 54, 57
Kaskowitz, Edwin, 114
Kaufman, Jay, 35

Kearl, Wayne, 137
Kefauver, Estes, 143
Kennedy, Edward, 105, 117, 206n136
Kennedy, John F., 15, 19, 67, 70, 105, 143
Kennedy, Robert F., 96, 143, 151
Kerry, John, 82, 197n142
Keyes, Paul W., 70–72, 73–74, 77, 81, 87, 192n22
Khan, Nahnatchka, 2
Kimmel, Jimmy, 165
King, Martin Luther, Jr., 143
Kissinger, Henry, 77, 194n87
Knight, Wayne, 164
Kogan, Julius, 36
Kohen, David, 1
Komack, James, 60
Kosciuszko Foundation, 39
Kusielewicz, Eugene, 39–40, 41

Lader, Lawrence, 53
Lafferty, Perry, 37,
La Guardia, Fiorello, 91
LaHaye, Beverly, 154
LaHaye, Tim, 154
Lakin, Rita, 138
Lamb, Brian, 77
Last Man Standing, 159, 162
Lavin, Linda, 119
Leachman, Cloris, 119, 121
Lear, Frances, 46–47, 53, 56, 111, 118, 124
Lear, Norman, 21, 36, 41, 87–88, 103, 105, 129, 166; and Archie Bunker's bigotry, 7, 27, 29, 30, 35, 38, 40, 42, 43–45, 93; and CBS, 25, 37, 53, 59–60, 62–63, 74, 139, 145, 150; and creation of *All in the Family*, 23, 25; and family viewing hour, 139, 142–44, 145–46, 149, 150, 156; legacy of, 9, 160–61; and reception of *All in the Family*, 26, 29, 125, 128, 131, 134; and themes of *All in the Family*, 5, 37, 44–45, 48–49, 51–52, 54–56, 58–60, 62, 74, 92, 113, 125; and women's movement, 46–47, 53, 54–56, 62–63, 111, 112, 115, 116, 118, 123–24
Lee, J. Bracken, 132
Lelyveld, Arthur J., 31–33, 36, 39, 44
Levine, Irving, 35
Lewine, Robert, 50

Lewis, Jerry, 32
Linden, Hal, 140, 143
Lindsay, John, 90–95, 98, 99, 101, 105, 106, 201n47
Linkletter, Art, 75
Little, Cleavon, 39
Long, Kermit L., 43
Louis-Dreyfus, Julia, 3

Macdonald, Torbert, 147, 149, 150–51
MacLaine, Shirley, 96, 103, 119, 198n183
MacRae, Meredith, 120
Macy, Bill, 49
Magnuson, Warren, 143
Manion, Clarence, 130
Mankiewicz, Frank, 96, 202n53
Mansfield, Mike, 93
Markey, Ed, 156
Married . . . with Children, 162
Martin, Dick, 71–72
The Mary Tyler Moore Show, 15, 30, 48, 60, 119, 128, 144, 152, 157
*M*A*S*H*, 15, 30, 60, 119, 128, 131, 134, 139, 152, 157
Maude, 49, 51–53, 57, 59, 61, 62, 131–34, 138, 152
McClanahan, Rue, 160
McCormack, Eric, 1, 2
McDade, Joseph, 126
McGovern, George, 76, 95–101, 102, 103, 105, 106, 201n48; and *All in the Family*, 84–86, 100–101; and Archie Bunker, 89–90, 98–101, 160, 205n95
McGraw, Ali, 14
McIntire, Carl, 130
McLuhan, Marshall, 71
Messing, Debra, 1, 2–3, 159
Miceli, Vincent P., 132
Mikulski, Barbara, 156
Minow, Newton, 19, 59
Mitchell, John, 77
Mitchell, Martha, 77
Mizell, Wilmer, 133
The Mod Squad, 7, 14
Moonves, Les, 165
Moore, Mary Tyler, 20, 48, 110, 119, 121, 143
Moore, Tom, 23

Morality in Media, 131
Morsell, John, 34, 36
Moses, Robert, 92-93
Moss, John E., 147
MTM Enterprises, 20, 144, 145
Mullally, Megan, 1
Murphy, George, 75
Murphy, John M., 156
Murphy Brown, 2, 163, 164
Murrow, Edward R., 7, 166
Muskie, Edmund, 91, 97, 98, 202n64, 202n66
Mutchnick, Max, 1

Nader, Ralph, 82
National Association for the Repeal of Abortion Laws (NARAL), 53, 57
National Association of Broadcasters (NAB), 9, 21, 48, 127; and *All in the Family*, 40-41; and family viewing hour, 135, 137-38, 140, 142, 145, 151, 153, 155
National Broadcasting Corporation (NBC), 2, 18, 19, 48, 133, 159, 162
National Conference of Christians and Jews, 34
National Council of Catholic Bishops, 52
National Council of Churches, 50
National Council on Aging, 114
National Organization for Women (NOW), 47, 52-53, 58, 110, 112, 115, 118, 123, 125
National Urban League, 33
Nicholl, Don, 54
Nielsen ratings, 24, 26, 33, 42, 134, 176n52. *See also* ratings
Nimoy, Leonard, 96
Nixon, Pat, 77
Nixon, Richard, 8, 14, 91, 95, 96, 101, 164; and *All in the Family*, 68, 73-75, 77-78, 83-86; and 1972 campaign, 75-78, 83-84, 86, 89, 98-101; and 1968 campaign, 71-72, 79; and television, 61, 67-72, 75-76, 90, 104-5; and television networks, 22, 76-77, 78-83, 87-88, 130-31
Novak, Robert, 72

Obama, Barack, 3
Obama, Michelle, 2

O'Connor, Carroll, 5, 8, 109, 118, 123, 142-43, 160; and bigotry, 29, 36, 40, 43; and Jimmy Carter; 102-4, 105; and John Lindsay, 93-95, 160; and George McGovern, 89-90, 99-101, 160; and Richard Nixon, 77-78. *See also* Bunker, Archie
O'Connor, John J., 28, 132
O'Neal, Ryan, 14
One Day at a Time, 2
O'Neill, John, 82, 197n142
O'Neill, Thomas "Tip," 163
Ossofsky, Jack, 114

Paar, Jack, 70-71
Packwood, Robert, 50, 186n33
Paley, William S., 18, 19, 74, 81, 86, 147, 155; and *All in the Family*, 17-18, 23, 24; and *Maude*, 52, 53
Parker, Everett C., 19, 40, 42
Parks and Recreation, 3, 164
Pastore, John O., 134-35, 143, 144, 150-51, 153, 155
Perry, Katy, 1
Phillips, Kevin, 130
Phyllis, 139
Poehler, Amy, 3, 164
Poindexter, David O., 49-51, 52, 57, 161, 185n29
Polish-American Guardian Society, 40
Population Institute, 49-52, 55, 57, 161
Postman, Neil, 164
Poussaint, Alvin F., 34
Prime Time Access Rule, 20-21, 61, 140, 145
Prinze, Freddie, 104
Procaccino, Mario, 92, 93
Proxmire, William, 44

Quayle, Dan, 164

Rafshoon, Jerry, 104
Rakolta, Terry, 162
Randall, Tony, 103
rape. *See* sexual assault
Rather, Dan, 79, 80
ratings, 15, 18, 24, 30, 83, 165
Raye, Martha, 96
Reagan, Ronald, 3, 76, 130

INDEX   255

Redford, Robert, 95, 119, 161
Reiner, Carl, 59–60
Reiner, Rob, 5, 86, 93, 109, 123, 160, 164–65, 166; and Democratic Party, 99, 163, 103–4; and Equal Rights Amendment, 163. *See also* Stivic, Mike
Reynolds, Gene, 141, 144
Rhine, Larry, 112
Rhoda, 119, 139
Rich, John, 29, 38, 43, 100, 113
Rizzo, Frank, 92
Rizzuto, Phil, 132
Robinson, Jackie, 92
Rockefeller, John D., III, 50
Rockefeller, Nelson, 91, 151
Rodino, Peter, 115–16
Rogers, Edward, 69–70
Rogers, Ginger, 75
The Rookies, 138, 140, 144, 156
Roseanne, 2, 159,
Rosenthal, Phil, 160
Ross, Michael, 38, 54
Ross, Tracee Ellis, 2, 3
Rowan, Dan, 71
Rowan and Martin's Laugh-In, 71–72, 81, 86
Rustin, Bayard, 34

Saarinen, Eliel, 13
Salant, Richard, 88
Sanders, Charles L., 34
Sanford, Isabel, 5
Sanford and Son, 59, 60, 104, 131
Santos, Nico, 2
Sarnoff, David, 18, 19, 74, 147
Sarnoff, Robert, 50
Sarnoff, Thomas W., 50
Scheuer, James H., 116
Schiller, Bob, 51–52
Schlafly, Phyllis, 124, 153
Schlosser, Herbert, 133
Schneider, Alfred, 63, 129, 137, 138, 140, 143
Schneider, John A., 17, 23, 26, 59, 61
Schorr, Daniel, 80, 196n126
Schreiber, Taft, 76–78, 82, 87
Schroeder, Patricia, 122
Schuller, Robert, 154

Schwartz, Walter J., 133
Schwarz, Fred, 153
Schwarzenegger, Arnold, 163
Scott, Hugh, 133
Screen Actors Guild, 76–77, 142
Segal, Robert E., 36
Segelstein, Irwin, 13
Seinfeld, 162, 164
sexual assault, 54–55, 57–58, 115–17
Shriver, Sargent, 100, 103
Silverman, Fred, 17, 25, 49
Sinatra, Frank, 77
Skelton, Red, 24, 75, 96, 132
Smothers, Dick, 80–82
Smothers, Tom, 80–82, 96
The Smothers Brothers Comedy Hour, 7, 14, 81–83
Snyder, Jimmy "The Greek," 96
Southern Baptist Radio and Television Commission, 153–54
Spelling, Aaron, 20, 138
Spelling-Goldberg Productions, 20
Staggers, Harley O., 133
standards and practices department, 48–49, 51, 62–63, 129–30, 139–40, 150; and *All in the Family*, 25, 37–39, 87–88
Stanton, Frank, 18, 50–51, 53, 80, 81, 86, 135, 136, 161
Stapleton, Jean, 5, 104, 109–12, 160, 210n86; and Equal Rights Amendment, 9, 117–24, 163. *See also* Bunker, Edith
Starger, Martin, 23
Star Trek, 14
Stewart, Mel, 5, 75
Stewart, Potter, 138
St. George, Katherine, 132
Stivic, Gloria, 5, 7, 55, 110–11, 128, 160; and bigotry, 38, 68; and 1972 election, 83–85, 100; and women's movement, 5, 57, 110–11
Stivic, Mike, 5–6, 37, 55, 57, 110, 113, 160, 164; and bigotry, 38, 39, 68; and 1972 election, 84–85, 100
Stop Immorality on TV, 131–34, 152–53
Streisand, Barbra, 76, 92
Struthers, Sally, 5, 34, 40, 55, 123, 160. *See also* Stivic, Gloria
Sullivan, Ed, 14

Superstore, 2
Swafford, Thomas, 137, 138–39

Tandem Productions, 26, 36, 48–49, 52–54, 62, 85, 116, 123, 131, 160; and family viewing hour, 145; origins of, 23; success of, 21, 47, 59–60, 62; and women's movement, 53, 55–56, 57–58, 112, 123, 188n92
Tanenbaum, Marc H., 36
Tankersley, William, 37, 63
Taylor, Arthur, 136–38, 148, 151–52, 153–54, 155
Television Code, 40, 143
Thomas, Marlo, 119
Three's Company, 157
Thurmond, Strom, 117
Till Death Us Do Part, 23
Tinker, Grant, 20, 144, 145, 150
Traviesas, Herminio, 63, 127, 137
Trump, Donald J., 1–3, 9, 159, 165–66
Ture, Kwame, 34, 82

Udall, Mo, 103
Urban Coalition, 34

Valenti, Jack, 76
Van Deerlin, Lionel, 149, 151, 156
Van Dyke, Dick, 59
Vaughn, Robert, 96
Viguerie, Richard, 130

Wagner, Robert, 93
Wallace, George, 91, 98
Wallace, Mike, 145
Warner, Jack, 76, 77
Washburn, Abbott, 147
Wasserman, Lew, 76
Waxman, Henry, 146–51, 154, 156
Wayne, John, 75, 77

Weiskopf, Bob, 51–52
Welk, Lawrence, 14
Wendt, George, 161
West, Bernie, 54, 60, 111
Westinghouse rule. *See* Financial Interest and Syndication Rules; Prime Time Access Rule
White, Betty, 160
White, Byron, 21
White, Theodore, 95
White, William S., 72, 92, 95
Wildmon, Donald, 154, 157, 162
Wiley, Richard E., 135–36, 137, 140, 142, 145, 151, 153–54, 155; and Congress, 126–27, 136, 147–48, 150
Wilkins, Roy, 34
Wilkinson, Ernest L., 132
Will & Grace, 1–2, 9, 159
Wilson, Demond, 39
Winkler, Henry, 120
Wirth, Timothy, 146, 156
Wood, Robert "Bob," 19, 30, 36, 38, 49, 59, 62, 74, 133, 161; and affiliates, 14–15, 24–25; and *All in the Family*, 13, 15, 17–18, 23–24, 26, 29, 37; and family viewing hour, 138–39, 141
Writers Guild of America (WGA), 142
Wurmbrand, Richard, 132
Wussler, Robert, 62

Yorkin, Bud, 21, 23, 34, 36, 60, 62, 111, 158, 205n95
Yorkin, Peggy, 56, 111
Yorty, Sam, 92
Young, Whitney M., Jr., 33–34, 37

Zanuck, Darryl F., 76
Zanuck, Richard, 77
Ziegler, Ronald, 72–73, 74–75, 79

www.ingramcontent.com/pod-product-compliance
Lightning Source LLC
Chambersburg PA
CBHW021853230426

43671CB00006B/370